The Frock-Coated Communist

TRISTRAM HUNT

The Frock-Coated Communist

The Revolutionary Life of Friedrich Engels

ALLEN LANE
an imprint of
PENGUIN BOOKS

ALLEN LANE

Published by the Penguin Group
Penguin Books Ltd, 80 Strand, London WC2R ORL, England
Penguin Group (USA) Inc., 375 Hudson Street, New York, New York 10014, USA
Penguin Group (Canada), 90 Eglinton Avenue East, Suite 700, Toronto, Ontario, Canada M4P 2Y3
(a division of Pearson Penguin Canada Inc.)
Penguin Ireland, 25 St Stephen's Green, Dublin 2, Ireland
(a division of Penguin Books Ltd)
Penguin Group (Australia), 250 Camberwell Road, Camberwell, Victoria 3124, Australia
(a division of Pearson Australia Group Pty Ltd)
Penguin Books India Pvt Ltd, 11 Community Centre, Panchsheel Park, New Delhi – 110 017, India
Penguin Group (NZ), 67 Apollo Drive, Rosedale, North Shore 0632, New Zealand
(a division of Pearson New Zealand Ltd)
Penguin Books (South Africa) (Pty) Ltd, 24 Sturdee Avenue, Rosebank, Johannesburg 2196, South Africa

Penguin Books Ltd, Registered Offices: 80 Strand, London WC2R ORL, England

www.penguin.com

First published 2009
1

Copyright © Tristram Hunt, 2009

The moral right of the author has been asserted

The author would like to thank Lawrence & Wishart for their kind permission to quote from
Marx Engels Collected Works (London 1975–2004)

Set in 10.5/14 pt PostScript Linotype Sabon
Typeset by Rowland Phototypesetting Ltd, Bury St Edmunds, Suffolk
Printed in England by Clays Ltd, St Ives plc

ISBN: 978–0–713–99852–8

www.greenpenguin.co.uk

To D. W. H. H.

Contents

List of Illustrations

Integrated illustrations

Acknowledgements

For their generous assistance with the research, writing and production of this book, the author would like to thank Alice Austin, Sara Bershtel, Phillip Birch, Georgina Capel, Michael V. Carlisle, Barney Cokeliss, Bela Cunha, Andrew and Theresa Curtis, Dermot Daly and the Cheshire Hunt, Virginia Davis and the Department of History, Queen Mary, University of London, Thomas Dixon, Orlando Figes, Gilés Foden, Tom Graves, Michael Herbert, Eric Hobsbawm, Julian and Marylla Hunt, Stephen Kingston, Nick Mansfield, Ed Miliband, Seumas Milne, Liudmila Novikova, Alastair Owens, Stuart Proffitt, Caroline Read, Stephen Rigby, Donald Sassoon, Sophie Schlondorff, Bill Smyth, Gareth Stedman Jones, Juliet Thornback, Benjamin and Yulia Wegg-Prosser, Francis Wheen, Bee Wilson, Michael Yehuda. In addition, the staff of the British Library; Engels-Haus, Wuppertal; the International Institute of Social History, Amsterdam; the London Library; the Marx Memorial Library, London; the People's History Museum, Manchester; the Working Class Movement Library, Salford.

NORTH SEA

DENMARK

SCHLESWIG

HOLSTEIN

MECKLENBURG

Hamburg

Bremen

HANOVER

Hanover

River Elbe

Amsterdam

NETHERLANDS

River Rhine

Barmen

Cologne

River Weser

SAXONY

Brussels

BELGIUM

PRUSSIA

Trier

Frankfurt

Paris

River Seine

(BAV.)

Rastatt

Stuttgart

BAVARIA

WÜRTEMBERG

Munich

BADEN

Innsbruck

FRANCE

SWITZERLAND

LOMBARDY

VENETIA

ADRIATIC

Central Europe, 1815–66

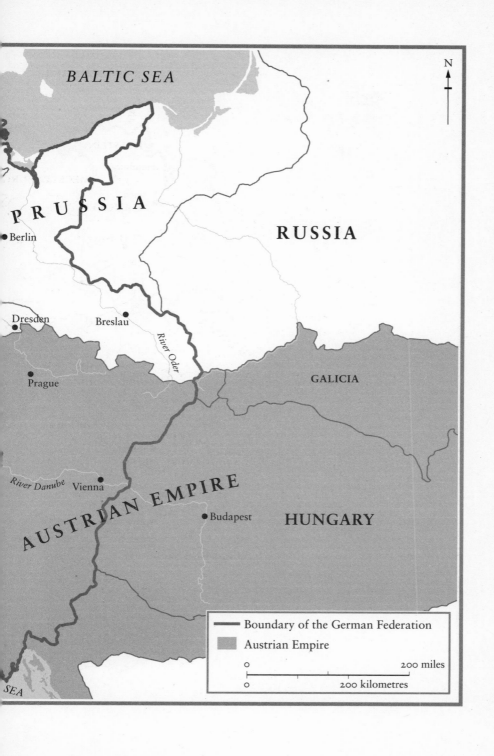

N

BALTIC SEA

PRUSSIA

• Berlin

RUSSIA

Dresden

Breslau

River Oder

Prague

GALICIA

River Danube Vienna •

AUSTRIAN EMPIRE

• Budapest

HUNGARY

SEA

—— Boundary of the German Federation

   Austrian Empire

0   200 miles

0   200 kilometres

Preface

On 30 June 1869 Friedrich Engels, a Manchester mill owner, gave up his job in the family business after nearly twenty years. Ready to greet him, on the path of his small cottage in the Chorlton suburbs, were his lover Lizzy Burns and houseguest Eleanor Marx, daughter of his old friend Karl. 'I was with Engels when he reached the end of his forced labour and I saw what he must have gone through all those years,' Eleanor later wrote of Engels's final day at work,

I shall never forget the triumph with which he exclaimed 'for the last time!' as he put on his boots in the morning to go to his office. A few hours later we were standing at the gate waiting for him. We saw him coming over the little field opposite the house where he lived. He was swinging his stick in the air and singing, his face beaming. Then we set the table for a celebration and drank champagne and were happy.[1]

Friedrich Engels was a textile magnate and fox-hunter, member of the Manchester Royal Exchange and president of the city's Schiller Institute. He was a raffish, high-living, heavy-drinking devotee of the good things in life: lobster salad, Château Margaux, Pilsener beer and expensive women. But for forty years Engels also funded Karl Marx, looked after his children, soothed his furies and provided one half of history's most celebrated ideological partnership: co-author of the *Communist Manifesto* and co-founder of what would come to be known as Marxism. Over the course of the twentieth century, from Chairman Mao's China to the Stasi state of the GDR, from the anti-imperial struggle in Africa to the Soviet Union itself, various manifestations of this compelling philosophy would cast their shadow over a full third of the human race. And as often as not, the leadership of the socialist world would look first to Engels rather than Marx to explain their policies, justify their excesses and shore up their regimes. Interpreted and misinterpreted, quoted and misquoted, Friedrich Engels – the frock-coated Victorian cotton lord – became one of the central architects of global communism.

Today, a journey to Engels begins at Moscow's Paveletsky rail station. From this shabbily romantic Tsarist-era terminal, the rusting sleeper train heaves off at midnight for the Volga plains hundreds of miles south-east of the capital. A grinding, stop–start fourteen-hour journey, alleviated only by a gurgling samovar in the guard's carriage, eventually lands you in the city of Saratov with its wide, tree-lined streets and attractive air of faded grandeur.

Bolted on to this prosperous, provincial centre is a crumbling, six-lane highway which bridges the mighty river Volga and connects Saratov to its unloved sister city, Engels. Lacking any of Saratov's sophistication, Engels is a grotty, forgotten site dominated by railway loading docks and the rusting detritus of light industry. At its civic centre squats Engels Square: a bleak parade ground encircled by housing estates, a shabby strip-mall dotted with sports bars, casinos and DVD stores, and a roundabout clogged with Ladas, Sputniks and the odd Ford. Here, in all its enervating grime, is the post-communist Russia of hyper-capitalism and bootleg Americana. And amidst this free-market dystopia stands a statue of Friedrich Engels himself – fifteen-foot high atop a marble plinth and with a well-tended municipal flowerbed at his heels, he looks resplendent in his trench coat clutching a curled-up copy of the *Communist Manifesto*.

Across the former USSR and Eastern bloc, the statues of Marx (together with those of Lenin, Stalin and Beria) have come down. Decapitated and mutilated, their remains are gathered together in monument graveyards for the ironic edification of Cold War cultural tourists. Inexplicably, Engels has been given leave to remain, still holding sway over his eponymous town. As a quick conversation with local residents and early evening promenaders in Engels Square reveals, his presence here is the product neither of affection nor admiration. Certainly, there is little hostility towards the co-founder of communism, but rather a weary apathy and nonchalant ignorance about the adamantine figure whose face they pass by daily. As with the nineteenth-century generals and long-forgotten social reformers on myriad plinths littering the squares of western European capitals, Engels has become an unknown and unremarkable part of the civic wallpaper.

At his birthplace in the Rhineland town of Wuppertal (now a commuter suburb for the nearby finance and fashion city of Düsseldorf), it is a similar story of disinterest. There is a Friedrich Engels Strasse and a Friedrich Engels Allee, but little sense of a town overly anxious to commemorate its most celebrated son. The site of Engels's Geburtshaus, destroyed by a Royal Air Force bombing raid in 1943, remains barren and all that marks the place of his arrival into the world is a dirty granite monument modestly noting his role as the 'co-founder of scientific socialism'. Covered in holly and ivy, it is edged into the shadowy corner of a run-down park, overlooked by rusting Portakabins and a vandalized phone booth.

In modern Russia and Germany, let alone in Spain, England or America, Engels has slipped the surly bonds of history. Where once his name was on the lips of millions – as Marx's fellow combatant; as the author of *Socialism: Utopian and Scientific* (the Bible of global communism); as the theoretician of dialectical materialism; as the name so regularly grafted on to city streets and squares by revolutionary insurgents and left-wing councils; as the man whose visionary, bearded features were stamped on to the currency, etched into textbooks, and alongside Marx, Lenin and Stalin stared down from vast flags and Soviet Realist hoardings on to May Day parades – it is now barely registered in either East or West. In 1972 an official GDR biography could naturally claim that 'nowadays there is hardly a corner of this earth of ours where Engels's name has not been heard of, where the significance of his work is unknown'.[2] Today, he is so innocuous, his statue isn't even pulled down.

The same cannot be said of his colleague, Karl Marx. Two decades on from the fall of the Berlin Wall and Francis Fukuyama's hubristic declaration of 'the end of history', Marx's reputation is enjoying a remarkable renaissance. In recent years he has been transformed from the ogre responsible for the killing fields of Cambodia and labour camps of Siberia to modern capitalism's most perceptive analyst.

'Marx's Stock Resurges on a 150-Year Tip' was how the *New York Times* marked the 150th anniversary of the publication of the *Communist Manifesto* – a text which, more than any other, 'recognized the unstoppable wealth-creating power of capitalism, predicted it would conquer the world, and warned that this inevitable globalization of national economies and cultures would have divisive and painful consequences'.[3] As Western governments, businesses and banks reaped the bitter harvest of free-market fundamentalism at the turn of the twenty-first century – financial meltdowns in Mexico and Asia, the industrialization of China and India, the decimation of the middle class in Russia and Argentina, mass migration and a worldwide 'crisis of capitalism' in 2007–9 – the Cassandra-like voice of Marx started to echo down the decades. The post-1989 neo-liberal settlement, Fukuyama's endpoint of mankind's ideological evolution, all set to be built on the historical wreck of communism, seemed to falter. And there was Marx waiting in the wings. 'He's back,' screamed *The Times* in the autumn of 2008 as stock markets plunged, banks were summarily nationalized and President Sarkozy of France was photographed leafing through *Das Kapital* (sales of which surged to the top of the German bestseller lists). Even Pope Benedict XVI was moved to praise Marx's 'great analytical skill'.[4] The British economist Meghnad Desai, in a work which formed part of an increasingly effusive literature on Marx, had already labelled the phenomenon, *Marx's Revenge: The Resurgence of Capitalism and the Death of Statist Socialism*.[5]

For it was now a universal truth that Marx was the first to chart the uncompromising, unrelenting, compulsively iconoclastic nature of capitalism. 'It has pitilessly torn asunder the motley feudal ties that bound man to his "natural superiors", and has left remaining no other nexus between man and man than naked self-interests, than callous "cash-payment",' as the *Communist Manifesto* put it. 'It has drowned the most heavenly ecstasies of religious fervour, of chivalrous enthusiasm, of philistine sentimentalism, in the icy water of egotistical calculation.'[6] It was Marx who revealed how capitalism would crush languages, cultures, traditions, even nations, in its wake. 'In one word, it creates a world after its own image,' he wrote long before globalization became a by-word for Americanization. In his bestselling 2005 biography, *Karl Marx ou l'esprit du monde*, the French politician-cum-banker Jacques Attali located Marx as the first great theorist of globalization. For Attali, Marx was 'an amazingly modern thinker, because when you look at what he has written, it is not a theory of what an organised socialist country should be like, but how capitalism will be in the future ... he considered that capitalism would end only when it was a global force ... when nations disappeared, when technology was able to transform the life of a country'.[7] Even the *Economist*, the great weekly promulgator of neo-liberal dogma, had to give him credit for 'envisioning the awesome productive power of capitalism', as the magazine conceded in a 2002 article entitled 'Marx after Communism'. 'He saw that capitalism would spur innovation to a hitherto-unimagined degree. He was right that giant corporations would come to dominate the world's industries.'[8] At the same time, Attali's book, together with Francis Wheen's popular biography of Marx as journalist and rapscallion (*Karl Marx*, 1999), helped to cast him in a sympathetic light as a struggling writer and loving father shamefully persecuted by the authorities.[9] Since the 1960s and Louis Althusser's 'discovery' of the 'epistemological break' between the young and the mature Marx – between the Marx of the *Economic and Philosophical Manuscripts* concerned with alienation and morality and the later, materialist Marx – we had already come to know of Karl Marx's early philosophical humanism. Now we were offered the biographical complement of a rounded, engaging and strikingly contemporary individual.

But where does Friedrich Engels fit within this generous new alignment? In the absence of a similar slew of biographies (with the last truly popular English-language life of Engels being the translation of Gustav Mayer's seminal work of 1934) and perhaps as part of a conscious post-1989 forgetting, Engels has been excised from the popular memory.[10] Or, more worrisomely, in certain ideological circles he has been landed with responsibility for the terrible excesses of twentieth-century Marxism-Leninism. For as Marx's stock has risen, so Engels's has fallen. Increasingly, the trend has been to separate off an ethical, humanist Karl Marx from a mechanical, scientistic Engels and blame the latter for sanctifying the state crimes of communist Russia, China and south-east Asia. Even in the mid-1970s, E. P. Thompson was noting the urge to turn 'old Engels into a whipping boy, and to impugn to him any sin that one chooses to impugn to subsequent Marxisms . . . I cannot accept the pleadings which always find Marx and Lenin innocent and leave Engels alone in the dock.'[11] Similarly, Richard N. Hunt commented on how 'It has lately become fashionable in some quarters to treat Engels as the dustbin of Classical Marxism, a convenient receptacle into which can be swept any unsightly oddments of the system, and who can thus also bear the blame for whatever subsequently went awry.'[12] Thus, the attractive Marx of the Paris notebooks is compared and contrasted unfavourably with the dour Engels of *Anti-Dühring*. The Marxist scholar Norman Levine, for instance, has been in no doubt that 'Engelism [*sic*] led directly to the dialectical materialism of the Stalin era . . . By asserting that a fixed path of development existed in history, by asserting that pre-determined historical development was moving towards socialism, Engelism made Soviet Russia appear as the fulfilment of history since it had already achieved socialism . . . During the Stalin era, what the world understood as Marxism was really Engelism.'[13] Suddenly, Engels is left holding the baby of twentieth-century ideological extremism while Marx is rebranded as the acceptable, post-political seer of global capitalism.

Of course it is true that we know about and are interested in Friedrich Engels largely because of his collaboration with Marx; a partnership in which the devoted Engels was always careful to cast himself as 'second fiddle'. 'Marx was a genius; we others were at best talented. Without him the theory would not be by far what it is today. It therefore rightly bears his name,' he announced conclusively after his friend's death.[14] It is equally true that much of the official ideology of Marxism-Leninism in the twentieth century sought its validity, however spurious, in elements of Engels's later codification of Marxism. But just as it is now possible, as the post-1989 polemical dust settles and the socialism of Marx and Engels is no longer automatically obscured by the long, Leninist shadow of the Soviet Union, to take a renewed look at Marx, so we can also begin to approach Engels afresh. 'Communism defiled and despoiled the radical heritage,' Tony Judt has written of the 'dictatorial deviation' which marked its perverted implementation during the twentieth century. 'If today we face a world in which there is no grand narrative of social progress, no politically plausible project of social justice, it is in large measure because Lenin and his heirs poisoned the well.'[15] As that historical tide at last begins to ebb, it is now possible and valuable to return to the lives and works of 'the old Londoners' to find elements of Marx and Engels's canon which we can examine in a world free for the most part of the state socialist experiments of the twentieth century. They offer not just an insightful critique of global capitalism but new perspectives on the nature of modernity and progress, religion and ideology, colonialism and 'liberal interventionism', global financial crises, urban theory, feminism, even Darwinism and reproductive ethics.

To all of which Engels contributed profoundly. Managing a mid-Victorian Manchester cotton business, dealing daily with the economic chain of world trade which stretched from the plantations of the American South to the Lancashire mills to the British Raj, it was *his* experience of the workings of global capitalism which made its way into the pages of Marx's *Das Kapital*, just as it was *his* experience of factory life, slum living, armed insurrection and street-by-street politicking which informed the development of communist doctrine. And, again, it was Friedrich Engels who was far more adventurous when it came to exploring the ramification of his and Marx's thinking in terms of family structure, scientific method, military theory and colonial liberation. As Marx immersed himself ever deeper in the second half of the nineteenth century in economic theory and primitive Russian communism, Engels ranged freely on questions of politics, the environment and democracy, with unexpectedly modern applicability. If Marx's voice is being heard again today, then it is also time we stripped away Engels's modesty and allowed his richly iconoclastic ideas to be explored beyond the memory of Marx.

Yet what makes Engels a fascinating source of biographical enquiry is the personal background to this philosophical prowess; the rich contradiction and limitless sacrifice which marked his long life. It was a life, moreover, set against the great revolutionary epoch of the nineteenth century: Engels was with the Chartists in Manchester, on the barricades in 1848–9, urging on the Paris Communards in 1871 and witness to the uncomfortable birth of the British labour movement in 1890s London. He was a man who believed in praxis, in living his theory of revolutionary communism as practice. Yet the miserable frustration of his life was that he so rarely got the chance, since from his earliest meetings with Marx he decided to relinquish his own ambitions for the sake of his friend's genius and the greater good of the communist cause. Over twenty long years, in the prime of his life, he endured a self-loathing existence as a Manchester millocrat in order to allow Marx the resources and freedom to complete *Das Kapital*. The notion of individual sacrifice, so central to communist self-definition, was there at the movement's birth.

This extraordinary deference to Marx's mind made great periods of Engels's adult life a time of painful contradiction. Symbolically, at the heart of the Marxist theory of dialectical materialism stood precisely this dynamic of contradiction – how the interpenetration of opposites and the negation of the negation explain the evolution of the natural, physical and social sciences. Right from his initial conversion to communism, Engels, the well-born scion of Prussian Calvinist merchants, lived that tension in a transparently personal way. And so this biography is also the memoir of a fox-hunting man: how a womanizing, champagne-drinking capitalist helped to found an ideology which was both contrary to his class interests and would, over the decades, morph into a dull, puritanical faith utterly at odds with the character of its founders. Engels himself would never admit any contradiction between his gentleman's lifestyle and egalitarian ideals – but his critics did then and certainly do now.

Perhaps any personalized account of an individual Marxist necessarily involves this kind of contradiction since – many Marxist historians would argue – one should focus on the history of the masses, not the biography of a single man. Yet this would be to succumb to a particularly restrictive interpretation of Marxism and neglect the attractively non-doctrinaire thinking of Engels himself. He not only had an abiding interest in biography (especially the lives of British army generals), but was adamant that 'men make their own history . . . in that each person follows his own consciously desired end, and it is precisely the result of these many wills operating in different directions and of their manifold effects upon the world outside that constitutes history'. History is therefore in part a question of individual desires.

The will is determined by passion or deliberation. But the levers which immediately determine passion or deliberation are of very different kinds. In part they may be external objects, in part ideal motives . . . personal hatred, or even purely individual whims of all kinds . . . the question also arises: What driving forces in turn stand behind these motives? What are the historical causes which transform themselves into these motives in the minds of the actors?[16]

It is the ambition of this biography to unpick those passions and desires, personal hatreds and individual whims – as well as the driving forces and historical causes – of a man who made his own history and who continues to shape ours.

I

Siegfried in Zion

'Rejoice with me, dearly beloved Karl, that the good Lord has heard our prayer and last Tuesday evening, the 28th, at 9pm presented us with a babe, a healthy well-shapen boy. We thank and praise Him from the fullness of our hearts for this child, and for the merciful assistance and care for mother and child during confinement.' In late November 1820, after his wife's difficult labour, the Rhineland businessman Friedrich Engels was delighted to announce to his brother-in-law Karl Snethlage the birth of his first son and namesake. Instantly anxious for the child's spiritual state, Engels also wrote of his hopes that the Lord 'grants us the wisdom to bring it up well and in fear of Him, and to give it the best teaching through our example!' This prayer would go spectacularly unanswered.[1]

The infant Friedrich was ushered into a family and a culture that offered no inkling of his revolutionary future – and soon clamoured to disavow it. There was no broken home, no lost father, no lonely childhood, no school bullying. Instead, there were loving parents, indulgent grandparents, plentiful siblings, steady prosperity and a sense of structured, familial purpose. 'Probably no son born in such a family ever struck so entirely different a path from it. Friedrich must have been considered by his family as the "ugly duckling",' mused Eleanor Marx in 1890, when the wounds of the Engels clan were still raw. 'Perhaps they still do not understand that the "duckling" was in reality a "swan".'[2]

Engels's upbringing in the Rhineland town of Barmen took place within a safe, cloistered neighbourhood that resembled something of a family compound. Across the road from his home stood the detached, four-storey, late-baroque house his own father was born in (now the threadbare Engels-Haus museum); nearby the homes of his uncles, Johann Caspar III and August; and dotted amongst them the steaming, stinking yarn bleacheries that had funded their showy mansions. Factories, workers' tenements and merchant houses mingled together in what resembled an early industrial model village. For Friedrich Engels was delivered straight into the furnace of the nineteenth century. The historic transformations he would make his life's work – urbanization, industrialization, social class and technology – were there at his birth. 'The factory and cottages of the esteemed family of Caspar Engels, together with the bleacheries, almost form a small semi-circular city,' confirmed an 1816 report on the state of Barmen's housing.[3] Leading down to the Wupper river, this damp, marshy district was officially called 'the Red Brook'; in the early 1900s it was still widely known as 'Engels' Brook'.

While the Engels line can be traced back to Rhineland farms of the late sixteenth century, the family's prosperity begins with the arrival of Johann Caspar I (1715–87), Engels's great-grandfather, in the Wupper valley in the latter half of the eighteenth century. Exchanging agriculture for industry, Caspar was drawn to the lime-free waters of the Wupper river – one of the tributaries of the Rhine – and the riches it promised from linen yarn bleaching. With just 25 thalers in his pocket and a pannier on his back (as family legend had it), he chose to settle in the tiny town of Barmen, which clings to the slopes of the high valley lining the Wupper. An assiduous entrepreneur, he built up a highly successful yarn business, complete with a bleachery, and then a workshop for a pioneering form of mechanical lace production. When he handed over the company to his sons, it was one of Barmen's largest enterprises.

Yet the commercial ethos of Caspar Engels und Söhne stood for more than just the cash nexus. In an era when gradations between workers and masters were subtler than full-throttle industrialization would later allow, the Engelses fused paternalism with profits and were widely renowned for the benevolence of their employment and refusal to use child labour. Down the generations, the Engelses provided homes, gardens and even schools for family employees, and a granary co-operative was set up during food shortages. As a result, Engels spent his early years mixing easily with ribbon-makers, joiners and craftsmen, fostering in him a class-free ease which would later serve him well in the Salford slums and communist clubs of Paris.

Johann Caspar's sons continued in the family firm, expanding operations to include the production of silk ribbons. By the time of his death in 1787 the Engelses' combination of commercial success and high-minded philanthropy had secured them a pre-eminent social position within Wuppertal society: Engels's grandfather, Johann Caspar II, was appointed a municipal councillor in 1808 and became one of the founders of Barmen's United Protestant Church.[4] But when the business was passed on to the third generation – Engels's father and uncles – the family dynamic crumbled. After repeated fallings out, in 1837 the three brothers drew lots to decide who would inherit the firm. Friedrich Engels senior lost and started up a new business, going into partnership with two Dutch brothers, Gottfried and Peter Ermen. There, he rapidly revealed his greater entrepreneurial gifts and his new company, Ermen & Engels, diversified from linen bleaching into cotton-spinning, setting up a series of sewing thread factories in Manchester and then in Barmen and nearby Engelskirchen in 1841.

This then was the world of the merchant-manufacturer elite (the so-called *Fabrikanten*) within which Engels grew up: a childhood encircled by industry and commerce, civic duty and family loyalty. Of course, such wealthy families as the Engelses – who lived, as one observer put it, in 'spacious and sumptuous houses, often faced with fronts of cut stone and in the best architectural styles' – were protected from the more nefarious effects of industrialization. But they could not avoid them altogether: following the steps of Johann Caspar along the Wupper had trudged tens of thousands of workers equally determined to share in the promises of industry.

Barmen's population grew from 16,000 in 1810 to over 40,000 in 1840. In Barmen and Elberfeld combined the population topped 70,000 – roughly the same size as 1840s Newcastle or Hull. The valley's workforce consisted of 1,100 dyers, 2,000 spinners, 12,500 weavers in various materials and 16,000 ribbon weavers and trimmings makers. The vast majority did their work in modest homes and small workshops, but a new generation of sizeable bleaching grounds and cotton mills was also starting up and by the 1830s there were nearly 200 factories operating along the valley. 'It is a long, straggling town, skirting both sides of the river Wupper,' as a visitor described it in the 1840s. 'Some parts are well-built, and are nicely paved; but the greater part of the town is composed of extremely irregular and very narrow streets ... The river itself is a disgusting object, being an open receptacle for all sewers, disguising the various tinctures contributed from the dyeing establishments in one murky impenetrable hue, that makes the stranger shudder on beholding.'[5]

What might once have been compared with the kind of pleasant rural-industrial mix seen in the mill towns of the Pennines or Derbyshire's Derwent Valley – high valleys topped with green fields and forests, bottomed out by clear, fast-running streams providing the initial water power for mills and workshops – soon came to resemble a polluted, overcrowded 'German Manchester'. 'The purple waves of the narrow river flow sometimes swiftly, sometimes sluggishly between smoky factory buildings and yarn-strewn bleaching-yards,' was how Engels would come to describe his birthplace. 'Its bright red colour, however, is due not to some bloody battle ... but simply and solely to the numerous dye-works using Turkey red.' From his earliest days, amidst the acrid stench of workshops and bleaching yards, Engels was exposed to this witches' brew of industrialization: the eye-watering, nose-bleeding pollution that blanketed the intense poverty and ostentatious wealth. As an impressionable young boy, he soaked it all up.[6]

Beyond the industry, visitors to the Wupper valley noticed something else. 'Both Barmen and Elberfeld are places where strong religious feelings prevail. The churches are large and well attended, and each place has its own bible, missionary, and tract societies.'[7] Contemporary sketches reveal a forest of church steeples jostling for space amongst the skyline of factory chimneys. For Engels, the Wupper valley was nothing less than the 'Zion of the obscurantists'. The spirit that dominated Barmen and Elberfeld was an aggressive form of Pietism, a movement within the German Lutheran (Protestant) Church which had first emerged in the late seventeenth century and stressed 'a more intense, committed and practical form of Christian observance'.[8] As the movement developed and diversified it often distanced itself from the formal structures and theology of the Lutheran Church and, along the Wupper valley, allied itself with a

Calvinist ethic which presaged sin, personal salvation and a renunciation of the world. On the one hand, this provided a religion of introspection which saw God's hand at work in all the tiny mysteries of life, as the letters which passed between Engels's parents clearly testify. In 1835, as Engels's mother, Elise, tended her dying father, her husband proffered to her the comfort of faith in God's omnipotent mercy. 'I am happy and thank God that you are coping with the illness of your beloved father in such a composed way,' he wrote from the family home. 'We all have good reason to thank the Lord for His guidance so far ... He [Elise's father] has enjoyed a generally happy life full of strength and health and now the good Lord seems to want to take the old man to him gently and without any pain. What can mortal man wish for more?' God's will could also be bathetically revealed in the most trivial occurrences. 'Things don't look good for your potatoes, my dear Elise,' Engels senior ominously warned his wife whilst she was on holiday in Ostend, 'they looked so fine but now have also been infected by this disease that is spreading everywhere ... it has never been seen before in this form and is now appearing in almost every country like a plague.' The lesson was clear. 'It is almost as if God wanted to show humanity in this godless age how dependent we are on Him and how much our fate rests in His hands.'[9]

In true Protestant fashion, the Wupper pietists subscribed to a priesthood of all believers finding salvation through unmediated, individual prayer alongside the difficult task of scriptural exegesis. The churches fulfilled a useful religious function, but it was through brotherhood and sermonizing, rather than celebration of the Eucharist, that they delivered their mission. The Barmen *Fabrikanten* displayed a Puritan-like morality (*Sittlichkeit*) which valued asceticism, studiousness, individual uprightness and personal reserve. Much of the psychological brittleness of Friedrich Engels senior can be traced to this deeply personal, often overweening faith. And, at least to begin with, his eldest son shared it. Engels was baptized at the Elberfeld Reformed Evangelical parish church, which was 'well known as an exemplary Reformed church, soundly Calvinist in its doctrine, well versed in Scripture, and reverent in worship'.[10] In 1837 Engels marked his Confirmation with a suitably evangelical poem.

Lord Jesus Christ, God's only son,
O step down from Thy heavenly throne
And save my soul for me.
Come down in all thy blessedness,
Light of Thy Father's holiness,
Grant that I may choose Thee.[11]

In contrast to such evangelical niceties, the other side of Pietism was a ruthless engagement with the material realities of the world drawn from the Calvinist notion of predestination: at the dawn of time, God had marked out the saved and the damned and, while no one could be certain of their status as chosen or condemned, one of the surest signs of election was worldly success. With a nod to Max Weber, the Protestant ethic and spirit of capitalism were hard at work among the churches and factories of the Wupper valley. Industriousness and prosperity were signs of grace and the most ardent pietists were often the most successful merchants – amongst them Johann Caspar II, whose sense of prudence and sobriety dictated both his religious and business ethos. 'We have to look to our own advantage even in spiritual matters,' he told his son Friedrich Engels senior in 1813. 'I think as a merchant in these matters too and seek the best price, as no person with whom I might like to waste an hour on trivial things can give me back a single minute of it.'[12]

If all time was God's time, and wasting a minute was a sin, then life was certainly not meant for enjoyment and socializing. As Engels's first biographer, Gustav Mayer, recorded, in the early nineteenth century the evangelical parishes in Elberfeld-Barmen petitioned the government against the erection of a local theatre, claiming that the allure of the stage could not coexist with industriousness in the Wupper valley. For the pietists, 'pleasure' was one of the heathen blasphemies.[13] The poet Ferdinand Freiligrath condemned Elberfeld as 'a cursed nest, prosaic, small-townish, sombre and reviled', and the adult Engels always recalled with a shudder its dour public culture.[14] 'Why, for us, the philistine Wuppertalers, Düsseldorf was always a little Paris, where the pious gentlemen of Barmen and Elberfeld kept their mistresses, went to the theatre, and had a right royal time,' he told the German Social Democrat Theodor Cuno, before adding sourly, 'But the sky always looks grey where one's own reactionary family lives.'[15] Such Puritan public morals were the product of a close alignment between political power and Church authority. Elberfeld's powerful Church elders, who governed the congregations, also held sway over the municipal institutions with a writ running right through the spiritual and secular realms.

And the Church's power was only growing in influence. In the wake of an agrarian crisis and economic downturn during the 1830s, the pietist message became more doctrinaire, mystical, even chiliastic. A revivalist sensibility gripped the Wupper valley, led by a charismatic preacher, Dr Frederick William Krummacher. 'He thrashes about in the pulpit, bends over all sides, bangs his fist on the edge, stamps like a cavalry horse and shouts so that the windows resound and the people in the street tremble,' recorded the young Engels. 'Then the congregation begins to sob; first the young girls weep, then the old women join in with a heart-rending soprano and the cacophony is completed by the wailing of the enfeebled drunken pietists . . . through all this uproar Krummacher's powerful voice rings out pronouncing before the whole congregation innumerable sentences of damnation, or describing diabolical scenes.'[16]

The Engelses were not such hot Protestants as that. Indeed, so zealous was this godly upswing that many leading Barmen families began to retreat from church activity during the 1840s to focus instead on hearth and home. Just as the evangelical revival in England led the way for the Victorian celebration of patriarchy and domesticity (think of the sentimental poetry of William Cowper, the garden aesthetic of John Claudius Loudon or the novels of Hannah More), so in the picturesque merchant homes of Barmen there was a renewed cultural stress on the value of a tight-knit household. This vehement championing of the family unit expressed itself in an almost suburban ethic: a high-bourgeois desire to draw the curtains tight, seal off the corrupting outside world and seek spiritual renewal in the simple pleasures of domestic ritual – reading, embroidery, pianoforte performances, Christmas celebrations and birthday parties. 'It is really nice and homely to have a piano!' Engels's father put it with almost Pooterish delight.[17] In the coming years, this parlour culture would be summed up in the cutting term *Biedermeier*, which combined the adjective *bieder*, a condescending designation of plainness, with the common surname, Meier, to describe the middle-class visual style, literature and values of the period.[18]

Despite the later sneers, this was a safe and caring if not always joyful environment for Engels, his three brothers and four sisters to grow up in. Best of all, their parents adored each other. 'You may not believe it but I was thinking about you all day and I could not find contentment in anything in the house,' Engels senior wrote to Elise, then visiting her parents in Hamm, before signing off with 'a few tender words for you ... Look, I suddenly feel like someone head over heels in love again. In all seriousness I can feel a spot of longing under my waistcoat (the one with the mother of pearl buttons, you know it). I don't think I will be able to last the four weeks.' Indeed, his correspondence from the early 1820s is replete with the most passionate protestations of love for his wife. 'Truthfully, dearest Elise, my heart yearns for us to be reunited, because I now feel a constant need to share everything with you.'[19] Engels's mother, descended from a family of intellectual rather than commercial bent (the van Haars counted headmasters and philologists amongst them), owned a far more generous, humorous, even subversive nature than her husband. One Christmas she went so far as to give Engels a book of Goethe's poetry – a writer generally dismissed in Barmen circles as 'a godless man', but for Engels 'the greatest of Germans'.[20] Meanwhile, Elise's own father, the pastor Gerhard van Haar, introduced the adolescent Engels to the legends of classical mythology – a subject which found fertile ground in his grandson's energetic imagination. 'O you dear Grandfather, who always treat us so kindly,' Engels began one poetic thank you note,

> Always helping us when our work isn't going so smoothly,
> While you were here, you told me many a beautiful story
> Of Cercyon and Theseus, and Argus the hundred-eyed monster,
> The Minotaur, Ariadne, and Aegeus drowned in the ocean,
> The Golden Fleece, the Argonauts and Jason defiant . . .[21]

Within this comfortable setting, Engels's father is traditionally portrayed as an unhappy, rigidly religious, money-hungry philistine thanks in no small part to his son's later bitter characterizations.

Philistine, it should be added, was a favoured term of abuse which Engels had co-opted from Goethe: 'A Philistine is an empty gut filled with fear who hopes that God will take pity on him.' But a reading of Engels senior's letters to Elise reveals a very different side to the man: commercial-minded, yes, patriotic and God-fearing, but also a loving son, doting father and uxorious husband, who shared numerous business decisions with his wife and frequently sought her advice. For all his puritanical reputation, he was also a keen musician who could play the piano, cello and bassoon and enjoyed few things more than a family concert. Nevertheless, it was his mother to whom Engels remained close long after his acrimonious split from his father. 'Were it not for my mother, who has a rare fund of humanity . . . and whom I really love,' Engels wrote some years later, 'it would not occur to me for a moment to make even the most paltry concession to my bigoted and despotic old man.'[22] If his childhood occasionally seemed to gasp for air under the weight of commerce and piety, there was also a warm foundation of music, laughter and love.

'Friedrich had a pretty average report last week. As you know, he has become more polite, outwardly, but in spite of the severe chastisements he received earlier, not even the fear of punishment seems to teach him unconditional obedience,' Engels senior wrote censoriously to Elise in August 1835 while she was back in Hamm caring for her dying father. 'Thus today I was again distressed to find in his desk a smutty book which he had borrowed from the lending library, a story about knights in the thirteenth century. The careless way he leaves such books about in his desk is remarkable. May God watch over his disposition, I am often fearful for this otherwise excellent boy.'[23]

Much to his father's chagrin, from an early age Friedrich started to chafe against the pietist strictures of Barmen life. His initial tutoring was in the local Stadtschule, where intellectual ambition was generally not encouraged. At age fourteen, he was transferred to the municipal Gymnasium in Elberfeld, where he lodged with a Lutheran schoolmaster. Purportedly one of the finest schools in Prussia, the more liberal Gymnasium certainly fostered Engels's gift for languages and, under the tutelage of a Dr Clausen ('the only one who can arouse a feeling for poetry among the pupils, a feeling which would otherwise be bound to perish miserably among the philistines of Wuppertal'), nurtured his growing interest in the myths and romance of ancient Germania. As his final school report put it, 'Engels showed commendable interest in the history of German national literature and the reading of the German classics.'[24]

Indeed, a romanticized patriotism was to be one of the earliest intellectual influences on the young Engels. In later decades he would often come to be unfairly decried as a dull, mechanistic Marxist – indeed, Marxism itself would frequently be described as a reductionist offshoot of Enlightenment thought – but the first seedlings of Engels's philosophical development are to be found in some of the most idealized writings in the Western cultural canon. Across Europe, part of the response to the political excesses of the French Revolution and the universalist rationalism of the Enlightenment was a flourishing of Romanticism. For the guiding principle of *Aufklärung* – as laid out in the French philosopher Marquis de Condorcet's icily Cartesian *Sketch for a Historical Picture of the Progress of the Human Mind*, with its prediction of infinite human development – was soon ridiculed as wildly hubristic. While the Enlightenment varied across national contexts, what the writings of Immanuel Kant, David Hume, Jeremy Bentham, Voltaire and the French *Encyclopédistes* shared was a collective reverence for the power of universal, human reason. Isaac Newton, whose gravitational discoveries had revealed God as a mathematician and the universe as clockwork, was their apostle. And in this new mechanical age, the differences of nations and cultures, along with the value of customary authority, religion and tradition, were put at naught in the face of an unbending scientific calculus. In this new cosmopolitan consensus, man was fundamentally the same in all times and all places and the job of legislators – Frederick the Great in Prussia; Joseph II in Austria; Catherine the Great in Russia – was to allow for the development of human self-expression through the liberation of reason.

Opposition to this Enlightenment ideal was as old as the movement itself and few led the reaction with more verve than the Whig politician and conservative philosopher Edmund Burke.[25] 'We are not the disciples of Voltaire,' he announced to his fellow Englishmen and, even before the rumbling of the tumbril through the streets of Paris, his

Reflections on the Revolution in France connected the awful rationality of Enlightenment thought with the bloodletting of the French Revolution. The insurgents of 1789, who 'despise experience as the wisdom of unlettered men' and 'reduce men to loose counters merely for the sake of simple telling', assumed that reason alone could construct a commonwealth. The so-called 'rights of man', Burke averred, were no substitute for the slow, elemental mystery of a state and civil society crafted down the generations. 'But the age of chivalry is gone. That of sophisters, economists, and calculators has succeeded; and the glory of Europe is extinguished for ever.'[26]

Yet the age of chivalry was exactly what the Romantics had in mind. From the late 1700s particularities of language, culture, tradition and custom confidently reasserted themselves across European intellectual life. In Scotland, the movement was led by the Celtic myth-maker James Macpherson and then by Walter Scott, author of the Waverley novels. In France, Chateaubriand's *Le Génie du Christianisme* venerated the much decried Catholic Church, while Joseph de Maistre excoriated the Enlightenment for its shallow understanding of human nature. And in England, the poetry of Wordsworth, Blake and Coleridge dwelled on the unique attributes of a national tradition with the 'Rime of the Ancyent Marinere', a conscious affront to any cosmopolitan notion of common culture, language and reason. 'In England, in Germany, in Spain, old native traditions, even superstitions, acquired a new force, a new respectability,' as Hugh Trevor-Roper put it. 'The old, customary organs of society, the old established beliefs, which had seemed so contemptible to the rationalists of the *Encyclopaedia*, now acquired a new dignity.'[27]

And nowhere more so than in Germany. As an aesthetic, cultural and political movement stretching over many decades and assuming simultaneously complementary and contradictory forms, Romanticism remains awkward to codify. However, if the Enlightenment was committed to a uniform and predictable human nature, Romanticism stressed the opposite – the irrational, emotional, imaginative and restless desire amongst its adherents to escape the narrow, prosaic present.[28] In terms of the German tradition one could begin with the work of the *Sturm und Drang* dramatists or Goethe's remarkable novel of passionate self-immersion, *The Sorrows of Young Werther*

(1774). Intellectually, German Romanticism might trace its roots to the mid-eighteenth-century writings of Johann Gottfried von Herder and J. G. Hamann, both of whom reacted to enlightened French civility by stressing the centrality of earthy German language to the construction of national culture. In his essay 'Treatise on the Origins of Language', Herder described language as a lyre with a tone all its own, with each national tongue the peculiar product of a specific people, or *Volk*. As such, it was traceable through a nation's primitive folk-tales, songs and literature; a peculiarly democratic notion of culture which helped to spur a growing interest in the German national, notably medieval past. Strasbourg's high Gothic cathedral, the pre-Reformation Catholic Church, hoary fairy-tales and the art of Dürer all became unique totems of Germany's communal greatness. As Madame de Staël put it in her bestselling history *Germania*, because the Teutonic people had never been conquered by the Romans and had passed straight from barbarism to medieval Christianity, 'Their imagination disports itself in old towers and battlements, among knights, sorceresses and spectres; and mysteries of a thoughtful and solitary nature form the principal part of their poetry.'[29]

Friedrich Schiller served to aestheticize this romantic impulse with his influential essay of 1795, 'On the Aesthetic Education of Man', presaging the role of art and culture in generating human self-formation (*Bildung*). Schiller suggested that the collapse of the organic cohesion of medieval society – that which Herder had venerated and Edmund Burke traced the disintegration of in revolutionary Paris – could be reversed only by a broad ethic of beauty and creativity. This was the call which the Schlegel brothers answered in 1798 when they launched the golden age of German Romanticism with their Jena-based journal, *Athenaeum*. Through its pages, the romantic artist, poet, wanderer or mystic appeared centre-stage embodying the spirit of the age whilst also battling with the awful personal angst which came from this higher calling. Caspar David Friedrich's moody paintings of heroic subjects confronting themselves in the face of vast forests and pounding waterfalls; E. T. A. Hoffmann's elusive, transcendent scores; and Schiller's poetry of freedom, rebellion and betrayal caught this introspective, romantic spirit in which individual experience was all.

But whilst Schiller and the Schlegels stressed the calling of the artist to rebind the social ties, their contemporaries the philosophers Novalis and Johann Gottlieb Fichte sought to revive the proto-nationalist ideas of Herder. His patriotic notion of the *Volk* ('the invisible, hidden medium that links minds through ideas, hearts through inclinations and impulses, the senses through impressions and forms, civil society through laws and institutions') proved particularly prescient in the aftermath of 1806 when Prussia succumbed to the might of the French Emperor Napoleon Bonaparte at the Battle of Jena.[30] Despite the generally enlightened nature of subsequent imperial French rule – with its Civil Code granting greater freedom of speech, constitutional liberty and Jewish rights than the Hohenzollern monarchy had allowed in Prussia – foreign occupation is rarely a popular condition and the years of French governance served only to intensify an aggrieved sense of Germanic identity. Fichte nursed this sentiment with a provocative series of lectures, 'Homilies to the German Nation', delivered at the Berlin Academy in 1807–8, in which he elevated Herder's idea of nationhood to emotional new heights. Only through the nation and its *Volk* could individuals realize their full freedom, he announced to a Berlin audience labouring under French rule, whilst the nation itself was a beautiful, organic entity with a soul and a purpose.

The result was a renewed outpouring of interest in the vernacular German past as embodied by the country's most famous philologists and fairy-tale aficionados, the brothers Jacob and Wilhelm Grimm. Having already published a journal entitled *Altdeutsche Wälder* (*Old German Forests*), which provided an archaeology of German customs, laws and language, in 1815 they issued a new appeal. 'A society has been founded that is intended to spread throughout all of Germany and has as its goal to save and collect all the existing songs and tales that can be found among the common German peasantry.' It was a work of 'imaginative state-building' and, despite the fact that many of the fairy- and folk-tales which the Grimms collated into their best-selling *Kinder- und Hausmärchen* came from middle-class ladies of French Huguenot origin, they had successfully added another inventive layer to the national German tradition.[31]

Behind the poetry and folk-tales, the operas and novels rumbled the hard-edged politics of Romanticism. When peace finally came to

Europe in 1815, following Napoleon's defeat at the Battle of Waterloo and the ensuing diplomatic carve-up at the Congress of Vienna, the Rhineland was annexed from France by Prussia. The free-thinking, industrial, urban world of the Rhine now fell subject to the Hohenzollern monarchy of Berlin and its dry, Junker ethos which set the merits of hierarchy and authority far above any democratic German culture. Yet across Prussia – as well as within the other principalities, kingdoms and free cities which would later constitute Germany – romantic, progressive patriots raised on the poetry of Novalis and nationalism of Fichte were mobilizing in support of a more unitary, more liberal German nation. Inspired by the legends and language of invented tradition, radicals now wanted to cleanse the memory of French occupation and Enlightenment hubris with a re-invigoration of national sentiment.

From 1815 in Jena, student *Burschenschaften* (fraternities or clubs) started to campaign for constitutional reform based on the idea of a Germanic *patria*. They decked themselves out in the black, red and gold colours of the Lützow volunteers (a patriotic Free Corps supposedly made up of armed students and intellectuals who heroically fought the French at the 1813 Battle of Leipzig) and swore loyalty to the fatherland – rather than to the indecisive Prussian King Frederick William III, who was then retreating from his earlier plans for constitutional reform. Part of this patriotic cult found expression in the 150 gymnastics clubs and 100,000-strong choral society movement which sprouted across Prussia, singing ballads and organizing festivals in praise of the fatherland. The movement's high point arrived in October 1817, when students from all over Germany gathered at Wartburg Castle (where Martin Luther had translated the New Testament into German) to celebrate the 300th anniversary of the Reformation and fourth anniversary of the Battle of Leipzig. Through a radical political culture built around a strong set of patriotic symbols, the Prussian war against Napoleon was being woven into a broader narrative of emerging German nationhood.[32]

All of which was deeply troubling to the kings and first ministers of Austria and the German Confederation, who fervently believed in dynasties not nations, monarchies not democracies. They responded with the Karlsbad Decrees of November 1819, which closed down the student societies, ended any talk of a written constitution, put the universities under police surveillance and quashed press freedoms. The 1820s then witnessed an accomplished campaign on behalf of the royal houses to snuff out the radicalism of German Romanticism – masterminded by the Machiavellian Austrian chief minister, Count Klemens von Metternich, whose relentless fear-mongering exercised a remarkable sway over the Prussian authorities.

How much of this Romanticism made its way into Barmen, that inward-looking Zion of the obscurantists? Here, remember, Goethe was just 'a godless man'. Yet encouraged by Dr Clausen and his own reading of medieval romances, the imagination of young Friedrich Engels was enlivened by this revival of German nationalism. In 1836 he penned a small poem altogether less godly than his Confirmation ode, eulogizing the deeds of such romantic legends as 'The Archer, William Tell', 'The warrior-knight Bouillon' and 'Siegfried', the dragon-slaying hero of the medieval *Song of the Niebelungs*. He wrote articles championing the democratic tradition of the German *Volksbüchner* and the work of the Brothers Grimm. 'These old popular books with their old-fashioned tone, their misprints and their poor woodcuts have for me an extraordinary, poetic charm,' he announced airily, 'they transport me from our artificial modern "conditions, confusions and fine distinctions" into a world which is much closer to nature.'[33] There were more poems venerating the life of the German national icon and father of printing, Johannes Gutenberg, and even pantheistic accounts of the divine glory of the German countryside ('gaze over the vine-fragrant valley of the Rhine, the distant blue mountains merging with the horizon, the green fields and vineyards flooded with golden sunlight . . .').[34] Throughout his long life, Engels never abandoned this youthful cultural patriotism. Even when he was championing the international solidarity of the proletariat and banned on pain of execution from his homeland, Engels retained an unexpected emotional empathy for the heroic world of Siegfried and the epic destiny he represented.

But it was never a sympathy shared by his father. Despite Engels's wish to stay on in school and glowing reports from his headmaster, in 1837 he was summarily withdrawn from the Gymnasium and ushered into the family business. Already concerned about his son's literary foibles and questionable piety, Engels senior had no qualms about removing him from the deviant intellectual circles surrounding Dr Clausen. Friedrich's hopes of studying law at university, perhaps entering the civil service, even becoming a poet – all hinted at in his final report from headmaster J. C. L. Hantschke, who spoke of how Engels was 'induced to choose [business] as his outward profession in life instead of the studies he had earlier intended' – were not to be.[35] Instead, for an arduous twelve months he was inducted into the dull mysteries of linen and cotton, spinning and weaving, bleaching and dyeing. In the summer of 1838 father and son embarked on a business trip around England to arrange silk sales in Manchester, *grège* (raw silk) purchases in London, and to look over the Ermen & Engels concerns. They returned via the northern German city of Bremen where Friedrich was set to embark on the next stage of his commercial apprenticeship: a crash course in international capitalism.

The coastal air of Bremen, a free town and Hanseatic trading city, proved altogether more congenial to Engels than the low Barmen mists. Of course, it too was a place of piety ('their hearts have been scrubbed with the teachings of Johann Calvin,' complained a resident of his fellow citizens), but as one of Germany's largest ports it was a centre of intellectual as well as commercial exchange. Apprenticed to the Saxon consul and linen exporter Heinrich Leupold, Engels worked as a clerk in the trading house and lodged with a friendly clergyman, Georg Gottfried Trevinarus. After the suffocating *Biedermeier* gentility of Barmen, the more relaxed Trevinarus household seemed a riot. 'We put a ring in a cup of flour and then played the well-known game of trying to get it out with your mouth,' he wrote to one of his sisters about a Sunday afternoon pastime.

We all had a turn – the Pastor's wife, the girls, the painter and I too, while the Pastor sat in the corner on the sofa and watched the fun through a cloud of cigar smoke. The Pastor's wife couldn't stop laughing as she tried to get it out and covered herself with flour over and over ... Afterwards we threw flour in each other's faces. I blackened my face with cork, at which they all laughed, and when I started to laugh, that made them laugh all the more and all the louder.[36]

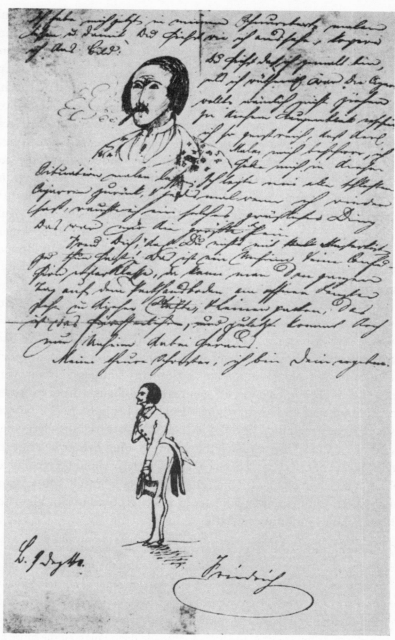

Engels's Bremen correspondence was a riot of doodles, puns and self-absorption. A letter of 6–9 December 1840 to Marie Engels.

This was just one of a series of letters to his favourite sibling, his younger sister or 'goose', Marie. They reveal a part of Engels's character which remained constant throughout his years: a roguish, gossipy, sometimes malicious sense of humour (which would meet its counterpart in Karl Marx) and an uncomplicated appetite for life. His correspondence is littered with nicknames, terrible puns, jottings, even musical chords, together with bragging accounts of doomed romances, alcoholic endurance and practical jokes. Unlike the cyclically despondent Marx, Engels rarely suffered from low spirits. Physically and intellectually, Engels was a Victorian man of action rather than of emotional reflection. Whether it was learning a new language, devouring a library or pursuing his Teutonic urge for hiking, Engels needed to be on the move, channelling his restless energies into seeking out the best of any situation. As the Victorian radical George Julian Harney noted, 'there was nothing of the "stuck-up" or "stand-offishness" about him . . . He was himself laughter-loving, and his laughter was contagious. A joy inspirer, he made all around him share his happy mood.'[37]

Engels's work in Bremen mainly involved handling international correspondence: there were packages to Havana, letters to Baltimore, hams to the West Indies and a consignment of Domingo coffee beans from Haiti ('which has a light tinge of green, but is usually grey and in which for every ten good beans, there are four bad ones, six stones and a half ounce of dirt . . .').[38] Through this clerking apprenticeship, he came to know the ins and outs of the export business, currency deals, and import duties – a detailed knowledge of capitalist mechanics which would, in years to come, prove of great worth to him as both businessman and communist. But for a wistful, young romantic like Engels, it was numbing stuff. And, as his father no doubt warned, idle hands made easy work for the devil. 'We now have a complete stock of beer in the office; under the table, behind the stove, behind the cupboard, everywhere are beer bottles,' he boasted to Marie. 'Up to now it was always very annoying to have to dash straight to the desk from a meal, when you are so dreadfully lazy, and to remedy this we have fixed up two very fine hammocks in the packing-house loft and there we swing after we have eaten, smoking a cigar, and sometimes having a little doze.'[39]

In addition to enjoying the relaxed working environment, Engels took advantage of Bremen's more liberal society. He signed up for dancing lessons, combed the city's bookshops (and helped to import some more politically risqué texts), went horse-riding, travelled widely and swam across the Weser, occasionally four times a day. He also took to the testosterone-ridden practice of semi-serious student fencing (*Mensurschläger*). Quick to take offence and even quicker to defend the honour of friends, family or political ideals, Engels liked his swordplay. 'I have had two duels here in the last four weeks,' he glowingly announced in one letter. 'The first fellow has retracted the insulting words of "stupid" which he said to me after I gave him a box on the ear . . . I fought with the second fellow yesterday and gave him a real beauty above the brow, running right down from the top, a really first-class prime.'[40]

Tempering his pugnacity, he also attended chamber concerts, attempted a few of his own musical compositions and joined the Academy of Singing – as much for the chance of meeting young women as exercising his baritone. For Engels was a suavely attractive, if not ruggedly good-looking, fellow: nearly six feet tall, with 'clear, bright eyes', sleek dark hair and a very smooth complexion. Encountering him in the 1840s, the German communist Friedrich Lessner described Engels as 'tall and slim, his movements ... quick and vigorous, his manner of speaking brief and decisive, his carriage erect, giving a soldierly touch'.[41] Accompanying his good looks came a shade of vanity. Engels's friends recalled him being especially 'particular about his appearance; he was always trim and scrupulously clean'.[42]

In future years, his youthful appearance would bring him numerous female admirers but in Bremen he tried to mitigate his boyishness with a determined facial hair strategy. 'Last Sunday we had a moustache evening [at the town-hall cellars]. For I had sent out a circular to all moustache-capable young men that it was finally time to horrify all philistines, and that could not be done better than by wearing moustaches.' Ever the poet, Engels composed a suitable toast for the heavy drinking which accompanied the evening.

> Philistines shirk the burden of bristle
> By shaving their faces as clean as a whistle.
> We are not philistines, so we
> Can let our mustachios flourish free.
> Long life to every Christian
> Who bears his moustaches like a man.
> And may all philistines be damned
> For having moustaches banished and banned.[43]

This masculine flamboyance constituted more than just fun and games. Joining a choral society and sporting a moustache (of which Engels was inordinately proud just as he would be of his beard in later years) were something of a political statement in the watchful, authoritarian era which followed Metternich's Karlsbad Decrees and then the equally repressive Six Articles of 1832. The denial of freedom of expression in newspapers and political associations resulted in a remarkable politicization of everyday life across Germany with clothes, insignia, music and even facial hair utilized as displays for republican patriotism – which provoked the Bavarian authorities to outlaw moustaches on security grounds. Engels embraced this *sotto voce* culture of subversion. In addition to his moustache and choral outings, he had Pastor Trevinarus's wife embroider a purse for him in the black, red and gold tricolour of the Lützow volunteers and he developed an ostentatious admiration for the great *German* composer Beethoven. 'What a symphony it was last night!' he wrote to Marie after attending an evening concert of the C Minor and *Eroica*, 'You never heard anything like it in your whole life . . . what a tremendous, youthful, jubilant celebration of freedom by the trombone in the third and fourth movement!'[44]

For amidst Bremen's cosmopolitan market of ideas, Engels had begun his political journey from Romanticism towards socialism with the discovery of 'the Berlin party of Young Germany'. Early nineteenth century Europe spawned an eclectic range of 'young' movements from Mazzini's *La Giovane Italia* to Lord John Manners' Young England cabal of aristocratic Tories to the Young Ireland republican circle, each of them championing a revival of patriotic sentiment based around a romanticized idea of nationhood. However, *Junges Deutschland* was far less of an identifiable political project and more a loosely aligned, 'realist' literary grouping, centred around the dissident and radical-liberal poet Ludwig Börne. Their unwritten manifesto demanded that the romantic Age of Art give way to the Age of Action, and Börne, a fierce opponent of Metternich's authoritarianism, was scathing towards the craven, political quietism which had been adopted by Goethe and other high-minded priests of Romanticism. 'Heaven has given you a tongue of fire, but have you ever defended justice?' he demanded of the Sage of Weimar whose career he ridiculed for its courtier-like servility towards princes and patrons.[45]

Börne's cause was cultural and intellectual freedom under a system of modern liberal governance, and he was highly dismissive of the nostalgic forests-and-ruins conservatism of traditional Romanticism. Exiled in Paris, having run foul of Metternich's censors, he moved towards republican politics whilst lobbing sarcastic barbs at the Prussian occupation of the Rhineland. Joining Börne in the Young Germany firmament were the poet Heinrich Heine, the novelist

Heinrich Laube and the journalist Karl Gutzkow. Gutzkow's notoriety came from his 1835 novel, *Wally the Skeptic*, which combined a racy narrative of sexual liberation with religious blasphemy and cultural emancipation. The lengthy ramblings of his 'new woman' heroine, Wally – with her liberal sentiments on marriage, domesticity and the meaning of the Bible – managed to encompass just about every known anathema to *Biedermeier* society. Metternich was not slow to act on such a dangerous affront to public morals and political stability and in 1835 he had the Diet of the German Confederation condemn the entire oeuvre of Heine, Gutzkow and Laube.

Engels identified enthusiastically with Young Germany's rejection of romanticized medievalism. Although he continued to be drawn to the heroic myths of the past on a literary level, he was equally convinced that Germany's political future could not entail a retreat to the feudal nostalgia of the Middle Ages. Instead, he expressed sympathy for a programme of radical, progressive patriotism which looked enticingly possible in the early years of the reign of Frederick William III. This was not a call for democracy but for the liberation of Germany from the parochialism of feudal, petty kingdoms and their absolutist rulers. Above all, as Engels wrote, what Young Germany wanted was 'participation by the people in the administration of the state, that is, constitutional matters; further, emancipation of the Jews, abolition of all religious compulsion, of all hereditary aristocracy, etc. Who can have anything against that?'[46]

Augmenting the radicalism of Young Germany, Engels's political consciousness was aroused by the poetry of the man he called 'the genius, the prophet', Percy Bysshe Shelley (whom he read together with Byron and Coleridge).[47] No doubt the office-bound Engels was excited by the heroic bravado of Shelley's rebellious, priapic lifestyle: the breach with his reactionary father, the doomed love affairs and devil-may-care nonchalance. But what also attracted him was Shelley's political philosophy. Not yet for Engels the 'recognizably pre-Marxist' writings of *An Address to the People on the Death of the Princess Charlotte* (1817) which, in contrasting public reaction to a royal death with the case of three recently executed labourers, directly connected political oppression to economic exploitation.[48] Rather, at this stage of his thinking, Engels was drawn to the radical republican, antireligious, socially liberal creed which Shelley explored in *Queen Mab* (1812):

> Nature rejects the monarch, not the man;
> The subject, not the citizen: for kings
> And subjects, mutual foes, forever play
> A losing game into each other's hands,
> Whose stakes are vice and misery.

No doubt he also enjoyed Shelley's thoughts on political economy.

> Commerce! Beneath whose poison-breathing shade
> No solitary virtue dares to spring;
> But poverty and wealth with equal hand
> Scatter their withering curses, and unfold
> The doors of premature and violent death,

Here was an idea of personal liberation tailor-made for Engels the radical romantic doomed to a life of commerce. Yet Shelley's celebration of political freedom in his 'Ode to Liberty' also touched a chord with Engels who responded with an 1840 poem, 'An Evening' (topped with Shelley's epigram, 'Tomorrow comes!')

> I, too, am one of Freedom's minstrel band.
> 'Twas to the boughs of Börne's great oak-tree
> I soared, when in the vales the despot's hand
> Tightened the strangling chains round Germany.
> Yes, I am one of those plucky birds that make
> Their course through Freedom's bright aethereal sea . . .

Shelley's Philhellenic epic *Hellas* similarly appealed to his accelerating nationalism. Indeed, the cause of Greek independence was a popular one in the Rhineland as dozens of local associations sprang up to assist in the 1820s struggle against the Ottomans, with the conflict used as something of a proxy for enthusiasts of Germany's own quest for national autonomy.[49] Engels himself had earlier penned a piece of narrative fiction, 'A Pirate Tale', which whimsically recounted a young man's struggle against the Turks and his 'fight for the freedom of the Hellenes . . . men who still have a taste for freedom'.[50] On multiple levels, the life and work of Shelley served as a source of inspiration for Engels and, stuck in Bremen during a dull summer in 1840, he even made plans to publish his own translations of *The Sensitive Plant*. Later, he would reveal to Eleanor Marx that at that time 'we all knew Shelley by heart'.[51]

Less loftily, developments in France were also sharpening Engels's political stance. He did not yet regard 1789 as the epoch-making event he later would and, at this stage, he was more enamoured of the bourgeois revolution of July 1830 – which had seen the ejection of King Charles X and his replacement with the constitutional monarch Louis-Philippe. For Young Germany, this had been the supreme example of 'freedom' in action. 'Each item was a sunbeam, wrapped in printed paper, and together they kindled my soul into a wild glow,' recalled Heine of receiving the news. 'Lafayette, the tricolor, the Marseillaise – it intoxicates me. Bold, ardent hopes spring up, like trees with golden fruit . . .'[52] Along the industrial settlements of the Rhineland, Paris's successful deployment of popular will against an aloof monarch was widely celebrated in a series of anti-Prussian riots. Once reviled for its occupation of the Rhineland, but now admired again for its national liberation, France and its July days stood for the overthrow of antiquated authoritarianism in the name of progress, freedom and patriotism. Compared with the revolutionary communism of his coming years, Engels's support for this bourgeois constitutionalism – with its commitment to the rule of law, the balance of power, the freedom of the press – was fairly mild stuff. But, at the time, it was exhilarating enough. 'I must become a Young German or rather, I am one already, body and soul,' he wrote in 1839. 'I cannot sleep at night, all because of the ideas of the century. When I am at the post-office and look at the Prussian coat of arms, I am seized with the spirit of freedom. Every time I look at a newspaper I hunt for advances of freedom.'[53]

In his free time in Bremen between the socializing, the Trevinarus family fun and games and the counting house, for the first time Engels began to write publicly of his hunt for freedom. Historically, Engels's style has been deemed inferior to Marx's: commentators are given to contrast the leaden, clinical prose of Engels with Marx's glittering, chiasmus-ridden wit. This is unfair. For Engels was, in fact, an elegant author in both his private and public writings until his work took a more doggedly scientific turn in the 1880s. That said, the case for the defence does not begin promisingly.

> Sons of the desert, proud and free,
> Walk on to greet us, face to face;
> But pride is vanished utterly,
> And freedom lost without a trace.
> They jump at money's beck and call
> (As once that had from dune to dune
> Bounded for joy). They're silent, all,
> Save one who sings a dirge-like tune . . .

'The Bedouin' – Engels's first published work – was an Orientalist poem eulogizing the noble savagery of the Bedouin people undone by their contact with Western civilization. Where once they walked 'proud and free', now they slavishly performed for pennies in Parisian theatres. Even for an eighteen-year-old it was a clumsy effort. Still it showed that under the dull routine of his commercial correspondence, Engels retained his romantic, Shelley-like ambitions. The work was, in fact, something of a tribute to Wuppertal's most celebrated poet-clerk, Ferdinand Freiligrath, who combined his work in the Barmen firm of Eynern & Söhne with a flourishing literary career. From the provincial banality of the Rhineland, Freiligrath conjured up a dreamland of exoticized tribes and sun-drenched landscapes typi-cally peopled by beautiful Negro princesses. Engels the bored clerk was enchanted and in numerous verses he shamelessly ripped off Freiligrath's tropes of Moorish princes, proud savagery and corrupt civilizations.

Yet he could not shake his youthful literary passion for the German mythical past and, in April 1839, he penned an (unfinished) epic play based around the life of the folk-hero Siegfried. It is full of demands for action and an end to reflection with battles entered and dragons slain. Most intriguing is the stress Engels lays on the psychological struggle between Siegfried and his father, Sieghard: while the former wants to run free ('Give me a charger and a sword / That I may fare to some far land / As I so often have implored'), the king thinks 'it's time he learned to be his age' ('Instead of studying state affairs / He's after wrestling bouts with bears'). After a war of words, the father finally lets go and Siegfried is free to follow his own path in life ('I want to be like the mountain stream / Clearing my route all on my own'). It doesn't require too much psychological insight to realize that, in the words of Gustav Mayer, this unfinished play represents 'the virtual embodiment of the battle that may have taken place in the Engels family in relation to Friedrich's choice of vocation'.[54]

More successful than his poetry was Engels's journalistic prose. 'The Bedouin' had been published in the Bremen paper *Bremisches Conversationsblatt*, and Engels – like any good hack – had immediately complained about the subs ruining his copy ('the fellow went and changed the last verse and so created the most hopeless confusion').[55] So he moved on to write for Karl Gutzkow's paper, *Telegraph für Deutschland*, and began to make his name as a precocious cultural critic from the Young Germany stable. Or rather, he began to make the name of his chosen, suitably medieval-sounding pseudonym, 'Friedrich Oswald' – an early indication of the tensions which would come to mark Engels's life. He wanted his opinions and criticisms to be heard, but at the same time he was keen to avoid the stress and anguish which would inevitably come from any open break with his family's values. For both his own financial security and his unwillingness to embarrass his parents publicly, Engels started out on his double life as 'Oswald'.

The *Telegraph*'s in-house style was the *feuilleton*: unable, due to Prussian censorship, to publish detailed political commentaries, the progressive papers embedded their criticism in literary and cultural pieces, even travelogues. The writer became an intellectual *flâneur*, interspersing social and political points among reflections on regional culture and cuisine, memory and myth. Landscapes, boat journeys and poetry provided Engels with just the romantic cover he needed to expound his liberal, nationalist sensibilities. Thus a travelogue on Xanten, 'Siegfried's Native Town', allowed Engels to mount a critique of conservatism in the name of freedom and youth. As our correspondent enters the town, the sound of High Mass filters from the cathedral. For the emotional 'Oswald' the sentiments are almost too much to take. 'You, too, son of the nineteenth century, let your heart be conquered by them – these sounds have enthralled stronger and wilder men than you!' He gives himself up to the myth of Siegfried, drawing from it a modern message: the need for energy, action and heroic contempt in the face of the petty, deadening bureaucracy of the Prussian state and its newly ascended monarch – the religio-conservative Frederick William IV. 'Siegfried is the representative of German youth. All of us, who still carry in our breast a heart unfettered by the restraints of life, know what that means.'[56]

Engels's most substantive writing for the *Telegraph* was markedly less high-flown. During the 1830s the Rhineland textile industry was finding it increasingly difficult to challenge the industrialized English competition. The old-fashioned outwork practices of the Barmen artisans – with textile goods produced by hand in home workshops – were proving no match for the efficient, mechanized manu-factories of Lancashire. Even within Germany, with its free trade *Zollverein* (Prussia-led Customs Union), the situation was bleak as the Rhenish advantage in textile goods fell away to competition from Saxony and Silesia. French demand for silk weaving and ribbon took up some of the slack, but it was a volatile, fashion-driven market subject to sharp drops in demand. These economic changes brought a steady worsening of conditions among Barmen workers and the gradual disintegration of the kind of paternalist corporate structures that the Engels family had traditionally prided itself on. Guilds were disbanded, incomes squeezed, working conditions undermined and the old social economy of apprenticeships, wage differentials linked to skill levels and properly paid male labour came under sustained assault. In their place sprang up a stark, new divide between worker and manufacturer which for those on the edges of the textile economy – handspinners, hosiers and weavers – meant a rapid diminishment of income and position.

This new economic reality was reflected in the growing usage of the terms 'pauperism' and 'proletariat' by journalists and social commentators in referring to the kind of rootless, propertyless, casual urban workers who lacked regular employment and security: the thousands of unemployed and under-employed knife-grinders, shoemakers, tailors, journeymen and textile labourers who crowded into the towns and cities of the Rhineland. In cities such as Cologne between 20 and 30 per cent of the population were on poor relief. The German social theorist Robert von Mohl described the modern factory worker – unlikely ever to be apprenticed, to become a master, inherit property or acquire a skill – as akin to a 'serf, chained like Ixion to his wheel'. The political reformer Theodor von Schön used proletariat as a synonym for 'people without home or property'.[57]

'Friedrich Oswald', however, did something rather different. In a style he would in the coming years define as his own, Engels got amongst the people to produce an extraordinarily mature piece of social and cultural reportage. No lofty social theories about the nature of pauperism and the meaning of the proletariat for this son of a factory owner. Instead his 'Letters from Wuppertal' – published in the *Telegraph* in 1839 – offered an unrivalled authenticity, an eye-witness experience of the depressed, drunken, demoralized region. When Engels contrasted the reality of Barmen life with his romanticized ideal of what the motherland was meant to be – the imagined nation of Herder, Fichte and the Brothers Grimm peopled by a lusty, patriotic *Volk* – the disappointment was tangible. 'There is no trace here of the wholesome, vigorous life of the people that exists almost everywhere in Germany. True, at first glance it seems otherwise, for every evening you can hear merry fellows strolling through the streets singing their songs, but they are the most vulgar, obscene songs that ever came from drunken mouths; one never hears any of the folk-songs which are so familiar throughout Germany and of which we have every right to be proud.'[58]

Written by a nineteen-year-old industrial heir, the *Letters* provided a magnificently brutal critique of the human costs of capitalism. Engels points to the red-dyed Wupper, the 'smoky factory buildings and yarn-strewn bleaching yards'; he traces the plight of the weavers bent over their looms and the factory workers 'in low rooms where people breathe in more coal fumes and dust than oxygen'; he laments the exploitation of children and the grinding poverty of those he would later term the lumpenproletariat ('totally demoralized people, with no fixed abode or definite employment, who crawl out of their refuges, haystacks, stables, etc., at dawn, if they have not spent the night on a dungheap or on a staircase'); and he charts the rampant alcoholism amongst the leather-workers, where three out of five die from excess schnapps consumption. Decades on, this memory of industrializing

Barmen continued to haunt him. 'I can still well remember how, at the end of the 1820s, the low cost of schnapps suddenly overtook the industrial area of the Lower Rhine and the Mark,' Engels wrote in an 1876 essay on the social effects of cheap alcohol. 'In the Berg country particularly, and most notably in Elberfeld-Barmen, the mass of the working population fell victim to drink. From nine in the evening, in great crowds and arm in arm, taking up the whole width of the street, the "soused men" tottered their way, bawling discordantly, from one inn to the other and finally back home.'[59]

The *Letters'* prose was biting, but did the high-living and studiously intellectual Engels, the moustachioed fencer and *feuilleton* author, feel any personal empathy for these Wuppertal unfortunates? Official communist biographies are unequivocal that Engels's politics 'rested on a profound and genuine feeling of responsibility vis-à-vis the lot of the working people. Their sufferings grieved Engels who was anything but a prosaic, cold, matter-of-fact person.'[60] Certainly, any reader of Engels's work always takes away a clear picture of injustice and its causes, but whether the author was emotionally affected or merely ideologically motivated by such misery remains unclear. At this stage, all that can be said is that his strength of feeling for the Barmen underclass was probably as much the product of a rebellious antagonism towards his father's generation as any considered sentiment for the workers' plight.

Whatever the motivation, the criticisms cascaded down the *Telegraph* columns – as if carefully noted and steadily accumulated since childhood. The miserly vulgarity of the Wuppertal employers was reflected in the town's design, with 'dull streets, devoid of all character', shoddy churches and half-completed civic monuments. To the now sophisticated eye of the Bremen-based Engels, the town's so-called educated elite were nothing more than philistines. There was precious little talk of Young Germany along the Wupper valley, which was filled instead with endless useless gossip about horses, dogs and servants. 'The life these people lead is terrible, yet they are so satisfied with it; in the daytime they immerse themselves in their accounts with a passion and interest that is hard to believe; in the evening at an appointed hour they turn up at social gatherings where they play cards, talk politics and smoke, and then leave for home at the stroke of nine.' And the worst of it? 'Fathers zealously bring up their sons along these lines, sons who show every promise of following in their fathers' footsteps.' It was already apparent that that was not a fate Engels was willing to chance.

Despite the *Letters*' critique of working conditions and the social costs of industrialization, Engels's real target was not capitalism *per se*. He had as yet no real understanding of the workings of private property, the division of labour or the nature of surplus labour value. The true focus of his ire was the religious Pietism of his childhood. Here was a conscious, studied rejection of the guiding ethic behind his family's lineage by a young man disgusted at the social costs of religious dogma. Learning, reason and progress were all stunted by the deadening, sanctimonious grip of Krummacher and his congregations. And the factory workers were embracing the pietist fervour in the same way they consumed their schnapps: as a mystical route out of their all-enveloping misery. Meanwhile those manufacturers who most ostentatiously advertised their godliness were well known as the most exploitative of employers whose personal sense of election seemed to absolve them of the need to abide by respectable human conduct. To Engels the romantic ideologue, Wuppertal was sinking beneath a tide of moral and spiritual hypocrisy. 'This whole region is submerged in a sea of pietism and philistinism, from which rise no beautiful, flower-covered islands.'[61]

'Ha, ha, ha! Do you know who wrote the article in the *Telegraph*? The author is the writer of these lines, but I advise you not to say anything about it, I could get into a hell of a lot of trouble.' Engels's 'Letters from Wuppertal' sparked a highly gratifying public storm along the Wupper valley. The personal criticism of Krummacher, together with the linkage of Pietism and poverty, was strong stuff – and, though delighted by the controversy, 'Friedrich Oswald' was not quite ready to be exposed as one of Barmen's leading sons. Instead, he was content to enjoy a knowing chuckle with some Wuppertal friends from the safety of Bremen.[62] His correspondents were his old class mates the Graeber brothers – Friedrich and William – sons of an Orthodox priest and themselves training for the priesthood. Through a typically candid series of letters which Engels wrote to them between

1839 and 1841, we are offered an insight into the most important intellectual shift of Engels's Bremen years: his loss of faith.

It is a cliché of nineteenth-century intellectual historiography that the road to socialism was paved by secularism. From Robert Owen to Beatrice Webb to Annie Besant, the disavowal of Christianity was a familiar rite of passage for those whose spiritual journey would culminate with the new religion of humanity. But its obviousness does not invalidate its truth. 'Well, I have never been a Pietist. I have been a mystic for a while, but those are *tempi passati*. I am now an honest, and in comparison with others very liberal, super-naturalist' was how Engels described his religious temperament to the Graebers in April 1839. He had long been dissatisfied with the narrow spiritualism offered by Wuppertal Pietism, but he remained, aged nineteen, a long way from rejecting the central tenets of Christianity. However, amidst the intellectual liberalism of Bremen life, Engels felt he now wanted more from his Church than predestination and damnation. He was increasingly troubled with the notion of original sin and hoped some-how to unite his Christian inheritance with the progressive, rationalist thinking he had absorbed from Young Germany. 'I want to tell you quite plainly,' he informed Friedrich Graeber, 'that I have now reached a point where I can only regard as divine a teaching which can stand the test of reason,' before then pointing out the numerous contradictions within the Bible, querying God's divine mercy and taking special delight in exposing a series of astronomical howlers in a recent Krummacher sermon.[63]

In the summer of 1839 he thought he might have found an accept-able compromise to his spiritual crisis in the teachings of Friedrich Schleiermacher whose redemptive theology, with its stress on an intuitive religion of the heart compatible with the modern demands of reason, seemed a very different faith from the hellfire and dam-nation of 'our valley of hypocrites'. For Engels, Schleiermacher was said to 'teach the word of Christ in the sense of "Young Germany"'. But even that paled after Engels came across *the* theological bombshell of early nineteenth-century Europe. David Friedrich Strauss's *The Life of Jesus critically examined* had appeared in 1835–6 and, to many young men, proved a terrifying, secular revelation. 'The spell that this book exercised over one was indescribable,' was how the liberal philosopher Rudolf Haym put it. 'I never read any book with so much pleasure and thoroughness . . . It was as though scales fell from my eyes and a great light was shed on my path.'[64]

Strauss's book directly questioned the literal truth of the Bible: he regarded the Gospels not as infallible holy scripture but rather as the historically and culturally contingent product of their time. It was preferable, he averred, to approach the Gospels as Jewish myths or imaginative representations expressive of a specific stage of human development – and, consequently, not applicable to the current age. In turn, the figure of Christ was best substituted for the idea of 'humanity'. The effect of *The Life of Jesus* was to open up the Bible to a more rigorous process of intellectual and scriptural enquiry, and Engels rushed to be in the vanguard. 'I am very busy at present with philosophy and critical theology. When you get to be eighteen years of age and become acquainted with Strauss . . . then you must either read everything without thinking or begin to doubt your Wuppertal faith,' he priggishly informed the Graebers. Over the next few months Engels returned again and again to biblical contradictions, the impact of new geological findings on Christian timelines and the question of original sin. But, as he recounted in a letter to Friedrich Graeber, shedding a lifetime's indoctrination was not an easy or comfortable process.

I pray daily, indeed nearly the whole day, for truth, I have done so ever since I began to have doubts, but I still cannot return to your faith . . . My eyes fill with tears as I write this . . . To be sure, you lie comfortably in your faith as in a warm bed, and you know nothing of the fight we have to put up when we human beings have to decide whether God is God or not. You do not know the weight of the burden one feels with the first doubt, the burden of the old belief, when one must decide for or against, whether to go on carrying it or shake it off.[65]

By October 1839 the doubts had passed. There was no autumnal, 'Dover Beach' tidal melancholy for Engels – once the decision was made, he embraced his new spiritual status with relish. 'I am now a Straussian,' he told William Graeber matter of factly. 'I, a poor, miserable poet, have crept under the wing of the genius David Friedrich Strauss . . . *Adios* faith! It is as full of holes as a sponge.'[66] Engels was, as he later put it, 'utterly and wholly lost' from the standpoint of orthodox Christianity. And, true to form, he now supported his newly adopted stance with total conviction, teasing Friedrich Graeber as the 'great hunter of Straussians'.[67]

Behind the banter Engels seemed relieved that his spiritual journey had come to a conclusion. Having lost one faith, he moved swiftly to assume another: the psychological vacuum left by the demise of his Christian convictions was filled by an equally compelling ideology. Strauss was just a stepping stone. 'I am on the point of becoming a Hegelian. Whether I shall become one I don't, of course, know yet, but Strauss has lit up lights on Hegel for me which makes the thing quite plausible to me.'[68] The purpose of Strauss's criticisms had never been to show that Christianity was false *per se*; rather, he had hoped to show that the doctrine was no longer adequate for the new scientific age. Strauss's ambition was to take his readers to the next stage of spiritual development after Christianity – which was Hegelian philosophy.[69] 'Now I'll study Hegel over a glass of punch' was how Engels wisely approached the work of Europe's most abstruse, arcane and brilliant philosopher. But it would prove worth the struggle: the writings of Hegel eventually shunted Engels along the path towards socialism. In the coming decades Marx's reinterpretation of Hegel's dialectics would loom large over communist ideology, but at this stage of Engels's self-tutelage it was Hegel's pure philosophy which was of such great interest.

At the core of the Hegelian system was an interpretation of history which consists of the realization or unfolding of 'Mind' or 'Spirit' (the notoriously untranslatable *Geist*). Spirit, or self-conscious reason, was perpetually in motion and constituted the only true reality in the world; its unfolding was the chronicle of human history. Engels was instantly attracted to this new sense of a rational, ordered development of the past as laid out in Hegel's *Philosophy of History*, a transcription of his lectures to the University of Berlin in 1822–3. 'What distinguished Hegel's mode of thinking from that of all other philosophers was the exceptional historical sense underlying it,' as he later put it.[70]

What dictated the history of Spirit was the concrete actualization of the Idea of freedom in human affairs, and the achievement of that freedom constituted Spirit's absolute and final goal. Yet true freedom could be the product only of reason and rationality – as evidenced in language, culture and the 'spirit of the people'. Only once humans had the capacity of judgement could they really be free. Therefore the passage of history consisted of the organic growth of freedom and reason in civilization in a teleological manner which ultimately culminated in the fulfilment of the Spirit. 'The history of the world is none other than the progress of the consciousness of freedom,' in Hegel's words. At every stage, history was advancing in that direction even when it seemed most wayward and hopeless. For beneath the chaos and anarchy of human affairs the sly cunning of reason remained steadily at work. Thus Hegel's analysis of the past fully begins only with the emergence of the Greek city-states in which he sees the emergence of freedom and reason.

Christianity was a part of this story of all-encompassing progress – it, too, fitted within the framework of rational development. In obvious historical terms, events such as the Protestant Reformation had markedly accelerated freedom and individuality. It was through the faculty of reason, which man shared with God, that man came to self-consciousness and was reconciled with God. Hegel rejected the old dualism of man and God, the immanent and the transcendent, embodied in the traditional teachings of orthodox Christianity, and instead proffered a reconciliation of the individual self with the absolute as the fulfilment of human experience in the world.[71] In the modern age this would take place through the supersession of religious faith by knowledge and cultivation; universities and schools were to subsume the work of the Church. In that sense, religion would become part of the everyday world, its values incarnate in the family, the state and culture. What Engels took from this was an idea of modern Pantheism (or, rather, Pandeism) which dissolved the pietist ethos of religious alienation and, instead, merged divinity and humanity together. God and reason became one in the unfolding of freedom and progress. 'Through Strauss I have now entered on the straight road to Hegelianism . . . The Hegelian idea of God has already become mine, and thus I am joining the ranks of the "modern pantheists",' Engels wrote in one of his final letters to the soon to be discarded Graebers.[72]

After the doubts and confusions of the previous few months, Engels embraced his new Hegelian faith with characteristic enthusiasm. In a classic *feuilleton* for Gutzkow's *Telegraph* entitled 'Landscapes' (1840), Engels compared the refreshing spray and glistening sun enjoyed on a voyage across the North Sea to 'the first time the divine Idea of the last of the philosophers [Hegel], this most colossal creation of the thought of the nineteenth century, dawned upon me, I experienced the same blissful thrill, it was like a breath of fresh sea air blowing down upon me from the purest sky'. Engels had found temporary solace in a new, animating, naturalistic God. As Gareth Stedman Jones puts it, Hegel offered 'a secure resting place to replace the awesome contours of his Wuppertal faith'.[73]

However, those other elements of Engels's intellectual make-up didn't simply fade away. Alongside the Hegelianism, there was still the passion for German Romanticism, the allure of Young Germany's liberal-constitutionalism and the republican impulses of Shelley and July 1830. These strands came together in one of his last Bremen articles. A review of the German author Karl Immerman's *Memorabilien* provided Engels with the occasion for a *cri de coeur* which wove together the 'new philosophy' with his favourite trope of Siegfried-like heroism. 'He who is afraid of the dense wood in which stands the palace of the Idea, he who does not hack through it with the sword and wake the king's sleeping daughter with a kiss, is not worthy of her and her kingdom; he may go and become a country pastor, merchant, assessor, or whatever he likes, take a wife and beget children in all piety and respectability, but the century will not recognize him as its son.'[74]

By early 1841 Engels had reached the conclusion that his own recognition as one of the century's sons was far from assured if he remained deskbound in Bremen. 'There is nothing to do but fence, eat, drink, sleep and drudge, *voilà tout*,' he wrote to Marie. He returned to Barmen, but his lofty romantic soul found the parental home and office work in the family firm even more tedious. So, in September 1841, he agreed to the Prussian state's demand that he fulfil his military duties and he 'volunteered' for one year's service with the Royal Prussian Guards Artillery, 12th Company. Berlin, the Prussian capital, would offer this bourgeois son of a provincial textile merchant just the stage he needed in support of the Idea. Here, at last, he could reveal himself as a latter-day Siegfried in the service of the modern age.

2

The Dragon's Seed

'Ask anybody in Berlin today on what field the battle for dominion over German public opinion is being fought,' Engels wrote in 1841, 'and if he has any idea of the power of the mind over the world he will reply that this battlefield is the University, in particular Lecture-hall No. 6, where Schelling is giving his lectures in the philosophy of revelation . . .'[1]

Even for such a bullish philosopher as Friedrich Wilhelm Joseph von Schelling, it must have been a daunting class to teach. It was, said another observer, 'an extraordinary audience . . . select, numerous and diverse'. Arrayed around the lecture hall sat some of the most gifted young minds of the nineteenth century: earnestly taking notes at the front was the autodidact Engels – happy, at this point, to describe himself simply as 'young and self-taught in philosophy'; alongside him perched Jacob Burckhardt, the nascent art historian and Renaissance scholar; Michael Bakunin, the future anarchist (who dismissed the lectures as 'interesting but rather insignificant'); and the philosopher Søren Kierkegaard, who thought Schelling talked 'quite insufferable nonsense'. But, far worse, the revered philosopher committed the cardinal academic crime of ending his lectures over the hour. 'That isn't tolerated in Berlin, and there was scraping and hissing.'[2]

Engels, however, was mesmerized by the grey-haired, blue-eyed Schelling and his relentless critique of his hero, Hegel. In a philosophical battle royal, week by week Schelling attempted to unpick Hegel's pantheism by insisting on the direct power of the divine in history. It was revelation versus reason. 'Two old friends of younger days, room mates at Tübingen theological seminary, are after forty years meeting each other again face to face as opponents; one of them ten years dead but more alive than ever in his pupils; the other, as the latter say, intellectually dead for three decades, but now suddenly claiming for himself the full power and authority of life.' And Engels had no doubts as to where his sympathies lay: he was in the lecture hall, he said, to 'shield the great man's grave from abuse'.[3]

Though his official remit in Berlin was military training in support of the Prussian monarchy, Engels spent his time garnering the ideological tools to undermine it. As often as possible he left behind the parade ground for the university campus to immerse himself in theorems that would prove far more deadly than a six-pounder cannon. And he did so in deeply hostile terrain.

The Berlin which Engels entered in 1841 was fast turning into a civic monument to the Hohenzollern dynasty. Its residents, number-ing some 400,000 by the mid-1840s, had witnessed much over the previous half-century: the flight of their king, Frederick William III, and Emperor Napoleon's 1806 victory march through the Branden-burg Gate; liberation by the Russians in 1813 and, with it, a steady churn of reform, Romanticism and then reaction. The forces of reaction had triumphed in the 1820s and 1830s as Frederick William marked the restoration of royal authority with a neo-classical build-ing boom. Under architect Karl Friedrich Schinkel, the modern Berlin of bombastic public spaces and royal grandeur was carved out: the Doric Schauspielhaus (now the Konzerthaus Berlin), his ornately sculptured Schlossbrücke and then, along Unter den Linden, the imperial Roman Neue Wache guardhouse and, finally, his master-piece, the Pantheon-inspired Altes Museum. This was the innately anti-intellectual Berlin of the court, the army and the Junker aristoc-racy of the east Prussian plains. In later years Engels remembered how utterly ghastly it all was, 'with its scarcely formed bourgeoisie, its loud-mouthed petit-bourgeoisie, so unenterprising and fawning, its still completely unorganized workers, its masses of bureaucrats and hangers-on of nobility and court, its whole character as mere "residence"'.[4]

But, as would so often be the case with this endlessly divided city, there was another Berlin. Close by the parade grounds of his

Kupfergraben barracks (renamed by the GDR in 1963 as the Friedrich Engels Barracks, home to the Wachregiment Friedrich Engels of the National Peoples' Army) lay a bustling public sphere of cafés, ale-houses and wine-cellars. By the mid-1830s Berlin boasted over one hundred cafés in the city centre alone, providing official and unofficial newspapers, debating clubs and drinking dens. This was the *Konditorei* culture of political and literary discourse in which over-opinionated and under-employed academics thrived. Each café attracted its own clientele: the Kranzler, on the corner of Friedrichstrasse and the Linden, was known as the 'Walhalla of Berlin Guard Lieutenants' for its officer regulars and swanky interior; the Courtin, near the Bourse, catered to the bankers and businessmen; and Stehely's, across the road from Schinkel's Schauspielhaus, was home to the city's artists, actors and 'literary elements'.[5]

Feeding the bars of the Gendarmenmarkt neighbourhood was the nearby Friedrich-Wilhelms-Universität – renamed in 1949 the Humboldt-Universität after its founder, Wilhelm von Humboldt. Charged by Frederick William III during a more liberal period of office in the early 1800s with crafting an educational system for an enlightened citizenry, Humboldt and education minister Baron von Altenstein brought together in Berlin an extraordinary constellation of talents. Engels's one-time favourite theologian, Friedrich Schleiermacher, was appointed a professor; the more reactionary Karl von Savigny taught law; Georg Niebuhr lectured in history; whilst in 1818 Hegel succeeded Fichte as chair of philosophy. With Hegel on the faculty, the university naturally became a leading centre of Hegelian thought – so much so that the poet Heinrich Heine, a regular at Stehely's, expressed his relief in 1823 at leaving a city of 'thick sand and thin tea' inhabited by a population of know-alls 'who have long comprehended everything under the sun . . . through Hegelian logic'.[6]

Not everyone regarded this profusion of Hegelian logic with such weary detachment – especially not the new king, Frederick William IV (who had succeeded his father in 1840), and his chief minister, Johann Albert Friedrich Eichhorn. After a brief flirtation with a free press and political reform, the Hohenzollern genetic distrust of pluralism reasserted itself. 'He [Frederick William] commenced with a show of liberality,' Engels recounted, 'then passed over to feudalism; and ended in establishing the government of the police-spy.'[7] And so in 1841, as part of a broader clampdown on left-wing thinking, Eichhorn recalled the greying, 66-year-old Schelling to Berlin 'to root out the dragon-seed of Hegelianism' in the very university where it had first been sown. This was the philosophical tussle Engels was so enjoying from his ringside seat in lecture hall No. 6.

Why was Hegelianism so feared by the Prussian authorities? It certainly hadn't unnerved von Humboldt and Frederick William III, who had consistently appointed known Hegelians to influential professorships and state posts. 'The Hegelian system,' Engels later remarked of this period, 'was even raised, as it were, to the rank of a royal Prussian philosophy of State,' while 'Hegelian views, consciously or unconsciously, most extensively penetrated the most diversified sciences and leavened even popular literature and the daily press.' But that official endorsement was now set to be withdrawn.[8]

The answer to this divergence lies in two, often contradictory, readings of Hegel. The first is conservative. According to Hegel, that which exists at any one point in time necessarily embodies Spirit (*Geist*), the unfolding of which constituted the progress of human history and the existing power of reason. 'What is rational is actual and what is actual is rational' was the famous Hegelian dictum. 'Once that is granted, the great thing is to apprehend in the show of the temporal and transient the substance which is immanent and the eternal which is present.'[9] If history is the process that oversees this triumphant march of reason towards freedom, then each consecutive era can be regarded as necessarily more progressive, rational and freer than the preceding one, and every component of that era – its art, music, religion, literature, forms of governance – represents a higher stage of reason than the last. This is most especially the case when it comes to the state, which Hegel took to mean an organic body encompassing elements of both government and civil society.

For Hegel, the state was the means by which the individual will was reconciled with the grander imperatives of universal Reason, through obedience to the law: 'in duty the individual finds his liberation . . . from mere natural impulse . . . In duty the individual acquires his substantive freedom.'[10] Such freedom came when man's subjective sensibilities were aligned with the progressive development of Spirit, as it manifests itself through the medium of the state. As Hegel put it in his *Philosophy of Right* (1820):

The state is the actuality of concrete freedom. But concrete freedom consists in this, that personal individuality and its particular interests not only achieve their complete development and gain explicit recognition for their right (as they do in the sphere of the family and civil society), but, for one thing, they also pass over of their own accord into the interest of the universal; they even recognize it as their own substantive mind; they take it as their end and aim and are active in its pursuit.[11]

In the Hegelian template, the modern state, in contrast to ancient states based around slavery, represented 'the realization of freedom, an end in itself, "the divine idea as it exists on earth" and the reality which alone gives value to the individual life'.[12] In theory, the modern state embodied progress, reason and the Idea of freedom.

And there seemed to be a brief moment, in the aftermath of the 1806 Jena defeat, when the Prussian state might in practice signify that Hegelian ideal of rational freedom as set out in *The Philosophy of Right*. For this was the era of liberal reform, which had been forced upon Frederick William III by his military humiliation in 1806 and then implemented by his progressive-minded ministers, Baron Karl von Stein and Prince Karl August von Hardenberg. Serfdom was reformed, hereditary service abolished, Jews emancipated, economic controls freed up and gentle moves made in the direction of democratic representation. As part of this liberalization project, Hegel was brought from the University of Heidelberg to the newly founded Berlin University (where he held the chair of philosophy until his death in 1831 from cholera) to give the movement his intellectual imprimatur. 'Hegel in turn hailed the reformed Prussian state as an example of a state that had attained world-historical stature by making the political actualization of Reason its inner purpose and essence,' according to Hegel's intellectual biographer John Edward Toews.[13] And there is no doubt that Hegel's philosophical elevation of the state granted a rich, spiritual dignity to the bureaucratic apparatus of Frederick William III.

His advocacy of the state as a living entity, possessing in its laws and political structures a defined purpose based upon Reason and freedom to which individuals had to submit themselves (so that their own will self-consciously became a part of the common will), dramatically elevated its purpose. The state was not just a necessary evil to protect private property, defend the realm and manage the rule of law. Instead, it now had a far loftier purpose encompassing no less than the realization of absolute reason. And while the finer phenomenology of Hegelian philosophy might have been lost on some of the Berlin court, they quickly realized the political opportunities this reverence for authority presented. 'His writings provided an exalted legitimacy for the Prussian bureaucracy, whose expanding power within the executive during the reform era demanded justification,' according to the historian of Prussia, Christopher Clark. 'The state was no longer just the site of sovereignty and power, it was the engine that makes history, or even the embodiment of history itself.'[14] Yet, by the 1820s, the era of Stein, Hardenburg and liberal reform had fallen prey to a court counter-attack by the reactionary old guard. In the face of a growing tide of Romanticism and nationalism, Frederick William III retreated towards monarchical conservatism. But even as the Prussian state rolled out the oppressive 1819 Karlsbad Decrees and curtailed press and legal safeguards – all a long way from Hegel's vision of a free, liberal, rational state – the same, now anachronistic Hegelian justifications were deployed.

Hegel's radical protégés, meanwhile, offered a more progressive interpretation of their master's work. Facing the actual, revanchist philistinism of the Prussian state – with its growing authoritarianism, religious restrictions and diminishing possibility of constitutional reform – many of Hegel's disciples could not accept that their mentor (who had once planted a Liberty Tree in honour of the French Revolution) really believed this state of affairs to be the pinnacle of reason. Indeed, history seemed to be moving in a decidedly unprogressive direction when, as Engels put it, in 1840 'orthodox sanctimony and absolutist feudal reaction ascended the throne' with the succession of Frederick William IV.[15] If not quite a subscriber to the divine right of kings, Frederick William IV certainly held an exalted idea of Christian monarchy, with the sovereign linked to the people by a mystical, sacred bond which no parliament or constitution could sully. Frederick William IV's watch was to be no epoch of progress – instead, a sturdy commitment to tradition, continuity and hierarchy. And it was increasingly apparent that the alternative, more radical Hegelianism being preached on the Prussian campuses was at odds with such conservative dogma.

When it came to Hegel, the danger was in the dialectic. 'Whoever placed the emphasis on the *Hegelian system* could be fairly conservative in both spheres; whoever regarded the *dialectical method* as the main thing could belong to the most extreme opposition, both in religion and politics,' was how Engels later described the difference. This 'dialectical progression' was how the march of history happened: each age and its ruling idea was negated and subsumed by the following epoch. 'Position, opposition, composition', as a young Karl Marx explained. 'Or to speak Greek we have the thesis, antithesis and synthesis. For those who do not know the Hegelian language, we shall give the ritual formula: affirmation, negation, negation of the negation.'[16] Thus, the realization of Spirit in history involved a perpetual critique of every preceding political system and form of consciousness – each era successively undermined by the tension within itself – until rationality and freedom prevailed. 'Therein lay the true significance and the revolutionary character of Hegelian philosophy,' as Engels put it, '. . . all successive historical states are only transitory stages in the endless course of development of human society from the lower to the higher . . . Against it [the dialectic] nothing is final, absolute, sacred.'[17]

This interpretation offered an extraordinarily powerful ideological solvent. For Hegel's more radical readership there now existed no immutable, eternal truths: every civilization had its own realities, philosophies and religion, all liable to be negated and subsumed. What was more, this was as much the case for Hegel's own thinking as for any previous philosophy. The publicly funded Berlin professor had made the crucial mistake of thinking that the reformist-era Prussian state – of Stein, Hardenberg and Humboldt – might have been the culmination of Reason in history. But, in fact, it was just another transitory stage now set to be negated. For those sceptical students sitting through Schelling's lectures, Hegel's philosophical method provided not a justification of the Prussian status quo, but tools for a progressive critique of the Hohenzollern state. To these 'Left' or 'Young Hegelians', Hegel's philosophy became a spur to action, his writings a demand for liberal reform.

As was so often the case with the origins of early socialism, it was religion which generated the sharpest attacks. Just as Hegel had regarded the Prussian state as the final fulfilment of Reason, so his Lutheran faith had led him to endorse a narrow conception of Protestant Christianity dominant in the 1820s as the *summum bonum* of spiritual life. Once again it appeared that history had conveniently managed to culminate precisely in the cultural and religious practices of Hegel's own era. And, just as with politics so with religion, the Young Hegelians criticized Hegel for not appreciating his own historicism, for not understanding that what he considered the realization of freedom was simply another step along the path towards the Idea. How, they asked, was modern European Christianity different from Roman paganism or the Hindu faith of ancient India? Was not each simply a product of its times? In an anonymous critique of Schelling's lectures, published in Leipzig in 1842 under the title 'Schelling and Revelation', Engels announced how the Young Hegelians would 'no longer regard Christianity' as off-limits for critical investigation. 'All the basic principles of Christianity, and even of what has hitherto been called religion itself, have fallen before the inexorable criticism of reason.'[18]

As we have seen, the groundwork for this religious critique had been laid by David Strauss's reinterpretation of the Gospels as myth. Bruno Bauer, a theologian and philosopher who had studied under Hegel, took the critique a stage further with a detailed analysis of Christianity as a cultural construct. Known as 'a very decided man who, under a cold exterior, burns with an inner fire', Bauer thought the dialectic could progress only through a process of violent intellectual assault. Each age's verities needed to be ripped down in the face of reason. And such a process of rational assault led Bauer to conclude that in the modern era Christianity was an obstacle to the development of self-conscious freedom. The worship of an exterior God, the submission to creed and dogma, alienated man from his true essence. There could be no chance of human self-consciousness or realization of freedom as long as the ritual demands of mystical subservience remained in place. Summoning the dialectic, Bauer declared that such alienation was hindering the onward march of history and had to be transcended.

Behind this lofty metaphysics lurked a direct political challenge to the Christian principles that legitimized the Hohenzollern monarchy and its right to govern. Once regarded as the very bulwark of the state, Hegelian philosophy was now being deployed to undermine Prussia's religio-political foundations. Unsurprisingly, Frederick William IV was appalled and, in March 1842, he had the subversive Bruno Bauer dismissed from his post at the University of Bonn. But it would take more than a departmental demotion to temper the Young Hegelian advance. The next salvo had already been launched by Ludwig Feuerbach's *The Essence of Christianity* (1841). It finally expunged any conservative remnants of Hegelianism. As Engels recalled:

With one blow it pulverized the contradiction, by plainly placing materialism on the throne again . . . Nothing exists outside nature and man, and the higher beings our religious fantasies have created are only the fantastic reflection of our own essence. The spell was broken; the 'system' was exploded . . . One must have experienced the liberating effect of this book for oneself to get an idea of it. Enthusiasm was universal: we were all Feuerbachians for a moment.[19]

Feuerbach too was a former pupil of Hegel and just as keen as Bauer to apply the dialectical method to Christianity. Expanding upon Bauer's notion of alienation, he argued that the advance of religion must be understood as the progressive separation of man from his human, sensuous self. In the Christian God-head man had created a deity in his own image and likeness. Yet so replete with perfection was this objectified God that man started to abase himself before its spiritual authority. Consequently, the original power relationship was reversed. 'Man – this is the secret of religion – projects his essence into objectivity and then makes himself an object of this projected image of himself that is thus converted into a subject.' And the more fervently man worshipped this exterior God, the more internally impoverished he became. It was a zero-sum relationship: for the deity to prosper, man had to be degraded. 'Religion by its very essence drains man and nature of substance, and transfers this substance to the phantom of an other-worldly God, who in turn then graciously permits man and nature to receive some of his superfluity,' as Engels put it. 'Lacking awareness and at the same time faith, man can have no substance, he is bound to despair of truth, reason and nature . . .' In his 1844 *A Contribution to the Critique of Hegel's Philosophy of Right*, Karl Marx would put it more succinctly: 'Religion is the sigh of the oppressed creature, the heart of a heartless world, and the soul of soulless conditions. It is the opium of the people.'[20]

True to the critical ethos of the Young Hegelians, Feuerbach then performed intellectual parricide by turning his fire on his former tutor, Hegel himself. What, Feuerbach wanted to know, was the substantive difference between the theology of Christianity and the philosophy (or 'rational mysticism') of Hegel? Were they not both metaphysical belief systems involving self-alienation – in order to elevate God in one case and the even more intangible *Geist* in the other? 'Speculative theology [i.e. Hegelianism] distinguishes itself from ordinary theology by the fact that it transfers the divine essence into this world. That is, speculative theology envisions, determines, and realizes in this world the divine essence transported by ordinary theology out of fear and ignorance into another world.'[21] Philosophy was nothing more than religion brought into the realm of thought.

In terms of separating man from the realities of life, Feuerbach suggested, there was little to choose between Hegelian philosophy and the Christian religion. Feuerbach advocated an end to both and, with it, the transference of Christ and *Geist* to humanity. In place of God or the Idea, he wanted Man: anthropology not theology. 'Whoever fails to give up the Hegelian philosophy, fails to give up theology. The Hegelian doctrine, that nature or reality is *posited* by the Idea, is merely the *rational* expression of the theological doctrine that nature is created by God.'[22] And both needed to be shed for man to regain his true essence, his 'species-being'. The idealistic Hegel had made the mistake of deriving being from thought, rather than thought from being, and, as such, had turned reality on its head. What Feuerbach urged was not idealism but materialism: in place of the metaphysical theorizing of Hegel and ethereal march of Spirit, a concentration on the lived reality of man's natural, corporeal, 'immediate' existence.

*

This was all heady stuff for a young artillery officer meant to be learning his way around a smooth-bore six-pounder and seven-pound howitzer. Yet the allure of parade-ground drilling and projectile arithmetic had quickly paled for Engels. Allowed, as a volunteer with a generous private income, to live in private lodgings rather than barracks, he spent his days at the lecture halls, reading rooms and beer cellars of *demi-monde* Berlin. There was only one element of military life he truly relished. 'My uniform, incidentally, is very fine,' he wrote to his sister Marie soon after his arrival in Berlin, 'blue with a black collar adorned with two broad yellow stripes, and black, yellow-striped facings together with red piping round the coat tails. Furthermore, the red shoulder-straps are edged with white. I assure you the effect is most impressive and I'm worthy to be put on show.' Engels liked nothing more than wowing polite society with his glittering attire. 'Because of this the other day I shamefully embarrassed Ruckert, the poet, who is here at present. I sat down right in front of him as he was giving a poetry reading and the poor fellow was so dazzled by my shining buttons that he quite lost the thread of what he was saying . . . I shall soon be promoted to bombardier, which is a sort of non-commissioned officer, and I shall get gold braid to wear on my facings.'[23]

He also acquired a dog – a handsome spaniel playfully named '*Namenloser*' or 'Nameless' – which he took to his favourite Rhineland restaurant to fill up on pork and sauerkraut. 'He had a great talent for boozing and if I go to a restaurant in the evening, he always sits near me and has his share, or makes himself at home at everybody else's table.' Too skittish to be trained properly, the dog had managed to learn only one trick. 'When I say "Namenloser" (that's his name) – "there's an aristocrat!" he goes wild with rage and growls hideously at the person I show him.' In 1840s Berlin this could have been a rather regular occurrence.[24]

In addition to evenings with his growling spaniel, Engels would pass his time thrashing out matters philosophical with the Young Hegelians over a glass of the capital's industrial-strength white beer. 'We would meet at Stehely's and, in the evenings, at this or that Bavarian ale-house in Friedrichsstadt or, if we were in funds, at a wineshop in the Postrasse . . .'[25] At various times the inner circle included Bruno Bauer and his brother Edgar, the philosopher of 'ego'

Max Stirner, the historian and Buddhist scholar Karl Köppen, political science lecturer Karl Nauwerck, journalist Eduard Meyen, renegade University of Halle lecturer Arnold Ruge and others. Their iconoclastic ethos extended seamlessly from the philosophical realm to their public personae. Known as 'Die Freien' ('The Free') – or 'beer literati', as Bauer termed them – this band of aggressive, arrogant intellectuals ostentatiously discarded modern morality, religion and bourgeois propriety.[26] In his memoirs, the proto-communist and apprentice typesetter Stephan Born recalled this world of 'Bruno Bauer, Max Stirner and the circle of noisy characters that surrounded them, who had called attention to themselves through their open dealings with emancipated women'. Edgar Bauer's penchant for pornography was especially disturbing to the strait-laced young Born. 'Already just upon entering his room, I was shocked by the obscene lithographs he had hung on the wall; and the conversation he began with me as he read the proofs [of his novella] was no less repulsive in character.'[27]

Engels, always liberal-minded in matters of sex and morality, embraced the lifestyle of The Free with alacrity. If his father had hoped that Engels might shed his youthful radicalism in Berlin's rigid court society, he could not have been more disappointed. Instead, Engels now dropped the prevaricating idealism of Young Germany (just as he had earlier discarded the religiosity of the Graeber brothers) and gave his heart and head to Bauer, Stirner, Köppen et al.[28] – with the attraction of the circle no doubt enhanced by the terrible shock such counter-culture camaraderie would have given his respectable parents. So enamoured was Engels with his new band of friends that he sketched a picture of The Free at one of their debauched drinking sessions. There are fallen chairs, half-empty wine bottles, an enraged Edgar Bauer smashing a table, a cool Max Stirner smoking, a grumpy (or sozzled) Köppen sitting at the table and a pugnacious Bruno Bauer marching towards Arnold Ruge with his fists raised. Rows, fights and splits were very much a part of the Young Hegelian ethic. In bitter tones Ruge later described this moment as Bauer and his cohorts 'screamed insult after insult in the Weinstube [wine cellar] and huddled together about me as I left. All this they find brilliant and free.'[29] Floating in the sky above the tussle are a squirrel, symbolizing the Prussian minister Eichhorn (in a play on the German Eichhörnchen for 'squirrel') and a guillotine, which is either an acknowledgement of Bruno Bauer as the 'Robespierre of Theology' or a signature reference to Engels himself.

Engels's sketch of 'The Free' enjoying a typically boozy Berlin evening.

For another of Engels's creative acts with The Free was a mock-epic poem co-authored with Edgar Bauer. *The Insolently Threatened Yet Miraculously Rescued Bible, Or: The Triumph of Faith* was written in protest at Bruno Bauer's dismissal from Bonn and took the form of a *Paradise Lost*-style meditation on the struggle between Satan and God for the souls of the Young Hegelians (who are all destined for hell). A heavy-handed medley of theology and philosophy, it reads now as little more than a cleverly done student skit. Still, the description of Bruno Bauer has about it something of the catchiness of Gilbert and Sullivan's 'I Am the Very Model of a Modern Major General'.[30]

> I've studied matters Phenomenological,
> Theological also, to my distress,
> Aesthetical too, Metaphysical, Logical,
> Not entirely without success

Similarly, Hegel's cameo appearance is wittily done.

> To Science I've devoted every hour,
> And I've taught Atheism with all my power.
> Self-consciousness upon the Throne I seated,
> And thought that God had thereby been defeated . . .

Behind the farce, some more revealing elements to these character sketches are discernible – not least, Engels's own depiction of himself. 'Friedrich Oswald', the aspirant Siegfried and author of high-flown *feuilletons*, had metamorphosed amidst the Berlin beer cellars into an altogether more fiery figure, nothing less than a French revolutionary Montagnard nursing his guillotine.

> Right on the very left, that tall and long-legged stepper
> Is Oswald, coat of grey and trousers shade of pepper;
> Pepper inside as well, Oswald the Montagnard;
> A radical is he, dyed in the wool, and hard.
> Day in, day out, he plays upon the guillotine a
> Single solitary tune and that's a cavatina,
> The same old devil-song; he bellows the refrain:
> *Formez vos bataillons! Aux armes, citoyens!*

And close behind him appeared another figure who, in the coming years, Oswald – and Engels – were to come to know rather well.

> Who runs up next with wild impetuosity?
> A swarthy chap of Trier, a marked monstrosity.
> He neither hopes nor skips, but moves in leaps and bounds,
> Raving aloud. As if to seize and then pull down
> To Earth the spacious tent of Heaven up on high,
> He opens wide his arms and reaches for the sky.
> He shakes his wicked fist, raves with a frantic air,
> As if ten thousand devils had him by the hair.[31]

What is there left to say of Karl Marx, the 'swarthy chap of Trier'? 'He is a phenomenon who made a most deep impression,' was how Moses Hess described him. 'Be prepared to meet the greatest, perhaps the only real philosopher living now. When he will appear in public he will draw the eyes of all Germany upon him . . . he combines deepest philosophical seriousness with cutting wit. Can you imagine Rousseau, Voltaire, Holbach, Lessing, Heine and Hegel combined – not thrown together – in one person? If you can, you have Dr Marx.' Gustav Mevissen, a Cologne businessman, depicted an equally mesmerizing figure: 'a powerful man of 24 whose thick black hair sprang from his cheeks, arms, nose and ears. He was domineering, impetuous, passionate, full of boundless self-confidence, but at the same time deeply earnest and learned, a restless dialectician who with his restless Jewish penetration pushed every proposition of Young Hegelian doctrine to its final conclusion.'[32]

Marx was born two years before Engels, into a similarly bourgeois household along the banks of another tributary of the Rhine (the Mosel, rather than the Wupper), but his upbringing was signally different from the tight Pietism of the Engelses. In this south-western region of the Rhineland, the post-1806 Napoleonic occupation had fostered a notably more liberal outlook amongst the middling sort. Marx's father, Heinrich, an attorney and small-scale vineyard owner, was imbued with the ideals of the French Enlightenment and precisely the kind of Rhineland liberalism which Ludwig Börne and others of the Young Germany school had sought to disseminate. He knew his Voltaire and Rousseau by heart, his heroes were Newton and Leibniz, and he was active in Trier's Casino Club, where like-minded progressives spent their evenings mulling over the political and cultural controversies of the day.

However, Heinrich was really Hirschel (or Heschel), having changed his name, abjured his Jewish faith and been baptized into the Lutheran Church in 1817. The Prussian annexation of Rhineland from the French in 1815 had deprived the Jews of Trier of their Napoleonic freedoms, subjecting them to a range of sanctions that forbade them to hold public office or practise law. Rather than becoming 'breadless', Heinrich converted. In doing so, he abandoned a rabbinical lineage stretching back to the early 1700s, which had included Karl Marx's grandfather and uncles as rabbis of Trier. However, Heinrich – the Enlightenment acolyte of Newton and father of nine hungry children – did not seem overly upset about extinguishing his Judaic lineage. His wife, Henriette, found it a more difficult departure: she spoke Yiddish and kept certain Jewish customs alive in the household long after she and the children had been baptized.

Despite Heinrich's politic conversion, his broad outlook could not have been more different from the evangelical conservatism of Friedrich Engels senior. He was also a more obviously affectionate father. His lengthy letters to the adolescent Karl are heartfelt, indulgent and full of earnest, paternal trepidation. His often febrile, anxious tone was aggravated by Henriette who turned a myopic love of family into a habit of congenital worrying. Nonetheless, Marx's childhood, like Engels's early years, was all in all a happy one spent making mud-pies with his sisters and getting into scrapes at school. But by the time Karl entered the University of Bonn at the age of seventeen, he had begun to distance himself from his family. Indeed, Marx's subsequent, steely separation from his parents and siblings was far more systematic than Engels's tortured efforts at detachment.

Instead, Marx directed his emotional energies towards another family altogether: the von Westphalens. Baron Ludwig von Westphalen was a Protestant in a predominantly Catholic Trier, a liberal-minded career civil servant within the Prussian government. Despite his aristocratic ancestry he became friends with the bourgeois Heinrich Marx and enjoyed taking his gifted son, Karl, on long country hikes during which he would recite great chunks of Shakespeare and Homer. However, Karl was more interested in Ludwig's daughter, the beautiful Jenny von Westphalen. And, to everyone's surprise, Jenny – the sophisticated daughter of a Prussian aristocrat and 'the most beautiful girl in Trier' – fell in love with the lively wit and dashing bravado of the hairy Jewish boy. In 1836 she broke with her officer fiancé and promised herself to the man she would come to call her 'wild black boar', her 'wicked knave' – and, the tag that finally stuck, her 'Moor' (or 'Mohr') with all its implications of Levantine mystery and hirsute Oriental 'otherness'. While Marx's own family expressed horror at his increasingly reckless activities, Jenny only revelled in his trouble-making, student radicalism and fiendish impetuosity. They married in 1843. 'Their love survived all the trials of a life of constant struggle,' in the words of Stephan Born. 'I have rarely known such a happy marriage, in which happiness and sorrow (mostly the latter) were shared and all pain was overcome in the assurance of complete, reciprocal belonging.'[33]

The young Marx was certainly wild. Indulged and scolded in equal measure by his parents, when he was given the freedom of campus life in 1835 the results were predictably transgressive. At Bonn, he skipped Law Faculty lectures to become president of the Trier Tavern Club, which involved raucous drinking sessions, nights in police cells and even a duel with a Prussian officer, from which he was lucky to escape with only a cut above the left eye. 'Is duelling then so closely interwoven with philosophy?' vainly enquired Heinrich. 'Do not let this inclination, and if not inclination, this craze, take root. You could in the end deprive yourself and your parents of the finest hopes that life offers.'

Engels's swordmanship was far more reliable – as was his constitution. While Engels was very rarely under the weather, Marx lived constantly at the very edge of his intellectual and physical capacities. 'Nine lecture courses seem to me rather a lot and I would not like you to do more than your body and mind can bear,' Heinrich warned him as he started university. 'A sickly scholar is the most unfortunate being on earth. Therefore, do not study more than your health can bear.' Marx took no notice as he embarked on his life-long habit of smoking, reading and working late into the night. When he combined this workload with prodigious drinking bouts the consequences were nearly lethal. After one 'almighty binge' many years later, the oxen-like Engels emerged punctually for work the next morning clear headed, while Marx was knocked out for two weeks.

After a wasted year at Bonn, Marx departed for Berlin to complete his legal studies. Heinrich despatched him with a warning of the intellectual perils awaiting him in the heartland of Hegelianism, where 'the new immoralists twist their words until they themselves do not hear them'. Naturally discarding such advice, Marx exchanged his legal training for philosophy just as swiftly as Engels would flee the parade ground for the lecture hall. His conversion to the Hegelian system was not long in coming. In true *Die Freien* fashion, he celebrated it in the beer cellars of Französische Strasse with the Young Hegelian circle. Together with Arnold Ruge and Bruno Bauer, he formed the heavy-drinking, heavy-philosophizing Doktorclub run out of Hippel's Weinstube.

At home in Trier, Heinrich was mortified. 'Alas, your conduct has consisted merely in disorder, meandering in all the fields of knowledge, musty traditions by sombre lamplight; degeneration in a learned dressing gown with uncombed hair has replaced degeneration with a beer glass,' he wrote to his son. 'Your intercourse with the world is limited to your sordid room, where perhaps lie abandoned in the classical disorder the love letters of a Jenny and the tear-stained counsels of your father . . .' But the philosophical fire had been lit and Marx now had even less time for the petty concerns of his parents – despite continuing to extract money from them. Despairing to his final days at the way his son's life was unfolding, Heinrich died of tuberculosis in 1838. Karl Marx failed to attend the funeral – and then, with characteristically lachrymose self-indulgence, carried a portrait of Heinrich with him for the rest of his days.

Freed from his father, the following year Karl abandoned his law degree and began a PhD on what appeared a dry-as-dust topic – 'The Difference between the Democritean and Epicurean Philosophy' – but which was, in fact, a comparative critique of contemporary German philosophy in the aftermath of Hegel in light of a similar period in Greek thought. Its conclusion embraced the Young Hegelian project of philosophical criticism in the name of ever-widening human self-consciousness. Under the beady eyes of Eichhorn, Schelling and the 'Right Hegelian' university administration, it had little chance of passing in Berlin, but the University of Jena was altogether more pliable, and in 1841 Karl Marx emerged with a doctorate dedicated to Baron von Westphalen.

The question was then, what to do next? Family funds were running low after his father's death, while plans for academic work with Bruno Bauer at the University of Bonn were quashed together with the latter's 1842 dismissal. The solution was journalism. Marx started channelling his philosophical analysis into more concrete political directions with a series of articles on censorship (which were instantly censored), property rights, economic distress and the Prussian administration. Slowly, Marx was turning his revolutionary intellect from philosophical reflection to social realities. He wrote initially for Arnold Ruge's *Deutsche Jahrbücher*, then joined the Cologne-based *Rheinische Zeitung*. By October 1842 his energy, political chicanery and obvious writing talent had secured him the editor's chair.

Under his stewardship, the paper's circulation doubled and it gained a national reputation for provocative, close-to-the-wind reporting. 'It was immediately clear that he had the qualities which are essential in all great journalists: a determination to speak truth to power, and absolute fearlessness even when writing about people whose friendship or support he might need.'[34] There is much in this assessment by Francis Wheen of Marx as editor and hack, but he was never above the usual journalistic weakness of keeping the proprietors happy. And, in this case, the funders of the *Rheinische Zeitung* – 'For Politics, Commerce and Industry' – were a Cologne-based mercantile elite committed to protecting the liberal advances of the Napoleonic years from Prussian absolutism. For commercial if not necessarily political reasons, they wanted to retain religious toleration, freedom of speech and constitutional liberty and to work towards national German unification. Marx was happy to do their bidding even if it meant ditching some old friends.

To these staid Rhineland liberals, the notorious Berlin antics of *Die Freien* – the atheism, loose lifestyles, political extremism and drunken rows – risked torpedoing their gently reformist agenda. Marx realized The Free were jeopardizing his career prospects. 'Rowdiness and blackguardism must be loudly and resolutely repudiated in a period which demands serious, manly and sober-minded persons for the achievement of its lofty aims,' the former president of the Trier Tavern Club and drunken stalwart of the Doctors' Club now sternly informed his readers. He was even blunter in a letter to Ruge complaining how irresponsible Young Hegelian contributors were raising the censor's hackles and the threat of closure.

[Eduard] Meyen & Co. sent us heaps of scrawls pregnant with world revolutions and empty of thought, written in a slovenly style and flavoured with some atheism and communism (which these gentlemen have never studied) . . . I declared that I considered the smuggling of communist and socialist ideas into casual theatre reviews was unsuitable, indeed, immoral, and a very different and more fundamental treatment of communism was required if it was going to be discussed at all.

Given this bad blood, it was little surprise that one of the most influential friendships in Western political thought got off to such a thoroughly unpromising start. When in November 1842, Engels dropped into the *Rheinische Zeitung* offices,

I ran into Marx there and that was the occasion of our first, distinctly chilly meeting. Marx had [meanwhile] taken a stand against the Bauers, i.e. he had said he was opposed not only to the *Rheinische Zeitung* becoming predominantly a vehicle for theological propaganda, atheism, etc., rather than for political discussion and action, but also to Edgar Bauer's hot air brand of communism . . . Since I corresponded with the Bauers, I was regarded as their ally, whereas they caused me to view Marx with suspicion.[35]

There was also, perhaps, not a little jealousy on Marx's part. He was notoriously touchy about any hint of ideological competition and by the early 1840s the young Engels had gained a name for himself. Despite the cloak of anonymity, his 'Letters from Wuppertal', pamphlet on 'Schelling and Revelation' and much of his journalism for the *Telegraph für Deutschland* and the *Rheinische Zeitung* had marked him out as an up-and-coming man in radical print. Trying hard to establish his own journalistic presence, Marx was not overly inclined to welcome the young Berlin officer.

Engels too was searching for a new role as he headed back to Barmen from Berlin. He had finished his military service in October 1842, receiving the standard approbation for his one year's volunteering and an acknowledgement that he 'conducted himself very well during his period of service in respect both of morals and service'.[36] Engels senior, though, was not convinced by such official commendation, and in a letter to his brother-in-law Karl Snethlage expressed grave concerns about how he and Elise were to manage his radical heir's homecoming. 'I have known since childhood his tendency to extremes and was convinced, although he never wrote to me about his views since he was in Bremen, that he would not keep to those ordinarily held.' But they were not willing to compromise their own beliefs. 'I shall make clear to him that merely for his sake or because of his presence I shall neither change nor conceal my views, either in respect of religion or politics; we shall continue entirely our former way of living and read the word of God and other Christian books in his presence.' The anxious, pious father could only be patient: 'His conversion must come from above.'. . . 'Until then it is hard to bear having a son in the house who is like a black sheep in the flock and adopts a hostile attitude to the faith of his fathers.' There was one possible solution. 'I hope to be able to give him a fair amount of work, and wherever he may be I shall watch over him unnoticed with the greatest care so that he does not take any dangerous step.'[37] The plan was to send Engels away to Manchester to look after the Ermen & Engels investment in Salford where he would learn something of the 'English commercial method' before returning to assist in the Engelskirchen factory. Surely the thunderous mills and dour merchants' parlours of 'Cottonopolis' would prevent any further radicalization? It was another forlorn hope. On his way to Manchester, Engels encountered communism.

Eric Hobsbawm has written of how late Marx and Engels arrived at communism; they were equally slow when it came to socialism.[38] In the 1830s and early 1840s, even though the terms were often used interchangeably, socialism and communism constituted relatively distinct philosophical traditions, each with a different intellectual and political lineage and each flourishing long before the arrival of our two Prussian protagonists.*

The origins of socialism are particularly slippery and, in variant

---

* A further word about socialists and communists. In the 1830s and 40s, the French followers of Saint-Simon and Charles Fourier were widely known as socialists. By contrast, the Parisian secret societies organized around the ideas of Etienne Cabet and Louis-Auguste Blanqui (see below, p. 73), who looked back to the French Revolution for inspiration, were described as communists. During the early to mid-1840s, Marx and Engels followed contemporary practice in often using the terms communist and socialist without clear demarcations. In the words of Raymond Williams, 'until c. 1850 the word [socialist] was too new and too general to have any predominant use'. As we shall see, Marx and Engels's political alliance with the militant, working-class Communist League and belief in a more 'proletarian' form of socialism, led them in the later 1840s to describe themselves specifically, for a number of years, as communists (as in the *Communist Manifesto*) to differentiate themselves from the more Utopian socialism of Fourier, Saint-Simon and Robert Owen. However, by the latter half of the nineteenth century, as communism often came in the popular mind to be associated with insurrection (notably in the aftermath of the 1871 Paris Commune) and Michael Bakunin's philosophy of anarchism gained traction, Marx and Engels were inclined to describe themselves as 'socialists' – or even 'scientific socialists'. The usage of 'communist' fully re-emerges only from 1918 with the renaming of the Russian Social-Democratic Labour Party to the All-Russian Communist Party (Bolsheviks) following the Russian Revolution of 1917 and its clear differentiation from European social democracy. For a good account, see Raymond Williams, *Keywords* (London, 1988).

forms, can be traced back to any number of sources: to Plato's *Republic*, to the spiritual equality proclaimed by the Old Testament prophet Micah, the brotherly love preached by Jesus of Nazareth, the Utopianism of Sir Thomas More and Tommaso Campanella, or to the radical levelling of the Putney Debates.[39] But in its modern form socialism emerges out of the religious and ideological anarchy of the French Revolution. In the 1790s and early 1800s the search for a new *pouvoir spirituel*, after the fall of the Roman Catholic Church and extensive de-Christianization across France, led to the development of a number of identifiably socialist sects.

One of the first was founded by Count Claude Henri de Rouvroy de Saint-Simon, the aristocratic French war hero turned revolutionary partisan turned property speculator turned scourge of the idle rich. Saint-Simon was a descendant of the court chronicler of Louis XIV's Versailles, and his starting point was his belief that society was entering a new, critical phase of science and industry which required new forms of governance and worship. He called for a 'science of mankind' which would understand societies as 'bodies organised . . . like physiological phenomena'.[40] This rational approach to the management of human affairs would avoid precisely the kind of anarchy France had experienced during the 1790s, but for it to succeed power had to be transferred from the hapless, nepotistic elites of the *ancien régime* to a hierarchy of industrialists, scientists, engineers and artists (a kind of technological version of Samuel Taylor Coleridge's vision of a ruling clerisy). They alone would be able to plan a society 'in which all individuals will be classed according to their capacities and remunerated according to their work'. As such, politics would become an exact discipline, changing 'from the conjectured to the positive, from metaphysics to physics'.[41] The political act of 'governing' would give way to the objective process of 'administering' society so every individual could realize his potential. As Saint-Simon put it, in a phrase that Marx would later so successfully adapt, 'From each according to his abilities, from each ability according to his work.'

At the core of Saint-Simon's ideal society was an ethic of industry. Saint-Simon's heroes were the 'industrial class' (*les industriels*), producers not parasites. His enemies were the traditional rulers of France – the aristocracy, clergy, government officials (those he termed *les oisifs*) – as well as the 'idlers' or 'consumers' of the new bourgeoisie who inherited wealth or leeched off the workers. In the coming scientific era man would stop exploiting man and, instead, unite to exploit nature. Existing patterns of private property, inheritance and competition would be abolished as society collectively, harmoniously put its shoulder to the wheel. 'All men will work; they will regard themselves as labourers attached to one workshop whose efforts will be directed to guide human intelligence according to my divine foresight. The Supreme Council of Newton will direct their works.'[42]

And what was this Supreme Council of Newton? Clearly indebted to Robespierre's secular theology of the Supreme Being, this was to be the governing body of the new society on which would sit *savants* – 'men of genius' who would act as 'torches illuminating mankind'. The Saint-Simonian system offered a sacerdocy of science in which a modern, rational society would be seamlessly organized by an elite technocracy which would preside over a *chambre d'invention* (manned by 200 engineers and 100 artists), a *chambre d'examination* (100 biologists; 100 physicists; 100 chemists) and a *chambre d'exécution* (the leading industrialists and entrepreneurs of the day). Just as Isaac Newton had reordered the universe around the principle of gravitational attraction, so the Supreme Council, chaired by a mathematician, would ensure society's smooth running along equally applicable universal laws.

In his 1825 work, *The New Christianity*, Saint-Simon took these ideas further to urge a secular religion of humanity. From the efficient governance of society would spring a new spirit of human harmony, immediately transcending the guilt and alienation of Christianity. Society could then return to the fundamental 'principle of Christian morality': brotherly love. From this followed the mission to 'improve the moral and physical existence of the poorest class', a goal which could never be achieved under the iniquitous, wasteful and inhuman system of competition that underpinned modern capitalism.[43] It was this promise of moral regeneration and spiritual growth through collective action that led to the Saint-Simonian sects and their popular gospel of fraternity. Some altogether more risqué ideas about the sanctification of the body, as opposed to the Christian renunciation of the flesh, also played a part in attracting adherents. If only mankind united together, Saint-Simon was convinced that its productive energies could be channelled into creating a 'New Harmony' here on earth.

Saint-Simon's vision of a post-capitalist, post-Christian Utopia was shared by the other leading French socialist of the early nineteenth century, Charles Fourier. One of the more likeable characters within the progressive pantheon, he was born in 1772 to a prosperous cloth merchant and spent his life as a silk broker and commercial salesman in southern France – notably in the silk-weaving districts of Lyons. 'I am a child of the marketplace,' he explained, 'born and brought up in mercantile establishments. I have witnessed the infamies of commerce with my own eyes.'[44] However, Fourier's socialism was not simply the product of experience. Describing himself as a new Columbus, after a year spent studying natural sciences at the Bibliothèque Nationale in 1799 he claimed to have discovered the true science of mankind which would, at a stroke, end the misery, exploitation and unhappiness of modern civilization. He recounted it all in his bizarre 1808 opus, *The Theory of the Four Movements*.

Between accounts of lemonade seas and mating planets, Fourier offered a simple proposition: men and women were governed by their natural, God-given passions. In fact, each individual could be slotted into one of precisely 810 different personality types, drawn from twelve passions, and lived in a world governed by the four movements of social, animal, organic and material which constituted the General System of Nature (as something of a sociological Linnaeus, Fourier was very good at lists). To attempt to repress any of these passions on the altar of an edified ideal of human conduct was the terrible mistake of contemporary society. 'Nature driven out through the door comes back through the window.' But this was exactly what nineteenth-century bourgeois France was doing with its artificial constructs, like monogamous marriage, which in true Newtonian fashion produced unwarranted counter-passions 'as malignant as the natural passions would have been benign'. The equal and opposite reaction to Church-sanctioned monogamy, for example, could be seen in the thirty-two different types of adultery evident in France. In Fourier's harmonious society, citizens would be allowed full sexual freedom, starting and ending relationships as they desired. Women would have control over reproduction and children would be given the opportunity to choose between real or adoptive fathers.[45] It was the same with economics as with sex. The subversion of benign passions had turned ambition into avarice, leeched work of all joy and allowed the exploitative, parasitic middlemen to flourish. Revolted by the unemployment, poverty and hunger of 1790s Marseilles, Fourier time and again revealed his detestation of the deadly vice of capitalism. 'It is falsehood with all of its paraphernalia, bankruptcy, speculation, usury and cheating of every kind.'[46] He especially despised the merchant class who neither toiled nor span, but walked away with vast, paper-money profits.

Capitalism's greatest crime, though, was that it sullied the soul of man by denying him pleasure. In the mangled ethic of modern civilization, it was monetary wealth that secured such luxuries as food, love and art. Only the rich could revel in the kind of sensuous gastronomic and amorous delights which might, in fact, have appealed to the passions of numerous others (such as, for example, Fourier).[47] This iniquitous state of affairs was bolstered by the Roman Catholic Church's hypocritical creed of chastity and holy poverty. Fourier, the frustrated, lonely travelling salesman, saw little virtue in impecuniousness or the banality of a monogamous married life.

Traditional politics had no answer to these human sufferings. There was no programme of reform or economic adjustment that addressed the unnatural repressions of modern society. So the answer was to leave the rotting corpse of nineteenth-century Europe behind and reorganize humanity in a series of autonomous communities to be known as 'phalansteries'. In contrast to the individual anarchy of revolutionary France, the phalanstery was to be efficiently run on the science of 'passionate attraction'. Working from how human nature was, rather than moralists' projections of how it should be, the phalanstery was organized to cater for each different personality type, passion and unity. As such, its ideal size would number 1,620. The guarantee of a 'sexual minimum' for all residents would remove the medley of frustrations and desires that distorted 'amorous' relationships in patriarchal, bourgeois society. Fourier delighted in describing the kind of highly choreographed orgies – modelled on a sensuous inversion of the Catholic Mass – which would take place in the phalanstery, catering to every form of sexual inclination (including incest).

Alongside a 'sexual minimum' came a 'social minimum'. Just as Fourier would restore respect to sexual love, so his system would revive the dignity of work. The problem of modern employment was that it, too, denied man the fulfilment of his natural passions – assigning him to tasks that were both monotonous and ill-suited to particular capacities. In the phalanstery, by contrast, residents would be able to work at up to eight different jobs a day in spontaneously formed groups of friends and lovers. This unleashing of abilities would produce an outpouring of talent as men and women marched out to the fields, factories, workshops, studios and kitchens eager to fulfil their industrious enthusiasms. Fourier, *contra* the Catholic Church, did not think human beings were born to suffer. Instead, all that was needed was the creation of new communities to allow man to flourish in accordance with his innate passions.

Nowhere in Saint-Simon and Fourier are there demands for radical equality ('a social poison' in Fourier's words) or calls for the violent seizure of power in the name of 'the people'. Their socialism was a noble, frequently eccentric but fundamentally inspiring vision of human fulfilment. Indeed, given their experience of and attitude towards the blood and horror of the French Revolution, both thinkers displayed very little interest in violently challenging existing social systems. Instead, they urged a programme of gradual moral reform which would be inspired by the example of harmonious communities separated off from the iniquities of existing society. As Engels put it, 'Society presented nothing but wrongs; to remove these was the task of reason. It was necessary, then, to discover a new and more perfect system of social order and to impose this upon society from without by propaganda, and, wherever it was possible, by the example of model experiments.'[48] America witnessed the most practical achievement of the Fourierist vision with the establishment from the 1840s of a series of communities at Brook Farm, Massachusetts; La Reunion in Dallas County, Texas; and Raritan Bay Union in New Jersey. However, these phalansteries fell rather short when it came to converting the rest of American society to the Fourierist project. Such failings would allow Engels to belittle Saint-Simon and Fourier (along with Robert Owen) as 'Utopian socialists' in contrast to his and Marx's rigorous, practical 'scientific socialism'. Whilst Engels would later reveal a profound indebtedness to Fourier's analysis of bourgeois marriage and greatly admired his social criticism ('Fourier inexorably exposes the hypocrisy of respectable society, the contradiction between its theory and its practice, the dullness of its entire mode of life'),[49] he criticized the Utopians' failure to understand the function of the proletariat or the revolutionary ratchet of history. 'These new social systems were foredoomed as Utopian; the more completely they were worked out in detail, the more they could not avoid drifting off into pure phantasies.'[50]

Early nineteenth-century France harboured other ideologues equally impatient with this rarefied nonsense of movements and phalansteries. These were the communists. Led by the likes of Etienne Cabet and Louis-Auguste Blanqui, these outlawed Parisian sects, active during the 1830s, concerned themselves much more with direct political change than social analysis. While Cabet advocated the path of peaceful transition to 'a society founded on the basis of the most perfect equality', Blanqui urged a revolution and lionized the martyrdom of 'Gracchus' Babeuf who, in the name of the people, had organized a doomed rebellion in 1796 against the inequality and poverty of post-revolutionary France. Their communism or 'Babouvism' was a radical, violent creed inspired by the pure, pre-industrial egalitarianism of Jean-Jacques Rousseau. They wanted to reshape existing society, not retreat to phalansteries and communes. Supported by sections of the disgruntled Parisian working class, the communists (a term which first gained its wider currency in the early 1840s) constituted a revival of the revolutionary republican tradition: they demanded an end to inheritance, the abolition of private property and 'a great national community of goods' forced on the people in the aftermath of revolution. A botched attempt by Blanqui and his supporters in 1839 to usher in the new Jerusalem by force ended up with a term of life imprisonment – from which he was intermittently released. Marx and Engels, enjoying their boozy evenings in Berlin and Bonn debating Hegelian philosophy, had little to do with these earnest, early communists. But one German who did was the so-called communist rabbi, or, as Engels would describe him, the 'first Communist of the party', Moses Hess.

*

Like Marx and Engels, Hess, too, was a child of the Rhineland, born in Bonn in 1812 when the city was under Napoleonic occupation and, as Isaiah Berlin puts it, 'the gates of the Jewish ghetto were flung wide open, and its inmates, after centuries of being driven in upon themselves, were permitted to emerge into the light of day'.[51] He shared with Marx an impressive Semitic heritage, with rabbis on both parents' sides. His father, however, had sought a life outside the synagogue as a sugar refiner in Cologne, and Hess was left in the care of his 'extremely orthodox' maternal grandfather, who brought him up on stories of the Jews' expulsion from Israel. 'The strict old man's snow-white beard would be drenched with tears at this reading; we children, too, of course, could not prevent ourselves from weeping and sobbing.'[52]

While Hess never fully freed himself from this over-emotional inheritance, he did lose his faith. 'My main problem was, naturally, religion: from it I moved later on to the principles of ethics. First to be examined was my positive religion [i.e. Judaism]. It collapsed . . . Nothing, nothing remained. I was the most miserable person in the world. I became an atheist. The world became a burden and a curse to me. I looked at it as a cadaver.'[53] Just as Engels *père* had little patience for Friedrich's Romanticism, so Hess's father had no use for his son's melancholic introspection and pressured him to join the family refining business. But Hess was reluctant to participate in what he saw as the moral compromises of commerce and he fled for a year of European travel. Isaiah Berlin affectionately describes him at this time as 'a generous, high-minded, kindly, touchingly pure-hearted, enthusiastic, not over-astute young man, ready, indeed eager, to suffer for his ideas, filled with love of humanity, optimism, a passion for abstractions, and aversion from the world of practical affairs towards which the more hard-headed members of his family were trying to steer him'.[54]

It was in Paris, in the early 1830s, that he discovered a cure for his atheism amongst the communist secret societies and increasingly outlandish Saint-Simonians. Like Engels before him, and many thousands after him, Hess filled the gap left by his abandoned religious heritage with the new socialist creed of humanity. He recounted his intellectual conversion in *The Sacred History of Mankind* (1837), which highlighted the growing social disparity between 'pauperism' and an 'aristocracy of wealth' and posited a Babouvist-inspired community of goods as the answer. The book was one of the earliest expressions of communist thought in Germany and enjoyed a favourable reception in liberal Rhineland circles. Long before Marx and Engels had codified their views, Hess and, following him, the artisan communist Wilhelm Weitling, were introducing German audiences to the idea of a radical, egalitarian communist future in which the spiritual and social crises of the day would be resolved. Hess's real breakthrough came when he attached these communist ideas to Young Hegelian thinking.

The final link in this intellectual chain was provided by the entrancing figure of August von Cieszkowski. Described by his biographer as 'a sort of Polish Alexander Herzen', Cieszkowski was a wealthy, cultivated aristocrat, educated at Cracow and then Berlin – where he participated in the Young Hegelian struggle against Schelling.[55] His military background inspired in Cieszkowski a demand for action and he soon lost interest in the endlessly arcane nature of Hegelian philosophizing. In 1838 he published *Prolegomena to Historiosophy*, which sought to turn Hegel's work from an analytical tool into a socially oriented plan for change. The dialectic, he suggested, was entering a new age of synthesis where thought would have to be combined with action. What Europe needed was 'a philosophy of practical activity, of "praxis", exercising a direct influence on social life and developing the future in the realm of concrete activity'.[56] The futile, beer-soaked discussion so beloved by the Young Hegelians had to be rechannelled into a programme of practical reform.

Hess was immediately taken by Cieszkowski's writings. 'The time has come for the philosophy of spirit to become a philosophy of action,' he proclaimed. In his book *The European Triarchy* (1841), Hess spelled out precisely what such a communist strategy would entail. In doing so, he returned to Ludwig Feuerbach's stress on the need to end religious alienation and developed his thinking a stage further. Of course, Hess agreed, man could regain his essence only by ending his subservience towards a Christian deity, but such a radical shift should not be attempted on an individual basis; what was needed was a broader, communal process of associational conversion.

'Theology is anthropology. That is true, but it is not the whole truth. The being of man, it must be added, is social, the co-operation of the various individuals towards a common aim . . . and the true doctrine of man, the true humanism, is the theory of human sociability. That is to say, anthropology is socialism.'[57] For what socialism or communism promised (and Hess, like Marx and Engels, used the terms interchangeably) was heaven on earth: everything that in Christianity had been represented prophetically would come to pass in a truly humane society founded upon the eternal laws of love and reason.[58]

To reach this sublime state of co-operation a confrontation needed to be occasioned with the contemporary capitalist system which was the cause of so much of modern man's dehumanization. As a result, Hess urged the abolition of private property and, with it, an end to the alienating effects brought about by the money economy. Only then could the prevalent culture of egoism and competition be curtailed and, in its place, arise a new sociability based on freedom and human fellowship. In the great historical movement towards socialism, each member of what he called the European triarchy – France, England and Germany – had a specific role to play: Germany was to provide the philosophical foundations of communism; France was already well advanced with the political activism; and industrializing England was to gather the social kindling. 'The antagonism between poverty and the aristocracy of money will reach a revolutionary level only in England, just as that opposition between spiritualism and materialism could reach its culmination in France and the antagonism between state and church could reach its apex only in Germany.'[59]

Hess was amongst the first to introduce this 'social question' – the human costs of industrial capitalism – into the political dynamic. In an article entitled 'On the Approaching Catastrophe in England', Hess explained how the gathering storm was the product of powerful socio-economic climacterics.

The objective causes that will provoke a catastrophe in England are not of a political character. Industry passing from the hands of the people into those of the capitalists, the trade that used to be carried out on a small scale by small traders more and more being controlled by large scale capitalists, adventurers and swindlers, land property concentrated by the laws of heredity in the hands of aristocratic usurers . . . all these conditions that exist everywhere, but principally in England and which constitute, if not the exclusive, at least the principal and essential causes of the catastrophe that threatens us, have a social and not a political character.[60]

Increasingly, Hess's practical, socially oriented theorizing was drawing the Young Hegelians in an overtly communist direction. By the autumn of 1842, according to Engels, some of the Young Hegelian 'party' (within which he included himself), 'contended for the insufficiency of political change and declared their opinion to be that a *social* revolution based upon common property, was the only state of mankind agreeing with their abstract principles'.[61]

What was equally obvious was that England – with its vast manufactories, wealthy mill owners and hideously brutalized proletariat – was all set to stage the Approaching Catastrophe. 'The English are the nation of praxis, more than any other nation. England is to our century what France has been to the previous one.'[62] And it was to England that Friedrich Engels was now heading. Before departing, he called in on Moses Hess himself, with whom he had begun an initial correspondence. Hess recalled the visit in a letter to his friend the Jewish poet Berthold Auerbach. Engels arrived, he wrote, as a shy, naive, ' "first year" revolutionary' (*ein Anno I Revolutionär*) of the French revolutionary, Montagnard type. By the time he had finished his tutorial with Hess and continued on his way to England, Engels the Young Hegelian had been converted into 'an extremely eager communist'.[63]

3

Manchester in Black and White

On 27 August 1842 an advertisement appeared on the front page of the *Manchester Guardian*. Beneath an announcement by William Ashworth, 'beerseller of Heywood', that he 'will not be answerable for any debt or debts that my wife, Ann Ashworth, may contract after this day', the firm of Ermen & Engels bought space to express 'their deep sense of obligation not only to the authorities, police, and special constables, but also to their kind neighbours, for the very efficient and preventive measures adopted, and ready assistance given, to afford protection to their works, and the people in their employ, during the late disturbances'. What was more, 'E. & E. beg to add, that these feelings are fully shared in by their people, to whom it is only due further to state, that they have without exception exhibited the best disposition and conduct during the recent general turn out.' In short, Engels's father and business partner wished to thank the British state for crushing the most invigorating display of working-class dissent since the days of Peterloo.[1]

The months before the 1842 'Plug Plot' riots were ones of political disenchantment and accelerating poverty across Manchester. 'Any man who passes through the district observing the condition of the people, will at once perceive the deep and ravaging distress that prevails, laying industry prostrate, desolating families, and spreading abroad discontent and misery where recently happiness and content were enjoyed,' reported the *Manchester Times*.[2] But such accounts of despair in Lancashire's cotton slums had little impact on the landowners, industrialists and merchants sitting in session at Westminster. Three months earlier MPs had summarily rejected a million-strong National Petition from the working-class Chartist movement and, with it, their demand for universal male franchise. And now they showed an equal disdain in the human cost of the 'hungry 40s'.

In fact, Manchester's millocrats had exploited working-class disarray in the aftermath of the petition's rejection to drive through a series of 50 per cent wage cuts, starting in Stalybridge. In response, the mill workers headed out to the Lancashire moors for mass rallies, renewed demands for the People's Charter and the rousing cry of 'a fair day's wage for a fair day's work'. Strikes followed in the mills and coalpits of the surrounding villages of Ashton and Hyde (with workers giving the riots their moniker by pulling the boiler plugs from factory steam engines), disturbances flared in Bolton, and by the morning of Wednesday 10 August 1842 some 10,000 men and women were ominously circling the vast mills of Manchester's Ancoats district. Despondent, armed and increasingly violent, the workers looted shops, torched factories and attacked the police.

Much to the admiration of the Ermen & Engels directors, the response of the authorities was swift and savage. The Riot Act was read, the army mobilized and special constables sworn in from across the middle classes, including members of the German merchant community who marched 'through the city with their cigars in their mouths and thick truncheons in their hands'.[3] The rioters were rounded up and, by late August, with 2,000 troops drafted in by train, Manchester resembled an occupied city.[4] 'In the streets there were unmistakable signs of alarm on the part of the authorities,' recalled the Chartist Thomas Cooper. 'Troops of cavalry were going up and down the principal thoroughfares, accompanied by pieces of artillery, drawn by horses.'[5] In the face of such military bravado, and the early signs of an economic upturn, the working-class mood quietened.

But the Plug Plot riots were merely the surface fury of a much deeper social malaise. Like few other nineteenth-century cities, industrial Manchester was experiencing openly aggressive class warfare between a prospering bourgeoisie and an impoverished proletariat. 'The modern art of manufacture has reached its perfection in Manchester ... the effects of modern manufacture upon the working class must necessarily develop here most freely and perfectly,' noted Engels. The result was that 'the enemies are dividing gradually into two great

camps – the bourgeois on the one hand, the workers on the other'.[6]
And no one thought they had seen the last of the struggle.

Manchester, this city of social division, would over the succeeding
century come to be inviolably associated with Engels: it would inspire
him to write one of the greatest works on the British industrial experience, *The Condition. of the Working Class in England* (1845), as
well as provide his home and workplace for some two decades. It
was also here in the mid-1840s that Engels would make a series of
intellectual and ideological advances instrumental to the development
of Marxism. Lancashire delivered to Engels the essential data to flesh
out his pre-existing philosophy. If Berlin had been a city of the mind
– with its lecture halls and beer-room debates – then Manchester was
about matter. Along Deansgate and Great Ducie Street, in the Salford
rookeries and Oxford Road enclaves, Engels harvested the 'facts,
facts, facts' of industrial England to devastating effect. Communism
took a step forward as he married his German philosophical inheritance to the class fissures and 'red in tooth and claw' capitalism he saw
at work on the streets of London, Leeds and Manchester. Hess's
theorizing became flesh as Engels realized that communism offered
the only credible settlement for such a grievous social state. And while
the French might have realized this truth 'politically' and the Germans
'philosophically', Engels believed the English were accepting this conclusion 'practically, by the rapid increase of misery, demoralization,
and pauperism in their own country'.[7] This was the breakthrough of
his Manchester days.

In Manchester it had been tangibly brought to my notice that the economic
facts which have so far played no role or only a contemptible one in historiography are, at least in the modern world, a decisive historical force. I learned
that economic factors were the basic cause of the clash between different
classes in society. And I realized that in a highly industrialized country like
England the clash of social classes lay at the very root of the rivalry between
parties and were of fundamental significance in tracing the course of modern
political history.[8]

Yet such political advances did nothing to alleviate the awkward
tensions of Engels's own status: residing in Manchester on the pay of
his father, he was there as a bourgeois, a mill owner apprentice, to

learn the business and extract value from the proletariat at a time when his politics were taking him in a very different direction. The young Engels, it would be fair to say, did not wholly share the sentiments of his Ermen & Engels colleagues when it came to crushing working-class resistance.

So much of what we think we know of Victorian Manchester is itself the product of Engels and his lacerating prose. Written when he was just twenty-four, *The Condition of the Working Class* would in the twentieth century come to serve as a literary shorthand for the horror, exploitation and class conflict of urbanizing Britain. However, Engels's work forms part of a much broader literature – some known, some unknown to Engels himself – on the industrial city and Manchester especially. 'As you enter Manchester from Rusholme, the town at the lower end of Oxford-road has the appearance of one dense volume of smoke, more forbidding than the entrance to Dante's inferno,' was a typical response to the phenomenon of Manchester by the co-operative pioneer George Jacob Holyoake. 'It struck me that were it not for previous knowledge, no man would have the courage to enter it.'[9]

To the Victorian mindset, 'Cottonopolis' stood for all the horrors of modernity: it was the 'shock-city' of the Industrial Revolution, an awful metonym for the terrifying transformations of the age of steam. Between 1800 and 1841 its population (including Salford) grew from 95,000 to over 310,000 on the back of a booming textile industry which flourished – like Barmen and Elberfeld – thanks to its technology clusters, reserves of labour power and helpfully damp climate. The entrepreneur and inventor Richard Arkwright – who had pioneered cotton production at his Cromford mills along the Derwent Valley – was the first to use steam power for the purposes of cotton-spinning in Manchester in the late 1780s. By 1816 his Shudehill mill had been joined by a further eighty-five steam-powered factories employing almost 12,000 men, women and children as Lancashire and Cheshire expanded to account for some 90 per cent of Britain's cotton production. By 1830 there were in excess of 550 cotton mills in Lancashire with well over 100,000 workers. However, unlike the surrounding towns of Oldham, Ashton and Stalybridge, Manchester was more than just a cotton capital. It was a marketplace, a

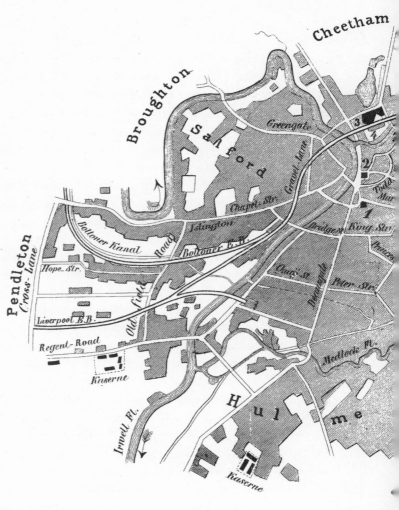

Map of Manchester
from the 1845 German
edition of *The Condition
of the Working Class in
England*.

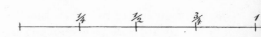

1. die Börse.

2. die alte Kirche.

3. das Arbeitshaus.

4. der Armenkirchhof
Zwischen Beiden der Liver-
pooler & Leedser E.B. Hof.

5. St. Michael's Kirche.

6. Scotland Bridge über d. Irk.

Die Strasse von 2 nach 6 heisst
Long Millgate.

7 Ducie Bridge über d. Irk.

8 Little Ireland.

¼   1½   engl. Meilen.
        69½ = 1° des Aequators.

zur rechten Hand abwärts schattirt.

distribution hub and a centre of finance, with even more investment and design value channelled into the warehouses of Portland
and Princess Streets than its notorious factories and mills. It was at
the centre of a mutually supportive web of north-west towns dependent as much upon its mercantile base, construction industry and
retail sector as its cotton mills. The city's wealthiest citizens were as
likely to be bankers, brewers or merchants as the mill owners of
Victorian lore.[10]

Nonetheless, the Cottonopolis image, with its smog-cloaked factories and stark contrasts of misery and Midas-like riches, made the
city a honey-pot for those wishing to decipher the meaning of industrialization. So, after he had studied democracy in America, Alexis de
Tocqueville in 1833 turned to 'this new Hades'. Approaching the city,
de Tocqueville spotted 'thirty or forty factories rise on the top of hills'
spewing out their foul waste. In fact, he heard Manchester before he
entered it as no visitor could escape from the 'crunching wheels of
machinery', 'the noise of the furnaces', 'the shriek of steam from
boilers', or the incessant 'regular beat of the looms'. Inside the sprawling, filthy city he found (as Engels had in Wuppertal), 'fetid, muddy
waters, stained with a thousand colours by the factories they pass'.
And yet, 'from this foul drain the greatest stream of human industry
flows out to fertilize the whole world. From this filthy sewer pure gold
flows.'[11]

The French *voyeur* was not alone. Partly through commercial connections as well as official requests for industrial intelligence, German
visitors – such as the historian Frederick von Raumer, the author
Johanna Schopenhauer, the Prussian bureaucrat John Georg May,
even Otto von Bismarck – were thick on the ground in Hulme, Chorlton and Ardwick. May was mesmerized by the 'hundreds of factories
in Manchester which tower up to five and six storeys in height. The
huge chimneys at the side of these buildings belch forth black coal
vapours and this tells us that powerful steam engines are used here
. . . The houses are blackened by it.'[12] A few years later a French
visitor, the liberal journalist Léon Faucher, was similarly appalled by
'the fogs which exhale from this marshy district, and the clouds of
smoke vomited forth from the numberless chimneys'. Equally disgusting was the state of the waterways. 'The river which runs through

Manchester is so filled with waste dye matter that it looks like a dye-vat. The whole scene is one of melancholy.'[13]

Accompanying the industrial pollutants were the infernal working conditions in which the helots of this city slaved. Manchester was renowned for its work ethic. 'Hast thou heard, with sound ears,' asked the Victorian sage Thomas Carlyle, 'the awakening of a Manchester, on Monday morning, at half-past five by the clock; the rushing-off of its thousand mills, like the boom of an Atlantic tide, ten thousand times ten-thousand spools and spindles all set humming there – it is perhaps if thou knew it well, sublime as a Niagra, or more so.'[14] The mill owners, as we shall see, were especially keen on effective time management. When the future Poet Laureate Robert Southey visited one Manchester factory he was proudly informed by the owner, 'There is no idleness among us.' The child workers came in at 5 a.m., had half an hour for breakfast, half an hour for dinner and left again at 6 p.m. – at which point they were replaced by the next shift of children. 'The wheel never stands still.'[15] The result, according to the German travel writer Johann George Kohl, was a new race of people. 'In long rows on every side, and in every direction hurried forward thousands of men, women and children. They spoke not a word, but huddling up their frozen hands in their cotton clothes, they hastened on, clap, clap, along the pavement, to their dreary and monotonous occupation.'[16] The French historian Hippolyte Taine thought Manchester resembled nothing more than 'a great jerry-built barracks, a "work-house" for 400,000 people, a hard-labour penal establishment'. The penning together of thousands of workmen, carrying out mindless, regimented tasks, 'hands active, feet motionless, all day and every day' was simply improper. 'Could there be any kind of life more outraged, more opposed to man's natural instincts?'[17]

Alongside the *favela* tourism of the day, there was a highly developed canon of indigenous urban criticism which Engels devoured. One of the most eloquent testimonials was from the physician to the Ardwick and Ancoats Dispensary, Dr James Phillips Kay. His 1832 polemic, *The Moral and Physical Condition of the Working Classes Employed in the Cotton Manufacture in Manchester*, was a part-Christian, part-scientific critique of the misery he confronted on his cholera rounds in 'the close alleys, the crowded courts, the overpopulated habitations of wretchedness, where pauperism and disease congregate round the source of social discontent and political disorder'.[18] Like Engels, the son of a Nonconformist mill owner, Kay was morally affronted by Manchester's combination of unnecessary suffering in the face of such unprecedented prosperity – 'a slumbering giant . . . in the midst of so much opulence'. Alongside such eyewitness accounts were the official publications of civil servant Edwin Chadwick, whose *Report on the Sanitary Conditions of the Labouring Population of Great Britain* (1842) gave a stark assessment of the effects of rapid industrialization on public health: 'The annual slaughter in England and Wales from preventable causes of typhus which attacks persons in the vigour of life, appears to be double the amount of what was suffered by the Allied Armies in the battle of Waterloo.'[19] Inevitably, Manchester came in for particularly strong censure from the city's assistant Poor Law commissioner, Dr Richard Baron Howard, who described how whole streets were 'unpaved and without drains or main-sewers' and were 'so covered with refuse and excrementitious matter as to be almost impassable from depth of mud, and intolerable from stench'. 'In many of these places are to be seen privies in the most disgusting state of filth, open cesspools, obstructed drains, ditches full of stagnant water, dunghills, pigsties etc., from which the most abominable odours are emitted.'[20]

There lurked, in the ill-conceived medical terminology of the day, moral miasmas as well as sanitary ones. While Manchester's working classes were notorious for their irreligion (or, worse, Catholicism amongst the Irish), sexual promiscuity, drunkenness and general depravity, the city's middle classes were equally infamous for their vulgar materialism. 'The all-absorbing feeling of the bulk of the inhabitants is a desire to acquire wealth; and everything is deemed worthless in their estimation, that has not the accomplishment of this object for its end.' The Manchester man, it was said, 'hears more music in the everlasting motion of the loom than he would in the songs of the lark or the nightingale. For him philosophy has no attraction, poetry no enchantment; mountains, rocks, vales and streams excite not his delight or admiration; genius shrinks at his approach.'[21] As even the usually loyal *Manchester Guardian* was forced to admit, 'If the English are held to be a nation entirely of shopkeepers, Manchester is supposed to be always behind the counter, and to view men and measures through an atmosphere of cotton.'[22] The German visitors concurred: 'Work, profit and greed seem to be the only thoughts here . . . One reads figures, nothing but figures on all the faces here.'[23]

The raw monetary divide between the proletariat and the bourgeoisie signified an unbridgeable social chasm. Canon Richard Parkinson could claim of Manchester that there was 'no town in the world where the distance between the rich and the poor is so great'. In fact, there was 'far less personal communication between the master cotton spinner and his workmen' than between 'the Duke of Wellington and the humblest labourer on his estate'.[24] This close-quartered urban division − physical proximity but yawning social disparity − forcibly struck Léon Faucher, who described how in Manchester there are 'two towns in one: in the one portion, there is space, fresh air, and provision for health; and in the other, every thing which poisons and abridges existence'.[25] Benjamin Disraeli placed this sense of class separation at the heart of his manifesto-cum-novel, *Sybil, or the Two Nations* (1845). There could now exist, he lamented, within one city two entirely different nations, 'between whom there is no intercourse and no sympathy; who are as ignorant of each other's habits, thoughts and feelings, as if they were dwellers in different zones, or inhabitants of different planets'. These two nations were 'formed by different breeding', fed by different food, and governed by different laws. They were 'THE RICH AND THE POOR'.[26] It was a prediction of imminent class conflict from the most fastidiously Tory of voices.

Of course, Manchester was not the only city to undergo such critical inspection. Similar accounts could be told of Glasgow, Liverpool, Birmingham and Bradford. Equally, there existed a well-developed European literature of urban discovery bringing to light the shanty-towns, hidden tribes and underbelly amorality of Lyons, Paris, Berlin and Hamburg. But Manchester was something else: it symbolized the *ne plus ultra* of industrialization and, thanks to the exponential growth of the cotton industry, the scene of the starkest social divides and sanitary horrors Europe had to offer. It was an extraordinary urban phenomenon – akin to the Chinese boom cities or vast African megalopolises of today – which attracted intellectuals, activists, philosophers, even artists. They all wanted to *experience* this terrifying future. But it was Friedrich Engels's gift to paint the city's social crisis upon an altogether grander historical canvas.

'Is a revolution in England possible or even probable? This is the question on which the future of England depends.'[27] Fuelled by Moses Hess's predictions of an English social crisis, from the moment Engels disembarked his ship on to the London docks in 1842 – 'the masses of buildings, the wharves on both sides . . . the countless ships along both shores . . . all this is so vast, so impressive, that a man cannot collect himself, but is lost in the marvel of England's greatness . . .' – he was on the lookout for any sign of the impending catastrophe.[28] And he instantly alighted upon that class of proletarians – accounts of whom were highly familiar to Engels from the German social debates of the 1830s – who had to pay the price for such commercial greatness and, as such, were the only class capable of transcending its injustices. 'For although industry makes a country rich, it also creates a class of unpropertied, absolutely poor people,' he wrote back in a series of articles for Marx's *Rheinische Zeitung* (indicating that their relationship was slowly progressing from the early chill), 'a class which lives from hand to mouth, which multiplies rapidly, and which cannot afterwards be abolished.' Faced by the awful reality of industrialization, Engels was shifting away from Young Hegelian notions of *Geist*, consciousness and freedom to the earthy language of political economy. 'The slightest fluctuation in trade leaves thousands of workers destitute; their modest savings are soon used up and then they are in danger of starving to death. And a crisis of this kind is bound to occur again in a few years' time.'[29]

But before the revolution, there was work to be done. The firm of Ermen & Engels had been established in 1837 when Friedrich Engels senior transferred the money he received from being bought out of the family firm into the Ermen brothers' enterprise. The guiding force behind the company, Dutch-born Peter Ermen, had come to Manchester in the mid-1820s and worked his way up from being a doubler in a small factory to establishing a multinational cotton thread business run with the help of his two brothers Anthony and Gottfried. Investment by Engels senior allowed the company to open a new mill in the Eccles district of Salford – a neighbourhood renowned for its fine count mercerized cotton along with the weaving of bookcloths, canvas fire hose and waterproof garments – for the production of cotton thread bearing their trademark of three red towers, the arms reportedly granted to the Ermenses' sixteenth-century ancestors. The mill was located next to Weaste station, alongside the Manchester and Liverpool railway line, and ideally situated both for cotton imports from the Mersey docks and for drawing water from the nearby river Irwell for bleaching and dyeing. Patriotically christened Victoria Mill in honour of the young queen then ascending the throne, this was where Engels joined a 400-strong workforce by starting off 'in the throstle-room'.[30] Though we don't know exactly, it seems that he lived close by in the Eccles neighbourhood where – 'during my residence there' – he once witnessed a battle between the brick makers of Pauling & Henfrey and the police. Local legend also has it that he was a regular at the Crescent public house, while F. R. Johnston, the Eccles historian, has even suggested Engels tried to form 'a Communist cell based on the Grapes Hotel'.[31] The Weaste mill, later reincarnated as the Winterbottom Bookcloth Company, lasted until the 1960s, when the construction of the M602 from Salford into Manchester necessitated the demolition of what was by then an industrio-socialist footnote. Yet the legacy has not altogether vanished: the left-leaning Eccles Metropolitan Borough Council was rather prouder of its association with a socialist hero than Wuppertal and named a block of council flats Engels House (none of which now meets the government's Decent Housing Standard).[32] The Church of England, however, chose to stick with the more respectable side of the partnership by christening a local school Godfrey Ermen Memorial Church of England Primary.[33]

Working for the family firm whilst living within a community exploited and perpetuated by cotton capitalism, Engels readily felt the contradictions of his calling. As he put it in a heartfelt letter to Marx some years later, 'huckstering is too beastly . . . most beastly of all is the fact of being, not only a bourgeois, but actually a manufacturer, a bourgeois who actively takes side against the proletariat. A few days in my old man's factory have sufficed to bring me face to face with this beastliness, which I had rather overlooked.'[34] But even if he worked for the bourgeoisie, Engels didn't have to socialize with them. 'I forsook the company and the dinner-parties, the port-wine and champagne of the middle classes, and devoted my leisure-hours almost exclusively to the intercourse with plain working men.'[35] His first call was to the plain working men of the Owenite Hall of Science.

Robert Owen was the final member of Engels's 'Utopian socialist' triumvirate, joining Charles Fourier and Saint-Simon in the pantheon of dreamers marred, as he would later see it, by an inadequate appreciation of the historical rigours of scientific socialism. Yet Owen himself could lay claim to a far more practical understanding of social justice than either Marx or Engels ever could. A textile manufacturer by trade and marriage, he had attempted to turn his New Lanark factories in Scotland into a model of equitable employment and community cohesion. Owen's starting point was that conditioning, not character, was the key to man, who 'is a compound being, whose character is formed of his constitution, or organisation at birth, and of the effects of external circumstances upon it, from birth to death'. Original sin was a fallacy and what was instead required was an educational and social ethos designed to draw out the co-operative best in mankind. At New Lanark he operated a beneficent commercial dictatorship, cutting working hours, eliminating underage employment, restricting alcohol sales, improving conditions and introducing free primary education. In *A New View of Society, or Essays on the Principle of the Formation of the Human Character* (1813–14), he detailed how his experiment could be magnified for society at large and, in so doing, helped to drive through the 1819 Factory Act limiting working hours in the textile industry.

Yet no matter how many ameliorative acts of Parliament were passed, politics as usual could never provide the answer to the structural poverty which afflicted Britain in the years following the Napoleonic wars. The underlying fault lay with organized Christianity (for keeping man in a backward state of superstition) and the competitive ethos of society – of which private property was an economic manifestation – which corrupted the nature of man. Straying a long way from his industrial reform roots, Owen now advocated a wholesale moral revolution in order to regenerate society: this meant retreating from the evils of the 'old immoral world' and, as with Fourier, creating new communities, built around agriculture and industry, where education and co-operation would kick-start the regenerative process. 'The children are not tormented with religious and theological controversies, nor with Greek and Latin,' Engels wrote admiringly of the early Owenite settlement at Queen farm in Hampshire, 'instead they become the better acquainted with nature, their own bodies and their intellectual capacities ... Their moral education is restricted to the application of the one principle: Do not do to others what you would not have them do to you, in other words, the practice of complete equality and brotherly love.'[36] However, just as with Fourier's phalansteries and the Saint-Simonian sects, planned Owenite communities proved disastrously and expensively shortlived both in England and America.

More productive was his following of Owenite socialists, with their particularist criticisms of modern competition, who grouped together under the aegis of the British Association for the Promotion of Co-operative Knowledge. 'The selfish feeling in man may fairly be called the competitive principle,' announced the leading Owenite William Lovett, 'since it causes him to compete with others, for the gratification of his wants and propensities. Whereas the co-operative may be said to be the social feeling that prompts him to acts of benevolence and brotherly affection.' An economy based on the competitive system was condemned as inherently inequitable and unstable: wealth was concentrated, trade cycles became more extreme and poverty deepened. While Robert Owen himself increasingly focused his efforts on reforming religion and ending 'the unnatural and artificial union of the sexes' in marriage, the Owenites during the 1830s built a political programme around co-operation and a moral sense of value based on labour-time and just transfer rather than 'the doctrine of wages'. This led to the establishment of a series of co-operative shops in London and Brighton, 'labour exchanges' for the direct marketing of goods, trade unions to advance the cause of labour, and a network of Halls of Science (under the banner of the Association of All Classes of All Nations) to nurture all men in the ways of socialism, fellowship and reason. One of the largest and most active branches, with 440 members and a purpose-built Hall of Science, was first of all in Salford and then, as interest in socialism surged across the north-west, relocated in 1840 to grander premises in Manchester's Campfield. The French critic Léon Faucher remembered it as

an immense building, raised exclusively by the savings of the mechanics and artisans, at a cost of £7,000, and which contains a lecture-hall – the finest and most spacious in the town. It is tenanted by the disciples of Mr Owen. In addition to Sunday lectures upon the doctrines of Socialism, they possess a day and Sunday-school, and increase the number of their adherents by oratorios and festivals – by rural excursions, and by providing cheap and innocent recreation for the working classes . . . The large sums of money they raise, prove that they belong to the wealthier portion of the working classes. Their audiences on Sunday evenings are generally crowded.[37]

Generous estimates put Manchester's 'socialist community' at 8–10,000 during the 1840s with an impressive 3,000 filling the hall on Sunday evenings – Friedrich Engels amongst them. Seated hugger-mugger with the respectable working classes, what struck this *Fabrikant* heir most forcefully was the British operatives' articulacy in contrast to the drunken Barmen artisans. 'At first one cannot get over one's surprise on hearing in the Hall of Science the most ordinary workers speaking with a clear understanding on political, religious and social affairs.'[38] Indeed, he had often heard 'working men, whose fustian jackets scarcely held together, speak upon geological, astronomical and other subjects, with more knowledge than most "cultivated" bourgeois in Germany possess'. This was, he thought, the product of their avaricious literary culture with Rousseau, Voltaire and Paine all firm favourites amongst Manchester's working but not middle classes. 'Byron and Shelley are read almost exclusively by the lower classes; no "respectable" person could have the works of the latter on his desk without his coming into the most terrible disrepute.'[39]

As with so many variants of socialism, this new religion of humanity subsumed into its practices – often abetted by former Methodists – the rites and rituals of Christian worship. 'In their form, these meetings partly resemble church gatherings; in the gallery a choir accompanied by an orchestra sings social hymns,' noted Engels admiringly. 'These consist of semi-religious or wholly religious melodies with communist words, during which the audience stands.' However, the sermons were of an altogether higher quality than the rantings of Krummacher. 'Then, quite nonchalantly, without removing his hat, a lecturer comes on to the platform . . . and then sits down and delivers his address, which usually gives much occasion for laughter, for in those speeches the English intellect expresses itself in superabundant humour.' At other times the Owenite gatherings seemed to resemble simple forums for working- and lower-middle-class socializing with Sunday evening parties 'of the usual supper of tea and sandwiches; on working days dances and concerts are often held in the hall, where people have a very jolly time'.[40] All of which sounds refreshingly like an old-fashioned Labour Party social.

Once in a while a crowd-puller would be booked. In late 1843 it was the celebrated mesmerist Spencer Hall who, to a sceptical audience of materialist Owenites, 'undertook magnetico-phrenological performances with a young woman in order to prove thereby the existence of God, the immortality of the soul, and the incorrectness of materialism, which was being preached at that time by the Owenites in all big towns'. Engels was clearly gripped by the demonstration and, on returning from the hall, attempted to conduct a similar experiment in this pseudo-science for himself. 'A wide-awake young boy twelve years old offered himself as subject. Gently gazing into his eyes, or stroking, sent him without difficulty into the hypnotic condition . . . Apart from muscular rigidity and loss of sensation, which were easy to produce, we found also a state of complete passivity of the will bound up with a peculiar hypersensitivity of sensation.' However, the co-founder of dialectical materialism was not easily fooled by such hocus-pocus. '. . . we discovered in the great toe an organ of drunkenness which only had to be touched in order to cause the finest drunken comedy to be enacted. But it must be well understood, no organ showed a trace of action until the patient was given to understand what was expected of him; the boy soon perfected himself by practice to such an extent that the merest indication sufficed.'[41]

Of greater intellectual value was the Owenite lecturer John Watts.

A ribbon weaver and former assistant secretary of the Coventry Mechanics' Institute, Watts was an Owenite missionary and fierce critic of political economy. Engels would learn much from this 'outstanding man' and his moral critique of competition. 'The nature of trade is evil,' Watts wrote in his influential tract, *The Facts and Fictions of Political Economists* (1842), 'and to it more than to aught else, we owe what we have of natural depravity.' The capitalist system of values and money wages – themselves based on the force and fraud, the appropriation and accumulation of the marketplace – was the root cause of the economic crisis gripping industrial Britain. It sought to deny the truth that 'labour is the source of all wealth'. Watts's solution was to return to a form of pre-industrial, co-operative system of exchange – 'i.e., a fixed return for labour, a return in kind, a certain and invariable proportion of the produce'. At the same time, *contra* Adam Smith, he railed against the deadening effects of the division of labour ('it cannot admit of long question, whether the clipping of the wire, or the pointing or heading of a pin, be fit employment for the life of a rational being') and the hideous state of factory life – 'Is this condition so much better than that of the negroes, that it deserves no exhibition of philanthropy, that it demands no sympathy? Yet the tendency of our Political Economy in the doctrine of wages, is to perpetuate this state of things.'[42]

Despite their undoubted strength within Manchester, by the late 1830s the Owenites were a waning force in national working-class politics. Their place had been taken by the Chartists with their easily understood, six-point demand: universal manhood suffrage, secret ballots, annual elections, equally populated constituencies, payment of MPs and the abolition of the minimum property requirement for MPs. In contrast to the Utopian ambitions of the Owenites, the Charter was a practical attempt to find a political solution to the working-class condition and found its warmest reception in Lancashire, where the Manchester Political Union organized torchlight marches and 'monster rallies' on Kersal Moor – the so-called 'Mons Sacer' of Chartism. In September 1838 some 30,000 turned out under their trade union banners to hear the Chartist leader Feargus O'Connor declaim that 'universal franchise' is 'the only principle which can stop the flowing of human blood . . . You will never be represented until every man is entrusted with that which nature has imprinted in the breast of every man, namely, the power of self-defence as implied in the vote of every individual.'[43] But such popular shows of force served only to heighten Establishment trepidation towards Chartism and in 1839 and again in 1842 their petitions were rejected by the House of Commons. In turn, such obvious contempt radicalized Chartist opinion, sparked a move away from middle-class alliances and a vociferous internal debate as to the merits of moral versus physical force. The 1842 Plug Plot riots were, in one sense, a wilful expression of this political impotence.

Nevertheless, Engels had few doubts as to Chartism's significance. Whilst modern interpretations tend to place weight on Chartism as an outgrowth of radical eighteenth-century politics which presaged demands for political transparency and a moral economy, to Engels's eyes it was 'a class movement' pure and simple which encapsulated the working-class 'collective consciousness'.[44] And he wanted to learn as much from it as possible. He gained two introductions to the movement: the first through Chartism's *enfant terrible*, George Julian Harney, who stood firmly on the physical force wing of the party and enjoyed riling his conservative comrades by flaunting the red cap of liberty at public meetings. In and out of jail, endlessly feuding with fellow Chartists and ultimately expelled from the party, the Robespierre-admiring Harney remained convinced that insurrection was the surest route to the Charter.[45] Decades later he remembered how Engels – 'a tall, handsome young man, with a countenance of almost boyish youthfulness' – had sought him out at his Leeds office; 'He told me he was a constant reader of *The Northern Star* [the Chartist paper] and took a keen interest in the Chartist movement. Thus began our friendship . . .'[46] As ever with Marx and Engels, the friendship would prove rocky, but it lasted – through an intermittent correspondence – for half a century, during which Harney provided one of the more damning responses to the condition of Manchester: 'I am not surprised to find you expressing your disgust at Manchester,' he wrote to Engels in 1850. 'It is a damned dirty den of muckworms. I would rather be hanged in London than die a natural death in Manchester.'[47]

Engels's other main contact was the Manchester hand-loom weaver turned Chartist activist, James Leach. Before being elected as South Lancashire's delegate to the National Charter Association, Leach, according to Engels, 'worked for years in various branches of industry, in mills and coal-mines, and is known to me personally as an honest, trustworthy, and capable man'.[48] He was also regarded as a 'terror, not only to the cotton lords, but every other humbug' – a reputation ably justified with his anonymous 1844 polemic, *Stubborn Facts from the Factories*. Dedicated to 'the working classes', it was a first-hand indictment of the nefarious practices deployed by mill owners, from wage robbery to fining pregnant women for sitting down to manipulating clocks to enforced prostitution. Much of this evidence would find its way into Engels's book – as well as the insight that the modern state was merely a front for bourgeois class interests. 'The working classes will ever look upon this [the state] as no better than a *brigand* system, that thus allows the employers to assume a power over the Law, and by their nefarious plotting, first create what they are pleased to term offences, and then punish them. They are both law makers, judges, and jurors.'[49] As Marx and Engels would later put it in the *Communist Manifesto*, 'The executive of the modern State is but a committee for managing the common affairs of the whole bourgeoisie.'[50]

Despite these close friendships and his own personal enthusiasm for working-class Chartism, Engels did not think the solution to Britain's crisis lay with the six points. First of all their socialism, in contrast to the advanced ideas on the continent (amongst the Fourierists, Saint-Simonians or Hess and his circle) was 'very little developed', but more importantly, 'social evils cannot be cured by People's Charters'.[51] Something altogether more fundamental than democratic tinkering was required. It was a sentiment majestically enunciated by another British mentor to the young Engels, Thomas Carlyle.

Sage, polemicist and reactionary, Carlyle was the only British intellectual whom Engels really admired. Perhaps it was his Germanophilia. His earliest work, as a critic for the *Edinburgh Review*, had been a translation of Johann Paul Richter, and from there he went on to immerse himself in the work of Goethe (with whom he corresponded regularly), Schiller and Herder, acting as a kind of cultural bridge bringing German Romanticism to a British audience. In doing so, Carlyle was drawn to contrast the miserable state of industrial England with its romantic and medieval forebears before mournfully concluding that 'This is not a Religious age. Only the material, the immediately practical, not the divine and spiritual, is important to us.'[52] The nineteenth century was 'the mechanical age' in which the social bonds which traditionally connected man to man had fallen apart in the quest for material riches. 'We call it a Society; and go about professing openly the totalest separation, isolation. Our life is not a mutual helpfulness; but rather, cloaked under due laws-of-war, named "fair competition" and so forth, it is a mutual hostility. We have profoundly forgotten everywhere that *Cash-payment* is not the sole relation of human beings.'[53] Which was why demands for the Charter and other political quick fixes – which Carlyle dismissed as 'Morrison's Pills' after a voguish quack doctor of the day – would make no real difference to the so-called 'condition of England' question (as to the social effects of industrialization). The solution, for Carlyle, was a combination of renewed religiosity and heroic, dictatorial leadership: on the walls of his Cheyne Row drawing room, he gave pride of place to portraits of Oliver Cromwell and Martin Luther's parents.

'We too are concerned with combating the lack of principle, the inner emptiness, the spiritual deadness, the untruthfulness of the age,' responded Engels (still then aligning himself with the radical wing of the Young Hegelians) in a review of Carlyle's contrast of medieval and modern Britain, *Past and Present*. However, religion, the opium of the people, was certainly not the answer. 'We want to put an end to atheism, as Carlyle portrays it, by giving back to man the substance he has lost through religion; not as divine but as human substance, and this whole process of giving back is no more than simply the awakening of self-consciousness.'[54] Carlyle's defining weakness, according to Engels, was that he had read German literature but not philosophy; Goethe without Feuerbach got you only so far. Yet what Engels did admire about Carlyle was both his extraordinary prose style – 'Carlyle treated the English language as though it were completely raw material which he had to cast utterly afresh' – and his Olympian denunciation of the misery wrought by capitalist society.[55]

In *The Condition of the Working Class*, Engels used the same historical metaphors as Carlyle (contrasting the position of a factory hand unfavourably with that of a Saxon serf under the lash of a Norman baron; highlighting the hypocrisy of liberal 'freedom' which meant little more than liberty to die by starvation), the same official sources, and quoted 'the sage of Chelsea' generously. 'The relation of the manufacturer to his operatives has nothing human in it; it is purely economic,' Engels wrote in a chapter on industrial relations taken straight from the pages of Carlyle's epic denunciation of mechanical, industrial England, *Signs of the Times*. 'The manufacturer is capital, the operative labour . . . he insists, as Carlyle says, that "cash payment is the only nexus between man and man".'[56]

Carlyle's denunciations of 'the mechanical age', the Owenites' call for moral renewal, the six points of the Charter, and Watts and Leach's attacks on competition were all instrumental to Engels's ideological evolution, but he was not in Manchester to read books. He was there to confront the *reality* of working-class life, to forsake 'the company and the dinner-parties, the port-wine and champagne' for the fellowship of 'plain working men'. But who was to be the guide of this boyish German *ingénu* to the proletarian netherworld? One street-walking companion was fellow socialist émigré George Weerth, then unhappily clerking in Bradford – 'the most disgusting manufacturing town in England'. To his horror, Weerth had discovered that this woollen boom town had 'no theatre, no social life, no decent hotel, no reading room, and no civilized human beings – only Yorkshiremen in torn frock coats, shabby hats and gloomy faces'. To escape the Yorkshire philistinism, he would set out across the Pennines to visit his ideological ally in Lancashire, where 'during the days, I wandered about with my friend Engels, investigating the sprawling Manchester'.[57] In addition, Engels had the personal attentions of a native of the city. Her name was Mary Burns – a vital consort to Manchester's undiscovered people and places and the first great love of Engels's life.

'She was a very pretty, witty, and altogether charming girl . . . Of course, as she was a Manchester (Irish) factory girl, quite uneducated, though she could read, and write a little, but my parents . . .

were very fond of her, and always spoke of her with the greatest affection.'[58] Eleanor Marx's sketchy, second-hand, childhood memories are sadly some of the fullest accounts we have of Engels's Mary. Born sometime between April 1822 and January 1823 (perhaps in Eltoft Street, off Deansgate), Mary was the daughter of the Irish dyer and factory-hand Michael Burns, who came to Manchester in the 1820s and took Mary Conroy as his first wife. At the time of the 1841 census, Michael surfaces as the husband of his second wife, Mary Tuomey, and living in grim conditions just off Deansgate – but without his daughters Mary and Lydia (known as Lizzy) Burns. A decade on, Michael and the second Mrs Burns had been lost to the workhouse on New Bridge Street, after which he became just another Manchester mortality statistic for 1858.[59] Mary, however, was prospering.

We know Engels met her in the early months of 1843, but there is much debate as to the exact nature of the encounter. With no obvious evidence, Edmund Wilson has asserted that Mary operated a 'self-actor' in the Ermen & Engels mill.[60] Similarly, the socialist Max Beer, who met Engels in the 1890s, described how 'he [Engels] lived, in free union, with an Irish girl of the people, Mary Burns, who had worked in his father's factory'.[61] Heinrich Gemkow has more vaguely described Mary Burns 'work[ing] in one of the city's many cotton factories'.[62] However, Engels himself was never particularly complimentary about the quality of his father's female employees, 'I do not remember to have seen one single tall, well-built girl; they were all short, dumpy, and badly-formed, decidedly ugly in the whole development of the figure.'[63] More probable, according to Roy Whitfield, is that Mary and Lizzy worked in a Manchester mill before then becoming domestic servants where they might have caught Engels's roving eye. Edmund and Ruth Frow, by contrast, have provided an altogether more romantic legend with Engels meeting Mary at a reception in the Owenite Hall of Science, where she was selling oranges.[64] This certainly helps to explain (but just a little too easily) the nature of George Weerth's idiosyncratic poem 'Mary', which recounts in deliciously laboured verse the life of a vivacious young Fenian girl selling oranges on the Liverpool docks.

From Ireland with the tide she came,
She came from Tipperary;
Warm, impetuous blood in her vein,
The young lass, Mary.
And when she boldly sprang ashore,
A cry from the sailors arose:
'The lass Mary, thank the Lord,
Is just like a wild rose!'[65]

The conjecture surrounding Mary is so varied because of the paucity of sources. She herself was illiterate and Engels later burned much of the correspondence from this period of his life. In addition, Engels was never especially keen to publicize his relationship with Mary – no missives to his 'goose' Marie about her namesake – as he had to retain both his own social position within Manchester and good relations with his censorious parents. Living in 'free union' with an illiterate Irish factory-hand could not be expected to further either objective. But there might also have been some sense of political embarrassment as to his own class status *vis-à-vis* Mary. For one of the many socialist charges laid against the cotton lords was their almost feudal exploitation of female workers. Engels himself touched upon it in the *Condition*. 'It is, besides, a matter of course that factory servitude, like any other, and to an even higher degree, confers the *ius primae noctis* upon the master ... his mill is also his harem.'[66] Even if Mary was never or no longer an employee of Ermen & Engels, in socialist circles this kind of sexualized power relationship of proletariat with bourgeois, mill-hand with mill owner, was widely frowned upon.

Whatever the social niceties, Engels and Mary were in each other's arms over 1843–4. And while there was, as later letters testify, deep affection between them there was also, for Engels, a very helpful entrée into the dark continent of industrial Manchester. Taking him by the hand, Mary Burns acted as his underworld Persephone, profoundly enriching Engels's appreciation of capitalist society. 'She introduced him to the life of the immigrant Irish community in Manchester,' according to Roy Whitfield, 'she escorted him on excursions through districts which would otherwise have been unsafe for any stranger to enter; she was a source of information about factory and domestic conditions endured by working people.'[67] Mary helped to provide Engels with the material reality for his communist theory.

Friedrich Engels's two worlds – of the mill owner and Mary Burns – profoundly influenced his journey from philosophy to political economy and, in turn, had a marked effect on the emergent shape of Marxism. Uniquely, Engels was able to fuse his real experience of industrial capitalism and working-class Chartist politics with the Young Hegelian tradition. 'German Socialism and Communism have grown, more than any other, from theoretical premises,' he noted censoriously. 'We German theoreticians still knew much too little of the real world to be driven directly by the real conditions to reforms of this "bad reality".'[68] In a seminal 1843 article for the *Deutsche-Französische Jahrbücher* (Marx's latest newspaper), 'Outlines of a Critique of Political Economy', he showed the fruits of his Manchester experience by dropping the Berlin theorizing for a hard-headed empirical analysis of the economic contradictions and social crises coming Europe's way. His work first of all betrayed the impact of John Watts's lectures by its critique, in tellingly biblical terms, of competition and exchange value. 'This political economy or science of enrichment born of the merchants' mutual envy and greed, bears on its brow the mark of the most detestable selfishness.' However, capitalism was an all-consuming beast ('all that is solid melts into air . . .') which necessitated the continuing, unending expansion of the British economy or the prospect of a terrible fiscal crisis. This explained Britain's unquenchable thirst for colonies – 'You have civilized the ends of the earth to win new terrain for the deployment of your vile avarice' – and the by-product of accelerating domestic concentrations of wealth: 'The middle classes must increasingly disappear until the world is divided into millionaires and paupers, into large landowners and poor farm labourers.' All of which at some point had to come to a bloody, climactic contradiction.[69]

However, Engels's most remarkable ideological advance came when he applied the Young Hegelian notion of alienation – which Feuerbach had discussed solely in terms of religious sentiments ('Man . . . projects his essence into objectivity and then makes himself an object of this projected image of himself that is thus converted into a subject . . .') – to the realm of political economy. For it wasn't just Christianity that demanded a denial of man's nature: competitive capitalism, through its systems of property, money and exchange, involved an equally disfiguring process of alienation from the authentic human essence. Under the aegis of political economy, man was divorced from himself and became the slave of things. 'Through this theory we have come to know the deepest degradation of mankind, their dependence on the conditions of competition. It has shown us how in the last instance private property has turned man into a commodity whose production and destruction also depend solely on demand . . .'[70] This was an insight garnered not only from Feuerbach and Hess, but from watching the thousands hunting for work outside the mill gates of Ancoats, condemned to poverty by the slightest fluctuation in world markets.

What drove this process of alienation, what stood at the root of political economy, and what the Owenites, Fourierists and Chartists had all overlooked was the role of private property. This was the essential insight of Engels's 'Outlines' and owed not a little to his recent reading of the French socialist-cum-anarchist Pierre-Joseph Proudhon's *What is Property?* (1840) – which he had answered with the celebrated response, 'It is theft.' It was private property in the form of unearned interest and rents from land which, Proudhon suggested, enabled one man to exploit another and underpinned the iniquities of modern capitalism. Taking aim at the parasitical, unproductive *oisifs* of the July monarchy, Proudhon's stress on the correlation of labour with ownership – alongside his conviction that political equality necessitated the abolition of private property – struck an immediate chord with the young Engels (despite the unacceptably anarchist trajectory of Proudhon's thinking). 'The right of private property, the consequences of this institution, competition, immorality, misery, are here developed with a power of intellect, and real scientific research, which I never since found united in a single volume,' he wrote of Proudhon's book.[71]

However, Engels took his conception of private property further than Proudhon had allowed himself and had it encompass all the myriad apparatus of political economy, 'e.g., wages, trade, value, price, money, etc.', which he had seen at work in Manchester.[72] He concluded that private property was the essential prerequisite of political economy and it too had to be eliminated: 'If we abandon private property, then all these unnatural divisions disappear.' Discord and individualism would melt away and the true nature of profit and value clarified. 'Labour becomes its own reward, and the true significance of the wages of labour, hitherto alienated, comes to light – namely, the significance of labour for the determination of the production costs of a thing.' The end of private property and personal avarice would conclude, in Hegelian fashion, with the end of history and arrival of communism: 'the great transformation to which the century is moving – the reconciliation of mankind with nature and with itself'.[73] All this in a short, precocious essay by a scarcely known 23-year-old apprentice manufacturer – no wonder, in his Left Bank apartment, Marx was taking notes on this 'brilliant essay'.[74] But 'Outlines' was just a foretaste of Engels's true monument to Manchester.

I have read your book again and I have realized that I am not getting any younger. What power, what incisiveness and what passion drove you to work in those days. That was a time when you were never worried by academic scholarly reservations! Those were the days when you made the reader feel that your theories would become hard facts if not tomorrow then at any rate on the day after. Yet that very illusion gave the whole work a human warmth and a touch of humour that makes our later writings – where 'black and white' have become 'grey and grey' – seem positively distasteful.[75]

So wrote Marx to Engels almost twenty years after the publication of *The Condition of the Working Class in England*. And he was right. Today, its uncompromising passion means it remains one of the most celebrated polemics in Western literature as well as a leading text – alongside Disraeli's *Sybil, or the Two Nations*, Carlyle's *Past and Present*, Dickens's *Hard Times* and Elizabeth Gaskell's *Mary Barton* – within the 'condition of England' canon. But what separated the work from those novels (with their milky Christian hopes for an eirenic absolution of class division) was its relentless condemnatory tone. It challenged the reader, as few other contemporary accounts dared, with the full, unvarnished horrors of *laissez-faire* industrialization and urbanization. 'I shall be presenting the English with a fine bill of indictment,' Engels announced mid-composition, 'I accuse the English bourgeois before the entire world of murder, robbery and other crimes on a massive scale.'[76] The work thus races across a range of subjects, mixing history and statistics, from 'The Great Towns' to 'Irish Immigration' to 'The Mining Proletariat', each of which encompasses a litany of crimes to be laid at the feet of the bourgeois. Alongside his own first-hand narratives and those culled from Leach, Engels especially enjoyed deploying the reams of official documentation coming out of Whitehall. And when there were no Blue Books available, 'I always preferred to present proof from Liberal sources in order to defeat the liberal bourgeoisie by casting their own words in their teeth.'[77] It was a polemical trick which Marx would perfect in *Das Kapital*. Thus the *Condition* is jam-packed with factory commission reports, court records, articles from the *Manchester Guardian* and *Liverpool Mercury*, and rosy accounts of merry, industrializing England from liberal protagonists such as Peter Gaskell and Andrew Ure.

The *Condition*'s strength lies in both its intellectual trajectory and empirical richness. What leaps off the page is the detailed accounts of the Manchester he had met with Mary Burns: its stink, noise, grime and human horror. 'Friedrich Engels had a clear bright head, free from any romantic or sentimental haze, that did not see men and things through coloured glasses or a misty atmosphere but always in clear bright air, with clear bright eyes, not remaining on the surface but seeing to the bottom of things, piercing them through and through,' was how the German social democrat Wilhelm Liebknecht would later describe Engels's approach.[78] The *Condition* was a shining product of this intellectual incisiveness combined with some obvious journalistic licence and his fierce urge to contrast the 'phantasms' and 'theoretical twaddle' of the Young Hegelians with 'real, live things'.[79] This combination of political philosophy with material reality would set the precedent for much of his polemical work. 'A knowledge of proletarian conditions is absolutely necessary to provide solid ground for socialist theories,' he declared.[80]

Engels's rhetorical blows, 'though aimed at the panniers, are meant for the donkey, namely the German bourgeoisie'.[81] For it was only a matter of time before the social crisis wrought by industrialization made its way on to the continent. 'While the conditions of existence of Germany's proletariat have not assumed the classical form that they have in England, we nevertheless have, at bottom, the same social order, which sooner or later must necessarily reach the same extremes as it has already attained across the North Sea, unless the intelligence of the nation brings about the adoption of measures that will provide a new basis for the whole social system.'[82]

Written back at his parents' house in Barmen in late 1844, the *Condition* was published in Leipzig in 1845 and primed for a German audience – being translated into English for an American edition only in 1885 and then for the British market in 1892. It was a *tour de force* of urban-industrial horrorism. In a passage that recalls his earlier account of Barmen's waterways in 'Letters from Wuppertal', Engels ascends Ducie Bridge overlooking Manchester's Irk to record a view 'characteristic for the whole district'. 'At the bottom flows, or rather stagnates, the Irk, a narrow, coal-black, foul-smelling stream, full of debris and refuse which it deposits on the lower right bank. In dry weather, an extended series of the most revolting brackish green pools of slime remain standing on this bank, out of whose depth bubbles of miasmatic gases constantly rise and give forth a stench that is unbearable even on the bridge forty or fifty feet above the level of the water.' Nearby, Engels retraces the steps of James Phillips Kay inside some of the insanitary hovels. 'In one of these courts there stands directly at the entrance, at the end of the covered passage, a privy without a door, so dirty that the inhabitants can pass into and out of the court only by passing through foul pools of stagnant urine and excrement.' Surrounding it are hundreds more of these 'cattle-sheds for human beings', where men are reduced to the state of animals, pigs share sties with children, hundreds cramp into dank cellars, railways slash through neighbourhoods, and privies, rivers and water supplies all seem to merge into one deadly mix.

Such is the Old Town of Manchester, and on re-reading my description, I am forced to admit that instead of being exaggerated, it is far from black enough to convey a true impression of the filth, ruin, and uninhabitableness, the defiance of all considerations of cleanliness, ventilation, and health which characterise the construction of this single district, containing at least 20–30,000 inhabitants. And such a district exists in the heart of the second city of England, the first manufacturing city of the world.[83]

Die Lage

der

arbeitenden Klasse

in

England.

Nach eigner Anschauung und authentischen Quellen

von

Friedrich Engels.

Leipzig.
Druck und Verlag von Otto Wigand.
1845.

Cover of the first edition of *The Condition of the Working Class in England.*

There was worse to come. On the south side of the city, just off Oxford Road, was where some of Manchester's 40,000-strong Irish immigrants huddled. Mary Burns's confrères were the most exploited, lowly paid and abused of all the city's residents; the most lumpen of the proletariat.

The cottages are old, dirty, and of the smallest sort, the streets uneven, fallen into ruts and in part without drains or pavement; masses of refuse, offal and sickening filth lie among standing pools in all directions . . . The race that lives in these ruinous cottages, behind broken windows, mended with oilskin, sprung doors, and rotten door-posts, or in dark, wet cellars, in measureless filth and stench, in this atmosphere penned in as if with a purpose, this race must really have reached the lowest stage of humanity.[84]

Despite having 'Tipperary' Mary Burns as his guide, Engels unquestionably acceded to the mid-Victorian caricature (much of it codified by Thomas Carlyle) of the immature, drunken, filthy Irish. Ignoring both the internal differences within Manchester's highly varied Irish community and their vital contribution to the Chartist movement (under the leadership of Feargus O'Connor and James Bronterre O'Brien), Engels depicted them en masse as a dissolute lumpenproletariat. 'The Irishman is a carefree, cheerful, potato-eating child of nature,' Engels explained, who was wholly unable to deal with the 'mechanical, egoistic, ice-cold hurly-burly of the English factory towns'.[85] The result was a swift descent into alcoholic torpor: 'The southern facile character of the Irishman, his crudity, which places him but little above the savage, his contempt for all humane enjoyments . . . his filth and poverty, all favour drunkenness.' His other weakness was livestock: 'The Irishman loves his pig as the Arab his horse . . . he eats and sleeps with it, his children play with it, ride upon it, roll in the dirt with it.'[86] But the Irish effect on urban life was far from benign since their minimal sustenance requirements inevitably forced down local wage rates. In every part of the economy where these 'wild Milesians' competed for jobs, impoverishment was the end result.

It was the base, insensate characteristics of the Irish which allowed them to cope with the terrible demands of industrial employment. With almost vicarious pleasure, Engels systematically listed the maiming and physical disfigurements that accompanied life on the factory floor. 'The knees are bent inward and backwards, the ankles deformed and thick, and the spinal column often bent forwards or to one side,' he wrote of the effects of the long hours spent in the cotton mill. In the mining industry, so heinous was the system of transporting coal and iron-stone that children's puberty was unnaturally delayed. And then there was the tyranny of time-management. 'The slavery in which the bourgeoisie holds the proletariat chained, is nowhere more conspicuous than in the factory system.' Engels had before him a copy of factory regulations, 'according to which every operative who comes three minutes too late, forfeits the wages for a quarter of an hour, and every one who comes twenty minutes too late, for a quarter of a day. Every one who remains absent until breakfast forfeits a shilling on Monday, and sixpence every other day of the week, etc.' But, as James Leach had first revealed, time was a variable phenomenon. '... operatives find the factory clock moved forward a quarter of an hour and the doors shut, while the clerk moves about with the fines-book inside, noting the many names of the absentees'. All of which meant that, in the radical idiom of the day, the working classes were 'worse slaves than the Negroes in America, for they are more sharply watched, and yet it is demanded of them that they shall live like human beings, shall think and feel like men'![87]

The result of such mental and physical torture – 'Women made unfit for childbearing, children deformed, men enfeebled, limbs crushed, whole generations wrecked, afflicted with disease and infirmity, purely to fill the purses of the bourgeoisie' – combined with filthy housing and debilitating hand-to-mouth existence, was an animalistic retreat into drinking and prostitution.[88] This was certainly the case in Sheffield. 'The younger generation spend the whole of Sunday lying in the street tossing coins or dog-fighting, and go regularly to the gin palace ... No wonder, then, that, as all witnesses testify, early, unbridled sexual intercourse, youthful prostitution, beginning with persons of 14–15 years, is extraordinarily frequent in Sheffield. Crimes of a savage and desperate sort are of common occurrence ...' The predicament facing the residents of the industrial city was exactly the sort of social disintegration Carlyle had warned of. 'The brutal indifference, the unfeeling isolation of each in his private interest becomes the more repellent and offensive ... The dissolution of mankind into monads, of which each one has a separate essence, and a separate purpose, the world of atoms, is here carried out to its utmost extreme.'[89] And what did the middle classes think of this wretched state of society? 'I once went into Manchester with such a bourgeois, and spoke to him of the bad, unwholesome method of building, the frightful condition of the working people's quarters, and asserted that I had never seen so ill-built a city. The man listened quietly to the end, and said at the corner where we parted: "And yet there is a great deal of money made here; good morning, sir."'[90]

On the surface, Engels's Manchester appeared to have no purpose or structure – 'a planless, knotted chaos of houses' – but, in reality, there existed a terrible logic behind the city's suffocating form. As Marx would later go beneath the veneer of freedom, equality and property in *Das Kapital* to depict capitalism's 'hidden abode of production', so Engels, in good Hegelian fashion, transcended the appearance of the city to elucidate its true essence. Yes, slum tenements went up haphazardly on the crumbling side of river banks and railways piled through old neighbourhoods, but these developments were part of a broader urban form which perfectly reflected the class divisions of industrial society. Like few before him, Engels appreciated the city's spatial dynamics – its streets, houses, factories and warehouses – as expressions of social and political power. The struggle between bourgeois and proletariat was not limited to the throstle room or Chartist rally, it was there in the street layouts, transport systems and planning process. 'The town itself is peculiarly built, so that a person may live in it for years, and go in and out daily without coming into contact with a working people's quarter or even with workers . . . This arises chiefly from the fact, that by unconscious tacit agreement, as well as with outspoken conscious determination, the working people's quarters are sharply separated from the sections of the city reserved for the middle class.' The social divides wrought by private property were embedded in the very flagstones of the city.

Engels's analysis of class zoning begins along the main thoroughfare of Deansgate, where the merchant princes and cotton lords came to make their deals. Like today, the road was in the 1840s a retail and commercial hub lined with high-end shops and showy warehouses.

And, as with so many modern city centres, 'the whole district is abandoned by dwellers, and is lonely and deserted at night; only watchmen and policemen traverse its narrow lanes with their dark lanterns'. But surrounding it, in the inner suburbs, lay the 'unmixed working people's quarters' of Manchester proper – Salford and Hume, Pendleton and Chorlton – 'stretching like a girdle ... around the commercial district'. And beyond that, 'outside this girdle, lives the middle bourgeois ... in regularly laid out streets in the vicinity of the working quarters; the upper bourgeois in remoter villas with gardens in Chorlton and Ardwick, or on the breezy heights of Cheetham Hill, Broughton, and Pendleton, in free, wholesome country air, in fine, comfortable homes'. And the finest part of the arrangement was that

the members of this money aristocracy can take the shortest road through the middle of all the labouring districts to their places of business, without ever seeing that they are in the midst of the grimy misery that lurks to the right and the left. For the thoroughfares leading from the Exchange in all directions out of the city are lined, on both sides, with an almost unbroken series of shops, and are so kept in the hands of the middle and lower bourgeoisie, which, out of self-interest, cares for a decent and cleanly external appearance and can care for it ... they suffice to conceal from the eyes of the wealthy men and women of strong stomachs and weak nerves the misery and grime which form the complement of their wealth.[91]

Engels, who in his Barmen corporate village had shared his neighbourhood with the local dyers, weavers and operatives, declared himself properly shocked: 'I have never seen so systematic a shutting out of the working class from the thoroughfares, so tender a concealment of everything which might affront the eye and the nerves of the bourgeois, as in Manchester.' And he was convinced this manipulation of urban form was not some accidental piece of planning: 'I cannot help feeling that the liberal manufacturers, the bigwigs of Manchester, are not so innocent after all, in the matter of this sensitive method of construction.'[92]

Of course, this notion of two nations in one city was a familiar one and Léon Faucher had earlier drawn attention to Manchester's geography of class division. But no one prior to Engels had managed to describe it with such acute percipience. He established a mode of reading the city through an entirely different lens: an appreciation that class power was the ultimate determinate of urban form. It was a subject he returned to some thirty years later in an analysis of Second Empire Paris which, thanks to the urban improvement of Baron Eugène Haussmann, had been transformed from a cobbled, decaying medieval city into a metropolis worthy of Emperor Napoleon III. Markets were erected, sewers laid, trees planted, churches and museums redecorated and, most monumentally of all, a series of boulevards driven through the traditional, working-class *arrondisse-ments*. In the process some 27,000 houses were demolished and tens of thousands of workers either forced or priced out of the city centre. In whatever way the scheme was dressed up – in terms of public health or transport efficiency – it was a far more obvious example of class-based urban planning in which the fabric of the city constituted a reification of bourgeois values. Engels termed it simply 'Haussmann'.

By 'Haussmann' I mean the practice which has now become general of making breaches in the working class quarters of our big towns, and particularly in those which are centrally situated, quite apart from whether this is done from considerations of public health and for beautifying the town, or owing to the demand for big centrally situated business premises, or owing to traffic requirements, such as the laying down of railways, streets, etc. No matter how different the reasons may be, the result is everywhere the same: the scandalous alleys and lanes disappear to the accompaniment of lavish self-praise from the bourgeoisie on account of this tremendous success, but they appear again immediately somewhere else and often in the immediate neighborhood.[93]

Ever since the publication of *The Condition of the Working Class*, Engels's civic gaze has helped to shape the way sociologists, journalists and activists approach the built environment. One can read clear echoes of his work in the 1920s Chicago School of urban theorists, with their concentric zone theory, or in any number of modern university courses on cultural criticism and social geography, with their derivative Henri Lefèbvre focus on the production or archaeology of space.[94] Such continuing relevance points to the role of ideology rather than reportage in Engels's account. Critics and biographers have often suggested that Engels simply walked the streets of 1840s Manchester, notebook in hand, writing down what he saw, with little premeditated sensibility. According to Steven Marcus, 'He [Engels] was choosing to write about his own experience: to contend with it, to exploit it, to clarify it, and in some literal sense to create it and thereby himself. For in transforming his experiences into language he was at once both generating and discovering their structure.'[95] Similarly, historian Simon Gunn has described how 'Engels developed a style of grimly detailed reportage in order to extract meaning from the profusion of sense impressions.'[96] Manchester historian Jonathan Schofield has gone even further in stressing how Lancashire transformed Engels's thinking and, with it, the nature of communism. 'Without Manchester there would have been no Soviet Union,' he declares. 'And the history of the 20th century would have been very different.'[97]

Much of this approach falls into a broader conception of Engels as the philosophically naive but socially acute reporter: the Marx collaborator whose only real achievement was to provide the data on capitalist conditions. Yet, following his 'conversion' to communism, Engels came to Manchester with a clear idea of the political significance of industrial society. He was so drawn to this city – 'where the modern art of manufacture has reached its perfection' – precisely because it promised to validate the communism he had taken from Moses Hess with its prediction of social revolution. Manchester's role was to confirm not create, the theory. Which meant that despite the book's dark vividness, what marked it out from contemporary urban travel literature was its polemical power rather than descriptive resonance.

This accounts for the *Condition*'s curious opening with its epic account of Britain's pre-history of industrialization – 'a history which has no counter-part in the annals of humanity'. It is a sweeping economic narrative taking in the spinning jenny, the steam engine, the digging of canals and the arrival of the railway. In true Moses Hess fashion, Engels declares, 'the industrial revolution [is] of the same importance for England as the political revolution for France, and the philosophical revolution for Germany'.[98] Slowly, inexorably, the old economy of guilds and apprenticeships with its thick social hierarchy was dismantled in favour of class division, of 'great capitalists and working men who had no prospect of rising above their class'. For the great crime of the British Industrial Revolution was that, thanks to the iniquity of private property, the technological and economic progress of the nineteenth century had not brought about the equitable enrichment of man. The end of the Malthusian spectre of famine and promise of abundance which had been offered by industrial capitalism was denied to the people by outmoded forms of property ownership. Instead, the final product of industrialization, the greatest iron hammered on the anvil, was the proletariat. Engels then outlines what would become the fundamental Marxist proposition that class was economically determined: 'The proletarian, who has nothing but his two hands, who consumes today what he earned yesterday, who is subject to every possible chance, and has not the slightest guarantee for being able to earn the barest necessities of life, whom every crisis, every whim of his employer may deprive of bread, this proletarian is placed in the most revolting, inhuman position conceivable for a human being.'[99] These desperate, miserable creatures, born of Britain's breakneck industrialization, are the callow heroes of the *Condition*. And their home is in the city.

So, despite all the bucolic 'idyllic simplicity' of pre-industrial peasant life – of farmers and fields, maypoles and harvesting – 'intellectually, they were dead', according to Engels. 'They were comfortable in their silent vegetation, and but for the industrial revolution they would never have emerged from this existence, which, cosily romantic as it was, was nevertheless not worthy of human beings.'[100] It is only once the working classes have been ripped from their villages and the idiocy of rural life and herded into factories that they come to appreciate their purpose as a proletariat. And here Engels provides one of the earliest accounts of the historic function of the proletariat as the harbingers of the communist revolution. Crucial to that was the state of their existence within the city, and Engels's breakthrough in 'Outlines of a Critique of Political Economy', that man was alienated from his human essence by capitalism, provided the essential ideological preamble. Engels's trawl through the slums of Salford and Little Ireland was an attempt, as Gareth Stedman Jones puts it, 'to validate, both metaphorically and literally, the Feuerbachian conception of the ontological loss of humanity associated with religious alienation and

– in the radical communist gloss added by Young Hegelians – with the establishment of money and private property'.[101] In the industrial city, man was precisely the alienated, de-humanized beast of burden which Hess and Engels regarded as the end product of capitalism – all of which helps to explain the ubiquitous animalistic imagery, the endless swine and cattle, that suffuses his text. As Engels says of Manchester's working-class accommodation, 'in such dwellings only a physically degenerate race, robbed of all humanity, degraded, reduced morally and physically to bestiality, could feel comfortable and at home'.[102] The city provides the raw, human evidence of capitalist alienation.

Such suffering was, however, necessary, since it was only once the impoverished masses reached their lowest ebb, once their very humanity had been taken from them, that they began to realize their class consciousness. 'Here humanity attains its most complete development and its most brutish; here civilization works its miracles, and civilized man is turned back almost into a savage,' as de Tocqueville described it.[103] As the birthplace of the labour movement, the city was thus the scene of immense sacrifice but also of redemption: through exploitation came ultimate liberation. 'Only the proletariat created by modern large-scale industry, liberated from all inherited fetters including those which chained it to the land, and herded together in the big cities, is in a position to accomplish the great social transformation which put an end to all class exploitation and all class rule,' as Engels later wrote in *The Housing Question*.

Through their delicate planning of the city, the middle classes hoped to have placed the working classes out of sight and out of mind. But the spatial configuration of the city – the creation of proletarian ghettos – only accelerated the nurturing of class consciousness. Thus Manchester was the scene of middle-class triumph but also doom. Every factory, slum and workhouse was a bourgeois *memento mori*: their glistening cities, tombs of the living dead. 'Hence the absurd freedom from anxiety, with which the middle class dwells upon a soil that is honeycombed, and may any day collapse.' From Glasgow to London, revolution was inevitable, 'a revolution in comparison with which the French Revolution, and the year 1794, will prove to have been child's play'.[104]

This sense of the city's purpose dictates Engels's seemingly rambling descriptions of 1840s Manchester. This was not simply a *feuilleton* or piece of journalistic slum tourism; it was also a politically persuasive work of supple communist propaganda. As such, everything had an ideological role to play: the landscape, people and industry. Hence, we never hear the working class speak in Engels's account, nor is there any sense of the multiple divisions within Manchester's labouring masses – street cleaners as distinct from cotton spinners, conservatives from liberals, Catholics from Protestants. The nuances of Manchester's multiple economies – distribution, services, construction, retail, as well as the cotton mills – are subtly elided for an overarching urban confrontation between solidified labour and capital. Similarly, the city's rich working-class civil society of Mechanics' Institutes, Friendly Societies and working men's clubs, of political parties and chapels, is absent. Instead, Engels offers one codified proletariat anxious to fulfil its historic destiny.

This focus on the historic role of the proletariat significantly marks out Engels's thinking from the Owenites and Chartists, who had little sense of the broader socio-economic forces that had given rise to the working class. Nor did their schemes for new harmonies, phalansteries or charters take account of the social revolution required. 'They acknowledge no historical development, and wish to place the nation in a state of Communism at once, overnight, instead of continuing political action until the goal is won and the movement can dissolve . . . They preach instead a philanthropy and universal love far more unfruitful for the present state of England . . . they are too abstract, too metaphysical, and accomplish little.'[105] What was needed was practicable action, the union of Chartism and socialism and, with it, the march of history. 'The revolution must come; it is already too late to bring about a peaceful solution,' Engels the Montagnard declared. The one hope was to lessen the accompanying violence by converting as much of the proletariat to communism as possible. 'In proportion as the proletariat absorbs socialistic and communistic elements, will the revolution diminish in bloodshed, revenge, and savagery.' For even if the working class had the specific task of delivering the communist future, the new society would embrace every class as old antagonisms melted away. 'Communism is a question of humanity and not of the workers alone.'[106]

With the clash between bourgeois and proletariat resolved in the communist future, the site of its struggle, the modern big cities, would similarly be rendered obsolete 'by the abolition of the capitalist mode of production'.[107] While the city might have witnessed the birth of the labour movement, the latter's triumph signalled the dissolution of the old antithesis between town and country. In future works Engels predicted that modern industrial techniques and a planned economy meant that commercial concentrations in urban areas would prove unnecessary. In turn, the poor sanitation and environment – 'the present poisoning of the air, water and land' – would be alleviated by the fusion of town and country. And so we have the irony that Engels, the great apostle of urban radicalism, ended his days advocating a hideously technocratic communist future devoid of civic life. 'Abolition of the antithesis between town and country is not merely possible. It has become a direct necessity of industrial production itself, just as it has become a necessity of agricultural production and, besides, of public health ... It is true that in the huge towns civilisation has bequeathed us a heritage which it will take much time and trouble to get rid of. But it must and will be got rid of, however protracted a process it may be.'[108]

The impact of *The Condition of the Working Class* was immediately apparent within German radical circles. 'As far as I know, I was the first to describe in German ... the social conditions created by modern large-scale industry,' Engels later recalled proudly, 'to provide an actual basis for German socialism, which was then arising and was expending itself in empty phrases.'[109] According to one Elberfeld communist, 'Friedrich Engels's book "The Condition of the Working Class in England", which abases all sacrosanct nonsense and iniquity, lies openly in taverns.'[110] Most bourgeois reviews, including that in the local *Barmen Zeitung*, were scathing, but the Prussian statistician Friedrich Ludwig von Reden was one exception, thinking it deserved 'particular attention both for its subject and its thoroughness and accuracy'. He was especially impressed by Engels's 'visibly truthful representation of the English bourgeoisie's attitude towards the proletariat: the despotism it practised in all important social issues, on the one hand, and the rage and frustrated bitterness of the propertyless on the other'.[111] Marx, as we have seen, was bewitched by the book and its helpful accumulation of data – from the mill owners' manipulation of factory clocks to the physical incapacity of operatives to the economic history of the cotton industry – to which he turned again and again for evidence of capitalism's inhumanity. 'As far as concerns the period from the beginning of large-scale industry in England down to the year 1845 I shall only touch upon this here and there, referring the reader for fuller details to Friedrich Engels's *The Condition of the Working Class*,' he wrote in an early note to the first volume of *Das Kapital*. 'The fullness of Engels's insight into the nature of the capitalist method of production has been shown by the factory reports, the reports on mines etc. that have appeared since the publication of his book.'[112]

But Engels contributed more than just facts. While Marxist scholars rarely give it full credit, *The Condition of the Working Class*, together with 'Outlines of a Critique of Political Economy', comprised a pioneering text of communist theory. Engels had, in the words of Wilhelm Liebknecht, 'deHegeled' himself: the human injustices he witnessed at first hand in industrializing Manchester took him beyond the 'mere abstract knowledge' of his Berlin days. With astonishing intellectual maturity, the 24-year-old Engels applied the Young Hegelian notion of alienation to the material realities of Victorian Britain and, in the process, crafted the ideological architecture of scientific socialism. The thin crust of theoretical communism he took from Moses Hess had been profoundly enriched by his Manchester days. So much of what would later be regarded as mainstream Marxist thought – class division, the unstable nature of modern industrial capitalism, the bourgeois creation of their own gravediggers, the inevitability of socialist revolution – was all first embedded in Engels's brilliant polemic.[113] Yet the *Condition* also proved one of his last substantive works of socialist ideology for thirty years. By the summer of 1844 Engels's apprenticeship in Manchester had come to an end and the son and heir to Ermen & Engels returned home to Barmen. On his way back, he stopped off in Paris for an altogether warmer meeting with Karl Marx. And, from then on, Engels's life's work was given over to managing 'Moor'.

4

'A Little Patience and Some Terrorism'

In the final moments of Honoré de Balzac's acid chronicle of bourgeois Paris, *Old Goriot*, the young hero Rastignac steps forward to confront the French capital. 'Lights were beginning to twinkle here and there. His gaze fixed almost avidly upon the space that lay between the column of the Place Vendôme and the dome of the Invalides; there lay the splendid world that he had wished to gain. He eyed that humming hive with a look that foretold its despoliation, as if he already felt on his lips the sweetness of its honey, and said with superb defiance, "It's war between us now!"'

Paris provided the glittering stage for the next phase of Engels's life. It was a city, he thought, whose 'population combines a passion for pleasure with a passion for historical action like no other people'. Like Rastignac, the ambitious, intellectually voracious and libidinous Engels wanted to taste all the city's delights. After the philistinism of Barmen and smoggy drizzle of Manchester, Paris promised countless opportunities for a young man of means. As Balzac marvelled: 'Paris is an ocean. Throw in the plummet, you will never reach bottom. Survey it; describe it. However conscientious your survey and careful your chart, however numerous and concerned to learn the truth the explorers of this sea may be, there will always be a virgin realm, an unknown cavern, flowers, pearls, monsters, things undreamed of, overlooked by the literary divers.'[1]

He wasn't alone in wanting to master this metropolis. For radicals, intellectuals, artists and philosophers, Paris was, in the words of Walter Benjamin, 'the capital of the nineteenth century'. The Young Hegelian Arnold Ruge called it 'the great laboratory where world history is formed and has its ever fresh source. It is in Paris that we shall live our victories and our defeats. Even our philosophy, the field where we are in advance of our time, will only be able to triumph when proclaimed in Paris and impregnated with the French spirit'.[2] True to Moses Hess's European triarchy, Paris's role was to draw on its revolutionary lifeblood and provide the vital spark in the struggle for communism. To the material injustices of England and the philosophical advances of Germany, France added the political dynamite – 'the crowing of the Gallic cock', as Marx excitedly called it.

The French metropolis provided the backdrop not just for a raffish display of Engels's carnal appetite, but for the formation of the modern Communist League. It was here that Engels learned the dark arts of machine politics: amidst the capital's boarding houses and workshops he started to craft the movement that one day would culminate in the worldwide Communist Party. Accompanying the politics – the vote-rigging and procedural gerrymandering – came Engels's collaboration with Marx on the nineteenth-century's most celebrated polemic, the *Communist Manifesto*. It all began over drinks at the Café de la Régence on 28 August 1844, when the bar which had once served Benjamin Franklin, Louis Napoleon and Voltaire himself, now played host to an increasingly dissolute pair of young Prussian philosophers.

Karl and a pregnant Jenny Marx had arrived in Paris in October 1843 following the rapid demise of his newspaper, the *Rheinische Zeitung*. No less a reader than Tsar Nicholas I had complained of the paper's anti-Russian tone and forced the Prussian authorities to revoke its printing licence. Marx's fellow editor, Arnold Ruge, suggested they leave Prussia to pursue their journalistic careers in France on the newly formed *Deutsche-Französische Jahrbücher*. Within weeks, though, Ruge was already regretting his continued co-operation with Marx as his colleague's editorial indiscipline quickly became apparent – 'he finishes nothing, breaks off everything and plunges ever afresh into an endless sea of books'.[3] But their divisions were more than just temperamental. After an intense period of research from autumn 1843 to spring 1844, Marx had distanced himself from Ruge's politics by defining himself as a communist and embracing the more activist elements of the Parisian working class. 'You should be present at one of the meetings of French workers so that you could believe the youthful freshness and nobility prevailing amongst these toil-worn people,' he wrote to Feuerbach in August 1844. 'It is among these "barbarians" of our civilized society that history is preparing the practical element for the emancipation of man.'[4] In addition, his study of the French Revolution as well as detailed reading of the classic works of political economy (notably, Adam Smith and David Ricardo alongside Engels's 'Outlines of a Critique of Political Economy') moved Marx on from a concern with religious alienation to the material realities of capitalist society. 'The years 1843–45 are the most decisive in his life,' declared Isaiah Berlin. 'In Paris he underwent his final intellectual transformation.'[5]

Less concerned with a critique of Hegelianism, he was now drawn to the effects which the division of labour and Carlyle's cash-nexus had on the nature of man. Like Engels's Manchester operatives, Marx regarded modern man as progressively alienated from himself by the nature of class-based capitalism. And, like Engels, he regarded the solution to this crisis of alienation as lying in the property-less hands of the very class created by capitalism, the proletariat. It was their historic function to return man to himself ('human emancipation') by transcending the poisonous iniquity which underlay political economy, the system of private property. 'Communism is the positive abolition of private property and thus of human self-alienation and therefore the real reappropriation of the human essence by and for man,' he wrote.[6] This obvious philosophical sympathy with Engels meant that by the time the two men downed their aperitifs at the Café de la Régence the memory of their chilly meeting at the *Rheinische Zeitung* offices had faded. Now, over ten beer-soaked days, they formed the emotional and ideological bond which would last a lifetime. 'When I visited Marx in Paris in the summer of 1844, our complete agreement in all theoretical fields became evident and our joint work dates from that time,' Engels definitively recalled.[7]

What was the nature of this meeting of minds, this companionship which in the words of Lenin 'surpassed the most moving stories of human friendship among the ancients'?[8] Unpersuasively, Edmund Wilson has written of Marx providing 'the paternal authority' which Engels had rejected in his own father. Alternatively, Francis Wheen has described Engels serving Marx 'as a kind of substitute mother'.

Less Freudianly, their relationship in familial terms is perhaps best approached as one of affectionate first cousins. Whilst sharing a background heritage of Rhenish, Prussian descent, each man brought markedly different but mutually supportive characteristics to it. 'Engels had a brighter, less contorted, and more harmonious disposition: physically and intellectually he was more elastic and resilient,' was how Gustav Mayer judged it.[9] Certainly, there was less of the 'dragon' about Engels: less 'Moorish' impetuosity, intellectual self-absorption and personal indignation at the human cost of capitalism. Engels was both more aloof and more rigorously empirical than his distracted, tortured collaborator. Marx's son-in-law Paul Lafargue called Engels 'methodical as an old maid'.[10] Physically, Engels was far more robust than the blister- and boil-ridden Marx, whose financial and personal stresses could be read like angry Braille across his body. Much has been made of how these differing characteristics revealed themselves in their handwriting, with Engels's studious, symmetrical script (elevated here and there by a neat, humorous illustration) contrasted by the furious, blotch-marked prose of Marx. Yet, in a neat metaphor for their friendship, it was often only Engels who could decipher Marx's meaning.

For the next forty years their relationship barely faltered, even amidst the most wretched of circumstances. 'Money, knowledge – everything was in common between them ... Engels extended his friendship to the whole of Marx's family: Marx's daughters were as children to him, they called him their second father. This friendship lasted beyond the grave,' was how Lafargue described it.[11] Fundamental to their friendship was a division of responsibility as, from the Paris meeting onward, Engels came to recognize Marx's superior ability to provide the ideological grounding of 'our outlook'. He accepted this intellectual demotion in a typically candid, matter-of-fact manner. 'I cannot deny that both before and during my forty years' collaboration with Marx I had a certain independent share in laying the foundations of the theory,' Engels wrote after his friend's death. 'But the greater part of its leading basic principles ... belongs to Marx ... Marx was a genius; we others were at best talented. Without him the theory would not be by far what it is today. It therefore rightly bears his name.'[12] This faith in Marx's genius was what convinced Engels to step back, sacrifice his own ideological development and play 'second fiddle' to 'so splendid a first fiddle as Marx'.[13] And the devoted Engels could never understand how anyone would have acted differently, 'how anyone can be envious of genius; it's something so very special that we, who have not got it, know it to be unattainable right from the start; but to be envious of anything like that one must have to be frightfully small-minded'.[14] But, crucially, Engels never needed to be converted to Marx's thinking. He had, according to Marx, 'arrived by another road ... at the same result as I' and was thus equally committed to exploring the theoretical and political implications of their philosophical stance. The difference was that 'Marx stood higher, saw further, and took a wider and quicker view than all the rest of us.'[15]

The first fruit of their relationship was a pamphlet entitled *A Critique of Critical Criticism: against Bruno Bauer and Co.* (1845) which revealed their shared impatience, in the wake of their Manchester and Paris experiences, with the idealistic remnants of the Young Hegelian school, along with a wish to announce publicly their newly held materialism. In intellectual terms, this materialism entailed a concentration on the lived reality of Man's natural, corporeal, 'immediate' existence and, with it, a primary focus on human economic activity and the social relations which result from that. In the face of the Bauer brothers' endless, futile philosophizing on religion and ethics – 'formulae, nothing but formulae' – the Berlin circle was now denounced as a self-indulgent impediment to progressive social change. 'A war has been declared against those of the German philosophers, who refuse to draw from their mere theories practical inferences, and who contend that man has nothing to do but to speculate upon metaphysical questions,' as Engels later put it in his increasingly strident tones.[16] In contrast to the 'beer literati', Marx and Engels wanted to focus on social and economic conditions and not chase the Hegelian shadow of Idea and Spirit: 'Real humanism has no more dangerous enemy in Germany than spiritualism or speculative idealism, which substitutes "self-consciousness" or the "spirit" for the real individual man.'[17] Marx's reading of political economy and Engels's time in the cotton mills of Manchester had revealed to both men the definitive role of private property in shaping modern society. It was material reality, not 'faded, widowed, Hegelian philosophy', which determined social structures and, if evidence were needed, one had only to consult the past. In an early, tentative exploration of the materialist interpretation of history, Engels countered the role of the Hegelian Idea in history by stressing the real contribution of flesh and blood humanity. 'History does nothing, has no "enormous wealth", wages no battles,' he wrote in criticism of Bruno Bauer. 'It is not "history" but live human beings who own possessions, perform actions and fight battles. There is no independent entity called "history", using mankind to attain its ends: history is simply the purposeful activity of human beings.'[18]

Despite its grandiose theme, the *Critique* was initially concocted as a short squib against Bauer et al. and Engels quickly churned out his copy before leaving Paris for Barmen in September 1844. 'Good-bye for the present, dear Karl,' Engels wrote on his departure, 'I have not been able to recapture the mood of cheerfulness and goodwill I experienced during the ten days I spent with you.'[19] Foolishly, he left the manuscript behind with dear Karl, where it quickly accumulated the tell-tale signs of Marx's stylistic incontinence. First of all, there was the length. 'The fact that you enlarged the *Critical Criticism* to 20 sheets surprised me not a little ... if you have retained my name on the title page it will look odd since I wrote barely 1½ sheets,' Engels noted. And, then, there was the disproportionate space given to denouncing political foes. 'The supreme contempt we two evince towards the *Literatur-Zeitung* is in glaring contrast to the 22 sheets we devote to it.' Evident also from the book's growth was Marx's crippling weakness for diverting himself from more substantive projects. 'Do try and finish your political economy book, even if there's much in it that you yourself are still dissatisfied with, it doesn't really matter; minds are ripe and we must strike while the iron is hot,' Engels pleaded in what would, over the following decades, become a wearily familiar refrain. 'Do as I do, set yourself a date by which you will *definitely have finished*, and make sure it gets into print quickly.' Finally, there was the journalistic knack of a catchy title: this time, Marx had crassly rechristened the pamphlet *The Holy Family: A Critique of Critical Criticism* in mock reference to the Bauer circle. 'Its new title ... will probably get me into hot water with my pious and already highly incensed parent, though you could not have known that.'[20]

Even prior to the publication of *The Holy Family*, the situation at home was hardly harmonious. Despite Engels's two-year absence and agreement to return to 'huckstering' (*schachern*) in the family firm, his relations with his father were increasingly tetchy as both found that atheistic communism and evangelical Protestantism did not rub along well. 'I can't eat, drink, sleep, let out a fart, without being confronted by this same accursed lamb-of-God expression,' he complained to Marx. '... today the whole tribe went toddling off to Communion ... this morning the doleful expressions surpassed themselves. To make matters worse I spent yesterday evening with [Moses] Hess in Elberfeld, where we held forth about communism until two in the morning. Today, of course, long faces over my late return, hints that I might have been in jail.' The situation was not helped by his sister Marie's engagement to another communist, Emil Blank. 'Of course, the house is now in a hellish state of turmoil.'[21] Those good pietists Friedrich and Elise were probably asking themselves where it had all gone wrong.

None of these domestic ructions diverted Engels from his missionary work. On his return journey from Paris through the Rhineland, he had been highly encouraged by the advanced state of socialist sentiment. 'I spent three days in Cologne and marvelled at the tremendous propaganda we had put out there.' Even along the Wupper valley, that Zion of obscurantists, there were signs of progress. 'This promises to be first-rate soil for our principles ... In Barmen the police inspector is a communist. The day before yesterday I was called on by a former schoolfellow, a grammar school teacher, who's been thoroughly bitten although he's had no contact whatever with communists.'[22] In an article for the Owenite journal, *The New Moral World*, Engels reported back on 'the rapidity with which Socialism has progressed in this country'. Gilding the lily somewhat, Engels announced that 'Socialism is the question of the day in Germany ... you cannot go on board a steamer, or into a railway carriage, or mail-coach, without meeting somebody who has imbibed at least some Social idea, and who agrees with you, that something must be done to reorganize society.' He went so far as to suggest that, 'among my own family —

and it is a very pious and loyal one – I count six or more, each of which has been converted without being influenced by the remainder'.[23] And, as a result of such successes, 'the clerical gentry have been preaching against us . . . for the present they confine themselves to the atheism of the young, but I hope this will soon be followed by a philippic against communism'.[24]

Of particular excitement to Engels was the growing number of agricultural uprisings and industrial strikes across the German states, the most celebrated of which was the revolt of Silesian weavers in Peterswaldau in June 1844. After years of intensifying impoverishment in the face of international and technological competition, these once wealthy and independent artisans stormed the local cotton mills in desperation. Across Silesia and Bohemia similar riots erupted as 'the social question' – the defining issue of poverty and exploitation in the face of accelerating industrialization – started to dominate public discourse. The Silesian weavers gained particular notoriety thanks to Heinrich Heine's sorrowful poem, *Song of the Silesian Weavers*. As the workers chant a lament for the 'old Germany' they weave a shroud for their vanishing society.

> The crack of the loom and the shuttle's flight;
> We weave all day and we weave all night.
> Germany, we're weaving your coffin-sheet;
> Still weaving, ever weaving!

Engels translated the verses into English before proudly announcing that 'Heinrich Heine, the most eminent of all living German poets, has joined our ranks.'[25]

Engels's political strategy was to channel this growing public concern about pauperism and class division in a consciously communist direction through a series of lectures he organized with his old mentor Moses Hess. The first, in February 1845, was to the liberal elite of Elberfeld at the popular Zweibrücker Hof. With an audience swelling to 200, the directors of local manufacturing and commercial firms, members of the court of law, and even the attorney general were invited to debate the nature of communism. Only the working class – the handmaidens of the communist future but not yet allowed into Elberfeld's best inns – was absent from discussing its predicament.

Engels thought the evening, which began with a reading of Shelley, an astounding success. 'All Elberfeld and Barmen, from the financial aristocracy to the *épicerie*, was represented, only the proletariat being excluded ... The ensuing discussion lasted until one o'clock. The subject is a tremendous draw. All the talk is of communism and every day brings us new supporters.'[26] One Elberfeld resident remembered the evening slightly differently:

In order to make the thing look harmless, some harpists had been engaged. At the beginning of the meeting, poems based on social themes were read. Then Hess and 'Friedrich Oswald' began their speeches. In the audience were manufacturers who had come for a thrill; they expressed their annoyance by laughter and jeers. The defence of capitalist society was left to the director of the local theatre. The more violently he attacked the possibility of communism, the more enthusiastically the notables drank his health.[27]

Engels enjoyed the rough and tumble of public speaking. 'Standing up in front of real, live people and holding forth to them directly and straightforwardly, so that they see and hear you is something quite different from engaging in this devilishly abstract quill-pushing with an abstract audience in one's "mind's eye".' In his speeches, Engels spelled out the iniquitous, competitive nature of capitalist society and its inevitable descent into class conflict as the divide between rich and poor widened and the middling classes were squeezed out of existence. 'The ruin of the small middle class, that estate which constituted the main foundation of states during the last century, is the first result of this struggle. Daily we see how this class in society is crushed by the power of capital . . .'[28] As the waste, bankruptcies and unemployment inherent in the capitalist mode of production mount up – on the back of cyclical trade crises and market failures – society would come to demand its reorganization along more rational principles of distribution and exchange. That future would necessitate a form of communism where competition was eliminated, capital and labour were efficiently allocated through a central authority, and crime disappeared alongside the tension between man and society. Moreover, productivity would rocket as industrial advances of the day were marshalled for the good of all rather than the profits of the few. 'The greatest saving of labour power lies in the fusing of the individual powers into social collective power and in the kind of organization which is based on this concentration of powers hitherto opposed to one another.'[29] In softly-softly tones, Engels explained the series of practical policies which would lead to this communist future – beginning with universal childhood education, followed by reorganization of the poor relief system and a progressive tax on capital. 'So you see, gentlemen, that it is not intended to introduce common ownership [*Gütergemeinschaft*] overnight and against the will of the nation, but that it is only a matter of establishing the aim and the ways and means of advancing towards it,' he reassured the conservative-minded Elberfeld elite.[30] Indeed, it was almost a question of old-fashioned paternalism. 'We must make it our business to contribute our share towards humanizing the condition of the modern helots,' suggested the young manufacturing heir.[31]

Despite the warm words, Engels's sermonizing brought him to the unwelcome attention of the authorities. The mayor of Elberfeld threatened to withdraw the licence of any hotel-keeper who provided a further meeting venue, and immediately despatched a letter to the Rhineland president, Freiherr von Spiegel-Borlinghausen, recounting the subversive communist debates and pinpointing Hess and Engels as the ringleaders. The mayor noted Engels's trips to England and France, which had provided the foundations of his communism, and described him as 'the eldest son of the highly esteemed father, the businessman Friedrich Engels senior'.[32] The security services were also on to him.

'Friedrich Engels of Barmen is a quite reliable man, but he has a son who is a rabid communist and wanders about as a man of letters; it is possible that his name is Frederick,' noted a police report to the Ministry of Interior.[33] On the basis of such intelligence the Prussian interior minister, von Arnin-Boytzenburg, issued a decree from Berlin banning all future communist meetings in Elberfeld-Barmen.

The unfortunate travails of Engels senior and his disreputable son were soon the talk of polite Barmen society. One Wuppertal notable, Georg Gottfried Gervinus, remarked on the looming perils of communist indoctrination in a letter to his friend Otto Freiherr von Rutenberg. He used Engels as stark evidence 'of how they are reeling in a young merchant over to philosophy, a young merchant who is independent and wealthy and completely fanatical, the son of a family from Barmen. I know him and . . . the father is very unhappy about his experience with his son; he told me: "You can't imagine how much this grieves a father: first my father endowed the Protestant parish in Barmen, then I built a church and now my son is tearing it down." – I replied: "That's the story of our times." '[34]

Engels's father was indeed furious with his son's political activities – 'my public appearance as a communist has fostered in him bourgeois fanaticism of truly splendid proportions' – and his avowed intention not to continue in the family firm. In response, he curtailed Engels's allowance, leaving the aspirant revolutionary 'leading a real dog's life' moping around the house.[35] 'He is now at terrible variance with his family,' Engels's Bradford friend George Weerth reported to his mother, 'he is considered godless and impious, and the rich father will not give his son another *pfennig* for his keep.'[36] So Engels retreated to his study to work on *The Condition of the Working Class in England* during the autumn of 1844. Even that aroused suspicion. 'If I sit in my room and work – communism, of course, as they know – the same expression.' But such was his devotion to Marx – then scrabbling together an exile's living in Brussels, having been deported from Paris as a political undesirable – he promised his new friend the book's fee. Catching wind of police plans to have him arrested and keen not to embarrass his parents any further in the eyes of the Barmen bourgeoisie, Engels decided to join Marx. It was a symbolic rupturing of family ties: by the time he stepped across the Belgian border in spring 1845, it was clear he would not easily be allowed back into Prussia – even for Marie's wedding to Emil. 'As you know, of all my brothers and sisters, I loved you the best and you were the one in whom I always had most confidence,' he wrote to his disappointed 'goose' in May 1845.[37] It was to be the first of many future instances placing the communist cause above the call of family and friends.

No sooner had he met up with Marx than the two of them left Belgium for a study trip to England. Engels reacquainted himself with Mary Burns (who would return with them to the continent), while Marx continued his studies in political economy. When the two young communists were not touring the industrial sores of Manchester, they spent their days boning up on the works of various liberal economists and official government publications. Their favoured reading spot was a bay window seat in Manchester's seventeenth-century Chetham's Library, whose 100,000 volumes they plundered for political and social data. 'In the last few days I have often been sitting at the quadrilateral desk in the small bow window where we sat 24 years ago,' Engels wrote to Marx in 1870. 'I like this place very much; because of its coloured window the weather is always fine there.'[38] The thick oak desk and stained-glass window are still there as they were in the 1840s, now encircled by the youthful bustle of the Chetham School of Music and overlooked by the skyscrapers, hotels and cranes of corporate Manchester. Today, the library acts as a popular shrine for communist pilgrims seeking some kind of direct, physical connection to the founding fathers. According to one tour guide, 'Whenever I bring people from the Chinese consulate here and get out the old books that Marx and Engels touched, they weep.'[39]

This time Marx and Engels didn't stay long in Britain and were back in Belgium by late summer 1845. The following months proved amongst the happiest the two spent together: living side by side in neighbouring Brussels apartments with their respective partners, they debated, laughed and drank long into the night. 'When I informed my wife of your very philosophical system of writing in couples till 3 or 4 o'clock in the morning, she protested that such philosophy would not suit her,' the Chartist Julian Harney joked to Engels in March 1846, 'and that if she was in Brussels she would get up a "*pronunciamento*" amongst your wives . . .'[40] Brussels offered Engels the opportunity to devote himself entirely to socialism. There was no prospect of huckstering in Belgium – instead, intoxicating evenings were spent in the bars with Marx, Moses Hess, George Weerth (who was delighted to exchange Bradford for Brussels), Stephan Born, the poet Ferdinand Freiligrath and the journalist Karl Heinzen. Firmly left out of the circle was the Russian aristocrat and future anarchist, Michael Bakunin, who described to his friend Georg Herwegh how 'The Germans, those craftsmen Bornstedt, Marx, and Engels – especially Marx – are plotting their usual mischief here. Vanity, malice, squabbles, theoretical intolerance and practical cowardice, endless theorizing about life, activity, and simplicity, and in practice a total absence of life, action, or simplicity . . . The single word bourgeois has become an epithet which they repeat *ad nauseam*, though they themselves are ingrained bourgeois from head to foot.'[41]

There was one minor social difficulty in this otherwise gregarious émigré scene: 'the small English woman from Manchester', in George Weerth's words. Described in correspondence of the period as either Engels's 'mistress' or 'wife', Mary Burns was clearly not to everyone's taste. Some socialists harboured an ideological objection to her relationship with Engels and resented the wealthy mill owner's son parading his proletarian lover through the salons of Brussels. According to Stephan Born, it was 'over confident of Engels to bring his mistress into this circle, which was frequented primarily by workers, thus invoking the accusation often made against rich sons of factory owners: namely, that they know how to draw the daughters of the common people into the service of their friends. *Noblesse oblige.*'[42] But it wasn't just Mary. Engels had a habit of introducing his other lovers – good-time girls amongst whom a 'Mademoiselle Josephine' and 'Mademoiselle Felicie' featured prominently – into the socialist circle. It was not a practice that Jenny Marx, daughter of the high-ranking Baron Ludwig von Westphalen and herself something of a blue-stocking, ever felt comfortable with. The Marxes, in the words of Max Beer, 'never in their heart of hearts regarded Engels and his female companions as their equals . . . Marx, one of the greatest revolutionists that ever lived, was in point of moral rectitude as conservative and punctilious as his Rabbinic forebears'.[43] This Puritanism or snobbery or moral rectitude came to a head during one of the numerous gala evenings the socialists put on in Brussels, at which Engels arrived with his current paramour. Stephan Born was there.

Among those present were Marx and his wife and Engels and his . . . lady friend. The two couples were separated by a large room. When I approached Marx to greet him and his wife, he gave me a look and a meaningful smile that let me know that his wife strictly refused all contact with this . . . lady friend. The noble woman was intransigent when it came to honouring *mores*. If anyone had had the impertinence to demand of her that she make a concession in this regard, she would have refused indignantly.[44]

Born recounted this scene many decades after the event and long after he had fallen out with both Marx and Engels, while Eleanor Marx, who was not there, always disputed what she called 'the idiotic Brussels story'. 'To begin with a person must have known my parents very little to ascribe to them the sleek-headed "morality" of the petit-bourgeois,' she wrote in a long letter to Karl Kautsky after the death of Engels. 'I know that occasionally the General [Engels] *did* turn up with queer acquaintances of the other sex, but, so far as I could ever learn, this only amused my mother, who had a rare sense of humour, and absolutely no middle-class hypocritical "propriety".'[45]

Out of this tight-knit, sometimes tense social maelstrom something very great emerged: *The German Ideology*. This joint manuscript by Marx and Engels was another commercial flop – never published in their lifetimes and famously abandoned 'to the gnawing criticism of the mice' (eventually gaining a readership only in 1932) – but it did achieve its purpose of intellectual self-clarification. The book was a further step along the road from idealism to materialism and, with it, another conscious act of distancing themselves from their Young Hegelian heritage. Characteristically, this literary path was pursued through a tedious bludgeoning of ideological rivals – the thinker in their sights this time being the philosopher of egoism, Max Stirner. And, equally typically, the level of abuse he sustained was precisely commensurate with the intellectual debt which Marx and Engels owed him.

An influential member of Berlin's Young Hegelian fraternity, Stirner had been unconvinced by Ludwig Feuerbach's critique of Hegelianism. Feuerbach had suggested that idealistic philosophy, namely Hegelianism, was little better than Christian theology when it came to impoverishing man's spiritual state. Both demanded that man worship something outside of himself – be it the Hegelian *Geist* or the Christian God. The solution, according to Feuerbach, was for man to worship humanity: anthropology not theology was the answer. But Stirner thought Feuerbach had fallen into the same trap of which he had earlier accused Hegel. In fact, Feuerbach had simply joined Hegel in elevating another enslaving theophany in place of the Christian deity: in Hegel's case it was Spirit and in Feuerbach's, 'Man with a capital M'. 'The HUMAN religion is only the last metamorphosis of the Christian religion,' in Stirner's judgement. By contrast, Stirner's 1845 book *The Ego and Its Own* advocated an absolute, self-conscious egoism completely free of any of the alienating effects of devotion to God, Man, Spirit or State. It was a supremely solipsistic, atheistic and ultimately nihilistic ethos in which the egoist 'does not look upon himself as a tool of the idea or a vessel of God, he recognizes no calling, he does not fancy that he exists for the further development of mankind and that he must contribute his mite to it, but he lives himself out, careless of how well or ill humanity may fare thereby'.[46] While Marx and Engels had no time for Stirner's advocacy of personal rebellion or the ahistoric nature of his individual man, their materialist inclinations were bolstered by his critique of Feuerbach's humanistic philosophy as little better than updated religion. As Engels explained in a rather strained letter to Marx, 'We must take our departure from the Ego, the empirical, flesh-and-blood individual, if we are not, like Stirner, to remain stuck at this point but rather proceed to raise ourselves to "man" . . . In short we must take our departure from empiricism and materialism if our concepts, and notably our "man", are to be something real; we must deduce the general from the particular, not from itself or, *à la* Hegel, from thin air.'[47]

This materialist ambition underpinned *The German Ideology*, which spelled out for the first time how Marx and Engels regarded social structures as the product of economic and technological forces. Each stage of production, from the primitive communism of early man to classical slavery to medieval feudalism to the industrial capitalism of the nineteenth century, was revealed in different 'forms of intercourse' in society – most notably, the property system, and in its wake social class, political forms, religion, even cultural movements. As Marx later put it, 'Social relations are closely bound up with productive forces. In acquiring new productive forces men change their mode of production; and in changing their mode of production, in changing the way of earning their living, they change all their social relations. The hand-mill gives you society with the feudal lord; the steam-mill society with the industrial capitalist.'[48]

And nowhere more so than when it came to the state which was simply 'the form in which the individuals of a ruling class assert their common interests, and in which the whole civil society of an epoch is epitomized'. This materialist interpretation of history suggested that each civilization was ultimately an expression of the modes of production which moulded it: the political and ideological superstructure was determined by the economic base as mediated through property forms, so-called 'relations of production'. 'The production of ideas, of conceptions, of consciousness, is at first directly interwoven with the material activity and the material intercourse of men . . . It is not consciousness that determines life, but life that determines consciousness.'[49] However, at a certain stage of development (e.g., the rising bourgeoisie during the English Civil War clashing with the medieval monarchy of King Charles I), the material forces of production come into conflict with existing property relations and their accompanying political, social and ideological superstructure – and then the moment is ripe for revolution. When the political systems were out of kilter with the economic fundamentals, then the former would have to readjust themselves to the latter in a series of often painful transformations. None of which meant that political change was either spontaneous or automatic. Given the opposition of the ruling elite, progress had to be fought for through political organizations, mass movements and practical agitation. Neither the 1650s English Commonwealth nor the 1790s Paris Commune was handed over willingly. 'A revolution is necessary, therefore, not only because the ruling class cannot be overthrown in any other way,' Marx and Engels explained, 'but also because the class overthrowing it can succeed only by revolution in getting rid of all the traditional muck and become capable of establishing society anew.'[50]

For the first time, *The German Ideology* made plain that the historic driver of such epochal shifts was class struggle and, in the context of the industrialized 1840s, it fell to the new proletarian class to instigate the coming revolution and usher in a communist future which promised not only their liberation, but a change in the entire human condition. As competition and private property gave way to communism 'the alienation between men and their products' would dissolve as men regained 'control of exchange, production and the mode of their mutual relationships'. In contrast to capitalist society, where the division of labour forces each man into 'a particular, exclusive sphere of activity', in the promised communist future 'where nobody has one exclusive sphere of activity but each can become accomplished in any branch he wishes, society regulates the general production and thus makes it possible for me to do one thing today and another tomorrow, to hunt in the morning, fish in the afternoon, rear cattle in the evening, criticize after dinner, just as I have a mind without ever becoming hunter, fisherman, cowboy or critic'.[51] But somehow this enviable future needed to be ushered in.

'The philosophers have only *interpreted* the world in various ways; the point is to *change* it,' Marx had declared in his 1845 *Theses on Feuerbach*, and the vehicle which he and Engels alighted on for delivering this change was the League of the Just (*Bund der Gerechten*). Founded in Paris in the 1830s, the league was part of an underground communist society run by émigré German tailors whose political inspiration could be traced back to the radical egalitarianism of 'Gracchus' Baboeuf during the French Revolution. In 1839 they collaborated with Louis-Auguste Blanqui in a doomed uprising which saw Blanqui jailed while other leaders of the league crossed the English Channel in search of political asylum. 'I came to know all three of them in London in 1843,' Engels later recalled of the exiled leadership in his history of the Communist League. The most impressive was Karl Schapper – 'of gigantic stature, resolute and energetic, always ready to risk civil existence and life, he was a model of the professional revolutionary'.[52] Schapper, the shoemaker Heinrich Bauer and the watchmaker Joseph Moll – 'these three real men' – established the German Workers' Educational Society in February 1840 in Great Windmill Street, Soho, as a front organization for the league. Most likely because of their continuing link to the Blanquists – and, with it, a futile belief in plots, conspiracies and putsches – Engels declined to join the league in 1843, but he and Marx did hold a series of meetings with them during their 1845 trip to England as part of an attempt to develop an international society of socialists or 'Fraternal Democrats'. Back in Brussels, this work was pursued with the establishment of a German Workers' Association and a Communist Correspondence Committee to co-ordinate socialist agitation and worker education across Europe. The league was to act as the recognized English arm of the movement.

Politically, the immediate aim of the Communist Correspondence Committee was the furtherance of democracy and, with it, the dissolution of *ancien régime* monarchies. 'Democracy nowadays is communism: democracy has become the proletarian principle, the principle of the masses,' Engels explained.[53] Democracy would ultimately and inevitably lead to the political rule of the proletariat and thence to communism. Indeed, the winning of suffrage rights would itself constitute a revolutionary event. 'Communism and communists were not binding words,' recalled Stephan Born (one of the founding members of the Committee), 'indeed, people hardly talked about them. Much more pertinent was the increasingly significant movement to reform electoral law in France.'[54] To destroy feudalism and head towards a democratic state, an alliance with the middle class was an uncomfortable necessity. 'To overthrow the nobility, another class is required, with wider interests, greater property and more determined courage: the bourgeoisie.'[55] From 1845 to the revolutions of 1848, Marx and Engels were unshakeable in their support for the establishment (by force if necessary) of bourgeois power and liberal democracy as a way stage to communism. There could be no overnight dictatorship of the proletariat – instead, a long process of political engagement which would see socialist commitment to a bourgeois-democratic revolution as a stepping stone towards communism. 'In a party one must support everything which helps towards progress, and have no truck with any tedious moral scruples,' the party leaders declared in almost Stalinist terms.[56] However, the bourgeoisie need not get too comfortable with this alliance. As Engels warned on the eve of 1848, 'So just fight bravely on, most gracious masters of capital! We need you for the present; here and there we even need you as rulers. You have to clear the vestiges of the middle ages and of absolute monarchy out of our path . . . In recompense whereof you shall be allowed to rule for a short time . . . – but do not forget that "The hangman stands at the door!" '[57]

However, there were those within the European communist movement who yearned for an immediate revolution, with its promise of rapturous human fulfilment, and regarded Marx and Engels's strategy as little better than weak-willed gradualism. Their leader was the itinerant tailor Wilhelm Weitling who, following the 1839 Blanquist uprising, had fled France for Switzerland and Austria, where he established League of the Just outposts and nurtured an enthusiastic plebeian following. There wasn't much Adam Smith, David Ricardo or Jeremy Bentham in Weitling's earthy politics. Instead, his doctrine encompassed a highly emotional mix of Babouvist communism, chiliastic Christianity and millenarian populism. Indebted to the work of the Christian radical Félicité de Lamennais, Weitling urged a physical-force adoption of communism on the back of a 40,000-strong army of ex-convicts. What followed would be a pre-lapsarian community of goods and societal harmony ushered in by the Christ-like figure of Weitling himself. While Marx and Engels struggled with the intricacies of industrial capitalism and modern modes of production, Weitling revived the apocalyptic politics of the sixteenth-century Münster Anabaptists and their gory attempts to usher in the Second Coming. It was a communist martyrology he liked emotionally to connect himself with by revealing to his audience the still livid scars he had suffered at the hands of Prussian jailers. His was a giddy, evangelical blend of proto-communist sympathies about the real nature of man which, much to Marx and Engels's fury, attracted thousands of dedicated followers across the continent. And the more Weitling was persecuted by official authorities, the brighter his halo of righteous martyrdom burned. 'He was now the great man, the prophet, driven from country to country,' Engels sneered, 'who carried a prescription for the realization of heaven on earth ready-made in his pocket, and who imagined that everybody was out to steal it from him.'[58]

Unsurprisingly, the continental socialist establishment was aghast at Weitling's facile approach. In London, the 'real men' of the league gave him short shrift, and so in 1846 he turned up in Brussels hoping to win over the Communist Correspondence Committee. It was to be a bruising encounter since Marx and Engels were always eager to denounce an ideological competitor. 'The tailor-agitator Weitling was a handsome fair-headed young man in a coat of elegant cut, a coquettishly trimmed small beard, more like a commercial traveller than the stern, embittered worker that I had expected to meet,' was how Pavel Annenkov, a Russian observer of the Brussels meeting, described Weitling's entrance. Around a 'small green table' the ideologues crouched.

Marx sat at one end of it with a pencil in his hand and his leonine head bent over a sheet of paper, while Engels, his inseparable fellow-worker and comrade in propaganda, tall and erect, as dignified and serious as an English-man, made the opening speech. He spoke of the necessity for people, who have devoted themselves to transforming labour, of explaining their views to one another and agreeing on a single common doctrine that could be a banner for all their followers who lacked the time and opportunity to study theory.

But before he could expound any further, the pent-up Marx – furious at the pretensions of Weitling – sprang up and demanded, 'Tell us, Weitling, you who have made such a noise in Germany with your preaching: on what grounds do you justify your activity and what do you intend to base it on in the future?' When Weitling, who liked to deal in abstracts and biblical imagery, failed to adopt the appropriate level of scientific rigour, Marx hit the table and screamed, 'Ignorance never yet helped anybody!'[59]

It wasn't enough just to crush Weitling; his acolytes also needed to be exposed. Chief amongst them was Hermann Kriege, who had tried to disseminate Weitling's views to the German community in America through his editorship of the New York-based *Der Volks-Tribun*. 'He founded a paper in which, in the name of the League, he preached an effusive communism of starry-eyed love, based on "love" and overflowing with love.' In the face of such ideological deviation, it was clearly far better to enforce party purity than enjoy broad public support. As a result of Kriege's political depredations, the Brussels Communist Correspondence Committee (at this stage, only eighteen-men strong) decided as one of its first public acts to expel a founding member. The 'Circular Against Kriege', signed by Engels, accused their former colleague of 'childish pomposity', 'fantastic emotionalism', damaging workers' morale and unacceptable deviation from the official communist 'line'. Kriege's crime, like Weitling's, was a hope-less inability to realize that their 'revolutionary movement of world-historical importance' had to be built on more than just vague aspirations about 'the great spirit of community'. The communism of Marx and Engels was a methodical, increasingly scientific process dependent upon the historical actions of the proletariat. So to silence Kriege, 'we let fly with a circular that did not fail to have its effect'. Soon after, 'Kriege vanished from the League scene.'[60] What the next 150 years brought in terms of expulsions, denunciations and political purges within left-wing parties is gloriously preordained in this chilling, three-point circular. And, from the outset, Engels was in the vanguard: over the decades, he would express his love and loyalty for Marx by taking delight in enforcing party discipline, pursuing ideological heretics and generally playing the 'Grand Inquisitor' when it came to upholding the true communist faith.

Of equal menace to Weitling's primitive communism was the 'true' or 'philosophical socialism' which drew much of its inspiration from the French philosopher Pierre-Joseph Proudhon. Initially, Marx like Engels had been highly impressed by Proudhon and his 1840 work, *What is Property?* What Proudhon taught Marx was that the solution to the iniquity of private property did not lie (as Weitling suggested) in some mystical 'community of goods'. Instead, he proposed the abolition of any income unjustified by productive work and the establishment of a system of fair exchange in which goods were equitably traded on the basis of the labour embodied in them. Marx was so enamoured of Proudhon's approach that, in May 1846, he invited him to join the Communist Correspondence Committee as its French representative. Engels added a 'PS' earnestly hoping that Proudhon, 'will approve of the scheme we have just put to you and that you will be kind enough not to deny us your cooperation. Assuring you of the deep respect your writings have inspired in me . . .' But Marx couldn't resist another little addition and the harmonious, cooperative mask of the committee suddenly dropped. 'I must now denounce to you Mr Grün of Paris. The man is nothing more than a literary swindler, a species of charlatan, who seeks to traffic in modern ideas.'[61]

Unfortunately, the Brussels agitators had overreached themselves as Proudhon was a close ally of the 'true socialist' popularizer Karl Grün, and he wrote back clearly judging the measure of Marx and Engels's political absolutism. 'Let us by all means collaborate in trying to discover the laws of society . . . but for God's sake, after we have demolished all the dogmatisms a priori, let us not of all things attempt in our turn to instil another kind of doctrine into the people . . . let us not set ourselves up as the leaders of a new intolerance, let us not pose as the apostles of a new religion.'[62] Marx and Engels did not take criticism well and the next few months saw an escalating tide of bile directed at Proudhon. It culminated in Marx's blistering pamphlet *The Poverty of Philosophy* (a characteristically chiasmatic response to Proudhon's *The Philosophy of Poverty*), with its attack on what Marx depicted as Proudhon's petit-bourgeois philosophizing, Utopian plans for labour exchanges and crippling inability to appreciate the historic role of the proletariat. This was the trouble with 'true socialism': it was a philosophy which wilfully ignored the social reality of working-class life and 'presupposed the existence of bourgeois society, with its corresponding economic conditions of existence, and the political constitution adapted thereto'.[63] Its attempts to preserve a petit-bourgeois quality of life in the face of international competition served only to hinder the final, communist summation of capitalism. It was a philosophy built around the narrow needs of an artisan class, wedded to a romantic notion of pre-industrial cooperation. Yet, however compelling Marx's philosophical critique, the irony was that Proudhon and Grün's followers were well dug in amongst the Parisian and German émigré working class, where their clear programme of co-operation, fairly priced products and universal employment enjoyed popular support. So that was where Engels, the Grand Inquisitor, was forced to take the fight.

'The scent of the great Revolution and of the July Revolution – a column to commemorate which had been erected on the square where the Bastille had stood – was still in the air,' was how Stephan Born remembered 1840s Paris. 'Unlike in Germany, where nothing of the sort existed at the time, the workers of Paris already formed a distinct opposition to the ruling bourgeoisie . . .'[64] Engels's posting to Paris in August 1846 came with a clear brief to win these workers over to the League of the Just and prevent any proletarians falling into the hands of Grün's 'true socialists' or Weitling's 'tailor communists'.

The French metropolis was just as seductive and dangerous as Balzac's Rastignac had described. And like industrializing Manchester, it was increasingly regarded as a divided city. Historically, Paris had always prided itself on the geographical intimacy of differing social classes – 'a palace opposite a stable and a cathedral next to a chicken-run', according to one US visitor. But now the rich were separating themselves off from the poor, leaving behind ghettos and no-go areas peopled by a dangerous residuum. Amongst the most notorious was the horribly overcrowded Île de la Cité – 'a labyrinth of obscure, crooked, and narrow streets, which extends from the Palais de Justice to Notre Dame' – which provided the opening scene for Eugène Sue's bestselling potboiler, *The Mysteries of Paris* (1842).[65] While the western enclaves of Paris cocooned themselves in wealth and privilege, the filthy *faubourgs* of the centre and east housed the city's increasingly restive *classes dangereuses*. Novelists of the era delighted in describing their capital as a hideous, decaying old harridan in which the heroism of the revolution was progressively tarnished by the awful reality of disease, prostitution, crime and mercantile bourgeois mores. The political economist Victor Considérant described Paris in 1848 as 'a great manufactory of putrefaction in which poverty, plague . . . and disease labour in concert and where sunlight barely ever enters. [It is] a foul hole where plants wilt and perish and four out of seven children die within their first years'.[66] In an age of empire, the language was one of lost world, monstrous tribes, new lands and unknowable cultures. Sue wrote of 'the barbarians . . . in our midst'; Balzac described his city 'like a forest in the New World where a score of savage tribes, the Illinois, the Hurons, struggle for existence; each group lives on what it can get by hunting throughout society'.[67]

Scratching a living just above this lumpenproletariat were the skilled émigré communities to whom Engels directed his attentions. The Industrial Revolution had come late to France but by the 1840s the economy was, at last, starting to pick up. The expansion of the defence sector and railway construction – together with the development of cotton, silk and mineral industries – led to a sustained surge in industrial production and foreign exports. However, within Paris the workshop system of manufacture continued to hold out against the production line of the factory. Skilled workers in firms of fewer than ten people selling into a fashion-oriented market dictated much of the city's employment patterns: in 1848 Paris contained 350,000 workers with one third in clothes and textile trades and much of the remainder divided between construction, the furniture trade, jewellery, metallurgy and domestic service. A large part of this workforce – some 60,000 by the late 1840s – was made up of Germans specializing in the print trade, tailoring and cabinet-making. Engels described them as 'everywhere', and such was their strength that in certain Parisian quarters barely a word of French was to be heard.[68]

The competition for their political affiliation was keen. As we have seen, France had long been a centre of socialist thought and, after the early years of Fourier and Saint-Simon, radical politics resurfaced in the 1840s on the back of 'the social question'. First there was Proudhon, but he was joined by Louis Blanc, Etienne Cabet, Pierre Leroux and George Sand – all offering the promise of a new society ranging from Owenite-style co-operation to full-blooded communism. Much of this theorizing found its keenest audience amongst the exploited, impoverished German community – so much so that in 1843 the Prussian government launched an inquiry into just how extensive and dangerous this contamination of expatriate Germans was. One consequence of this was Marx's expulsion from France in 1845. 'We must purge Paris of German philosophers!' was King Louis-Philippe's understandable reaction to the subversive pamphleteering infecting his capital.

Engels entered this tight political market supported only by his own self-confidence (and his parents' continuing allowance), but gamely set to work trying to rid the Parisian working class of the deviant socialist strains of Grün and Weitling. His target was the so-called *Straubingers* – the German artisans and journeymen inclined to 'true socialism' – gathered in the Faubourg St Antoine manufacturing district. For students of entryism, Engels's tactics at their weekly political meetings were textbook stuff: a brutally successful medley of threats, divide and rule, denunciations and ideological bullying. 'By dint of a little patience and some terrorism I have emerged victorious with the great majority behind me,' he boasted to Marx before recounting how he 'went into action, so intimidating old Eisermann [a joiner and member of the League of the Just] that he no longer turns up'. The one worry he had was the primitive level of ideological understanding amongst the *Straubingers* – 'the fellows are horribly ignorant' – as their relative prosperity was hindering the development of their class consciousness. 'There is no competition among them, wages remain constantly at the same wretched level; the struggle with the master, far from turning on the question of wages, is concerned with "journeymen's pride", etc.' Ideally, Engels would have had them a great deal poorer and more desperate.

At his next meeting Engels decided to set out the real meaning of communism to these myopically contented workers. In doing so, he embarked on his career as one of the most prolific and intelligible popularizers of Marxist doctrine. Its aims, he explained, were clear:

1. to ensure that the interests of the proletariat prevail, as opposed to those of the bourgeoisie;
2. to do so by abolishing private property;
3. to recognize no means of attaining these aims other than democratic revolution by force.

He then called a vote so the group could decide whether they were proper, committed communists or some fanciful debating society which he would not waste any more time over. 'At the beginning I had nearly the whole clique against me and at the end only Eisermann and the three other Grünians.' Engels denounced the anti-proletarian, petit-bourgeois sentiments of Grün and his disciples in such strident tones that the meeting eventually acceded to his definition of communism by a majority of thirteen to two (which also gives some sense of the intimacy of the gatherings).[69]

In Paris as in Elberfeld, his achievements did not go unnoticed by the authorities. Among those taking an interest were the city police, who used the growing number of social disturbances in the St Antoine neighbourhood as an excuse to crack down on the subversive *Straubinger* cells. Grün's men fingered Engels as the agitator and he soon had a motley collection of spies and informers trailing him across Paris. Perhaps tiring of the nightly debates and votes on procedural motions, Engels used this police harassment as a welcome excuse to exchange socialist study evenings for a high-society plunge into Paris's carnal delights. 'If the suspicious individuals who have been following me for the past fortnight are really informers, as I am convinced some of them are, the Prefecture must of late have given out a great many entrance tickets to the *bals* Montesquieu, Valentino, Prado, etc.,' he boasted to Marx. 'I am indebted to Mr Delessert [Prefect of the Paris police] for some delicious encounters with *grisettes* [prostitutes] and for a great deal of pleasure, *car j'ai voulu profiter des journées et des nuits qui pouvaient être mes dernières à Paris* [since I wanted to take advantage of the days and nights which might well be my last in Paris].'[70]

By his mid-twenties Engels was a well-versed Lothario whose silky good looks and raffish demeanour had earned him a string of lovers. No sooner had he left the earthy embrace of Mary Burns in Manchester than he was writing to Marx of 'a love affair' he had 'to clear up'. By January 1845 it had come 'to a fearful end. I'll spare you the boring details, nothing more can be done about it, and I've already been through enough over it as it is.'[71] In Brussels over the summer he was back with his 'wife', Mary, but during the autumn in Paris prudish Stephan Born was aghast at his companion's Bacchanalian urges. 'Notwithstanding his communist doctrine, Engels, too, was a staunch individualist . . . He had no appreciation for the fine arts, and for music in particular; . . . It never occurred to Engels to show me the artistic treasures of Paris; I visited the galleries of the Louvre without him. While he watched the wildest burlesques at the theatre of the Palais Royal, I admired Rachel in the role of Phèdre at the *Théâtre français*.'[72] Engels took a series of mistresses (apparently his 'insolent manner' was found to 'work well with the female sex'), spent boozy evenings with a louche cadre of artists and, like so many of his class and epoch, had no compunction about paying for sex. Barely one year later he would condemn prostitution as 'the most tangible exploitation – one directly attacking the physical body – of the proletariat by the bourgeoisie', but no such reservations concerned him now. 'It is absolutely essential that you get out of *ennuyante* [boring] Brussels for once and come to Paris, and I for my part have a great desire to go carousing with you,' he urged family man Marx. 'If I had an income of 5000 francs I would do nothing but work and amuse myself with women until I went to pieces. If there were no Frenchwomen, life wouldn't be worth living. *Mais tant qu'il y a des grisettes, va!* . . . [But so long as there are prostitutes, well and good!]'[73] Happily for Engels, when it came to female relationships the personal and the ideological fused gratifyingly together: he had a strong libido, a love for the company of women, and also an innate, anti-*Biedermeier* distaste for the bourgeois morality of monogamous marriage. In time this would develop into a coherent theory of socialist feminism, but in his mid-twenties it remained a product of an ongoing reaction to the dowdy philistinism of his Barmen upbringing, along with a young man's obvious enjoyment of Parisian nightlife.

There was, however, an altogether less attractive aspect to Engels's womanizing. Since the start of his friendship with Marx, Engels's attitude to Moses Hess had been hardening. The 'communist rabbi' who had first brought him into the socialist current was increasingly disparaged as an ideologically confused ditherer whose sympathy for Grün's 'true socialism' provided clear evidence of his suspect philosophical tendencies. But, like a pair of playground bullies, Marx and Engels decided to make the political personal by directing their attention towards Hess's wife. Sibylle Hess, née Pesch, was, according to Cologne police reports, a former prostitute turned seamstress whom Hess rescued from the gutter as much out of political conviction as emotional attachment – 'he wished to perform an act expressive of the need for love among men and for equality between them', according to Isaiah Berlin. However, Sibylle had a wandering eye.[74]

In July 1846 Engels agreed to help Hess by smuggling the passport-less Mrs Hess across the border from Brussels into France. No sooner had the two arrived in Paris than Engels was taking her name in vain in a series of unchivalrous letters to Marx. 'Mrs Hess is on the look-out for a husband. She doesn't give a fig for Hess. If there should happen to be someone suitable, apply to Madame Gsell, Faubourg St Antoine. There's no hurry since the competition isn't keen.' By September it seemed Engels had taken upon himself the conjugal role after he boasted to Marx of consigning Mrs Hess 'cursing and swearing' back to the 'furthest end of the Faubourg St Antoine'. What gave him especial pleasure were the steps which the unknowingly cuckolded Hess (now little more than a Falstaff figure to Engels's Prince Hal) was at the same time taking to renew their friendship. When Hess eventually turned up in Paris in January 1847, 'my treatment of him was so cold and scornful that he will have no desire to return. All I did for him was to give him some advice about the clap he had brought with him from Germany.' Unsurprisingly, the friendship broke down terminally when Hess discovered Engels's seduction of his wife and he returned to Brussels to rubbish his one-time protégé. Engels adopted an air of lofty nonchalance. 'Moses brandishing his pistols,

1. Friedrich and Elise Engels: a model of bourgeois parental rectitude.

2. 'Zion of the obscurantists'. Engels's home town of Barmen in the early 1800s.

3. Georg Wilhelm Friedrich Hegel at the University of Berlin in 1828, sowing his dragon-seeds.

4. 'With one blow it pulverized the contradiction.' Ludwig Feuerbach, author of *The Essence of Christianity*.

5. 'The wild black boar', 'the wicked nave', 'the Moor': a young Karl Marx.

6. 'I am very busy at present with philosophy and critical theology.' Self-portrait of Engels the questing intellectual, aged nineteen.

7. 'King Cotton': design from the mill of John Marshall & Sons, depicting the civilizing wonders of the cotton trade, c. 1821.

8. Reels from the Ermen and Engels mill with their three towers trade mark.

9. 'The Juggernaut of Capital': The Ermen and Engels mill in Weaste, alongside the Manchester to Liverpool railway line.

10. Oswald the Montagnard. Portrait of Engels the romantic visionary, 1840.

11. Face to face with the proletariat: child labour in the Victorian cotton industry.

12. 'And yet there is a great deal of money made here; good morning, sir.' The wealth of mid-Victorian Manchester.

13. Engels's other world: the Albert Club on Dover Street, Manchester, renowned for its smoking room, card rooms and billiard tables.

14. 'The quadrilateral desk in the small bow window', Chetham's Library, Manchester, where Marx and Engels spent the summer of 1845 reading up on political economy.

15. The 1848 Revolution: Dresden in revolt against the King of Saxony. Amongst the rioters were Michael Bakunin and Richard Wagner.

16. Berlin's March revolution. 'All that is missing is the guillotine,' muttered Queen Elisabeth.

parading his horns before the whole of Brussels . . . must have been exquisite,' he wrote to Marx. However, what certainly did unsettle Engels was Hess's 'preposterous lie about rape [*Notzucht*]'. This was, he assured his friend, utter nonsense. 'I can provide him with enough earlier, concurrent, and later details to send him reeling. For only last July here in Paris this Balaam's she-ass [Sibylle] made me, *in optima forma* [in due form], a declaration of love mingled with resignation, and confided to me the most intimate nocturnal secrets of her ménage! Her rage with me is unrequited love, pure and simple.' Boorishly, he went on to suggest that 'the horned Siegfried' was 'perfectly at liberty . . . to avenge himself on all my present, past and future mistresses', which he helpfully listed. But if Hess wanted to take this matter of honour further, then Engels, who learned his duelling amongst the wealthy of Bremen, 'will give him fair play'.[75]

Did Engels really rape Moses Hess's wife? With his self-styled 'insolent manner', Engels was certainly something of a sexual predator during his time in Paris, but it seems unlikely to have carried itself over into violence. Most probably, it was an affair – elements of which were bound up with Engels wanting to humiliate Moses Hess – which went wrong. Nonetheless, there does exist a rather curious passage in Eleanor Marx's 1898 letter to Karl Kautsky in which she writes of a Paris incident unusually hushed up within the otherwise open-minded Marx household. 'That there was a woman in the case I *did* most certainly know, and from some words I heard, apparently a rather disreputable one at that. But what it all was – except that it was an episode to be passed over and covered up – I don't know.' It was, she assured herself and Kautsky, 'some silly young fellow's nonsense'.[76]

Impressively, Engels managed to get some politics done between his skirt chasing. In June 1847 the League of the Just held a congress in London to which Marx and Engels (as newly signed-up members) were invited. Its purpose was for Schapper, Bauer and Mill to join forces with the Brussels Committee and drop the old secret society mentality for a more open political programme. With Marx's finances at another characteristic low, the Brussels contingent was represented by Wilhelm Wolff, whilst Engels had to battle through a meeting of the Paris branch to ensure his selection as their representative. 'I realised that it would be very difficult to get Engels nominated, though he hoped to be,' recalled Stephan Born; 'there was strong opposition against him. I only succeeded in getting him elected by asking – against the rules – that those who were against, not for, the candidate raise their hands. This trick strikes me as loathsome today. "Well done," Engels said to me as we went home.'[77]

The congress represented a seminal moment in the development of the Communist Party: the name was changed from League of the Just to the Communist League; and the mission statement from 'All Men Are Brothers' to the altogether more bombastic, 'Working Men of All Countries, Unite!' Engels was tasked by the congress with drawing up a 'revolutionary catechism' for the league, outlining their politico-philosophical stance. The result was the 'Draft of a Communist Confession of Faith' which, in its very title, revealed that blend of religious zealotry and underground paranoia which still marked out the early communist movement.

> Question 1: *Are you a Communist?*
> Answer: Yes.
> Question 2: *What is the aim of the Communists?*
> Answer: To organise society in such a way that every member of it can develop and use all his capabilities and powers in complete freedom and without thereby infringing the basic conditions of this society.
> Question 3: *How do you wish to achieve this?*
> Answer: By the elimination of private property and its replacement by community of property.[78]

The draft confession, continuing to Question 22, was a compromise document including much of the sort of 'true' or Utopian socialism Marx and Engels abhorred. But it also contained inklings of the very brilliant, popularizing touch that would culminate in the *Communist Manifesto*. The coming of the proletariat and their historic function in ushering in the socialist revolution was at the core of the catechism. Equally, Engels's text was replete with the materialist interpretation of history and society which he and Marx had been developing over the previous five years. Political revolution, the document declared, was contingent upon a disjuncture between property relations and the mode of production (whether the political and social superstructure was in accordance with the economic base) – but that did not mean change could not be worked for. 'If, in the end, the oppressed proletariat is thus driven into a revolution, then we will defend the cause of the proletariat just as well by our deeds as now by our words.' However, the first step along the path to 'the political liberation of the proletariat' was the securing of 'a democratic constitution'. Following that would come the limiting of private property, creation of national workshops, universal state education and some potential reforms to the marriage system.[79]

With the congress concluded, Engels threw himself into an intensive round of shuttle diplomacy from which Marx was barred by a number of official travel bans. He returned from London to Brussels to shore up the Marxist position in the face of attempts by rival German factions to usurp the communist network, then back to Paris to sell the 'Confession of Faith' to the local Communist League branches. 'I at once set up a propaganda community and I rush round speechifying,' he reported to Marx. 'I was immediately elected to the district [district Committee of the Communist League] and have been entrusted with the correspondence.' To get the 'Confession' through the committees he needed to outmanoeuvre Moses Hess, who was hawking around an alternative version. Once again, his wily political skills came to the fore as he played 'an infernal trick on Mosi'. 'Last Friday at the district I dealt with this [Hess's version], point by point, and was not yet halfway through when the lads declared themselves *satisfaits*. Completely unopposed, I got them to entrust me with the task of drafting a new one which will be discussed next Friday by the district and will be sent to London behind the backs of the committees. Naturally not a soul must know about this, otherwise we shall all be unseated and there'll be the deuce of a row.'[80]

The next draft, composed by Engels in October 1847, was entitled 'Principles of Communism' in preparation for the second Communist League congress scheduled back in London for 28 November. While much of the 'Principles' is similar in tone and content to the 'Confession', there is a perceptible ratcheting up of the materialism and downplaying of the earlier Utopian socialism. The necessity of a thorough proletarian revolution is more openly advocated and a new emphasis on the unstoppable, global character of capitalism leads to a call for international worker solidarity. 'So if now in England or France the workers liberate themselves, this must lead to revolutions in all other countries, which sooner or later will also bring about the liberation of the workers in those countries.' Socialism in one country was not an option. Yet the destructive processes of globalized capitalism were in the meantime to be embraced: 'precisely that quality of large-scale industry which in present society produces all misery and all trade crises is the very quality which under a different social organization will destroy that same misery and these disastrous fluctuations'.

Engels retained the earlier commitment to the abolition of private property and the inauguration of a democratic constitution, but now offered an expanded list of transitional steps towards socialism. One of these, in something of a throwback to the Fourierist and Owenite tradition, was a pledge to erect 'large palaces on national estates as common dwellings for communities of citizens engaged in industry as well as agriculture, and combining the advantages of both urban and rural life without the one-sidedness and disadvantage of either'. Equally radical was Engels's suggestion that the coming communist order would transform relations between the sexes, since 'it abolished private property and educates children communally, thus destroying the twin foundation of hitherto existing marriage – the dependence through private property of the wife upon the husband and of the children upon the parents'.[81]

Unpublished until 1914, 'Principles of Communism' was the draft document with which Engels returned to London and the basis of the *Communist Manifesto*. 'This congress must be a decisive one,' Engels urged Marx before meeting him in Ostend and travelling together across the Channel. 'Give a little thought to the Confession of Faith. I think we would do best to abandon the catechetical form and call the thing Communist Manifesto.' Holed up inside the headquarters of the German Workers' Education Association, above the Red Lion pub in Great Windmill Street, the second congress picked apart the 'Principles' over the course of an exhausting ten days in November 1847. But Marx carried the meeting. 'His speech was brief, convincing and compelling in its logic. He never said a superfluous word; every sentence contained an idea and every idea was an essential link in the chain of his argument.'[82] By the end, 'All contradiction and doubt were finally over and done with, the new basic principles were adopted unanimously, and Marx and I were commissioned to draw up the manifesto. This was done immediately afterwards.' 'Since then,' Engels proudly noted looking back from the 1880s, 'it [the *Manifesto*] has travelled round the world, has been translated into almost all languages and still today serves in numerous countries as a guide for the proletarian movement.'[83]

From the rough, sometimes leaden drafts of the 'Confession of Faith' and 'Principles of Communism' emerged the seamless prose of the *Communist Manifesto*. 'This irresistible combination of utopian confidence, moral passion, hard-edged analysis, and – not least – a dark literary eloquence was eventually to become perhaps the best-known and certainly the most widely translated pamphlet of the nineteenth century,' in the fine words of Eric Hobsbawm. Marx and Engels began working together on the *Manifesto* in London and then Brussels. But it was Marx who delivered the final edition and it is this gratifying absence of a committee consensus which makes the *Manifesto* read so well. From its epic opening lines – 'A spectre is haunting Europe – the spectre of Communism' – to its challenging finale – 'The proletarians have nothing to lose but their chains. They have a world to win. WORKING MEN OF ALL COUNTRIES, UNITE!' – it is a polemic written out in one heroic breath. Yet much of the hard intellectual grind, in league meetings and drafting sessions, had been carried out by Engels. The German SPD leader Wilhelm Liebknecht had it right: 'What was supplied by one, what by the other? An idle question! It is of one mould, and Marx and Engels are one soul – as inseparable in *The Communist Manifesto* as they remained to their death in all their working and planning . . .'[84]

Perhaps the most obvious debt to Engels's work was the *Manifesto*'s account of the emergence of the proletariat, 'a class of labourers, who live only so long as they find work, and who find work only so long as their labour increases capital'. This socio-economic narrative, premised heavily on the accelerating function of the Industrial Revolution, could have come straight from the pages of *The Condition of the Working Class in England*. The unique history of the English

der

Kommunistischen Partei.

Veröffentlicht im Februar 1848.

Proletarier aller Länder vereinigt Euch!

London.

Gedruckt in der Office der „Bildungs-Gesellschaft für Arbeiter"
von J. E. Burghard.

46, LIVERPOOL STREET, BISHOPSGATE.

Cover of the first German 23-page edition of the *Manifesto of the Communist Party*.

proletariat suddenly became a universal template of working-class development.[85] At the same time Marx and Engels's Young Hegelian heritage was slyly jettisoned as they outlined a highly materialist schema – 'the history of all hitherto existing society is the history of class struggles' – inexorably culminating in the abolition of private property and the instigation of a proletarian revolution.[86]

Within the body of the *Manifesto* was much that Engels had already outlined, beginning with the immoral nature of bourgeois society – 'It has pitilessly torn asunder the motley feudal ties that bound man to his "natural superiors", and has left remaining no other nexus between man and man than naked self-interest, than callous "cash-payment"' – to the class fig-leaf of bourgeois government – 'The executive of the modern State is but a committee for managing the common affairs of the whole bourgeoisie' – to the deadly irony of the bourgeois producing, above all, 'its own grave-diggers'. Whilst the core demand of the communists could be 'summed up in the single sentence: Abolition of private property'. However, Marx did drop some of Engels's hobby-horses, including plans for agrico-industrial communes and the dissolution of marriage (an open goal for communist critics). In their place, he scaled the kind of rhetorical heights which Engels could never master. Echoing his celebration of the potential abundance promised by the Industrial Revolution, Marx's genius was on full show as he recounted the stunning achievements which the bourgeoisie had wrought as they unleashed capitalism and accelerated history.

It [the bourgeoisie] has been the first to show what man's activity can bring about. It has accomplished wonders far surpassing Egyptian pyramids, Roman aqueducts, and Gothic cathedrals; it has conducted expeditions that put in the shade all former Exoduses of nations and crusades.

The bourgeoisie cannot exist without constantly revolutionizing the instruments of production, and thereby the relations of production, and with them the whole relations of society . . . All fixed, fast-frozen relations, with their train of ancient and venerable prejudices and opinions, are swept away, all new-formed ones become antiquated before they can ossify. All that is solid melts into air, all that is holy is profaned, and man is at last compelled to face with sober senses, his real conditions of life, and his relations with his kind.[87]

Despite such giddy predictions, on its publication the *Manifesto* made no impact at all. It came off the London presses of the German Workers' Educational Society in February 1848 to a 'conspiracy of silence'. Some few hundred members of the Communist League read it and an English edition (translated by Helen Macfarlane) was serialized in Harney's *Red Republican* in 1850, but it was neither widely on sale nor obviously influential at the time. Not least, because history was already overtaking it. Marx's bourgeoisie, who had already achieved so much, were about to add another string to their bow: the extinguishing of the monarchy of King Louis-Philippe of France. On the morning of 24 February 1848 Alexis de Tocqueville walked out of his Parisian townhouse, turned his face to the chill wind and declared he could 'scent revolution in the air'. By the afternoon, with the Boulevard des Capucines caked in blood and trees along the Champs-Élysées being felled for barricades, the July monarchy of 1830 had melted into air. 'Our age, the age of democracy, is breaking. The flames of the Tuileries and the Palais Royal are the dawn of the proletariat,' Engels exclaimed.[88] The Gallic cock was crowing; Paris was fulfilling its destiny: revolution had arrived.

5

The Infinitely Rich '48 Harvest

'At half-past twelve at night, the train arrived, with the glorious news of Thursday's revolution, and the whole mass of people shouted, in one sudden outburst of enthusiasm, Vive la République!'[1] As the French monarchy crumbled, Marx and Engels were in the wrong place at the wrong time, milling around a Brussels train station snatching at the latest titbits of intelligence. It was to be a familiar pattern over the next eighteen months as the two aspirant insurgents chased the tail of the great 1848 revolutions across the continent – sometimes catching it, occasionally pulling it, but more often being led by it. It was a moment laden with promise and ridden with frustration.

From Marx and Engels's perspective, the startling events of 1848 looked to be a textbook bourgeois-democratic revolution. Europe's archaic political and legal systems were out of sync with the ever quickening capitalist modes of production and would be forced to adjust themselves to the new economic realities. This disjuncture between industrializing structure and feudal superstructure meant that a revolution led by the rising bourgeoisie was the next step in the epic trek towards communism. The bourgeois revolution would, in turn, be succeeded by proletarian rule after the middle classes had done the dirty work of disposing of the old world.

After all the talk of the last decade – 'formulae, nothing but formulae' – what 1848 offered was the tantalizing prospect of praxis and the chance to give history a helping hand. Leaving precious little to the inevitability of progress, Marx and Engels sought to accelerate the coming revolution through an exhaustive programme of political organization, newspaper propaganda, pamphleteering and, eventually, military insurrection. As the *Communist Manifesto* came off the presses, Marx and Engels criss-crossed Europe – from Brussels to Berne, Paris to Cologne – dodging arrest warrants and Prussian spies to urge the evisceration of Europe's crumbling, feudal *anciens régimes*.

Engels himself would leave the battlefield particularly enriched: for, at last, the self-styled Montagnard, the student fencer and barrack-room boxer enjoyed some front-line military experience. A boy's own adventure fulfilled, he raised the red flag over his home town of Barmen and launched raiding parties against Prussian infantry troops – before fleeing, under fire, through the Black Forest. It was a blooding on the barricades, a life-and-death struggle for revolution against counter-revolution, which, over the coming decades, he would rarely allow friends or enemies to forget.

Despite such personal heroics, the cumbersome reality was that the 1848–9 revolutions – in Denmark, Sicily, Sardinia, Piedmont, France, Prussia, Saxony, Hungary and Austria – were far from Marx and Engels's idealized class uprising. Instead, they rose and fell from a multiplicity of motives ranging from economic insecurity to national identity to republican ideology to popular aspirations for liberty. These uprisings, *frondes*, rebellions or revolutions – call them what you will – were also subject to rapid reverses in fortune depending upon the level of worker support, radical leadership and strength of the reactionary fight back. Such shifting, ultimately unfulfilled fortunes led A. J. P. Taylor to describe 1848 as the turning point when Europe 'failed to turn'. And for Marx and Engels, this much vaunted 'age of democracy' represented a signal moment both of personal disappointment and ideological re-evaluation.

The epic storm which broke over Europe in the spring of 1848 began, with a cloud no bigger than a man's hand, in the city of Palermo, where simmering noble discontent with the Bourbon king, Ferdinand II, and his aloof, Naples-based regime led to rioting in January of that year. Dissatisfied with decades of distant and aggressive Neapolitan rule, the leading Sicilian families played on widespread economic discontent to urge the restoration of their autonomous, pre-1816 parliament. Well-organized street demonstrations quickly spilled over into attacks on the police before the barricades went up, the king's troops deserted their barracks for the mainland and the

Bourbon dynasty was deposed. Within weeks a provisional government was formed and a new parliament elected.

Sicily was the first, but stresses were appearing in royal courts across
Europe as social pressures piled up and falling revenues necessitated
the calling of parliaments to levy new taxes which, in turn, demanded
constitutional reform. This was the era of 'pre-revolution' (*Vormärz*)
in which ill-defined expectations for significant power shifts abounded
in newspapers and Diets across the continent's capitals. Fermenting
much of this instability was the preceding decade of poor harvests,
high grain prices, economic depression and the spectre of famine.
Extensive crop failure in 1845 had undercut numerous rural economies, whilst an advancing credit crisis saw a collapse of confidence in
urban markets, illiquidity in the banks and the inability of businesses
to trade. Food prices rose, disposable incomes fell and unemployment
mounted. All of which fostered a popular sense of dissatisfaction
at the existing systems of arbitrary and monstrously unresponsive
monarchy which had ruled Europe since the 1815 Vienna Conference.
But, as Marx first predicted, it would take the crowing of the Gallic cock
to transform such sullen resentment into a European conflagration.

France's February revolution of 1848 – the lightning abdication
and then ignominious flight of King Louis-Philippe to England –
placed the Parisian workers back in the forefront of European communism. In the wake of the Palermo uprising and political discontent
brought on by the economic hardship, French radicals started to
organize outdoor banquets demanding universal manhood suffrage
and economic reform. Against a backdrop of renewed republican
nostalgia for the great events of 1789, revolutionary anthems were
belted out by Parisian theatre crowds and chanted menacingly outside
high-society balls. King Louis-Philippe's heavily reviled prime minister, the liberal historian François Guizot, reacted to the crisis by
banning the banquets and calling out the National Guard. It did no
good: Guizot, on 23 February 1848, was in turn offered up as a
political sacrifice to the mob. Events soon succumbed to Parisian street
tradition and, after the accidental shooting of republican protesters
by nervous soldiers, the capital embarked on its familiar choreography
of revolution.

Marx and Engels, stuck in Belgium, were desperate that Brussels should not miss out on this revolutionary impetus sweeping the continent – or, as they put it in a letter to Julian Harney, 'to obtain through the ways proper to Belgian political institutions the advantages which the French people have won'. To Marx's mind such 'peaceful but vigorous agitation' meant meetings outside the town hall, petitions to the town council and, more covertly, channelling arms to Belgian workers with money collected from his late father's estate.[2] However, the wily King Leopold I had no desire to follow Louis-Philippe's flight across the Channel, and the Belgian police quickly clamped down on their troublesome German guests. On 3 March 1848 Marx was ordered to quit the kingdom within twenty-four hours and, not long after, Engels followed.

As befitted the capital of the nineteenth century, Paris was the trigger, and across Europe popular grievances were now transformed into political revolts as the language of liberty and democracy, nationalism and republicanism sought to dismantle the post-1815 monarchical settlement. On the back of bread riots and rural rebellions, radicals saw a glorious opportunity to drive home constitutional reform and national self-determination. In Vienna, at the beginning of March 1848, the Austrian Diet was hijacked by student activists and workers leading to the assembling of barricades, then a bloody counter-attack by Habsburg troops before the eventual flight of that embodiment of *ancien régime* arrogance, Chancellor Metternich. As the Habsburg monarchy tottered, the northern states of Italy rose up with the urban poor of Lombardy, Piedmont, Venice and Milan leading the rebellion. Milan was to suffer a particularly fierce fight back by the Austrians, under Marshal Radetzky, during the celebrated 'Five Days' when 1,500 barricades went up overnight and the city's narrow streets became the setting for savage urban warfare. But it was to Paris, the laboratory of revolution and now host to the Second Republic, that Marx and Engels headed.

The city that had once harassed and deported them now embraced Marx, Engels and the executive committee of the Communist League with official ardour. A provisional government was in place staffed by a cadre of moderate republicans – such as the socialist philosopher Louis Blanc and the radical journalist Ferdinand Floçon (to whose paper, *La Réforme*, Engels had formerly contributed) – proud to welcome the communist revolutionaries. Engels, more used to being harried by police informers through the back-streets of Paris, revelled in the change of circumstance. 'Recently I lunched at the Tuileries, in the Prince de Joinville's suite, with old Imbert who was a refugee in Brussels and is now Governor of the Tuileries,' he boasted to his brother-in-law Emil Blank.[3] True to form, the remainder of the letter was then filled with a denunciation of the prevarications, stupidity and weaknesses of the newly installed administration.

For all its glamour and official hospitality Paris was only a holding post. As he explained in a letter to Marx, Engels's heart yearned for Germany. 'If only Frederick William IV digs his heels in! Then all will be won and in a few months' time we'll have the German revolution. If he only sticks to his feudal forms! But the devil only knows what this capricious and crazy individual will do.'[4] Engels was not alone in hoping to transplant the revolution back to the homeland: Paris's vast German émigré community was equally keen to cross the Rhine and inaugurate their longed-for democratic republic. To that end, a German Legion of artisan volunteers had emerged from the Parisian *faubourgs* ready to march on Prussia and launch a series of military attacks. Understandably, the provisional French government was more than happy to see the back of these *Straubinger* troublemakers and offered them a 50 centimes a day subsidy to get to the frontier. To Marx and Engels, this ill-conceived, terrorist strategy was doomed to fail (as it duly did), and in response they founded an alternative German Workers' Club of ideologically attuned proto-revolutionaries and set out their more considered approach in *The Demands of the Communist Party in Germany*. Curiously, given the urgency of the *Communist Manifesto*'s tone, it laid down no demands for immediate revolution or an all-out assault on private property. Instead, it sought to further the ambitions of a bourgeois revolution – a complex process that could not be ushered in overnight by a brigade of cack-handed émigrés. The priority was to dispossess Germany's Junker classes of their political and military power and then work towards a bourgeois republic based on manhood suffrage, rule of law and parliamentary authority. At this stage, the Communist League's ambition was to unite Germany's bourgeois, petit-bourgeois, working classes and even peasantry in a cross-class coalition for democracy. It was much more a question of propaganda and organization than of violent political action and, to prepare the ground, the Workers' Club surreptitiously sent back to the Rhineland some 300 communist activists.

There they found the soil well prepared. Part of the phenomenon of 1848 was the speed with which popular politics responded to events across Europe as the steam train and the telegraph ensured the rapid movement not just of troops and armaments, but also of information and ideas. 'Telegraphic despatches' and a fast-expanding newspaper industry offered a rolling news service of revolution – and the torching of the Paris Tuileries in February 1848 was all the encouragement the angry, radicalized German masses needed. Since the mid-1840s, a series of crop failures combined with a downturn in the business cycle had led to substantial increases in the price of foodstuffs alongside a falling standard of living. Escalating peasant unrest and attacks on government officials, bread riots in cities and growing unemployment produced a treacherous political terrain for the aristocratic administrations of princely Germany. In Bavaria, news of the February revolution led to the swift replacement of King Ludwig I – who had ignored widespread peasant distress for the bawdy delights of his mistress Lola Montez (née Betsy Watson) – with his son Maximilian II. In Saxony, King Frederick Augustus II gave in to liberal demands for a reform-minded 'March ministry' with an expansion of the suffrage and calling of a national assembly. Across the German states, 'public meeting democracy' flourished as petitions were drawn up, monster rallies held, and vast crowds of journeymen, peasants, workers and students picketed town halls and palaces. According to James J. Sheehan, 'With the possible exception of the months immediately prior to World War I, there is no other period in German history so full of spontaneous social action and dramatic political possibilities.'[5]

Revolution officially arrived in Prussia in mid-March 1848. Berlin had suffered particularly badly from the economic downturn with the collapse in manufacturing leading to dramatic and dangerous levels of unemployment. In turn, the usual recourse of petitions, rallies and meetings had steadily metamorphosed into a threatening array of encampments and anti-military skirmishing across the capital. In response, King Frederick William IV didn't dig his heels in as expected but wisely looked to steer a course through the rebellion by offering

(as in Saxony) a similarly liberal 'March ministry' package of constitutional reforms and easing of censorship. When the concessions were
announced, the mood in Berlin instantly lightened with cheering
crowds thronging into Palace Square to catch sight of their benign
sovereign. While Frederick William was soaking up the applause, his
less enlightened military commanders were planning to clear the
square with a squadron of dragoons. As the troops closed in, the guns
of Grenadier Kühn and Warrant Officer Hettgen both discharged. No
one was hurt but the capital's febrile crowds – rightly suspicious of
Berlin's officer class – thought the army had turned on them and they
responded with barricades and makeshift missiles. The result was
one of Europe's bloodiest March revolutions, with over 300 dead
protesters (mostly artisans and labourers employed on public works
projects) and nearly 100 military casualties. In the aftermath of the
massacre, Frederick William IV was forced to return to Berlin to
inspect the dead. As he and his wife, Queen Elisabeth, stood 'white
with fear' in front of the crowds, she is said to have whispered, 'All
that is missing is the guillotine.'[6] To avoid just such a Terror, the king
ceded further ground by withdrawing troops from the city and issuing
a humiliating address, 'An mein Volk und an die deutsche Nation',
promising greater liberalization of the Prussian state and declaring his
support for the calling of an all-German National Assembly as a step
towards unification and liberal democracy.

With the monarchy in retreat, the time was now ripe for bourgeois
revolution. Marx and Engels chose the Rhineland city of Cologne for
their reentry into German politics rather than the bloodied streets of
Berlin – a city they did not remember fondly for 'its cringing petty
bourgeoisie' and 'mass of bureaucrats, aristocrats and court riff-raff'.
Moreover, from his days in the newspaper industry, Marx still had
useful connections in Cologne, and its extensive industrialization,
expanding proletariat and wealthy manufacturing elite made the city
'in every respect the most advanced part of Germany at that time'.[7]
The urban, industrial Rhineland was destined to be in the forefront
of the impending revolution – and its relaxed censorship regime made
it the perfect base for Marx's scheme to revive the Rheinische Zeitung.

Yet the location was not without its difficulties. Chief amongst
them was Andreas Gottschalk, a Jewish butcher's son and gifted slum

doctor, who had bravely led the March revolution in Cologne by invading the town hall and demanding voting reforms, abolition of the standing army and freedom of the press. For his troubles, he was arrested, jailed and then released in the liberal aftermath of the Berlin riots. By the time Marx and Engels arrived, Gottschalk stood at the front of an 8,000-strong, grass-roots Workers' Association and was able to dictate much of the city's politics. Naturally, such proletarian authenticity infuriated Marx, who responded by splitting the city's working-class movement with a Democratic Society founded in direct opposition to Gottschalk's Workers' Association. In fairness, there was more to the Gottschalk spat than the habitual internecine strife of communist politics. Gottschalk was a follower of Moses Hess, Karl Grün and the 'true socialist' school of thought which advocated a peaceful reordering of the capitalist system towards an equitable mode of exchange. Pragmatically ignoring much of the philosophical abso-lutism of Marx and Engels's communism, Gottschalk's socialism avoided the dynamic of class struggle and historical progression towards proletarian revolution. Instead, the Workers' Association subscribed to a mixture of co-operation and mutualism based on a harmonious ideal of humanity beyond party politics – a programme which Marx and Engels variously dismissed as petit-bourgeois, Utopian or naive.

Ironically, such a stance actually made the true socialists *more* antagonistic to the ruling bourgeoisie than Marx and Engels since Gottschalk saw no need for an intervening period of bourgeois-democratic rule. He wanted to move straight from the remnants of a feudal polity to socialism. 'You have never been serious about the emancipation of the repressed,' Gottschalk taunted the two Prussian intellectuals. 'The misery of the worker, the hunger of the poor has for you only a scientific, a doctrinaire interest . . . You do not believe in the revolt of the working people, whose rising flood begins already to prepare the destruction of capital, you do not believe in the perma-nence of the revolution, you do not even believe in the capacity for revolution.'[8] The pursuit of constitutional government was, in the words of Karl Grün, 'an egotistical wish of the possessing classes' which true socialists would have nothing to do with. As a result, they boycotted the approaching elections for the all-German National

Assembly – a decision which instantly placed the Cologne Workers' Association on a collision course with Marx and Engels's carefully crafted plans for a bourgeois-democratic revolution.[9]

Marx and Engels had returned to Prussia to deliver a bourgeois democracy as part of the transition towards communism and they were in no mood for any indulgent nonsense about worker co-operatives. Backward, feudal Germany – in contrast, say, to advanced, industrial England with its developed working class – was not yet ready for a proletarian revolution. Their hostility to such futile scheming became quickly evident in the pages of Marx's *Neue Rheinische Zeitung*, which gave ostentatiously little space to covering strikes, radical congresses and any signs of proletarian insurrection. Indeed, so hostile was the newspaper to the city's radical working class that Oscar J. Hammen has even suggested it was produced using casual printing labour with wages far lower than its reactionary rival the *Kölnische Zeitung*.[10] Marx and Engels's political strategy was clear: to turn the *Neue Rheinische Zeitung* into 'the organ of the democratic movement' – but, according to Engels, 'of a democracy which everywhere emphasized in every point the specific proletarian character which it could not yet inscribe for all on its banner'.[11] And such democratic initiatives would, in the long run, help bring the proletariat to greater consciousness and arm them with the political tools to take on the bourgeoisie when the time was ripe. Week in, week out, the paper hurled insults at Prussian bureaucrats and Junker aristocrats and made the case for moderate reforms based around universal suffrage, the dismantling of feudalism and assistance for the unemployed. For all of Marx's fiery journalese, the paper was in fact advocating a very moderate, bourgeois-friendly programme as a first stage to revolution. And it proved a great success, surging to daily sales of almost 5,000 copies.

Given their newly consensual liberal stance, neither Marx nor Engels thought it would be too hard to drum up some investment for the paper from the region's middle classes. So, while Marx settled into the editor's chair in Cologne, Engels was despatched to Barmen to butter up the Wupper valley bourgeoisie. It was another difficult homecoming. 'C. and A. Ermen were quaking visibly when I walked into their office today. I, of course, am not meddling in anything but waiting to see what happens,' he reported mischievously to Emil Blank. Unsurprisingly, the fund-raising was not a success since the Barmen bourgeoisie were well aware of the communist programme. 'The fact is, *au fond*, that even these radical bourgeois here see us as their future main enemies and have no intention of putting into our hands weapons which we would very shortly turn against themselves.' Engels even had the chutzpah to ask his family for *Neue Rheinische Zeitung* funding despite his uncle, August Engels, being a notable reactionary on Barmen Town Council and his brother Hermann commanding a troop of the counter-revolutionary Home Guard. As for his father: 'Nothing whatever is to be got out of my old man. To him even the *Kölner Zeitung* is a hotbed of agitation and sooner than present us with 1,000 talers, he would pepper us with a thousand balls of grape.'[12]

The precious few investors whom Marx and Engels did entice into supporting the paper deserted in droves after Engels used the first issue to deliver a sarcastic diatribe against the newly elected National Assembly sitting in Frankfurt – 'and by the end of the month we no longer had any [investors] at all'.[13] But the paper somehow struggled on, with Engels concerning himself mainly with foreign and military matters and Marx providing the bulk of the German political coverage. For, despite the fears of shareholders, the *Neue Rheinische Zeitung* was in principle extremely supportive of the Frankfurt assembly. They just wanted its representatives to go further and faster in transforming Germany into a unitary, bourgeois state as a preliminary step towards revolution. The problem was the assembly's 'parliamentary cretinism' with its endless introspective debates and dizzying array of verbose lawyers, officials and academics. After one futile session, Engels dismissed it as 'nothing but a stage where old and worn-out political characters exhibited their involuntary ludicrousness and their impotence of thought as well as action'.[14] Such waffling was not without cost: the precious moment of revolution had to be grabbed if Germany's scatterboard of feudal, princely statelets was to be moulded into a single bourgeois republic. And, as the Frankfurt delegates speechified about procedures and protocol, the forces of reaction were regrouping. In Paris, they had already struck.

*

The French provisional government's political honeymoon did not last long. The April 1848 elections to France's Constituent Assembly saw a resurgence of provincial, conservative opinion loyal to the deposed monarchy in response to the republican administration's decision to raise taxes to bolster the deteriorating public finances. At the polls, the socialists and republican candidates lost heavily with barely 100 of the 876 deputies elected. And, once in power, the conservatives swiftly and vengefully acted to dismantle the cornerstone policy of the provisional government: Louis Blanc's national workshops (*ateliers nationaux*). The scheme had been conceived as 'true socialism' in action with unemployed male residents of Paris offered either decently paid, public works-style jobs or generous unemployment benefit. But the result was that tens of thousands of workers, idlers and chancers moved to Paris hoping to profit from this gigantic system of out relief, while furious private employers had to hike wages to compete. Facing ruinous costs and a residuum of well-paid loafers, the newly conservative assembly announced its intention to close the workshop system, force unemployed workers to enlist for the army or return to their jobs in the provinces. Fearing a popular backlash, it also enacted a series of measures against radical political clubs and open-air banquets. On 22 June 1848 the government issued an ultimatum to Paris's 120,000-odd workers to sign up or go home. In the poverty-stricken eastern *faubourgs* of Paris, the workers responded with street riots under the banners of 'Work or Death!' and 'Bread or Death!' By the following morning, the 15-foot-high barricades were back up.[15]

Infuriatingly, as the revolution rekindled itself, Engels was stuck in Cologne. However, such geographical difficulties were not going to interfere with his breathless reports on events in Paris for the *Neue Rheinische Zeitung*, as if the bullets were whizzing past him. For Engels, what was so invigorating about June 1848, in contrast to February, was that 'the insurrection is purely a workers' uprising' as France moved from a bourgeois to a proletarian revolution with delicious alacrity. 'The people are not standing on the barricades as in February singing "*Mourir pour la patrie*." The workers of June 23 are fighting for their existence and the fatherland has lost all meaning for them.' Comparing the uprising to the great slave revolts of ancient

Rome, Engels the Jacobin *manqué* celebrated a 'Paris bathed in blood' and admired how the 50,000-strong insurrection was 'growing into the greatest revolution that has ever taken place, into a revolution of proletariat *versus* the bourgeoisie'.[16] In his *Class Struggles in France*, Marx would later claim the June days amounted to 'civil war in its most terrible form, the war between labour and capital'. Yet whilst modern scholarship is generally sceptical about the level of proletarian involvement in the uprising (positing it more as a traditional artisan-led revolt), what remains in no doubt is the naked class antagonism of the government's response.

The counter-attack was overseen by the bloodthirsty Algiers veteran and newly appointed minister of war, Louis-Eugène Cavaignac, who carefully marshalled his forces before crushing the *faubourg* insurgency. It was a gruesome, butcherous affair as Cavaignac's troops cleared the boulevards with cavalry charges, peppered barricades with grapeshot, and concluded the day with a barrage of shells and incendiary Congreve rockets. Engels recounted it all, from second-hand sources, with a journalism dripping in socialist martyrology and nationalist sentiment. 'A strong detachment of the national guard made a flanking attack upon the barricade of the rue de Clery,' he reported in the *Neue Rheinische Zeitung* of 28 June 1848.

Most of the barricades' defenders withdrew. Only seven men and two women, two beautiful young *grisettes*, remained at their post. One of the seven mounts the barricades carrying a flag. The others open fire. The national guard replies and the standard-bearer falls. Then a *grisette*, a tall, beautiful, neatly-dressed girl with bare arms, grasps the flag, climbs over the barricade and advances upon the national guard. The firing continues and the bourgeois members of the national guard shoot down the girl just as she has come close to their bayonets. The other *grisette* immediately jumps forward, grasps the flag, raises the head of her companion and when she finds her dead, furiously throws stones at the national guard. She, too, falls under the bullets of the bourgeoisie.[17]

Anarchy on the streets of Paris played perfectly into the hands of embattled authorities across Europe. By late summer 1848 Prussia's reactionaries were becoming much bolder in countering the liberal ambitions of the National Assembly, marching troops through radical neighbourhoods and clamping down on republican and socialist clubs. The staff of the *Neue Rheinische Zeitung* faced extra persecution with Marx and Engels brought before the magistrates on an almost weekly basis to be charged either with 'insulting or libelling the Chief Public Prosecutor', 'incitement to revolt' or various other acts of subversion. The Cologne Workers responded to the looming, counter-revolutionary putsch by establishing a Committee of Public Safety and then organizing a mass meeting on Fühlinger Heide near Worringen, a heath to the north of Cologne, in September 1848. Travelling in barges, with red flags fluttering at the prow, some 8,000 workers and socialists journeyed up the Rhine to hear a rousing address from Engels in which he vowed that in the coming struggle with the Prussian authorities the people of Cologne stood 'ready to sacrifice their lives and property on the side of Germany'.[18] Ten days later the city was placed under martial law, with public gatherings banned, the civic militia disbanded and all newspapers suspended.

Luckily for him, Marx had not taken part in the Worringen meetings, but warrants for high treason were issued for the rest of the *Neue Rheinische Zeitung* editorial board. Wilhelm Wolff fled for the Bavarian Palatinate; George Weerth made for Bingen in Hesse-Darmstadt; unlucky Karl Schapper went straight to jail. Cologne's chief public prosecutor, Herr Hecker, was especially keen to get his hands on the 'merchant' Friedrich Engels with – as the highly descriptive arrest warrant put it – his 'ordinary' forehead, 'well proportioned' mouth, 'good' teeth, 'oval' face, 'healthy' complexion and 'slender' figure. Unfortunately, Engels's mother caught sight of this 'wanted' poster. 'Now you have really gone too far,' the mortified Elise upbraided her son after suffering the indignity of reading his warrant in the *Kölnische Zeitung* over her morning coffee. 'So often have I begged you to proceed no further but you have paid more heed to other people, to strangers, and have taken no account of your mother's pleas. God alone knows what I have felt and suffered of late.' The public humiliation was enough to break a mother's heart. 'I can think of nothing else but you and then I often see you as a little boy still, playing near me. How happy I used to be then and what hopes did I not pin upon you.' The only solution was for him to get away from the dangerous influence of his friends and start a new life in commerce across the Atlantic. 'Dear Friedrich, if the words of a poor, sorrowing mother still mean anything to you, then follow your father's advice, go to America and abandon the course you have pursued hitherto. With your knowledge you will surely succeed in finding a position in a good firm . . .'[19] She could hardly have known him less.

Like Wolff and Weerth, Engels was now on the run. After scampering back to Barmen (where, thankfully, his parents were absent) he left for Brussels. But the Belgian authorities were all too familiar with his type and after news of his and fellow communist Ernst Dronke's arrival reached the police, 'the inspector took them to the Town Hall and from there to the prison of the *Petit-Carmes*, whence after an hour or two they were transported in a sealed carriage to the Southern Railway Station'.[20] On 5 October 1848 the two freedom fighters were put on a train to Paris after the authorities used their powers to disperse 'vagabonds' – a favoured tactic for dealing with communists. As they travelled through the night, Europe was alight: a titanic struggle between the forces of revolution and counter-revolution was intensifying across the continent's capitals. In France, the dictatorial Louis Napoleon was beginning his march to power; in Vienna, imperial troops were moving in the heavy artillery to shell the revolutionaries out; in Prague, the Czech rising had been crushed by Habsburg forces, who were soon to turn their attentions to re-invading northern Italy; in Berlin, the Prussian army was on the verge of retaking the city; and in Cologne, Marx's *Neue Rheinische Zeitung* was demanding 'revolutionary terrorism' as the only way to avenge 'the useless butcheries of the June and October days'.[21] And what did Friedrich Engels do to help see in the promised proletariat dawn? Did he return to the struggle? Propagandize in Paris? Support a workers' defence fund? No, he got away from it all on a walking holiday.

His journey began in Paris – and his heart instantly sank at the effects of Cavaignac's fusillade. 'Paris was dead, it was no longer Paris. On the boulevards, no one but the bourgeoisie and police spies; the dance-halls and theatres deserted . . . it was the Paris of 1847 again, but without the spirit, without the life, without the fire and the ferment which the workers brought to everything in those days.'[22] He had to leave. Turning his back on this 'beautiful corpse' of a city, Engels headed into *la France profonde*. The 28-year-old fugitive had had enough, it seemed, of the demands of revolution; the sensuous, almost Fourierist side to his character reasserted itself as he abandoned the tedious demands of insurgent life for an escapade through the sexual and gastronomic riches of rural France. What was more, he chronicled this meandering, cross-country journey from Paris to Geneva in a marvellously self-conscious *feuilleton* reminiscent of his most purple prose for the *Telegraph für Deutschland*. Within this unpublished travelogue there are flashes of political commentary, such as when he encounters some former denizens of the Parisian national workshops – now forcibly returned to the provinces – and is horrified by their fallen ideological state. 'Not a trace of concern with the interests of their class and with current political issues which touch the workers so closely. They appeared not to read any papers any more . . . They were already on the point of turning into rustics, and they had only been there for two months.' It only confirmed Engels's distaste for the contented conservatism of the peasant – 'a barbarian in the midst of civilization'.[23]

However, the body of the journal was less exercised about politics and far more concerned with wine, women and the natural beauty of the Loire valley. 'The avenue is lined with elms, ashes, acacias or chestnuts; the valley floor comprises luxuriant pastures and fertile fields, amongst stubble a second harvest of the richest clover was sprouting . . .' At times his entries read little better than an upmarket wine society tour brochure. 'And what wine! What a diversity, from Bordeaux to Burgundy . . . from Petit Macon or Chablis to Chambertin . . . and from that to sparkling champagne! . . . With a few bottles one can experience every intermediate state from a Musard quadrille to the Marseillaise, from the exultation of the cancan to the tempestuous fever heat of revolution, and then finally with a bottle of champagne one can again drift into the merriest carnival mood in the world!' As revolutionaries were offering up their lives on barricades across Europe, Engels allowed himself a small joke on entering the town of Auxerre 'robed in red'.

It was not just one hall here but the whole town which was decorated in red . . . dark-red streams filled even the gutters and bespattered the paving stones, and a sinister-looking blackish, foaming-red liquid was being carried about the streets in great tubs by sinister bearded men. The red republic with all its horrors appeared to be working continuously . . . But the red republic of Auxerre was most innocent, it was the red republic of the Burgundian wine-harvest . . .

Would his fellow revolutionaries have appreciated the joke? Never mind: 'the 1848 harvest was so infinitely rich . . . better than '46, perhaps even better than '34!' Ever the taxonomist, the women he encounters in France's vineyards and villages are as variable as the wines, with Engels recording his personal preference for 'the cleanly-washed, smoothly-combed, slimly-built Burgundian women from Saint-Bris and Vermenton' in contrast to 'those earthily dirty, tousled, young Molossian buffaloes between the Seine and the Loire'. Engels, however, does not cast himself as overly selective in his favours. 'It will therefore readily be believed that I spent more time lying in the grass with the vintners and their girls, eating grapes, drinking wine, chatting and laughing, than marching up the hill . . .'[24]

By the time the well-satiated Engels crossed the French border into Switzerland in early November the counter-revolution in Germany was well on its way to overturning the advances of March 1848. Frederick William IV had abandoned his liberal reforms for the reactionary strategy of General Brandenburg, who marched the army straight back into Berlin, prorogued the Prussian parliament, banned radical newspapers and declared martial law. Although the crackdown had yet to reach Rhenish west Prussia, Engels was not keen on returning to Cologne to face charges of high treason. Instead, he bunkered down in Berne (assisted by secret funds from his mother, worried about him catching a cold in the Swiss winter), half-heartedly involved himself in the local Workers' Association, and spent most of his time catching up on the revolutionary events he had missed whilst rolling around with those slim-built Burgundian women.

Engels was particularly interested in the ongoing Hungarian uprising led by Lajos Kossuth. This nationalist rebellion against the Austro-Habsburg monarchy had been slowly fermenting since a Romantic resurgence of the Magyar language and culture in the late eighteenth century, which had been accompanied by an increasingly vocal prejudice against the millions of transnational Slavs resident within the Habsburg Empire. Over the decades this developed into a cohesive political and social reform movement with an enlightened Hungarian nobility championing national determination free from foreign, Austrian interference. Inspired by the upheavals in Paris and Vienna, a bloodless revolution in Pest allowed Kossuth and his fellow nobles to take control of the Diet and restore Hungarian sovereignty. However, Hungary had never been the unitary ethnic state of Romantic imagination and, in response to this Magyar upsurge, leaders of the disaffected Serb, Croat and Romanian minorities joined with Habsburg forces to crush the so-called 'Hungarian Spring'. The winter of 1848–9 thus witnessed a series of dramatic back and forth battles between the Austro-Croatian forces and Kossuth's nationalist Magyar army.[25] It was a campaign with multiple attractions for Engels. Despite earlier criticisms of Thomas Carlyle and his 'great man' theory of history, Engels was bewitched by heroic military statesmen – with Wellington, Napoleon and Cromwell as particular heroes. Similarly, he regarded Kossuth as 'a truly revolutionary figure' fighting an obviously righteous cause. Ignoring criticisms that the Hungarian nobles were little more than an aristocratic *fronde*, Engels championed the Magyar cause for its nationalist ambitions, republican spirit and revolutionary violence.

In a rather less pleasant vein to modern eyes, he also supported its visceral anti-Slav sensibility. Exchanging a materialist analysis of class for an unscientific mix of race and national heritage, Engels branded the Slavs as part of that sub-group of humanity he labelled 'historyless' or 'non-historic' peoples prone to interfere with revolutionary progress and so needing to be excised. It was an unbecoming ethnophilosophy which Engels had earlier alluded to in the run-up to the September 1848 Cologne rallies. Part of the uproar then gripping the Rhineland was the result of the Frankfurt National Assembly signing the Armistice of Malmö – a humiliating treaty pressed on Prussia by Russia and England, forcing it to retreat from the Duchy of Schleswig and agree to its annexation by Denmark. For revolutionary nationalists, it was a debilitating setback for moves towards a united Germany, and Engels used the treaty controversy as an excuse to berate the 'brutal, sordid, piratical, Old Norse national traits' which made up Scandinavian culture with its 'perpetual drunkenness and wild berserk frenzy alternating with tearful sentimentality'. Behind this boorish stereotyping was a more unnerving argument in favour of Prussia's ethno-national supremacy over the duchies. 'By the same right under which France took Flanders, Lorraine and Alsace, and will sooner or later take Belgium – by that same right Germany takes over Schleswig; it is the right of civilization as against barbarism, progress as against stability.'[26]

Roman Rosdolsky long ago suggested that Engels owed his theory of 'non-historic' people to Hegel, who, in his *Philosophy of Mind*, argued that only those people who were able – thanks to inherent 'natural and spiritual abilities' – to establish a state could be regarded as part of historical progress. 'A nation with no state formation . . . has, strictly speaking, no history – like the nations which existed before the rise of states and others which still exist in a condition of savagery.'[27] It was an arbitrary, binary division which laid down only vague criteria for what constituted 'national viability' which seemed to centre mainly around a country's capacity to produce a bourgeoisie and then, in its wake, entrepreneurs, capitalists and workers. Yet what the concept did allow Engels to do was dismiss various stateless peoples as counter-revolutionary, non-historic remnants – amongst whom he included the Bretons in France, the Gaels in Scotland, the Basques in Spain and, of course, the Slavs. 'There is no country in Europe which does not have in some corner or other one or several ruined fragments of peoples,' he wrote in an essay on 'The Magyar Struggle'. And it was no surprise that 'these residual fragments of people always become fanatical standard-bearers of counter-revolution and remain so until their complete extirpation or loss of their national character, just as their whole existence in general is itself a protest against a great historical revolution'.[28] Perhaps the best example of this struggle between ancient ethnicities and historic progress was taking place in North America where the United States was wrenching control of California, Texas and other territories from Mexico's hands. Engels was wholly in favour of this colonial land-grab. Is it in any way unfortunate, asked Engels, 'that splendid California has been taken away from the lazy Mexicans, who could not do anything with it?' Were the Mexicans capable of exploiting gold mines, building cities up the Pacific coastline, constructing railways and transforming global trade? Not a bit of it. 'The "independence" of a few Spanish Californians and Texans may suffer because of it, in some places "justice" and other moral principles may be violated; but what does that matter compared to such facts of world-historic significance?'[29]

For Engels, the subjugation of 'non-historic' people was especially suitable for the Slavs, who had committed the ultimate counter-revolutionary crime of allying themselves with the Habsburgs and Tsarist Russia against Kossuth's Magyars. As so many gruesome dictators, echoing his call, would do during the twentieth century, Engels advocated a policy of ethnic cleansing on the altar of progress and history. 'I am enough of an authoritarian to regard the existence of such aborigines in the heart of Europe as an anachronism,' he wrote years later of the Slavs in a letter to Eduard Bernstein, '. . . they and their right of cattle stealing will have to be mercilessly sacrificed to the interest of the European proletariat'.[30] It was an ugly, imperialist ideology which would provide intellectual succour in the succeeding century for the liquidation of any number of 'backward', 'feudal' or 'reactionary' peoples. And there is something deeply chilling about Engels's bloodcurdling call, just weeks after he had returned from his Arcadian walking tour, for 'bloody revenge on the Slav barbarian'. 'The next world war will result in the disappearance from the face of the earth not only of reactionary classes and dynasties, but also of entire reactionary peoples. And that, too, is a step forward.'[31]

But Engels soon had enough of standing on the sidelines of the 1848 revolutions and wanted to return to 'the movement'. 'Now that Gottschalk and Anneke have been acquitted, shan't I be able to come back soon?' he wrote plaintively to Marx in Cologne in December 1848 testing the legal waters. The attractions of a reflective life in Berne – 'lazing about in foreign parts' – had started to pale. 'I am rapidly coming to the conclusion that detention for questioning in Cologne is better than life in free Switzerland.' And despite General Brandenburg's best efforts, the Rhenish revolutionary spirit had not completely succumbed to Prussian revanchism. Indeed, to keep the democratic flame alive a left-wing faction of the Frankfurt National

Assembly had recently formed the Central March Association (*Centralmarzverein*) to defend the liberal settlement of March '48. By the spring of 1849 it had some 950 branches and over half a million members. The struggle was far from over.

Meanwhile, the *Neue Rheinische Zeitung* had found its true voice after Marx took the paper in a dramatically left-wing direction. Now openly blaming the weak-willed liberals for the 'failure' of 1848, Marx looked to develop an independent political line for the working classes that would be distinct from the bourgeois-democratic movement. For Engels, Marx's achievements on the *Neue Rheinische Zeitung* constituted perhaps his finest hour. 'No German newspaper, before or since, has ever had the same power and influence or been able to electrify the proletariat masses as effectively as the *Neue Rheinische Zeitung*. And that it owed above all to Marx.'[32] Engels was delighted with the paper's militant turn and, in one of his first articles after returning to Cologne in January 1849, he demanded to know, 'Why after the revolution in France and in Germany did we show so much generosity, magnanimity, consideration and kindheartedness, if we did not wish the bourgeois again to raise its head and betray us, and the calculating counter-revolution to plant its foot on our neck?'[33]

Inspired by Kossuth, Engels now sought to import the insurgent tactics of Hungary into Germany. His vision, in early 1849, was for Frankfurt and southern Germany to rise in revolt and join the broader Magyar rebellion. It was a strategy which would require a much more sophisticated appreciation of guerrilla insurgency and asymmetrical warfare since the Rhenish revolutionaries could never hope to beat the Prussian army in open battle. The lessons from Hungary were clear. 'Mass uprising, revolutionary war, guerrilla detachments everywhere – that is the only means by which a small nation can overcome a large one, by which a less strong army can be put in a position to resist a stronger and better organized one.'[34] And now was the moment to implement this underdog tactic since, in March 1849, the parliamentary cretins in Frankfurt finally did something historic by voting to adopt a fully fledged Imperial Constitution for Germany. This was a seismic political decision laying the groundwork for a genuine constitutional monarchy and bringing the various states of Germany together under a single currency, tariff structure and unified defence policy. After years of debate, a coherent liberalism had emerged with concrete, progressive policy proposals. But it all rested on the willingness of the Prussian king, Frederick William IV, to accept the German imperial crown and, with it, the parameters of a constitutional monarchy acting in concert with a democratic parliament. Needless to say, the great feudal sovereign and faithful believer in the divine right of kings was having none of it. 'This so-called crown is not really a crown at all, but actually a dog-collar, with which they want to leash me to the revolution of 1848,' was his haughty response to the parliament's offer.[35]

For radical groups in the Central March Association and elsewhere, the Imperial Constitution was the symbol of everything they had struggled for. And they were not going to let it fall away lightly. As Rhenish Westphalia rose in support of the constitution, Frederick William unleashed the Prussian *Landwehr* on the workers. By April 1849 revolution was once again talked of in western and southern Germany as communists and socialists assumed leadership posts once held by middle-class democrats and bourgeois constitutionalists. As political solutions crumbled, violent unrest resurfaced. 'Everywhere the people are organizing themselves into companies, electing leaders, providing themselves with arms and ammunition,' Engels reported excitedly.[36] On 3 May, Dresden erupted after the king of Saxony, Frederick Augustus II, closed the state parliament and followed Frederick William in refusing to recognize the Imperial Constitution. Workers, revolutionaries and Polish officers flooded on to the streets to battle both Saxon and Prussian troops. Amongst those manning the barricades was Engels's former Berlin classmate and now active anarchist, Michael Bakunin; the prudish, precious Stephan Born, who had spent the previous months running a Workers' Brotherhood in Berlin; and the newly appointed conductor of the Dresden Opera, Richard Wagner. The Rhineland took its cue from the south as Düsseldorf, Iserlohn, Solingen and even the Wupper valley itself joined the rebellion. After his detailed research into revolutionary warfare and guerrilla insurgency, after his youthful articles denouncing the Prussian state and long evenings spent with Moses Hess outlining the promise of communism to guffawing industrialists, the moment of violent contradiction had arrived. 'The *Neue Rheinische Zeitung*, too, was represented at the Elberfeld barricades,' as Engels, the native child of the Wupper, proudly put it.[37]

In May 1849, with opposition to the Prussian authorities spreading through the Rhineland, workers in Elberfeld gathered in a beer hall overlooking the city to hear rousing speeches from democrats and radicals urging a campaign of resistance. The result was the formation of a revolutionary militia which the local civic guard wisely demurred from disarming. When a troop of soldiers arrived from Düsseldorf to challenge the insubordination, the mayor ordered them back. By 10 May the county commissioner had fled and Elberfeld, that once pious, loyal Zion of the obscurantists, was in a state of armed revolt.[38] 'From the middle of Kipdorf and lower Hofkamp everything was closed off with barricades,' recalled the Elberfeld surgeon Alexander Pagenstecher. 'Here, there were fellows busy repairing and reinforcing the old barricades and setting up new ones; and, with them, groups of armed, adventurous *sans culottes* with all manner of shooting, hacking and stabbing weapons.'[39] To co-ordinate the resistance, the Elberfeld Political Club established a Committee of Public Safety which included (to the disgust of many revolutionaries) members of the existing city council.

Into this delicate situation stepped Engels. Adhering closely to protocol, on his arrival in Elberfeld – 'with two cases of cartridges which had been captured by the Solingen workers at the storming of the arsenal of Gräfrath' – he reported to the committee. His revolutionary reputation having far preceded him, they wanted to know what precisely his motives were. Engels replied falsely that he had been sent from Cologne and innocently suggested he might be able to provide some military assistance against the inevitable Prussian response. But, far more importantly, 'having been born in the Berg Country, he considered it a matter of honour to be there when the first armed uprising of the people of the Berg Country took place'. And the good burghers of Elberfeld had no need to worry about his red, radical politics. 'He said that he desired to concern himself exclusively with military matters and to have nothing to do with the political character of the movement . . .'[40] Unwisely taken in by such sophistry, the committee gave him the task of inspecting the barricades, positioning artillery installations and completing the fortifications. Drawing together a company of sappers, Engels reconfigured various defences, strengthening all possible entry points along the narrow Wupper valley.[41] But this 'dyed in the wool' radical was not going to let the revolutionary promise of the Elberfeld barricades escape his presence.

'After I had climbed over the barricade by the Haspeler Bridge, which was armed with three or four small Nuremberg-calibre salute cannons, I was stopped in front of the nearby house that acted as a barrier,' continued the worried Pagenstecher. 'It had been transformed into a sentry room, and Dr Engels from Barmen was in command.'[42] And he had decorated the site in a suitable manner. 'On the barricade by the mayor's house, a piece of red material torn from one of his curtains had been put up, and young men had made themselves sashes and bands from this same material; these signs were taken as proof that all of this was for the Republic – the red one, naturally.'[43] At the Committee for Public Safety the penny had finally dropped: this was the red-radical takeover, instigated by the town's most infamous communist turncoat, they had all feared. 'When the flags of the red republic finally fluttered on the barricades in our bleak streets, it fell like scales from the eyes of our well-meaning Elberfelders,' was how one local paper reviewed the events of May 1849.[44]

A loving array of myths and legends surrounds Engels's time on the Elberfeld barricades. The finest story is that of Friedrich Engels senior encountering his rebel son directing the gunners on the Haspeler Bridge. The fraught meeting, as witnessed by local resident and Barmen manufacturer Friedrich von Eynern, between the 'barricade-mounting son' and 'old, dignified factory owner' (on his way to church no less) feels almost too pathos-ridden for reality.[45] And, indeed, evidence for this encounter seems fairly thin. Similarly, Alexander Pagenstecher has suggested Engels was involved in the capture and ransom of the Elberfeld minister Daniel von der Heydt, along with his mother and brother. Again, apart from the aggrieved Pagenstecher, the supporting sources are sketchy. What is certainly true is that Engels's time in Elberfeld was both shortlived and widely resented. To one member of the Committee for Public Safety, barrister Höchster, Engels was 'a dreamer, one of those who ruin everything'.[46] And his replacement of the German tricolour with the red flag had not gone down well at all – according to his fellow insurrectionist, the drawing instructor Joseph Körner, 'people were so upset early the next morning that a counter insurrection and Engels's maltreatment could only be avoided through the speedy clearing away of the red scraps and Engels's "removal from the city"'.[47] It fell to Höchster to deliver the ultimatum: he approached Engels and stated that (in Engels's own version) 'although there was absolutely nothing to be said against his behaviour, nevertheless his presence evoked the utmost alarm of the Elberfeld bourgeoisie; they were afraid that at any moment he would proclaim a red republic and that by and large they wished him to leave'.[48]

Engels was furious at his summary removal from his birthplace and setting of such potential heroics and demanded 'that the above-mentioned request should be presented to him in black and white, over the signatures of all members of the Committee for Public Safety'. If this was an attempt to call the bourgeoisie's bluff, it failed miserably as they swiftly returned with a signed statement which, to deepen the public humiliation, they posted around Elberfeld:

WHILE FULLY APPRECIATING *THE ACTIVITY HITHERTO SHOWN IN THIS TOWN BY CITIZEN FRIEDRICH ENGELS OF BARMEN, RECENTLY RESIDENT IN COLOGNE, IT IS REQUESTED THAT HE SHOULD FROM TODAY LEAVE THE PRECINCTS OF THE LOCAL MUNICIPALITY* SINCE HIS PRESENCE COULD GIVE RISE TO MISUNDERSTANDINGS AS TO THE CHARACTER OF THE MOVEMENT.

It could not have been any clearer. According to Engels, 'The armed workers and volunteer corps were highly indignant at the decision of the Committee for Public Safety. They demanded that Engels should remain and said they would "protect him with their lives"'.[49] Selfless to the end, Engels accepted the verdict and decided to leave Elberfeld with a last shred of dignity and allow the town to return to its habitual moderation. When, one week later, Prussian forces arrived, ready to storm the Wupper valley, they found the barricades dismantled, red flags and all. But as Engels departed Elberfeld he received a stinging rebuke from his family. In a letter which gave full vent to the repeated humiliations of public arrest warrants, police searches of the family home and endless neighbourhood gossip about the wayward son, Engels's brother-in-law Adolf von Griesheim ripped into him as a hapless 'hounded dog'. 'If you, besides, had a family and worried about them, like me, you would change your restless life and, in the friendly circle of your loved ones, you would gain more from this short life than you ever can receive from a heartless gang of cowardly, ungrateful, troublemakers . . . It is as if you still have this thankless idea of sacrificing yourself for irredeemable Mankind, to become a social Christ and to devote all your egoism to achieving this goal.'[50]

With another arrest warrant out for Engels ('special characteristics: speaks very rapidly and is short-sighted') and the *Neue Rheinische Zeitung* firmly shut down after a melodramatic final edition printed in red ink, the communist influence over the German uprising looked finished. But as long as the chance for revolution remained, Marx and Engels refused to give up. They trudged from Cologne to Frankfurt and thence to Baden, Speyer, Kaiserslautern and Bingen in support of the spluttering armed struggle for the Imperial Constitution. It was in the south-west corner of Germany, in Baden-Palatinate, that Engels thought the last remaining chance of insurgency appeared most favourable. 'The entire people were united in their hatred for a government that broke its word, engaged in duplicity and cruelly persecuted its political adversaries. The reactionary classes, the nobility, the bureaucracy and the big bourgeoisie were few in numbers.'[51]

All too typically, the revolution was already being betrayed by a timid petit-bourgeois leadership – in this case a lawyer called Lorenz Peter Brentano – which could not shed its fear of committing high treason. Moreover, there appeared a distinct lack of revolutionary rigour within the higher echelons of the provisional government. 'People yawned and chatted, told anecdotes and made bad jokes and strategic plans and went from one office to another trying as well as they could to kill time.' As ever, Marx and Engels let their views about the competency of those in charge be known – at one point, Engels was so precise in his analysis of the leadership's weaknesses and so explicit in describing the coming Prussian onslaught that he was arrested as a spy on the grounds that only an enemy of the regime could be quite so damaging to morale. He spent a day in jail, before the intervention of various communist activists secured his release. Seeing no real hope for this revolution, at this point Marx abandoned the struggle and headed back to Paris. Engels was ready to do the same when the former Prussian officer and now rebel commander August von Willich and his 800-strong volunteer company of worker and student soldiers marched into Kaiserslautern. 'Since I had no intention of letting slip the opportunity of gaining some military education . . . I too buckled on a broadsword and went off to join Willich.'[52] For Engels, who was quickly commissioned as his aide-de-camp, Willich was one of the few figures of any worth within the Baden-Palatinate revolutionary army. In battle, Engels thought him 'brave, cool-headed and adroit, and able to appreciate a situation quickly and accurately'. Outside of the war zone, he was a terrible bore – 'plus ou moins tedious ideologist and a true socialist'.[53] Nevertheless, after the enforced exit from Elberfeld, here was a chance for real combat as the Prussian forces started to encircle this last redoubt of the 1848 revolution.

'Every man thinks meanly of himself for not having been a soldier, or not having been at sea,' was the judgement of Samuel Johnson. And Engels certainly thought a great deal more of himself having been in combat. In a long letter to Jenny Marx in the aftermath of the Baden campaign, Engels was full of it. 'The whistle of bullets is really quite a trivial matter,' he reported back insouciantly, 'and though, throughout the campaign, a great deal of cowardice was in evidence, I did not see as many as a dozen men whose conduct was cowardly in battle.'[54] Engels was involved in four engagements, 'two of them fairly important', but most of his time was spent in a futile cycle of skirmishing and retreat. 'We had scarcely climbed the bushy slope when we came to an open field from the opposite wooded edge of which Prussian riflemen were loosing off their elongated bullets at us. I fetched up a few more of the volunteers, who were scrambling around the slope helpless and rather nervous, posted them with as much cover as possible and took a closer look at the terrain . . .', reads a fairly typical account of Engels's war record from his Campaign for the German Imperial Constitution.[55] And whilst he had a great deal of admiration for Willich, some of the officers and the worker corps within the company, he had the autodidact's total disdain for the student contingent. 'During the course of the entire campaign the students generally showed themselves to be malcontent and timid young gentlemen; they always wanted to be let into all the plans of operation, complained about sore feet and grumbled when the campaign did not afford all the comforts of a holiday trip.'[56]

It was at the Rastatt Fortress, along the River Murg, south of Karlsruhe and on the very western edges of Germany, that Engels took part in the largest battle of the campaign – and discovered, as he put it to Jenny, 'that the much vaunted bravery under fire is quite the most ordinary quality one can possess'.[57] Facing a Prussian contingent some four times the size of the 13,000-strong revolutionary force, Engels fought with mettle and distinction. He led the Besançon workers' company of Willich's troops into battle with the 1st Prussian Army Corps and took part in a series of skirmishes along the Murg. Indeed, throughout the campaign Engels was widely praised by fellow soldiers for his easy willingness to muck in with the troops and 'energy and courage' in battle.[58] But the cause was doomed as the Prussians systematically outgunned and outmanoeuvred Willich's men and Rastatt proved a bloody defeat, with the Communist League founder member Joseph Moll amongst the fallen.

In the wake of the rout the last, straggling remnants of the revolutionary army sped south through the Black Forest towards the Swiss border. While Willich and Engels argued for making a last stand, they could no longer command the support of the wounded and exhausted troops. 'We marched through Lottstetten to the frontier, bivouacked that night still on German soil, discharged our rifles on the morning of the 12th [July] and then set foot on Swiss territory, the last of the army of Baden and the Palatinate to do so . . .'[59] From its hapless inception through to its divided leadership and woeful logistics, the Baden-Palatinate campaign was a doomed enterprise. But, for Engels, it served a vital purpose: he had tasted blood and could now look in the eye any fellow revolutionary. '*Enfin*, I came through the whole thing unscathed, and *au bout du compte*, it was as well that one member of the *Neue Rheinische Zeitung* was present, since the entire pack of democratic blackguards were in Baden and the Palatinate, and are now bragging about the heroic deeds they never performed.'[60] Marx, too, realized the campaign's significance in terms of their public image. 'Had you not taken part in the actual fighting, we couldn't have put forward our views about that frolic,' he wrote from Paris. And Marx now urged Engels to write up this authentic episode of revolutionary endeavour as swiftly as possible as he was positive 'the thing will sell and bring you money'.[61]

Back in safe but dull Switzerland, along with thousands of other political refugees seeking asylum, Engels followed Marx's advice and churned out *The Campaign for the German Imperial Constitution* both to cement his reputation for heroic conduct under fire and to establish the contours of the post-1848 blame game. For the unredeemed villains of the piece – indeed, the object of opprobrium for allowing the entire '48 harvest to go to waste – were the petit-bourgeois who led the workers down the garden path of insurgency and then abandoned them the moment the counter-revolution surfaced. In a blistering opening chapter, Engels branded them 'faint-hearted, cautious and calculating as soon as the slightest danger approaches; aghast, alarmed and wavering as soon as the movement it provoked is seized upon and taken up seriously by other classes'. There was no failure on the part of the radical democrats, the communists or the proletariat. Instead, it was the 'stab in the back' from the bourgeoisie which betrayed the promise of revolution. In the coming months, this contempt for bourgeois prevarication – 'as soon as there is the slightest chance of a return to anarchy, i.e. of the real, decisive struggle, it retreats from the scene in fear and trembling' – would harden into a political ideology.[62] After Europe's failure to turn, Marx and Engels came to the realization that the two-step model of bourgeois-democratic and then proletarian revolution would have to be rethought in its entirety. And they now had the time to do so.

Marx had been in Paris only a month when the forces of reaction caught up with him. Threatened by the Bonapartist authorities with banishment to 'the Pontine marshes of Brittany', he chose exile in London. 'So you must leave for London at once,' he wrote to Engels now festering in Lausanne. 'In any case your safety demands it. The Prussians would shoot you twice over: 1) because of Baden; 2) because of Elberfeld. And why stay in a Switzerland where you can do nothing

... In London we shall get down to business.'[63] But it was not so easy for a wanted man in an era of counter-revolution to make his way across a still cindering Europe. France and Germany were out of bounds, so he headed for Genoa via Piedmont to catch a ride with Captain Stevens aboard the *Cornish Diamond* sailing for London. Engels, the bloodied veteran of the Baden campaign, hurried to Marx's side to join a diaspora of émigrés, exiles, revolutionaries and communists huddled together in the capital of the one country that so spectacularly failed to rise to the '48 revolution. Far removed from the turmoil of the continent, conservative mid-Victorian England was to be his home for the next forty years.

6

Manchester in Shades of Grey

On Saturday I went out fox-hunting – seven hours in the saddle. That sort of thing always keeps me in a state of devilish excitement for several days; it's the greatest physical pleasure I know. I saw only two out of the whole field who were better horsemen than myself, but then they were also better mounted. This will really put my health to rights. At least twenty of the chaps fell off or came down, two horses were done for, one fox killed (I was in AT THE DEATH) . . .[1]

Barely a decade after raising the red flag over the Barmen barricades, Friedrich Engels seemed to have undergone a startling character change. The revolutionary of '49 was now a stalwart of Manchester society: riding out with the Cheshire Hunt; member of the prestigious Albert Club and Brazenose Club; resident of a salubrious city suburb; and a respectable, hard-working employee of Ermen & Engels, with good prospects of making partnership. 'I am very glad you have left and are well on the way to becoming a great COTTON LORD,' Jenny Marx wrote admiringly to her husband's friend.[2] Finally, it seemed Elise and Friedrich Engels might finally rest easy as their 'black sheep' son settled into his rightful place within the family firm. Had he, like so many young radicals, turned from firebrand to fogey? Or, like the youthful 'Oswald', was it just another front?

In truth, the middle decades of Engels's life were a wretched time. He was exiled back to Manchester, humiliatingly forced to return to Ermen & Engels, and the twenty years he then spent in the cotton trade was an era of nervous, sapping sacrifice. Karl Marx called them Engels's time of 'Sturm und Drang' – and he was not a little to blame. Heroically, between 1850 and 1870 Engels sacrificed much of what gave him meaning in life – intellectual enquiry, political activism, his close friendship with Marx – to serve the cause of scientific socialism. 'The two of us form a partnership together,' Marx soothingly explained, 'in which I spend my time on the theoretical and party side of the business,' while Engels's job was to provide the financial support by busying himself at commerce.[3] To support Marx, Marx's growing family and, most importantly of all, the writing of *Das Kapital*, Engels willingly offered up his own financial security, philosophical researches and even his good name. The Manchester years demanded a heavy price of the self-appointed second fiddle.

In retreating north, Engels turned his back on his favoured habitat of émigré radicalism and political machinations for the respectable life of a mid-Victorian bourgeois. And this was where the eye of the storm and stress really lay: in squaring his two diametrically opposed public and private lives as exploitative cotton lord and revolutionary socialist, as frock-coated member of the upper-middle class and ardent disciple of the low life. To retain his office job, keep Marx out of penury and the communist cause afloat Engels was forced to maintain a façade of painful propriety. It nurtured a contradiction between public commitments and personal beliefs which proved impossible to maintain as he spiralled towards illness, depression and eventual breakdown.

'If any one had conceived the idea of writing from the outside the inner history of the political émigrés and exiles from the year 1848 in London, what a melancholy page he would have added to the records of contemporary man,' the Russian exile Alexander Herzen wrote in his memoirs. 'What sufferings, what privations, what tears ... and what triviality, what narrowness, what poverty of intellectual powers, of resources, of understanding, what obstinacy in wrangling, what pettiness of wounded vanity ...'[4]

When Engels stepped off the *Cornish Diamond* in 1849 and rented some rooms in Chelsea and then Soho, he reentered precisely this scene of exile fratricide, failing newspapers, futile politicking and ever-present Prussian spies. 'We cannot make a single step without being followed by them wherever we go,' Engels publicly protested in a letter written in his hand under Marx's name to the *Spectator* in June 1850. 'We cannot get into an omnibus or enter a coffee-house without being favoured with the company of at least one of these unknown friends ... the majority of them look anything but clean and respectable.'[5] Meanwhile, the days passed with selection battles for the Communist League Central Committee, fights over membership of the London German Workers' Educational Society and a tussle over dispersing charitable funds for impoverished émigrés. Marx and Engels had quickly reverted to type by undermining the existing German Refugee Relief Committee and establishing their own Social Democratic Relief Committee for German Refugees. After fleeing Prussian sharpshooters and enduring the ennui of Switzerland, this rats-in-a-sack politics was a welcome return to the Brussels and Paris good time. 'All in all, things are going quite well here,' Engels wrote to his publisher friend Jakob Schabelitz in Paris. '[Gustav] Struve and [Karl] Heinzen are intriguing with all and sundry against the Workers' Society and ourselves, but without success. They, together with some wailers of moderate persuasion who have been thrown out of our society, form a select club at which Heinzen airs his grievances about the noxious doctrines of the Communists.'[6] Happy days.

This beery, smoke-filled world centred on Great Windmill Street amused itself in a political time-warp. 'After every unsuccessful revolution or counter-revolution, feverish activity develops among the émigrés who escaped abroad,' Engels later wrote.

Party groups of various shades are formed, which accuse each other of having driven the cart into the mud, of treason and of all other possible mortal sins. They also maintain close ties with the homeland, organize, conspire, print leaflets and newspapers, swear that it will start over again within the next 24 hours, that victory is certain and in the wake of this expectation, distribute government posts. Naturally, disappointment follows disappointment ... recriminations accumulate and result in general bickering.[7]

The full enormity of the 1848 failure – the collapse of a bourgeois-democratic revolution in the face of an *ancien régime* fight back – and the hegemony of counter-revolutionary sentiment on the continent had simply failed to sink in. The Great Windmill Street communists still believed the overthrow of monarchism was imminent. 'The revol-

ution is advancing so rapidly, that every one *must* see its approach,'
Engels confidently predicted of the French political scene in March
1850 (as Bonaparte's Second Empire lurked in the wings).[8] Marx and
Engels hoped to use this narrow, pre-revolutionary breathing space
to reaffirm their demands for a more organized, autonomous working-
class movement. The 'stab in the back' thesis they had been
adumbrating since the failure of the continental revolutions – of a
liberal bourgeoisie willing to sacrifice the workers' cause at the first
hint of a settlement with the ruling classes – evolved into a broader
political strategy to outmanoeuvre the petit-bourgeois democrats. In
their 1850 'Address of the Central Authority to the League', Marx
and Engels explained how only a system of workers' associations
could exploit the political gains of the coming bourgeois revolution
without falling into the trap of a liberal alliance. 'In a word, from the
first moment of victory, mistrust must be directed no longer against
the defeated reactionary party, but against the workers' previous
allies,' they enjoined.[9] What this necessitated, in a phrase Leon Trotsky
would later appropriate, was a 'permanent revolution' and a far more
aggressive proletarian commitment to grabbing the levers of power.
To avoid any prospect of bourgeois consolidation, there could be no
moment of calm after the initial democratic revolution.

Yet, at the same time, the revolution could not be rushed if the
socio-economic fundamentals were not in place. And as the reactionary fallout from 1848 continued to gather pace, with ever-decreasing
signs of an economic crisis precipitating political revolution, the
chances for insurrection diminished. Marx and Engels began to fear
that the materialist preconditions would not be ripe for some years to
come; the moment of contradiction had been lost, as the economic
crisis passed. Just as previously in Cologne, this political hesitancy
placed them at odds with the broader membership of the Communist
League led in London by Karl Schapper and Engels's old commander,
August Willich, both of whom advocated immediate military action.
To Marx and Engels, this was tinpot terrorism and a premature threat
to the communist cause. In addition to which, Marx could not abide
Willich's cocky bravado and war-veteran aura (nothing infuriated him
more than authentic, revolutionary credentials). Naturally, he ended
up challenging the decorated class warrior to a duel before transferring

the Central Board of the Communist League back to Germany in a fit of pique.

But it wasn't just Willich and Schapper. Marx and Engels couldn't get on with the German community leaders Gottfried Kinkel and their supposed old friend from Berlin days Arnold Ruge either. Nor did they care for Struve and Heinzen, for the exiled Italian nationalist Giuseppe Mazzini, the French socialist Louis Blanc, their one-time hero Lajos Kossuth, or even their Chartist ally Julian Harney. Obdurate to a T, Engels embraced the prospect of complete political isolation. 'At long last we again have the opportunity – the first time in ages – to show that we need neither popularity, nor the SUPPORT of any party in any country.' Instead, their role as communist ideologues was to chart the march of history and highlight the approaching contradictions of capitalism in order to ready the proletariat for their revolutionary duty. Deep down, this political loneliness seemed to appeal to Engels's instinctive, almost Puritan, ardour for sacrifice and martyrdom. 'How can people like us, who shun official appointments like the plague, fit into a "party"?' he asked Marx.[10]

What was less appealing was the poverty that accompanied the Soho wilderness. Jenny Marx had followed her husband across the Channel in September 1849 with her three small children and a fourth on the way – Heinrich Guido (nicknamed 'Fawksey'), who earned his incendiary soubriquet by being born on 5 November 1849. But with only irregular funds from freelance journalism, niggardly publishing contracts and a doomed attempt to relaunch the *Neue Rheinische Zeitung*, Marx was in no position to support his family. Jenny Marx later described this period as one of 'great hardship, continual acute privations, and real misery'.[11] Guido's infancy of poverty and fatigue – crammed together with undernourished brothers and sisters in a series of grotty flats – cut his life horribly short. 'Since coming into the world, he has never slept a whole night through – at most, two or three hours. Latterly, too, there have been violent convulsions, so that the child has been hovering constantly between death and a miserable life. In his pain he sucked so hard that I got a sore on my breast – an open sore; often blood would spurt into his little, trembling mouth,' Jenny wrote in a desperate, fund-raising letter to their communist friend Joseph Weydemeyer.[12] For a lady of Jenny von Westphalen's lineage, there was also the indignity of an existence spent harried across London by bakers, butchers, milkmen and bailiffs as Marx dodged bills and blagged new lodgings. It was a debilitating, humiliating, sickening time and young Guido suffered the effects. 'Just a line or two to let you know that our little gunpowder-plotter, Fawksey, died at ten o'clock this morning,' Marx wrote to Engels in November 1850. 'You can imagine what it is like here . . . If you happen to feel so inclined, drop a few lines to my wife. She is quite distracted.'[13] Jenny and Karl Marx were to lose two other children, Franziska and Edgar ('Colonel Musch'), to exactly the same noxious cocktail of poverty, damp and disease.

During the time he lodged at Macclesfield Street, down the road from Marx's flat on Dean Street in Soho, Engels's finances were in no better shape as he raised money for the refugee community and pursued various publishing contracts. While he lacked Marx's brood of dependants, he faced a similar absence of income since his usually indulgent parents had finally cut off the financial tap after one arrest warrant too many. 'It might be convenient to send you money to live on,' Elise wrote after another request, '. . . but I find quite extraordinary your demand that I should give financial support to a son who is attempting to spread ideas and principles which I regard as sinful.'[14] Facing diminishing opportunities in Soho and increasingly anxious about Marx's descent into the belittling poverty of émigré life, Engels readied himself for the inevitable: the only way he could feed himself and help Marx and their cause was to bend the knee, reconcile himself with his family and return to commerce. His sister Marie deftly managed the family diplomacy. 'The thought has come to us that you may perhaps wish to enter business seriously for the time being, in order to ensure yourself an income; you might drop it as soon as your party has a reasonable chance of success and resume your work for the party,' she wrote to Engels in an elegantly crafted letter sent with the blessing of her parents.[15] It might not be pleasant, his father added, but it would be useful for the family business. With few other options available, Engels agreed to the deal with the proviso of a short-term, rolling contract to allow him to return to the barricades when the workers' revolution called. 'He [Engels's father] will need me here for three years at least, and I have entered into no long-term obligations, not even for three years, nor was I asked for any, either with regard to my writing, or to my staying here in case of a revolution. This would appear to be far from his mind, so secure do these people now feel!'[16] As well they might: Engels ended up working nineteen years for the family firm.

The failure of the '48 revolutions had been mourned nowhere more keenly than in Manchester. The farrago of Kennington Common – where the Chartist dream of marching on Parliament to press home the Six Points collapsed under public inertia, government repression and rain – signalled a lengthy collapse of English working-class radicalism. The 150,000 demonstrators for democracy had been met by 85,000 special constables, 7,000 troops, 5,000 police, 1,231 Chelsea pensioners and even the Duke of Wellington. It was a drizzly, damp squib of an affair with the Chartists reduced to scurrying across the Thames in cabs to present their petition to Parliament. Whilst Europe's capitals had gone up in flames, the class-conscious English proletariat had spectacularly failed to rise. Across the mills and moors of Lancashire, where the Chartist call for social and political reform had resounded most loudly, the disappointment was evident. But it was all in tune with a changing city.

The repeal of the Corn Laws in 1846 had marked the triumph of 'the Manchester School': England's landowning, aristocratic governance was giving way to the middle-class, free-trading, Nonconformist vision of John Bright and the 'Cottonocracy'. With a Tory Party split and the Chartists in disarray, liberalism had seen off both conservatism and radicalism. Manchester, the city that had once portended a terrifying future of class warfare, industrial unrest and proletarian revolution, settled into its new role as the prosperous embodiment of the mid-Victorian boom. It became the age not of lockouts, strikes and torch-lit rallies, but of baths and wash-houses, libraries and parks, Mechanics' Institutes and Friendly Societies. The revolutionary moment had eased and the 'shock city' of the Industrial Revolution now looked set to be transformed into a middle-class imperium.

As Engels retraced his steps, *The Condition of the Working Class* would have already felt dated. In place of Little Ireland, all around him sprung new signs of mercantile hubris: well-endowed Dissenting chapels; multi-storey warehouses modelled on Renaissance *palazzi*; and, most symbolically of all, the foundations of the Free Trade Hall, callously erected on the site of the 1819 Peterloo massacre, to commemorate the Corn Law victory. Modelled on the Gran Guardia Vecchia in Verona, the hall was, in A. J. P. Taylor's phrase, 'dedicated, like the United States of America, to a proposition – one as noble and beneficent as any ever made . . . The men of Manchester had brought down the nobility and gentry of England in a bloodless, but decisive, Crecy. The Free Trade Hall was the symbol of their triumph.'[17] So neutered was radical Manchester that in October 1851 the city became fit for a queen. Victoria and Albert's successful civic progression, across Victoria Bridge and under a canopy of Italianate arches, was transformed into a pageant of bourgeois pride and provincial self-regard, culminating in a ceremony bestowing various honours on the council. The meaning of Manchester – commerce and industry, religious toleration, civil society, political self-government – was now granted royal approbation. The city had shown itself, according to the *Manchester Guardian*, as a 'community based upon the orderly, sober and peaceful industry of the middle classes' and had proved to its detractors that 'social importance and political power have passed into the hands of those classes upon whose shoulders the burden of maintaining the national edifice has shifted'.[18]

For Engels, this bourgeois self-satisfaction was an awful welcoming party. Even his old friend and mentor, the Owenite lecturer John Watts, had thrown his lot in with the enveloping smug liberalism. 'Recently I went to see John Watts; the fellow seems skilled in sharp practice and now has a much larger shop in Deansgate,' Engels wrote to Marx. 'He has become a consummate radical mediocrity . . . From a few instances he gave me, it transpired that he knows very well how to boost his tailoring business by parading his bourgeois liberalism.'[19] Most shamefully of all, Watts was selling up that great *agora* of radical intent, the Owenite Hall of Science, to provide space for a new library and reading room. 'The free traders here are exploiting the prosperity or semi-prosperity to buy the proletariat, with John Watts for broker.'[20]

The Chartist Thomas Cooper was similarly disturbed by the bourgeois tendencies of his former comrades. 'In our old Chartist time, it is true, Lancashire working men were in rags by thousands; and many of them often lacked food. But their intelligence was demonstrated wherever you went,' he wrote in his autobiography. 'You could see them in groups discussing the great doctrine of political justice ... Now, you will see no such groups in Lancashire. But you will hear well dressed working men talking, as they walk with their hands in their pockets, of "Co-ops" and their shares in them, or in building societies.'[21] Miserably, Engels watched this embourgeoisification take place before his very eyes. 'The English proletariat is actually becoming more and more bourgeois, so that the ultimate aim of this most bourgeois of all nations would appear to be the possession, alongside the bourgeoisie, of a bourgeois aristocracy and a bourgeois proletariat,' he grumbled.[22] In the early 1850s Engels put some faith in the leadership of the socialist Ernest Jones and his attempts to resuscitate the Chartist cadaver. He was even minded 'to start up a small club with these fellows, or organise regular meetings to discuss the Manifesto with them'.[23] But after Jones's failure to subscribe to the Marx-Engels canon in its entirety and after one too many compromises with middle-class reformers, Engels disowned him. 'The English proletariat's revolutionary energy has completely evaporated,' he concluded in 1863.[24]

Driving the mid-Victorian boom and sapping of proletariat ambition was a resurgent cotton industry. Profits were up thanks to new markets in America, Australia and China, while improvements in technology ensured sustained productivity gains. The economic upswing was particularly evident in Lancashire, where wage-rates and employment rose as the county's 2,000 mills kept their 300,000 power looms beating day and night. In 1860, at the zenith of its power, the cotton industry accounted for almost 40 per cent of the total value of British exports. Ermen & Engels took a profitable chunk of that trade thanks to the invention of the sewing machine and increased demand for just their type of sewing thread. The firm's fortunes improved again when Gottfried Ermen patented an invention for the polishing of cotton thread which allowed their product to be marketed under the exclusive banner of 'Diamond Thread'. With surging orders, the company moved offices to 7 Southgate (into a warehouse overlooking the courtyard of the Golden Lion public house) and purchased the

Bencliffe Mill in Little Bolton, Eccles to add to their Victoria Mill at Salford.

However, behind the healthy balance sheet, there was the usual corporate infighting. Ermen & Engels was owned by four partners – Peter, Gottfried and Anthony Ermen together with Friedrich Engels senior. The Manchester branch of this Anglo-German conglomerate was run exclusively by Peter and Gottfried Ermen, while Engels senior spent his time at the Engelskirchen factory in the Rhineland. Besides, running Ermen & Engels, Peter and Gottfried operated a separate printing mill and bleachworks business on the side. This company, Ermen Brothers, was technically independent of Ermen & Engels but was run from the same office and just happened to be a leading supplier of products to Ermen & Engels. Engels senior was convinced he was being ripped off by this cosy arrangement and wanted his son – employed simply as a corresponding clerk and general assistant – to unpick the company finances and expose any sharp practice.

Understandably, the Ermenses were not overly delighted at the prospect of an internal auditor on the staff and made life as difficult as possible for their new clerk. They remembered well Engels's apprenticeship in the office eight years earlier when 'he worked for the firm as little as possible and spent most of his time at political meetings and on studying the social conditions in Manchester'.[25] And now, in Engels's words, Peter Ermen was 'going round in circles like a fox that has left its brush in a trap, and [is] trying to make things too hot for me here – the stupid devil imagines he could annoy me!' Yet the Ermenses had their own problems as Peter was simultaneously trying to prevent his impatient brother Gottfried taking over the management of the firm. 'See that you entrench yourself firmly between the two warring brothers,' was Jenny Marx's advice on office politics for Engels (after he had posted her a large parcel of cotton thread), 'their tussle is bound to place you in a position of indispensability vis-à-vis your respected Papa, and in my mind's eye I already see you as Friedrich Engels Junior and partner of the Senior.'[26]

What no one had expected was just how industrious and effective Engels would prove at his job. He went through the books, tried to untangle Ermen & Engels from Ermen Brothers and generally looked after the Engels family concern with exemplary diligence. 'My old man is enchanted with my business letters and he regards me remaining here as a great sacrifice on my part,' the unlikely capitalist informed Marx.[27] Indeed, thanks to this blossoming professional relationship, father and son were well on the way to a rapprochement. In June 1851 they met again in Manchester for the first time since the apocryphal Barmen bridge incident. 'I think it is probably better that you should not be together all the time, for you can't always be talking business, and it is better to avoid politics, on which you have such different views,' was his nervous mother's advice prior to the reunion.[28] She was right. The trip was generally deemed a success, but Engels thought that 'had my old man stayed here a few days longer, however, we'd have been at each other's throats . . . on the last day of his visit, for example, he sought to take advantage of the presence of one of the Ermens . . . to indulge himself at my expense by intoning a dithyramb in praise of Prussia's institutions. A word or two and a furious look were, of course, enough to bring him back to heel . . .'[29]

Despite renewed family relations, the fun of goading the Ermen brothers, and even the initial intellectual challenge of bookkeeping, there was no avoiding the reality that Engels had returned to the beastly business of huckstering. His letters of the time are filled with references to 'accursed commerce' and 'filthy commerce' as office life progressively impinged on his journalism, scholarship and socialism. It was a dull, tedious existence. 'I drink rum and water, swot and spend my time 'twixt twist and tedium,' he wrote to his friend Ernst Dronke in 1851. To Marx he was even franker, 'I am bored to death here.'[30] Politically, the job also had its costs since Engels's position, as a bourgeois mill owner, was obviously in danger of compromising his and Marx's standing within the backbiting communist world. 'You wait and see, the louts will be saying, what's that Engels after, how can he speak in our name and tell us what to do, the fellow's up there in Manchester exploiting the workers, etc. To be sure, I don't give a damn about it now, but it's bound to come . . .', he confided to Marx.[31] And it was certainly a charge levelled at him from the youthful Barmen industrialist and family friend Friedrich von Eynern, who visited Engels in 1860, taking him on a walking tour of Wales (during which Engels sang verses of Heine's *Die Heimkehr* by the Menai Straits in

Bangor) and peppering him with questions. 'Encouraged by his debating ways,' Eynern recalled,

I had not failed to point out to him that his position as a manufacturer, as co-owner of one of the period's worst 'big capitalist businesses', must put him at sharp odds with his theories, if he didn't practically utilise his considerable means to help the 'disowned' entrusted to his direct care. However, since according to his teachings the goals of universal economic freedom could only be achieved through the systematic cooperation of the international labour force, he dismissed such trifling help as pointless and disruptive to all circles of the movement. He showed no inclination to allow any limits to be placed on the basic freedom of his existence: to use his private earnings by himself, as he saw fit.[32]

The criticisms were not without foundation since when it came to the 'direct care' of his employees, Engels could be something of a bully. 'Gottfried has taken on three fellows for me who are absolutely hopeless . . . I shall have to sack one or two of them,' he wrote to Marx in 1865 in a spirited defence of flexible labour laws. A month later the dismissal followed after an administrative error. 'That was the last straw as far as his slovenliness was concerned, and he was sacked.'[33] To be fair, in contrast to the de-classed clerks, the more obviously working-class mill-hands of Ermen & Engels were said to enjoy better working conditions than the average. A report from the 1871 Annual Meeting of the Bencliffe Sick and Burial Society – where the second Ermen & Engels mill was located – referred to 'the stream of clean and well-dressed young women passing through the village' and commented that 'in few mills were the hands so profitably and regularly employed'.[34]

Engels's own employment was equally profitable. For all the banality and self-loathing the job entailed, it provided a decent salary beginning at £100 p.a. combined with an 'expenses and entertainment allowance' of £200 p.a. and then, from the mid-1850s, a 5 per cent profit share growing to 7.5 per cent by the end of the decade. In 1856 Engels's cut of the company profits stood at £408, rising to a sizeable £978 by 1860, thereby taking his annual wage over £1,000, which is not far off £100,000 in today's money. To provide some kind of context, the social commentator Dudley Baxter analysed the 1861 census to produce a class analysis of mid-Victorian England relative to income. To scrape into the middle class was to earn over the taxable threshold of £100, with parsons, army officers, doctors, civil servants and barristers usually operating in the £250–£350 salary range.[35] Baxter thought that to join the comfortable upper-middle classes one had to take home an annual salary of £1,000–£5,000. In contrast to Engels's riches, another great Victorian writer, poor old Anthony Trollope, was having to get by on £140 a year at his day job as a post office clerk.

Yet the awkward truth was that Engels's lucrative income was the direct result of his exploitation of the labour power of the Manchester proletariat. The very evils which he and Marx had so meticulously decried funded their lifestyles and philosophy. Engels was always more perturbed by this political contradiction than Marx (often the chief beneficiary of Ermen & Engels's market dominance), but he still cashed the cheque. The defence was that without the money from the mill workers Engels could never have funded Marx and, with it, his seminal advances in the scientific analysis of capitalism. 'The opponents of the working class would, of course, have preferred Engels to give up his job and renounce his income,' was the later official communist line on Engels's profiteering. 'He would have been unable to support Marx in this case, *Das Kapital* would not have been written, and the process of the working classes becoming politically and theoretically independent would have been delayed.' But, thankfully, 'Engels looked on the profits he made as a factory owner and merchant as a contribution toward the working class's fight for emancipation, and used them accordingly all his life.'[36]

In the first letter we have from Engels in Manchester sent to Marx in London, he is already promising his salary and raiding the expenses' account. There was never any explicit agreement between Engels and Marx that his toiling in the cotton trade would fund Marx's intellectual exertions, just an implicit recognition that this was how their partnership was set to work. And the profits cascaded south like a spring torrent for the rest of Engels's professional life. There were post office orders, postage stamps, £5 notes, a few pounds snaffled from the Ermen & Engels cash box (when Gottfried Ermen was out of the office), and then far more weighty sums when pay-day arrived.

In addition to which there were generous hampers, crates of wine and birthday presents for the girls. 'Dear Mr Engels,' as Jenny was apt to address him, was regularly allocating over half his annual income to the Marx family – totalling between £3,000 and £4,000 (£300,000–£400,000 in today's terms) over the twenty-year period he was employed. Yet it was never enough. 'I assure you that I would rather have had my thumb cut off than write this letter to you. It is truly soul-destroying to be dependent for half one's life,' begins a typical letter from Marx before pleading for an emergency loan.[37] 'Considering the great efforts – greater, even, than you can manage – that you make on my behalf, I need hardly say how much I detest perpetually boring you with my lamentations,' starts another. 'The last money you sent me, plus a borrowed pound, went to pay the school bill – so that there shouldn't be twice the amount owing in January. The butcher and *épicier* made me give them IOUs, one for £10, the other for £12, due on 9 January . . .'[38] When Marx was in an especially cowardly frame of mind, he had his wife write the begging letter. 'It is for me a hateful task to have to write to you about money matters. You have already helped us all too often. But this time I have no other recourse, no other way out,' Jenny pleaded in April 1853. 'Can you send us something? The baker warned us that there'd be no more bread after Friday.'[39]

As numerous biographers have pointed out, Marx was not poor. In the measured judgement of David McLellan, 'his difficulties resulted less from real poverty than from a desire to preserve appearances, coupled with an inability to husband his financial resources'.[40] The subsidy from Engels combined with income from journalism, book deals and the odd inheritance totalled some £200 p.a. which meant that, after the needy Soho years, his financial position was far sounder than that of many middle-class families. But Marx was terrible with money ('I don't suppose anyone has ever written about "money" when so short of the stuff') and went from feast to famine in a hopeless cycle of financial gorging and retrenchment. With every windfall, the family moved to a new and larger house – from Soho to Kentish Town to Chalk Farm – with the associated costs adding up for Engels to sort out. 'It is true my house is beyond my means, and we have, moreover, lived better this year than was the case before,'

Marx wrote to Engels after an upgrade to fashionable Modena Villas. 'But it is the only way for the children to establish themselves socially with a view to securing their future . . . even from a merely commercial point of view, to run a purely proletarian house-hold would not be appropriate in the circumstances . . .'[41] Here was the rub: Karl and Jenny Marx were far more concerned about keeping up appearances, marrying their daughters well and holding their place in polite society – in short, being bourgeois – than the bohemian Engels ever was. 'For the sake of the children,' Jenny Marx explained defensively (and without acknowledging Engels's generosity), 'we had already adopted a regular, respectable middle class life. Everything conspired to bring about a bourgeois existence, and to enmesh us in it.'[42] Marx, the prophet-philosopher, was never going to sully himself with a profession to support his family – so it was Engels who was chained to the office treadmill to fund their aspirational lifestyle. Which is why it is wrong to paint Marx as a real-life Mr Micawber desperately hoping something would turn up; thanks to Engels he always *knew* something would turn up. 'Karl was tremendously pleased when he heard the postman's portentous double KNOCK,' Jenny wrote to their benefactor in 1854, '"*Voila* Frederick, £2, we're saved!" He cried.'[43] No wonder that behind his back Marx called Engels 'Mr Chitty'.

Accompanying the cash was a gripping correspondence. While both Marx and Engels, who spent years with each other at close quarters in Paris, Brussels and Cologne, desperately resented the distance between them, posterity has been the beneficiary. The 1850s and 60s provide the golden years of their letter-writing as they exploited the mid-Victorian postal revolution – of penny blacks, post offices and pillar boxes – to the full: a letter posted in Manchester before midnight would reach Marx the following day by 1 p.m.; a letter sent by 9 a.m. would be in his hands by 6 p.m. the same day. And this cache of letters provides an unequalled insight into their individual neuroses, frustrations, disappointments and passions. Stories of royal flatulence, cuckolded émigrés and drinking marathons abound – in the words of Francis Wheen, 'a gamey stew of history and gossip, political economy and schoolboy smut, high ideals and low intimacies'.[44] The letters are also a telling commentary on the depth of affection between the two men as they provide consolation in bereavement, encouragement in work, and criticism over political strategy, as well as a touching exchange of photographs. For Engels at his office and Marx in his study, the post was a highlight of the day. 'The two friends wrote to each other almost every day,' Eleanor Marx recalled, 'and I can remember how often Moor, as we called our father at home, used to talk to the letters as though their writer were there. "No, that's not the way it is"; "You're right there," etc., etc. But what I remember best is how Moor used sometimes to laugh over Engels's letters until tears ran down his cheeks.'[45]

It was the drooling prospect of an economic crash which consumed a large chunk of the initial Manchester–London correspondence. Part of the reason behind Marx and Engels's conflict with the Willich–Schapper faction in the Communist League was their conviction, as good materialists, that revolution could occur only given the appropriate economic circumstances. Attempts at insurrections and putsches were all doomed if the socio-economic preconditions were not in place – as the events of 1848–9 had so frustratingly shown. What revolutionary socialism required was advance warning of any looming financial collapse so Marx and Engels could ready themselves for the political consequences. And luckily the movement had a man stationed behind enemy lines: from his seat in the counting houses of Cottonopolis, Engels became the main source of intelligence on the state of international capitalism.

'Speculation in railways is again reaching dazzling heights – since 1 January most shares have risen by 40%, and the worst ones more than any. *Ça promet!*', he reported back to Marx six months into the job. Clearly, capitalism's denouement was just around the corner: the East India market was overstocked while the British cloth industry was being hit hard by a flood of cheap cotton. 'If the Crash in the market coincides with such a gigantic crop, things will be cheery indeed. Peter Ermen is already fouling his breeches at the very thought of it, and the little tree-frog's a pretty good barometer,' Engels wrote in July 1851. Bankruptcies were starting to pick up in London and Liverpool, overproduction glutting the market, and Engels was adamant the crash would arrive by March 1852.[46] 'But all this is guess-work and we could just as well have it in September. It should, though, be a fine how-d'ye-do, for never before has such a mass of goods of all descriptions been pushed onto the market, nor have there ever been such colossal means of production,' he forecast on 2 March 1852, slightly readjusting predictions for an autumn–winter meltdown. The only possible fly in the ointment was a strike for improved working conditions by the Amalgamated Society of Engineers, which was holding up machine-building. Engels, the champion of the workers, thought such irredeemably selfish behaviour would 'hold it [the crash] up for at least a month'.[47] And yet as April followed March and 1852 bowed to 1853, the day of reckoning was inexplicably averted. Instead, production increased, exports surged, wages rose, standards of living improved and the mid-Victorian boom ground relentlessly on.

By September 1856 the prophet of the Manchester Exchange had rediscovered his voice. 'This time there'll be a *dies irae* such as has never been seen before; the whole of Europe's industry in ruins, all markets over-stocked . . ., all the propertied classes in the soup, complete bankruptcy of the bourgeoisie, war and profligacy to the nth degree.' At last Engels was partly right: over-production in the textile markets combined with an unexpected hike in raw material costs had led to a collapse of confidence in the cotton industry, followed by a run on the banks and a spate of commercial insolvencies. The mid-Victorian global economy, from America to India via Britain and Germany, was rocked as sugar, coffee, cotton and silk prices plummeted. 'The American Crash is superb and not yet over by a long chalk,' Engels wrote rapturously in October 1857. 'The repercussion in England would appear to have begun with the Liverpool Borough Bank. *Tant mieux*. That means that for the next 3 or 4 years, commerce will again be in a bad way. *Nous avons maintenant de la chance*.' The conditions for revolution were ripe: they had to strike! Despite Ermen & Engels's extensive corporate losses, the veteran of the Baden campaign cared little for commercial difficulties as he sensed insurrection in the air. 'A period of chronic pressure is needed to get the people's blood up.' It was now clearer than ever that 1848 had been a false dawn, but this was the real thing – 'a case of do or die'. But two months into the crash the proletariat was still failing to realize its calling. 'There are as yet few signs of revolution, for the long period of prosperity has been fearfully demoralizing,' Engels noted gloomily in December 1857. And by the following spring, business had picked itself up again on the back of developing markets in India and China.[48]

Engels's last and best hope lay with the American Civil War. In April 1861 Union forces started to blockade the Southern ports, ratcheting up the cost of freight, insurance and, above all, the price of Middling Orleans cotton, with knock-on effects for production and employment in the UK. Imports from the American South fell from 2.6 million bales in 1860 to fewer than 72,000 in 1862. Hundreds of thousands of Lancashire operatives, valiantly supporting the ideals of Abraham Lincoln and the anti-slave North, were placed on short-time and then sacked. Their reduced earnings started to undermine the wider north-west economy as shops closed, savings collapsed and food riots broke out. By November 1862 almost 200,000 workers were receiving support from various relief committees across Lancashire. Modern economic historians now suggest the Lancashire 'cotton famine' was as much a product of an over-saturated global market as the direct result of the Civil War embargo – but either way the results were the same. 'You will readily understand that all the philistines are in a cold sweat,' Engels reported in April 1865 as the Liverpool import–export industry shuddered and 125,000 unemployed mill-hands wandered the Manchester streets. 'A lot of people in Scotland are finished as well, and one fine day it's bound to be the turn of the banks, and that'd be the end of the matter.'[49] Like many other cotton-based businesses, Ermen & Engels was directly affected as they introduced half-time in the mills, saw profits evaporate on unsold stock and even slashed directors' salaries. For Engels, no matter the personal costs, here was another chance for revolution. 'The distress up here is gradually becoming acute,' he noted as cases of typhoid, pneumonia, malnutrition and tuberculosis mounted. 'I imagine by next month the working people themselves will have had enough of sitting about with a look of passive misery on their faces.'[50]

In fact, the exact opposite occurred: the Manchester cotton operatives were to become a symbol of the mid-Victorian settlement and patted on the head for the dignified resolve with which they endured their poverty. It was an exemplary display of self-control in the interests of a greater moral calling. 'The leaders of the operative class are in general strongly favourable to the Northern policy, firm in their hatred of slavery, and firm in their faith in democracy,' wrote R. Arthur Arnold in his *History of the Cotton Famine*.[51] One government inspector thought that, 'at no period in the history of manufactures have sufferings so sudden and so severe been borne with so much silent resignation and so much patient self-respect'.[52] Rather than rioting, they accepted the vagaries of the global marketplace with unsettling stoicism and it seemed to Victorian official opinion that the respectable, self-helping working class had at last come of age. John Watts, former radical turned bourgeois apologist, thought such endurance revealed the beneficial influence of Sunday schools, improving literature and co-operative sentiments.[53] Everything Engels had first feared about the Manchester proletariat's debilitating lack of appetite for class struggle was being proved horribly right.

With revolution postponed, Engels returned to the day job – or rather, jobs, since what the Marx-Engels correspondence also reveals is the full extent to which Marx depended upon his collaborator to carry out the only piece of professional work for which he was personally contracted. In early 1851 Charles Dana, a former Fourierist and now managing director of the progressive, anti-slavery *New York Daily Tribune*, asked Marx to contribute to the paper on English and European affairs. The problem was Marx's grasp of written English remained so poor that Engels had to translate his copy from German into English – which all too often meant just writing it himself. 'If you could possibly let me have an article on conditions in Germany by Friday morning, that would make a splendid beginning,' Marx loftily wrote to his friend on receiving news of his column.[54] To which Engels obediently answered, 'write and tell me soon what sort of thing it should be – whether you wish it to stand on its own or to be one of a series, and 2) what attitudes I should adopt . . .'[55] It was a healthy salary (at £2 per article) for a good newspaper with over 200,000 US readers, but Marx clearly thought it grubby work for a philosopher. 'The continual newspaper muck annoys me,' he fumed when actually forced to write his own articles. 'It takes a lot of time, disperses my efforts and in the final analysis is nothing.'[56] But it was all right for his harried comrade slogging away in Manchester. 'Engels really has too much work, but being a veritable walking encyclopaedia, he's capable, drunk or sober, of working at any hour of the day or night, is a fast writer and devilish quick in the uptake . . .', Marx explained majestically to his American friend Adolf Cluss.[57]

He was not wrong. Engels was a gifted journalist able to turn around articles on most topics to length and time. 'This evening I shall translate the final part of your article and shall do the article on "Germany" tomorrow or Thursday,' reads a typically dutiful Engels response.[58] But it was banal hack work and very few of the *New York Daily Tribune* pieces rise to the usual heights of Engels's intellect. Back and forth the letters sped between Manchester and London with translations, suggestions for new articles, pleas for information on unknown subjects, demands for brevity ('You really must stop making your articles so long. Dana can't possibly want more than 1–1.5 columns'), stylistic criticisms ('you must colour your war-articles a little more seeing that you are writing for a general newspaper') and urgent requests to make sure the copy made the Liverpool steamer.[59] But Marx was always happy to take the credit. 'How do you like my husband creating a stir with your article throughout western, eastern and southern America,' asked Jenny indelicately after Engels's history of 1848–9, 'Revolution and Counter-Revolution in Germany', was well received by the *Tribune* readership.

But the traffic was not all one way. What the letters also reveal is the degree to which Marx shared the development of his thinking on *Das Kapital* with Engels. Much of the initial spur for the book had come from Engels himself. As early as 1851 he was already chiding Marx, 'the main thing is that you should once again make a public debut with a substantial book . . . it's absolutely essential to break the spell created by your prolonged absence from the German book market . . .'[60] Nine years later and with still no obvious sign of publication, Engels reminded him of the 'paramount importance' of the work which he was needlessly holding up with minor intellectual quibbles. 'The *main* thing is that it should be written and published; the weaknesses which you think of will never be discovered by those donkeys; and if an unsettled period sets in what will you be left with if the whole thing is interrupted before you get *Capital* finished as a whole?'[61]

Eventually, from his daily perch at seat 07 in the British Museum

Reading Room, Marx got down to writing his opus – and soon started pestering Engels with requests for technical data as well as some philosophical ballast. While the British Museum yielded much, it was no substitute for the commercial realities of the Manchester cotton trade when it came to understanding the functioning of capitalism. 'I have now reached a point in my work on economics where I need some practical advice from you, since I cannot find anything relevant in the theoretical writings,' Marx wrote in January 1858. 'It concerns the *circulation* of capital – its various forms in the various businesses; its effects on profit and prices. If you could give me some information on this, then it will be very welcome . . .' There then followed a series of questions on machinery costs and depreciation rates, the allocation of capital within the firm and calculation of turnover in the company bookkeeping. 'The theoretical laws for this are very simple and self-evident. But it is good to have an idea of how it works in practice.'[62] Over the next five years, the requests for real-life information kept coming as Engels's grafting at Ermen & Engels helped to construct the empirical foundations of *Das Kapital*. 'Could you inform me of all the different types of workers employed, e.g., at your mill and in what proportion to each other?', Marx enquired in 1862. 'For in my book I need an example showing that, in mechanical workshops, the division of labour, as forming the basis of manufacture and as described by A[dam] Smith, does not exist . . . All that is needed is an example of some kind.'[63] 'Since practice is better than all theory, I would ask you to describe to me *very precisely* (with examples) how you run your business,' began another round of queries.[64]

Engels's contribution went beyond the statistical. 'Let me say a word or two about what will, in the text, be a lengthy and complex affair, so that you may LET ME HAVE YOUR OPINION on it,' Marx began his letter of 2 August 1862, which then launched into a detailed explanation of the difference between constant capital (machinery) and variable capital (living labour) and his early idea of the theory of surplus value, which would become the bedrock of his explanation, in *Das Kapital*, of how the capitalist made a profit by exploiting the labour of the worker (see below, p. 238). Engels responded to his friend's philosophical queries in kind and it was he who, in a crucial letter of 26 June 1867, first pointed out one of the more puzzling economic lacunae in Marx's system – notably, that his friend's theory failed to take account of the surplus value produced by machinery, nor did it answer the criticism of those who would simply equate the value of labour with the labour-wage paid by the employer: 'if the capitalist only pays the worker the price of six hours for his twelve hours' labour, no surplus-value can be produced, since in that case each hour of the factory worker's labour counts only = ½ an hour's labour, = the amount which has been paid for, and only that value can be embodied in the value of the labour product'. Atrociously superficial though this argument may be, Engels averred, 'I do, nevertheless, find it surprising that you have not already taken it into account, for you will most certainly be immediately confronted with this objection, and it is better to anticipate it.'[65] Marx's rather unsatisfying answer was that such criticisms could not properly be treated 'prior to the 3rd book . . . if I wished to refute all such objections in advance, I should spoil the whole dialectical method of exposition'.[66] Despite all the reams of correspondence concerning *Das Kapital*, pursuing such complex themes on paper could sometimes prove just too trying. 'Can't you come down for a few days?' Marx asked on 20 August 1862. 'In my critique I have demolished so much of the old stuff that there are a number of points I should like to consult you about before I proceed. Discussing these matters in writing is tedious both for you and for me.' And even the sprightly Engels could find Marx's requests for enlightenment a little arduous after a day in the office. 'What with the cotton bother, the theory of rent has really proved too abstract for me,' he replied wearily in September 1862. 'I shall have to consider the thing when I eventually get a little more peace and quiet.'[67]

Amidst this treasury of intellectual, professional and personal material, there is an uncomfortable silence in the correspondence which points to Engels's most generous sacrifice. 'In the early summer of 1851 there occurred an event which I shall not touch upon further, although it brought about a great increase in our private and public sorrows,' was how Jenny Marx alluded to the delicate history of Henry Frederick Demuth.[68] His mother, 28-year-old Helene 'Lenchen' Demuth (or 'Nim'), had long been a part of the Marx family household

THE FROCK-COATED COMMUNIST

– passed down the von Westphalen line – as live-in housekeeper. Even in their most cramped Soho lodgings, Nim always found her place. Indeed, it was that very intimacy which sparked the crisis: when Jenny Marx travelled to the continent in 1850 on a family fund-raising mission, Marx took advantage of the maid. And, on 23 June 1851, their progeny, Freddy Demuth, duly entered the world to no great acclaim.

He was Marx's son, the birth certificate remained blank, but it was Engels who unofficially acknowledged the paternity. For the good of Marx's marriage and the broader political cause (émigré groups enjoyed nothing more than discrediting enemies via sexual scandal), Engels allowed Marx's son to take his Christian name and, in the process, sully his own good name. Marx behaved abominably when it came to Freddy's upbringing: he was packed off to unsympathetic foster-parents in east London, never received a proper education or enjoyed the kind of intellectual riches – the Shakespeare dramas, boisterous picnics on Hampstead Heath, low socialist banter – Marx bestowed on his half-sisters. He spent his professional life as a skilled fitter and turner and member of the Associated Society of Engineers, and his political life as a member of the Hackney Labour Party. When Engels later moved to London and, after Marx's death, hired Nim as his own housekeeper, Freddy and his son Harry used the tradesman's entrance to visit, the latter recalled, 'a motherly sort of person' in 'a basement'. Engels, however, was always careful to absent himself on such occasions.

Only Eleanor (or 'Tussy', as she was now known within the family) seemed moved by Freddy's plight. 'It may be that I am very "sentimental" – but I can't help feeling that Freddy has had great injustice all through his life,' she wrote in 1892. Nor could she account for the hostile and distant attitude of Engels towards his son when he was, in all other respects, so generous and warm-hearted to everyone else in their extended familial circle. To Tussy's horror, on Engels's death-bed all was revealed. In an 1898 letter located in the Amsterdam archives of the International Institute of Social History – the veracity and origins of which are much disputed amongst Marx-Engels scholars – Engels's final housekeeper and companion, Louise Freyberger, describes how on the eve of his death Engels confirmed to Tussy the real identity of Freddy's biological father. 'General [Engels] gave us

... permission to make use of the information only if he should be accused of treating Freddy shabbily. He said he would not want his name slandered, especially as it could no longer do anyone any good.' In the succeeding years Tussy tried desperately to repair the damage by befriending Freddy, and through the tormented, final months of her relationship with Edward Aveling, Freddy Demuth proved her most trusted and sympathetic correspondent. However, the damage to Engels's reputation – as a shoddy father – was done. Although he was characteristically unperturbed by the innuendoes, it was a telling indication of the personal sacrifices Engels was willing to endure to protect his friend and expedite the slow march of socialism.[69]

Such white lies were just another layer of mist to the miasma of subterfuge which encircled his middle decades. For Engels led little short of a double life: by day the respectable Dr Jekyll, clerk in the cotton trade; by night Mr Hyde, the revolutionary socialist. Bestriding the two worlds meant an exhaustive existence of psychological division and obfuscation which he was ultimately unable to sustain as the rebellious fun of being 'Oswald' – anonymously pulling the tail of the bourgeoisie from inside the parapet – started to pale.

The anchor of his private life, his real life, was his long-time lover, Mary Burns, and her sister, Lizzy. However, to retain his place within Manchester society and avoid the disapproval of his parents, Engels felt compelled to hide his relationship with the earthy Irish sisters from business colleagues and family alike. Another letter from his troublesome brother-in-law Adolf von Griesheim, complaining about the connection and its damaging effects on the Engelses' social standing suggests such secrecy was not wholly successful.[70] On his arrival in Manchester, he boarded with an 'old witch of a landlady', Mrs Isabella Tatham, at 70 Great Ducie Street in the Strangeways district close to where the hulking Victorian jail now stands along the Bury New Road. Joining him in this insalubrious establishment were a clogger, a waste dealer and a silversmith-cum-salesman. After a short-term hire of some more expensive lodgings to convince his visiting father he was spending his allowance wisely (rather than funnelling it to Marx), in March 1853 Engels moved in with the Burnses. Thanks to Roy Whitfield's meticulous reconstruction of Engels's Manchester years, we know that the poor rate books for the districts of Chorlton on Medlock and Moss Side show a certain Frederick Mann Burns (a very Engels-style pun) as the occupant of 17 Burlington Street and then 27 Cecil Street in the early 1850s.[71] But in April 1854 disaster struck. 'The philistines have got to know that I'm living with Mary,' a furious Engels reported to Marx as he was driven back into 'private lodgings again'.[72]

From 1854 onwards, after the discovery of his proletarian ménage, the cash-strapped Engels was forced to run two separate public and private, official and unofficial premises: he took an official residence at 5 Walmer Street in Rusholme – for entertaining business associates, correspondence and reasons of bourgeois propriety – whilst hiding the Burns sisters at Cecil Street. In 1858 he moved his official base to Thorncliffe Grove (demolished in 1971, after Manchester's Medical Officer of Health designated this elegant Victorian house 'unfit' for habitation and the university swallowed it up), which is where the 1861 census has him down as a 'short-sighted Prussian merchant'.[73] Meanwhile, he rehoused the sisters in two smaller, jerry-built terraces in the expanding working-class suburbs of Hulme and Ardwick. The rate book has the occupants of these addresses – 7 Rial Street and 252 Hyde Road – living under the assumed names of Frederick and Mary Boardman, together with a certain 'Elizabeth Byrne'. Deftly, Engels had managed to locate his lover and her sister just half a mile from his official residence.

These were only the first of numerous properties Engels would surreptitiously take for the Burnses over the next fifteen years. 'I'm living with Mary nearly all the time now so as to spend as little money as possible,' he explained to Marx in 1862. 'I can't dispense with my lodgings, otherwise I should move in with her altogether.' But it wasn't easy. 'You are right, I am very broke,' Engels responded later that year to another financial demand from Marx. 'In the hope that, by leading a domesticated life in Hyde Road, I shall be able to make good the deficiency, I enclose herewith a £5 note . . .'[74] In 1864 the caravan moved on again after Engels fell out with his Thorncliffe Grove housemaid, and he relocated his public residence to a flat in Dover Street, in the affluent Oxford Road neighbourhood, and his demi-monde to nearby Mornington Street. Keeping the different addresses going, making sure no one transgressed the separate silos of his life, managing the finances of leases and rates were all unwelcome additions to Engels's workload and he complained endlessly about the expense and annoyance. Yet one also gets the sense that the aggressively independent Engels enjoyed the freedom of manoeuvre these two, distinct worlds provided.

It was in his private, unofficial surroundings that the revolutionary Mr Hyde (of Hyde Road) could reveal himself. Here Engels gathered together a regular Manchester coterie of socialist believers and intellectual sparring-partners to drink beer, adumbrate over the latest philosophical advances and lament the bourgeois compromise they saw all around them. Wilhelm Wolff ('Lupus'), the Brussels communist turned tutor to the children of middle-class Manchester, was a close friend. 'For several years Wolff was the only comrade I had in Manchester with the same views as myself,' Engels later recalled; 'no wonder that we met almost daily and that I then again had more than ample opportunity of admiring his almost instinctively correct assessment of current events.'[75] George Weerth, back clerking in 'beastly' Bradford, was again part of the circle during the early 1850s before commerce took him abroad and death took him in Havana. Another close favourite was Darmstadt-born Carl Schorlemmer, who lectured in organic chemistry at Owens College, was a Fellow of the Royal Society and an expert on paraffin hydrocarbons – which, much to Engels's amusement, frequently resulted in explosive burnings to his 'bruised and battered face'.[76] He was also a committed socialist who was trusted enough by Marx and Engels to correct proofs of *Das Kapital*. On a Saturday night he could be found with Engels propping up the bar of the Thatched House Tavern in Newmarket Place, round the corner from the Royal Exchange.[77] Engels's other great friend and Dover Street flatmate was Samuel Moore, whom he became acquainted with through his uncle, Isaac Hall, a leading figure in the Lancashire and Cheshire Volunteers. Moore was a failed cotton trader, then barrister and Marxist (honoured with the task of translating *Das Kapital* into English) before incongruously concluding his professional life in Asaba as chief justice of the territories of the Royal Niger Company. Alongside these fixed friends, there was a smattering of German émigrés, unemployed communists, distant cousins and, of course, the visits from Marx himself. Occasionally, these boozy evenings could get out of hand, as when Engels, 'at a drunken gathering . . . was insulted by an Englishman I didn't know; I hit out at him with the umbrella I was carrying and the ferrule got him in the eye'. Unfortunately for Engels, Mr Daniells then took him to court on charges of assault, demanding £55 in compensation and costs. Engels duly stumped up the sum in the desperate hope of avoiding 'a public scandal and a ROW with my old man'.[78]

Engels's official existence was a world away from such bar-room brawls. The Cheshire Hounds, one of the grandest meets in Victorian Britain, 'composed of the first gentlemen in that aristocratic county', dated from 1763 when the Hon. John Smith-Barry brought together a pack from the Belvoir and Milton bloodlines. And they met, according to *The Field*, in some of England's most hunt-friendly settings. 'Cheshire abounds with parks, and mansions, and the aristocracy have from time immemorial been most devoted patrons of fox-hunting; indeed there is no country in England where that feeling can prevail more universally among the higher classes.'[79] From Tatton Hall, south of Manchester, to Crewe Hall, to the east of Crewe; from Norton Priory, alongside the river Mersey, to Alderley Park, just outside Macclesfield, the Cheshire Hounds criss-crossed the county two to three times a week during the November to April season. But it was not a cheap hobby: a subscription fee to the Cheshire Hunt Covert Fund, as it was known, was £10 p.a., while stabling fees could nudge £70 p.a. (taking annual costs into the region of £8,000 in today's money). Then there was the price of a good hunter. 'I saw Murray the horse-dealer on Saturday and asked him if he had anything . . . carrying 14 stone with hounds at about £70. He seemed to think he had . . .', began a note to Engels from one James Wood Lomax, who seems to have been his horse-agent.[80] Thankfully, when it came to funding respectable activities like hunting, he could always draw on the resources of his father. 'For my Christmas present my old man gave me the money to buy a horse and as there was a good one going, I bought it last week,' Engels wrote crassly to Marx in 1857. 'But I'm exceedingly vexed that I should be keeping a horse while you and your family are down on your luck in London.'[81]

It is unclear who first introduced Engels to the Cheshire Hounds, but he became a regular fixture in the field alongside some of England's most elevated nobility. For he had joined the hunt during the period known as 'The Cheshire Difficulty' which followed the affair of the Master of Foxhounds, Captain Mainwaring, with a married lady. The leading Cheshire landowners then boycotted the hunt in disgust until 1858, when Hugh Lupus, otherwise known as Earl Grosvenor (and future first Duke of Westminster), took over as MFH with his aristocratic chums, the Earls Cholmondeley and Crewe. This was the very cream of the English nobility with whom Engels – the scourge of Prussia's Junker class – found himself riding out. As Paul Lafargue, Marx's son-in-law, remembered it: 'He was an excellent rider and had his own hunter for the fox chase; when the neighbouring gentry and aristocracy sent out invitations to all riders in the district according to the ancient feudal custom he never failed to attend.'[82] In 2004, when the Labour government introduced legislation to ban fox-hunting as an out-of-date toffs' sport, Engels's membership of the Cheshire Hunt was cited in its defence. 'The idea of joining the class war with fox hunting is pathetic as well as nasty, as was very well demonstrated by no less an authority on both subjects than Friedrich Engels,' Lord Gilmour of Craigmillar told the House of Lords during a debate on the Hunting Bill. 'I think that shows that, at least in some ways, old communism was much more sensible than new Labour.'[83] And Engels was not the only Victorian left-winger with a penchant for the saddle: Michael Sadler, leader of the Factory Reform movement; Joseph Arch, the farmworkers' leader; and Robert Applegarth, the General Secretary of the Carpenters and Joiners, all rode to hounds.*

Engels tried to justify his hobby on revolutionary grounds as 'the best school of all' for warfare. Indeed, he thought one of the few saving graces of the British cavalry was its background in chasing old Charlie – 'being, most of them, passionate huntsmen, they possess that instinctive and rapid appreciation of advantage of ground, which the practice of hunting is sure to impart', he wrote in a review of British military strategy.[84] But however he dressed it up, what clearly

---

* My thanks for this information to Nick Mansfield, who also tells me that as late as 1940, the National Union of Seamen allowed the Leconfield hounds in Sussex to use the grounds of their wartime headquarters.

aroused Engels was the thrill of the chase: 'That sort of thing always keeps me in a state of devilish excitement for several days; it's the greatest physical pleasure I know.'[85] And he was never afraid to front the field. 'He was always among the leaders in clearing ditches, hedges and other obstacles,' according to Larfargue.[86] 'Let me tell you that yesterday I took my horse over a hedge and bank measuring 5 feet and some inches, the highest jump I've ever done,' he boasted to a sedentary Marx festering in the British Museum. Even with a nasty bout of piles, Engels would happily put himself through a 28-mile hack in pursuit of his quarry. Indeed, over the years, he obviously developed something of a bloodlust. 'Yesterday I let myself be talked into attending a coursing meeting at which hares are hunted with greyhounds, and spent seven hours in the saddle. All in all, it did me a power of good though it kept me from my work . . .'[87]

Engels's other pursuits were noticeably less savage. 'Everyone up here is an art lover just now and the talk is all of the pictures at the exhibition,' he wrote to Marx in the summer of 1857, having visited the celebrated Art Treasures Exhibition at Trafford Park and fallen for Titian's portrait of Ariosto. '*S'il y a moyen*, you and your wife ought to come up this summer and see the thing.'[88] As a leading Manchester merchant, his was a sophisticated, high-bourgeois lifestyle of galleries, dinners, clubs, charitable events and networking focused on the respectable German quarter near to his Thorncliffe Grove and Dover Street residences. Manchester had been a Mecca for Prussian merchants since the 1780s and by 1870 there were some 150 German business houses operating in the city. The 1851 census recorded 1,000 persons of German birth as resident and the most elevated of this community congregated nightly at the Schiller Anstalt along Oxford Street.[89] Engels himself had attended the original Schiller Festival in 1859 – commemorating the centenary of Friedrich Schiller's birth – with its concert of Beethoven, Mendelssohn, Schiller readings and Mozart directed by Manchester's most celebrated German resident, Charles Hallé, in the Free Trade Hall. The Anstalt, or Institute, was set up after the concert to give the German community a club for socializing and a little bit of cultural comfort from the homeland. By the mid-1860s it boasted 300 members, a 4,000-volume library, a skittle alley and billiard room, a gymnasium, a well-stocked reading room and a prodigiously busy calendar of events from male-voice choir concerts to public lecture series to amateur dramatics productions. Engels joined in 1861 and immediately fell out with the management over a book recall notice from the librarian. 'When I had read this missive, it was as though I had been suddenly transported home.' And not for the right reasons. 'It was as though, instead of a communication from the Librarian of the Schiller Institute, I were holding a peremptory summons from a German inspector of police ordering me, on pain of a heavy penalty, to make amends for some kind of violation "within 24 hours".'[90] For Engels, the victim of any number of police summons, an innocent library fine was altogether too reminiscent of the Prussian state.

Overdue notices didn't keep him away for long and he soon entered enthusiastically into the Schiller Anstalt circle, was elected on to the governing body and finally made chairman. He proved himself a good committee man, introducing beer into the directors' meetings, chairing numerous subcommittees and successfully overseeing the purchase of 6,000 volumes from the Manchester Subscription Library.[91] These negotiations concerned Engels greatly since, 'to be "done" in business, to get yourself "sold" is naturally here the worst thing that can happen to you. Now it is a great triumph and gives me the opportunity I wanted to withdraw with honour from official participation in the affair . . .'[92] But the following year Engels was out altogether after the Anstalt extended an invitation to the science popularizer Karl Vogt. Unbeknownst to them, Vogt featured prominently on Marx and Engels's extensive blacklist as a suspected Bonapartist spy and Engels immediately resigned.

Luckily, he had a number of other institutions to patronize. Together with Samuel Moore, he was a member of the Albert Club, 'christened appropriately after the husband of our most gracious Queen'. Renowned for its smoking room – 'we believe it to be, without exception, the best room of the kind in Manchester' – the club housed an equally impressive array of card rooms, private dining rooms and billiard tables. The names of Schaub, Schreider, von Lindelof and König pointed to its 50 per cent German membership.[93] In 1858 Engels put his clerking colleague from Ermen & Engels Charles Roesgen up for membership. In addition, Engels belonged to the Athenaeum, the

Brazenose Club, the Manchester Foreign Library and even the Royal Exchange. 'So now you're a member of the Exchange, and altogether respectable. My congratulations,' Marx wrote with a light pasting of sarcasm. 'Some time I should like to hear you howling amidst that pack of wolves.'[94] Despite this busy calendar of lectures, dinners and concerts, Engels always remained pained by the provincialism of Manchester life. 'For six months past I have not had a single opportunity to make use of my acknowledged gift for mixing a lobster salad – *quelle horreur*; it makes one quite rusty,' spoke the original champagne communist.[95]

By the mid-1850s the workload combined with Jekyll-and-Hyde double life was beginning to test even Engels's endurance. 'I now have three lads to keep in control and am forever checking, correcting, telling off and giving orders,' he complained to Marx in 1856. 'Add to this the running battle with manufacturers over bad yarn or late delivery, and my own work.' The mountain of arrears, business queries and competing demands of his father and Gottfried Ermen meant that Engels was having 'to slave away in the office until 8 o'clock each evening and can't start work till 10 o'clock, after supper'. His journalism was suffering, attempts at learning Russian falling behind and socialist theorizing non-existent. 'This summer things have got to be re-organized,' he announced in March 1857.[96] Yet that was the very moment Marx decided to pile on the pressure by accepting a ridiculous, if lucrative, contract to contribute to Charles Dana's latest publishing scheme, *The New American Cyclopaedia*. Engels was, of course, delighted with the money – 'now everything is going to be alright again' – but he was the one who would have to do the legwork. By early summer 1857 Engels's body was giving way. 'I'm sitting at home with linseed poultices on the left-hand side of my face in the hope of getting the better of a nasty abscess . . . I have had continual trouble with my face for the past month – first toothache, then a swollen cheek, then more toothache and now the whole thing has blossomed out into a furuncle.' By mid-summer he was suffering from exhaustion and full-blown glandular fever (a worrying development in Victorian England) and being nursed by his sister Marie in London. 'I'm one of your really miserable figures, stooped, lame and weak and – for example as at present – beside myself with pain.'[97] And what was Marx's response to his friend's debilitating illness? 'As you will understand, nothing could be more distasteful to me than TO PRESS UPON YOU while you are ill,' but he needed the *Cyclopaedia* articles and sharpish. It was only when Engels suffered a total collapse that Marx eased up on the demands. 'The chief thing for you at present is naturally to recover your health. I shall have to see how I can put Dana off again,' he wrote sheepishly in July 1857.

It would be wrong to suggest that Marx did not care about Engels's health. Indeed, discussions of illness, medication, therapies and doctors often comprised the most detailed and impassioned section of their correspondence. Like any good hypochondriac, the two of them positively revelled in their ailments. 'How are things in regard to "coughing"?' was an early enquiry when Marx learned of Engels's deterioration. After pursuing some 'meticulous medical studies' in the British Museum (always keen to put off the writing of *Das Kapital* if at all possible), he asked him to 'let me know whether you are taking iron. In cases such as yours, as in many others, iron has proved stronger than the affliction.'[98] Engels was unconvinced and replied with a lengthy disquisition on the merits of iron versus cod-liver oil – before revealing a personal preference for the Norwegian variety. But this was the exception: most times it was Marx who demanded the lion's share of medical advice on account of a persistent strain of psychosomatic illnesses (from liver complaints to headaches to insomnia) as well as his all-too-real struggle against the boils that took apart his body like landmines. A small hint of the miseries Marx went through is given in an 1866 letter to Engels when the carbuncles had encircled his crotch: 'The itching and scratching between my testis and posterior over the past 2½ years and the consequent peeling of the skin have been more aggravating to my constitution than anything else,' he revealed with just a tad too much information. Marx's preferred remedy was to go at every eruption with a razor until the blood and pus spurted forth. Engels advocated a less invasive strategy involving phosphate of lime – or, at least some arsenic. He even brought in advice from a new friend he had made in Manchester, the paediatrician Edward Gumpert, who 'has used it [arsenic] in one case of carbuncles and one of very virulent furunculosis and achieved a complete cure in approximately 3 months'.[99]

Engels's own recovery from glandular fever came less from medical alleviation than the economic crash ripping through Manchester in 1857. Seeing Peter Ermen and the other tree-frogs fouling their breeches as cotton prices tumbled was just the tonic. 'The general appearance of the Exchange here was truly delightful last week. The fellows are utterly infuriated by my sudden and inexplicable onset of high spirits.'[100] However, he was still fragile and the death in March 1860 of his father sent him into a relapse. What affected Engels was not so much the loss – his filial affection being notably tepid – but the ensuing family dispute over the Ermen & Engels finances. For Gottreid Ermen wasted no time in trying to lever Engels junior out of the firm. Relations quickly broke down at the Southgate office as Engels tried desperately to negotiate his future and hold on to his job. Up against the wily skills of Ermen, 'while physically so indisposed that I was incapable of making one single urgent decision in a sound frame of mind and with faculties unimpaired', he knew he would be unable to secure a decent settlement. Humiliatingly, he called in his brother Emil – 'clear of eye, firm of resolve and in full command of the situation' – to do the deal.[101]

However, whilst securing his English prospects, his brothers Rudolf and Hermann seized the moment when their mother fell ill with a suspected case of typhoid to carve Engels, the eldest son and heir, out of the more lucrative family business in Engelskirchen. 'For seven weeks now I've been living in a state of continual tension and excitation which has now reached a climax – never has it been so bad,' he wrote to Marx in May 1860.[102] Outmanoeuvred by his own brothers, Engels agreed to a wholly inequitable settlement – forcing him to cede all rights to the German component of Ermen & Engels – just to please his ailing mother. 'Mother dear, I have swallowed all this and much more for your sake. Not for anything in this world would I contribute in the smallest way towards embittering the evening of your life with family disputes over inheritance,' her first-born wrote lovingly. 'I might acquire a hundred other businesses, but never a second mother.' But he wanted her to know that 'it was extremely disagreeable for me to have to withdraw from the family business in this way'.[103] What Engels walked away with, in exchange for his brothers placing £10,000 in the Manchester firm, was a commitment to a partnership in Ermen & Engels by 1864. Given his enfeebled state, it was all he could hope for.

Incredibly, between housing the Burns sisters, clerking at Ermen & Engels and riding to the Cheshire Hounds, Engels did manage to make some significant contributions to the Marxist canon, beginning with 'historical materialism'. For Engels, this approach to studying the past – in which, as *The German Ideology* had first outlined, modes of production determined property relations and thence the broader contours of society – was one of Marx's seminal achievements. Marx had discovered, Engels wrote, 'the great law of motion of history': 'that the whole of history hitherto is a history of class struggles, that in all the manifold and complicated political struggles the only thing at issue has been the social and political rule of classes of society'; and consequently that 'the conception and ideas of each historical period are most simply to be explained from the economic conditions of life and from the social and political relations of the period, which are in turn determined by these economic conditions'.[104] Or, as Marx himself put it in his Preface to *A Contribution to the Critique of Political Economy*, 'The mode of production in material life determines the social, political and intellectual life processes in general . . . It is not the consciousness of men that determines their being, but, on the contrary, their social being that determines their consciousness.'[105] All of which helped to explain the phenomenon of false consciousness ('a consciousness that is spurious') whereby the true, materialist motives behind a political or intellectual shift in history – the Reformation, say, or Romanticism – were wrongly attributed to the autonomous role of ideas or religion rather than the indelible result of socio-economic forces. Similarly, to analyse political economy without revealing the true nature of exploitation, as Adam Smith and David Ricardo had, amounted to a partial understanding, a false conscious-ness of the present derived from a failure to delve below the political superstructure of ideas to the materialist base of society.

In *The German Ideology*, Marx and Engels had dissected capitalist society through a materialist lens. Now they turned their attentions to the past, arguing that it was a period's economic condition (the base) – its levels of technology, division of labour, means of production, etc. – that moulded its law, ideologies, religion, even art and science (the superstructure). Certainly, historical actors as lone individuals had free will and could still make choices. But what Marx and Engels were concerned with was mass phenomena and social change as the product of numerous individual decisions defined by structural economic conditions. 'The will is determined by passion or deliberation. But the levers which immediately determine passion or deliberation are of very different kinds.' Marx, again, had the more vivid phrasing. 'Men make their own history, but they do not make it just as they please,' he wrote in *The Eighteenth Brumaire of Louis Bonaparte*, 'they do not make it under circumstances chosen by themselves, but under circumstances directly found, given and transmitted from the past. The tradition of all the dead generations weighs like a nightmare on the brain of the living.'[106] Marx and Engels did away with Carlyle's 'great man' view of history for 'the fact that such and such a man, and he alone, should arise at a particular time in any given country, is, of course, purely fortuitous'.[107] In the absence of a Napoleon, someone else would simply have taken his place. Instead, class and class warfare (master/slave, lord/serf, capitalist/worker) – themselves products of historical phases in the development of the modes of production – became the defining prism for Marxist historiography. As Hegel had traced the march of Spirit through the pages of history, now Marx and Engels charted the rise and fall of class struggle within an equally teleological framework. History was a story of both bondage and liberation: progressive immiseration until a final, redemptive ending with the triumph of the proletariat and the end of class warfare. Indeed, the end of history itself.

Engels was an early practitioner of this discipline – not least because the approach was heavily influenced by the pioneering account of economic history he first provided in *The Condition of the Working Class in England*. But in his final years, he would worry that the strategy had been debased by lesser minds wanting to boil everything down to narrow economic causes. 'According to the materialist view of history, the determining factor in history is, *in the final analysis, the production and reproduction of actual life,*' he wrote in a letter to the Berlin student Joseph Bloc von Boegnik in 1890. 'More than that was never maintained by Marx or myself. Now if someone distorts this by declaring the economic moment to be the only determining factor, he changes that proposition into a meaningless, abstract, ridiculous piece of jargon.' In the same letter, Engels went on to introduce a new variable into the historical materialist template by suggesting that the superstructure – those ephemeral forms of law, philosophy and religion – somehow had a 'reciprocal influence' on the economic structure and then, in turn, on historical development: 'all these factors also have a bearing on the course of the historical struggles of which, in many cases, they largely determine the form. It is in the interaction of all these factors and amidst an unending multitude of fortuities ... that the economic trend ultimately asserts itself as something inevitable.' History, he now suggested in a significant reappraisal of Marxist historiographical thinking, was a lot more fluid than the materialist stereotype first posited. For the dialectical process was not simply a question of cause and effect, but the mutual interaction of opposites: so, while the economic context is 'ultimately decisive', he now thought politics, culture, even 'tradition', could play a part in shaping man's decisions and history. The past is 'made in such a way that the ultimate result is invariably produced by the clash of many individual wills of which each in turn has been made what it is by a wide variety of living conditions'. Such were the caveats introduced into the notion of historical materialism that it seemed almost neutered as a credible intellectual, let alone political, tool. By then aged seventy and firmly ensconced as Europe's leading communist seer, Engels was in reflective mode, conceding that the battle against idealist history might have earlier led him and Marx to overemphasize the materialist component. 'If some younger writers attribute more importance to the economic aspect than is its due, Marx and I are to some extent to blame. We had to stress this leading principle in the face of opponents who denied it, and we did not always have the time, space or opportunity to do justice to the other factors that interacted upon each other,' he wrote no doubt realizing that his historical theorem was in danger of becoming either a banal truism (in the sense that one should, of course, take some account of the economic context of a period) or an unattractive species of economic reductionism.[108]

In 1850s Manchester Engels was as yet untroubled by such nuances. Instead, he penned a positively bludgeoning work of historical materialism, *The Peasant War in Germany* (1850), which attempted to demonstrate, as he put it, 'the political structure of Germany at that time, the revolts against it, and the contemporary political and religious theories not as causes but as results of the stage of development of agriculture, industry, roads and waterways, commerce in commodities and money then obtaining in Germany'.[109] His aim, in fact, was an old-fashioned plundering of history (as well as the recent work of historian Wilhelm Zimmerman) to assist in current political battles – in this case, framing the 1520s peasant wars as inspiration for the German radicals discouraged by the 1848–9 setbacks. 'In the face of the slackening that has now ensued almost everywhere after two years of struggle, it is high time to remind the German people of the clumsy yet powerful and tenacious figures of the Great Peasant War.'[110] He did so with all the crassness of a first-grade materialist.

Ironically, the hero of Engels's history was a Carlylian 'great man', the 'magnificent figure' of the Protestant radical Thomas Müntzer. An itinerant mystic in the German chiliastic tradition, in the early 1520s Müntzer attempted to combine the radical wing of the Reformation with a traditional peasants' revolt to form a Christian League of the godly against the godless. His emphasis on the suffering of God, his stress on social equality alongside spiritual equality and his attack on the 'burgher reformation' of Martin Luther galvanized an impoverished peasantry angry at high clerical tithes and unpopular land reforms. Müntzer was trained in the priesthood, student at Wittenberg, many years a preacher in Allstedt, Prague and Zwickau, and his politics and vision of social reform were inextricably informed by his Protestant theology. But Engels was having none of that. Of course, 'the class struggles of those days were clothed in religious shibboleths', he conceded, but that was to forget the materialist underpinnings.[111] And Engels went on to recount in fastidious detail the economic fundamentals of early sixteenth-century German society and how class divisions – between the feudal nobility, the bourgeois Protestant reformers and the peasantry – dictated this revolutionary epoch. Yet only Müntzer was able to bring the plebeian elements to an understanding of their class consciousness. Properly understood, he was an embryonic Marxist agitator successfully marshalling the most advanced section of the peasantry towards class conflict. 'As Müntzer's religious philosophy approached atheism, so his political programme approached communism ... By the kingdom of God, Müntzer meant a society with no class differences, no private property and no state authority independent of, and foreign to, the members of society.'[112] But, sadly, he had got ahead of the modes of production: 'the worst thing that can befall the leader of an extreme party is to be compelled to assume power at a time when the movement is not yet ripe'.[113] Despite his heroic oratory and political organization, neither the feudal social system nor the agricultural economy were ready in early sixteenth-century Germany for revolutionary communism. And on the fields of Frankenhausen in eastern Germany in 1525, his rag-bag peasant army was put to the sword by Luther's allies – in this case, Engels's familiar refrain of the bourgeois 'stab in the back' being all too real.

The failures of 1525 and 1848–9 were not just a question of economic base and political superstructure being out of kilter, they were also the product of extensive military blunders. Thus the study of warfare became a second area of academic interest for Engels. Within months of moving to Manchester, he was writing to Joseph Weydemeyer in Frankfurt asking for some books on military history (which he later secured by buying up the library of a retired Prussian military officer) so that he could 'take it [military science] at least far enough to be able to join in theoretical discussion without making too much of a fool of myself'.[114] Warfare became Engels's 'special subject' and with typical rigour he immersed himself in studying the function of leadership, the nature of strategy and the role of topography, technology and army morale. And despite his theoretical aversion towards 'great men', Engels couldn't help himself when it came to the great generals. He admired Garibaldi and Napier with schoolboy ardour, but it was the Manichean clash between Napoleon and Wellington which truly bewitched him. Against every one of his materialist inclinations, Engels revered the hero of Waterloo – 'he would be a genius if common sense were not incapable of rising to the heights of genius' – and publicly lamented the passing of Britain's most reactionary general-politician in 1852.[115]

The years spent studying military history reaped dividends in the mid-1850s when the Crimean Peninsula became a miserable quagmire for Russian, British and French troops and Engels began a successful second career as one of England's leading armchair generals. He even hoped his military punditry might offer a route out of Manchester. When war broke out in 1854, Engels immediately fired off a job application to the editor of the *Daily News*. 'Perhaps I am not mistaken in supposing that at the present moment an offer to contribute to the military department of your paper may meet with some favour . . .' He went on to provide a short military résumé beginning with his service in the Prussian artillery before outlining his 'active service during the insurrectionary war in South Germany'. While he hoped the Russians would get a sound beating, he promised to mix his politics up 'as little as possible with military criticism'. But despite such assurances, the job never materialized. 'It's all off with the *The Daily News*,' he wrote angrily to Marx as he saw another lifeline out of Ermen & Engels slipping away. Everything seemed settled – the fee, the proofs, the terms – and then, 'today, the answer finally arrives saying that the articles are too professional' and he should approach a specialized, military journal. In a rare burst of pure fury, Engels blamed émigré gossip in London for belittling his military experience and queering his pitch; 'nothing was easier than to represent Engels, the MILITARY MAN, as no more than a former one-year volunteer, a communist and a clerk by trade, thus putting a stop to everything'.[116] All the horrible, huckstering indignity of his position flooded back to taunt him. But whilst there is little proof of any whispering campaign against him, there is abundant evidence (in the *Daily Tribune* ghostwriting he was forced to return to) of the dry, fact-heavy, over-analytical tone of his military journalism. His account of the charge of the Light Brigade, one of the most gory and dramatic moments in the entire campaign, is a case in point. After describing how 'the Earl of Cardigan led his light brigade up a valley opposite his position', Engels then very matter-of-factly recounts their obliteration. 'Of the 700 men that advanced, not 200 came back in a fighting condition. The light cavalry brigade may be considered destroyed, until reformed by fresh arrivals.'[117] It was small wonder the *Daily News* passed on such leaden copy.

Mercifully, Engels's style matured well and, in the late 1850s, the growing tension between Prussia, Austria and France over the issue of Italian unification allowed him to reenter the field with an anonymous pamphlet entitled *Po and Rhine*. With a deft overview of political intelligence, Alpine geography and war readiness, Engels outlined what Prussia's stance should be in the face of various military scenarios resulting from a Franco-Austrian war. 'Have read it all,' Marx wrote on receiving the paper, 'exceedingly clever; the political side is also splendidly done and that was damned difficult. The pamphlet will have a great success.'[118] And so it did, garnering adulatory coverage in the German and Austrian press and, it was rumoured, bought in bulk by General Giuseppe Garibaldi. Indeed, *Po and Rhine* was so well informed that the anonymous author was the object of numerous army headquarters' guessing games. 'Your pamphlet is considered in high, if not the highest, military circles (including, *inter alia*, that of Prince Charles Frederick) to be the product of an anonymous Prussian general,' a delighted Marx reported back to Engels.[119] But, frustratingly, the Manchester clerk remained unknown.

The looming hostilities between France and Austria were just one element of the dramatic diplomatic consequences of Bonaparte's rise to power. From the outset of his reign, Napoleon III was keen to extend the dominion of imperial France and, by the late 1850s (after a botched assassination attempt with tenuous British connections), some in the military staff thought Bonaparte's ambition might entail an English invasion. Following a highly jingoistic press campaign, on 12 May 1859 Britain's local volunteer corps – last called up to beat off uncle Napoleon I in 1804 – were re-formed to counter the new French threat. The tens of thousands of volunteers who signed up constituted a remarkable example of spontaneous, military association on behalf of the British people with 'Irish Corps', 'Artisans Corps', 'Borough Guards' and even a 'Press Guard' springing into action.[120] As Lord Palmerston erected a series of forts along the Solent (his so-called 'Follies') to prevent an invasionary fleet, Britain's parade grounds and parks resounded to the ill-disciplined step of the volunteer corps and their rousing anti-French songs. Engels had always been confident of the martial spirit of the British people – 'nowhere are there more hunters and poachers, i.e. semi-trained light infantry and sharpshooters' – and he enthusiastically endorsed this grassroots resistance movement against the reactionary Bonapartist regime.[121] He was especially supportive of the training the volunteers went through. For one thing the veteran of Baden had learned was the importance of logistical support, a proper chain of command and basic military skills. 'Experience teaches us that no matter how intense the patriotism of the masses may be, the fact that they, as a general thing, have no arms, and do not know how to use them if they had, renders their disposition in an emergency of very little value,' he wrote in an article for the *Daily Tribune* melodramatically entitled 'Could the French Sack London?'[122] But the authorities were well on their way to countering such a prospect with a highly effective inspection and drilling programme. 'All in all, the experiment is to be regarded, after three years, as completely successful,' Engels surmised in 1862. 'Almost without any expense to the Government, England has created an organized army of 163,000 men for the country's defence.'[123] This enthusiasm was tempered only when, on a railway journey from London back to Manchester, he 'had the added pleasure of a rifle-bullet shattering the window and flying through the carriage not 12 inches from my chest: some volunteer probably wished to demonstrate yet again that he ought not to be entrusted with a firearm'.[124]

However, Engels's support for the volunteers was another example of his occasional class confusion as an obsessive anti-Bonapartism got the better of his communist ideology. While the corps were indeed the first line of resistance against a French invasion, they were also an inherently reactionary force. For it was not the workers who signed up en masse; rather, only those persons who could furnish their own arms, 'defray all expenses' and be available for up to twenty-four days' training per year. This was a rich man's army led by local aristocrats and industrialists which working-class radicals in Rochdale and Oldham branded a 'Tory device' for diverting attention from political reform. The Preston Volunteer Corps was notable for its 'total absence of the working-class element', while the 40th (Manchester) Lancashire Rifle Volunteers was overwhelmingly dominated by 'gentlemen', tradesmen, clerks and artisans.[125] The volunteer corps were, in fact, another component of the bourgeois hegemony of mid-Victorian Britain: a middle-class voluntarist association subtly helping to embed a stratified class structure. Engels, who instinctively took the view of the officers' mess, was entirely deaf to this subaltern voice as his focus remained on military preparedness against the Bonapartist enemy.[126]

No doubt to the intense disappointment of the volunteers, Bonaparte's game-plan never involved crossing the Channel. Instead, he set himself on a collision course with continental Europe's other expansive power, Bismarck's Prussia. The Chancellor of the North German Confederation had already gone to war against Austria in 1866 over the convoluted question of Schleswig-Holstein and, by the end of the decade, a clash with France looked unavoidable. Engels had horribly misread Bismarck's character at the start of the Iron Chancellor's rise to power and, in a notable misjudgement, even thought Austria would win the 1866 tussle. But by July 1870 he no longer harboured any misapprehensions as to the bellicosity and strategic prowess of Bismarck. As it turned out, the Franco-Prussian war would prove the high point of Engels's career as a military pundit as, again and again, he called it right and so earned his Marx family nickname, 'General Staff' – or just 'The General'.

This time, he had a proper outlet for his views thanks to Marx setting him up as military commentator on the *Pall Mall Gazette*. 'I suppose I would like to write two articles weekly on the war for the *Pall Mall Gazette* for good cash payment,' was how Engels responded to the offer of work, still obviously smarting from the *Daily News* débâcle. So he began filing his copy from Manchester, charting the steady routing of Bonaparte's forces by the Prussians, based on reports from the front and a cross-section of European papers. But at the end of July Engels got a scoop on German troop manoeuvres thanks to the deployment of a cousin of his friend Edward Gumpert, 'a company commander in the 77th regiment', which led him accurately to predict that one of the first major engagements between French and Prussian forces would take place near Saarbrucken. 'Enclosed you will find the plan of the Prussian campaign. Please get a CAB immediately and take it round to the *Pall Mall Gazette*, so that it can come out on Monday evening. It will make me and the *Pall Mall Gazette* tremendously famous,' Engels the freelance hack, desperate for his exclusive, commanded Marx. 'Delay is now fatal for articles of this sort.' He was proved right when all the London papers – from *The Times* to the *Spectator* – followed up the story. 'If the war lasts a certain time, you will soon be acknowledged as the foremost military authority in London,' Marx replied with pride.[127] In fact, Engels's authority grew further when in August 1870 he forecast the defeat of the French troops at Sedan and the capture of Bonaparte.

There was more to Engels's analysis than an audit of firepower and strategy. Thanks to Lenin's later reprints of some *New York Daily Tribune* articles on insurrection, Engels is often regarded as a pioneer theorist of guerrilla warfare. He did, indeed, describe insurrection as 'an art quite as much as war' which had various, vague rules: once you enter upon it, 'act with the greatest determination, and on the offensive. The defensive is the death of every armed rising . . . surprise your antagonists while their forces are scattering, prepare new successes, however small but daily . . . force your enemies to a retreat before they can collect their strength against you; in the words of Danton, the greatest master of revolution policy yet known: *de l'audace, de l'audace, encore de l'audace!*'[128] But Engels remained at root deeply sceptical of guerrilla combat in part because of his unhappy Baden experience but largely because he favoured a materialist approach to military science.

The reason the British had bungled in the Crimea and why Bonaparte was being smashed by Bismarck was that their military edifices reflected their antiquated socio-economic fundamentals. To the materialist-minded Engels, warfare was another component of the superstructure – like religion, politics or culture – and, as such, it was determined by the economic base. 'Armaments, social composition, organization, tactics and strategy are above all dependent on the level of production and communications that has been reached.' It achieved its modern form in the years following the French Revolution when, he suggested, the rising bourgeoisie and the emancipated peasantry produced the money and men for the colossal war machines of the nineteenth century. As such, the development of various European armies constituted a history of those nations' socio-economic development – their class systems, technological capacity, property relations

– in which 'the influence of commanders of genius is at most restricted to adapting the methods of fighting to the new weapons and fighters'.[129] An obvious example was the modern battleship which was 'not only a product, but at the same time a specimen, of modern large-scale industry, a floating factory . . .'[130]

However, in the case of the British army, the state of its troops also exposed an outdated political system in all its hideous finery. 'Like old England herself, a mass of rampant abuses, the organization of the English army is rotten to the core,' he wrote of the Crimean forces before going on to list the selling of commissions, absence of professionalism, officer and soldier class divisions and unnatural enthusiasm for corporal punishment as all-too-prevalent in Her Majesty's regiments.[131] In materialist terms, the charge of the Light Brigade was less about Cardigan's individual failures in the field, and more the consequence of structural failings within the British elite as they failed to adjust to the modern industrial era. The incompetence, the needless casualties, 'the miserable leadership of the British army is the inevitable result of rule by an antiquated oligarchy'.[132]

That so much of the warfare Engels reported on in the mid-nineteenth century was imperial in origin naturally led him into thinking more broadly about the nature of colonialism. In the twentieth century this topic would prove amongst Marx and Engels's most dramatic political legacies as 'freedom fighters' from Mao to Ho Chi Minh to Castro embraced Marxism as an essential component of colonial liberation. However, just as with their conversion to communism, Marx and Engels came late to these ideas. While a critique of the brutality and jobbery of imperialism had been a staple part of British radicalism since Thomas Paine and William Cobbett, Engels had been more noteworthy for his high-handed dismissal of those 'non-historic' peoples – those ethnic rumps fighting the tide of history, as the Slavs had during the 1848 revolutions – who had been resisting colonial aggression. 'The conquest of Algeria is an important and fortunate fact for the progress of civilization,' he had written of the French push into Africa in 1848. 'And if we may regret that the liberty of the Bedouins of the desert has been destroyed, we must not forget that these same Bedouins were a nation of robbers.' We should remember, he went on, that 'the modern bourgeois, with civilization, industry, order and at least relative enlightenment following him, is preferable to the feudal lord or to the marauding robber'.[133] The benefits of capitalist imperialism – the forcible induction of backward peoples into the slipstream of history and thus setting them on their way to class consciousness, class struggle and all the rest – outweighed the unfortunate acts of invasionary forces. As Marx and Engels put it in the *Communist Manifesto*, 'The cheap prices of its [capitalism's] commodities are the heavy artillery with which it batters down all Chinese walls, with which it forces the barbarians' intensely obstinate hatred of foreigners to capitulate.'

This was certainly their view in regard to south Asia. 'Indian society has no history at all, at least no known history,' Marx wrote in an article which drew on the thinking of the political economists James Mill and Jean-Baptiste Say, as well as Hegel, to classify the people of the subcontinent as stationary, non-historic and in need of forcible liberation. 'What we call its history, is but the history of the successive intruders who founded their empires on the passive basis of that unresisting and unchanging society.' As such, the British Empire had to fulfil a double mission in India: 'one destructive, the other regenerating – the annihilation of old Asiatic society, and the laying of the material foundations of Western society in Asia'.[134] Similarly, Engels the mill owner spoke with positive relish of India's 'native handicrafts . . . finally being crushed by English competition'.[135] When it came to the Indian Mutiny (or first war of independence) of 1857, Marx was quick to place the account of atrocities in the context of decades of imperial abuse. 'However infamous the conduct of the Sepoys, it is only the reflex, in a concentrated form, of England's own conduct in India . . .'[136] But neither Marx nor Engels felt able to support fully the struggle for independence since the demands of economic progress and imperial modernity superseded any narrow Indian rights to self-governance.

By way of contradiction, for over a decade Marx and Engels had condemned the oppression of Poland by Germany and Russia as both a denial of democratic self-determination and an ugly chauvinism which undermined proletarian sensibility in the aggressor nations. 'A people that oppresses others cannot emancipate itself. The power it needs to oppress others is ultimately always turned against itself.'[137] The cause of Poland was the cause of the German working class, they declared; Poland would never shake off the shackles of feudalism until the German workers shed their colonial mindset and realized their common cause with the Polish people. At some point during the late 1850s, this belief in the shared fortunes of working-class solidarity and national liberation was generously extended from the 'old, cultured nations' of the West to non-European peoples. At the same time, Marx and Engels reinterpreted the economics of colonialism: no longer an aid to primitive capitalist accumulation, it was now seen as an iniquitous component of global capitalism whereby raw material and unprotected markets shored up the ruling classes of the metropole. Rather than a force of modernization, it was a tool of bourgeois hegemony. It was, after all, the push by British commerce into virgin colonial markets which had prevented the great crash of 1857 from spiralling into revolution.

As Engels abandoned his notion of non-historic peoples, he began to endorse the principle of colonial resistance. Whereas once he would have championed the advance of European civilization, by 1860 he supported the Chinese in their struggle against the British during the second opium war. Equally, he was shocked at the brutality of Governor Eyre's troops during the Morant Bay rebellion ('Every post brings news of worse atrocities in Jamaica. The letters from the English officers about their heroic deeds against unarmed niggers are beyond words') and sarcastically praised the grotesque atrocities of 'Belgium's humane, civilizing Association Internationale' in the African Congo.[138] In a total about turn, he even celebrated the resistance of 'Arab and Kabyle tribes' in Algeria (surely, the backward Bedouin of old?) whilst condemning France's 'barbarous system of warfare . . . against all the dictates of humanity, civilization, and Christianity'.[139] In countries which are 'inhabited by a native population, which are simply subjugated, India, Algiers, the Dutch, Portuguese, and Spanish possessions', Engels now advocated a programme of revolutionary working-class insurgency which would lead 'as rapidly as possible towards independence'. The U-turn complete, here was the pioneer Marxist vision of proletarian-led colonial resistance which would prove so inspirational in the twentieth century.[140]

But however assiduously Engels tried to cordon off his professional from his political life, there was a glaring contradiction in this newly radical colonial stance since his livelihood from Ermen & Engels made him a knowing accomplice in the commercial–imperial complex. The mid-Victorian boom in the Manchester cotton trade, which so enriched Engels personally, was fuelled by a foreign export market oriented around the colonies. Cheap, raw cotton came in from the slave plantations of the Southern United States and was re-exported as finished goods to the ends of Empire. By 1858–9, India was the destination of 25.8 per cent of British cotton exports (followed by America, Turkey and China) boosting profits and helping to act as a vital counterweight to the usual cyclical depression. Meanwhile, Indian calico remained banned from European nations by penal tariffs, while Asian markets were forced to accept English imports. In the aftermath of the 1857 Indian Mutiny, the final remnants of the subcontinent's cotton autonomy were crushed. 'The astounding growth of trade with India compelled the cotton industry to reject the anti-imperialism of [Richard] Cobden and to support the expensive military budget of India as well as the opium trade with China,' according to the cotton historian D. A. Farnie.[141] The mills and merchant world which Engels inhabited were a part of this political settlement. Inevitably, he blamed the misguided English proletariat for pocketing the imperial lucre – 'the workers gaily share the feast of England's monopoly of the world market and colonies' – but never quite dared question his own place within the colonial nexus.[142]

Such hypocrisies were of little matter for Engels in the grisly winter of 1863.

Dear Moor,
Mary is dead. Last night she went to bed early and, when Lizzy wanted to go to bed shortly before midnight, she found she had already died. Quite suddenly. Heart failure or an apoplectic stroke. I wasn't told this morning; on Monday evening she was still quite well. I simply can't convey what I feel. The poor girl loved me with all her heart.

Still weakened from his 1860 depression, the sudden death of Mary was a terrible blow. For all his womanizing and raffish exterior, he was a devoted partner to Mary. They had been together – off and on – for twenty years ever since the fresh-faced Young Hegelian first turned up in Manchester to work at the Salford mill. It was she who had provided his entrée into the Cottonopolis underworld and it was with her and her sort that Engels had felt most relaxed. For Engels, her death felt as though 'I was burying the last vestige of my youth'. But what was just as unsettling was Marx's response to Mary's passing. He began his commiseration letter appropriately enough by announcing how 'the news of Mary's death surprised no less than it dismayed me. She was so good-natured, witty and closely attached to you.' And, having cleared his throat, he then launched into an extraordinarily selfish tirade about his own bad luck – expensive school fees, rent demands – in a wholly misjudged jokey-cum-morose tone. 'It is dreadfully selfish of me to tell you about these *horreurs* at this time. But it's a homeopathic remedy. One calamity is a distraction from the other . . .' he wrote before signing off with a cheery '*Salut!*' Perhaps because the Marx family had never accepted Mary as a social equal or worthy companion for the General, he thought her death was of little instance. Engels was staggered by his callous disregard and it resulted in the greatest breach of their friendship. 'You will find it quite in order that, this time, my own misfortune and the frosty view you took of it should have made it positively impossible for me to reply to you any sooner,' he replied after a five-day hiatus. Even Engels's 'philistine acquaintances' – the ones he had spent years hiding Mary from – had displayed greater sympathy and affection than his dearest friend. 'You thought it a fit moment to assert the superiority of your "dispassionate turn of mind". *Soit!*'

Marx was suitably shamed. 'It was very wrong of me to write you that letter, and I regretted it as soon as it had gone off. However, what happened was in no sense due to heartlessness,' he responded a week later before explaining the letter's genesis and the wretched state of his household. However couched and contextualized, this constituted a rare apology from Marx and the bruised Engels accepted it with alacrity. 'Thank you for being so candid,' he wrote back. 'One can't live with a woman for years on end without being fearfully affected by her death . . . When your letter arrived she had not been buried . . . Your last letter made up for it and I'm glad that, in losing

Mary, I didn't also lose my oldest and best friend.' The row passed and to reaffirm their friendship Engels pilfered £100 from the accounts to bail Marx out.[143]

Engels was not one to dwell on the past: he forgave Marx and slowly got over Mary. By the autumn of 1864 there were a growing number of enquiries from Marx as to the health and happiness of 'Madame Lizzy'. It was a common enough Victorian practice for a man to move on from a deceased wife to her spinster sister and, at some point over those eighteen months, Engels did precisely that by upgrading Lizzy Burns from housekeeper to lover. We know much more about Lizzy than Mary mainly thanks to the 'staunch friendship' she struck up with Tussy. 'She was quite illiterate and could not read or write,' was how Tussy described her in a letter to Karl Kautsky, 'but she was as true, as honest, and in some ways as fine-souled a woman as you could meet . . . It is true she and Mary in later years both drank to excess: but my parents always said this was as much the fault of Engels as of the two women.'[144] Engels, meanwhile, chose to emphasize her Marxist qualities, describing her as of 'genuine Irish proletarian blood' and, in a touchy acknowledgement of her illiteracy, recounting how 'her passionate feelings for her class, a feeling that was inborn, was of immeasurably greater value to me . . . than anything of which the priggishness and sophistry of the "heddicated" and "sensitive" daughters of the bourgeoisie might have been capable'.[145] Both of these descriptions hint at the calming and enriching influence Lizzy had on Engels's life from the mid-1860s.

The first notable consequence of Lizzy succeeding the more prickly Mary was much improved relations between the Marx and Engels households. Whereas Marx himself had generally ignored the existence of Mary, his letters were now replete with 'my best compliments to Mrs Burns' and other such fripperies. Engels, in turn, was far more open about his companionship with Lizzy, calling her 'my dear spouse' and forwarding her best regards – and the odd shamrock – to Mrs Marx and the daughters. The Marx sisters – Laura, Jenny and Tussy – were the key to this blossoming friendship. From an early age Tussy had adored her 'uncle Angel': 'She looked upon him as a second father: the giver of good things. From him had flowed wine and stamps and jolly letters all her childhood.'[146] And now she included 'Auntie'

Lizzy within her embrace. In the summer of 1869 she spent a very jolly few weeks with Engels and Lizzy shopping, visiting the theatre and strolling around Manchester. 'I walk about a good deal with Tussy and as many of the family, human and canine, as I can induce to go with us,' as Engels described it to Jenny Marx. 'Tussy, Lizzy, Mary Ellen [or "Pumps", Lizzy's niece], myself and two dogs, and I am specially instructed to inform you that these two amiable ladies had two glasses of beer a-piece.'[147] For despite her later disparaging comments about Lizzy's alcoholism, Tussy was not averse to a drop herself and enjoyed a freedom of conduct in the Engels-Haus unknown in the more straitlaced Marx residence. On one summer's day it was so hot that, according to Tussy, the ladies of the house 'laid down on the floor the whole day, drinking beer, claret, etc.', which was how Engels found them when he came home: 'Auntie [Lizzy Burns], Sarah [Parker, a servant], me and Ellen [Pumps] . . . all lying our full length on the floor with no stays, no boots and one petticoat and a cotton dress on and that was all.'[148] Engels adored this louche, bohemian, female-dominated environment and often felt at his happiest around the various Marx daughters: officiating at their weddings, encouraging their journalism, revelling in their philosophical-intellectual wordplay, and giving their portraits pride of place on his 'chimney-piece'. Only this affection can explain Jenny Marx's ability to wheedle out of Engels his inner secrets in the form of the highly popular, mid-Victorian parlour game 'Confessions'. For a biographer, the result offers an invaluable mind-map:

Favourite virtue:	jollity;
in a man:	to mind his own business;
in a woman:	not to mislay things;
Chief characteristic:	knowing everything by half;
Idea of happiness:	Chateau Margaux 1848;
Idea of misery:	going to a dentist;
The vice you excuse:	excess of all sort;
The vice you detest:	cant;
Your aversion:	stuck-up, affected women;
The characters you most dislike:	[Charles Haddon] Spurgeon [influential Baptist preacher];

Favourite occupation:	chaffing and being chaffed;
Favourite hero:	'none';
Favourite heroine:	too many to name one;
Favourite poets:	Renard the Fox, Shakespeare, Ariosto;
Favourite prose:	Goethe; Lessing, Dr Samuelson;
Favourite flower:	bluebell;
Favourite colours:	any one not Aniline [cotton dye];
Favourite dishes:	'cold: salad; hot: Irish stew';
Favourite maxim:	not to have any;
Motto:	take it easy.[149]

As with Engels, part of the attraction of Lizzy for the Marx girls was her Irish proletarian blood. Tussy and Lizzy, according to Engels, liked to spend their Manchester evenings 'getting their tea ready . . . and after that there will be a reading of Irish novels which is likely to last until bedtime or nearly so, unless relieved by a bit of talk about the "convicted nation".'[150] Engels might mock this melancholy Emerald Isle *aligorning*, but with his love of Irish stew he was as susceptible to talk of 'the benighted isle' as any of the Marx sorority. For the two decades he had spent with the Burns sisters had turned his thinking on the Irish question in a far more sophisticated direction. The crass, racial caricature he had once offered of the Irish in *The Condition of the Working Class in England* – much of it drawn from Thomas Carlyle – gave way to a far more materialist reading of Anglo-Irish relations heavily enriched by his colonial theorizing.

Most importantly of all, Engels visited the island, travelling, in 1856, with Mary Burns from Dublin to Galway and, in 1869, returning with Lizzy and Tussy to tour the Wicklow mountains, Killarney and Cork. Always the scholar, Engels planned to write a history of Ireland and mugged up on his Gaelic before filling fifteen notebooks with jottings on the country's law, geography, geology, economics and folksongs. It was to be an epic account of the topographical, cultural and economic struggle of a nation and a people for whom he had developed an unexpected empathy. 'The weather, like the inhabitants, has a more acute character, it moves in sharper, more sudden contrasts; the sky is like an Irish woman's face: here also rain and sunshine succeed each other suddenly and unexpectedly and there is none of the grey English boredom,' was one of the more purple passages of Engels's aborted history.[151]

Perhaps because they had yet to let him down, he felt far more passionately about the condition of the exploited Irish peasantry than about the English working class. 'I had never imagined famine could be so tangibly real,' he wrote during his 1856 trip. 'Whole villages are deserted; in between the splendid parks of the smaller landlords, virtually the only people still living there, lawyers mostly. Famine, emigration and clearances between them have brought this about.' The Westminster-induced potato famine followed by the 'clearances' – 'the mass eviction of the Irish from house and home' – had produced a pasturage economy which decimated the agricultural proletariat. For unexplained reasons, Engels did not regard this as a progressive, modernizing intervention of a greater nation upon a backward, non-historic people (à la Mexico and America, Algeria and France), but rather unwarranted subjection. Indeed, Engels argued that Ireland had been reduced to the state 'of a completely wretched nation' by systematic English plundering stretching back to the Norman Conquest.[152] And whereas previously such aggression had been sanctioned when it came to the Magyars and the Slavs or the Americans and Mexicans, in the case of the Gaels it was somehow different. Indeed, what made the Irish people heroic was their continued, if faltering, resistance to this English imperialism.

Long before Marx came to codify his thinking on Ireland and English radicalism, Engels connected the British class structure with its imperial suzerainty across the Irish Sea. 'Ireland may be regarded as the earliest English colony,' whereby 'the English citizen's so-called freedom is based on the oppression of the colonies'.[153] The riches and power Ireland offered, from the plantations of Queen Elizabeth I to the vast estates of the Victorian landowners, immeasurably strengthened the hand of the imperial ruling classes. It enriched England's leading nobility and provided a vital kick-start towards industrialization. 'Ireland is the bulwark of the English landed aristocracy,' as Marx later put it. 'The exploitation of this country is not simply one of the main sources of their material wealth; it is their greatest moral power. Ireland is, thus, the grand moyen by which the English aristocracy maintains its domination in England itself.' In addition, the gutting of the Irish economy led hundreds of thousands of immigrants to flood Britain's industrial cities where they undercut wages, impoverished the working class and diverted the revolutionary spirit of the proletariat down chauvinist blind alleys. 'In relation to the Irish worker, he [the English worker] feels himself to be a member of the ruling nation and therefore, makes himself a tool of the aristocrats and capitalists against Ireland, thus strengthening their domination over himself.'[154] Just as the progress of the German working class depended upon the liberation of Poland, so revolution in Britain depended upon Irish independence. Ireland was England's weakest point, the loss of which would start the unravelling of the British Empire and the unleashing of class war in England.

But, as ever, the political conditions were not yet quite right. Founded in March 1858, the Irish Republican Brotherhood or 'Fenians' (a reference to the Fianna army in the medieval saga of Fionn Mac Cumhaill) were an Irish-American secret society committed to the violent overthrow of British rule and the establishment of a democratic and independent Irish republic. The Fenians were led by the sons of middle-income farmers, shopkeepers and the small-town petits-bourgeois, and their 'central motivation revolved round the view of England as a satanic power upon earth, a mystic commitment to Ireland, and a belief that an independent Irish republic, "virtually" established in the hearts of men, possessed a superior moral authority'.[155] What this led to in practice was a series of doomed 'risings' easily quelled by the British authorities, followed by a campaign of terrorist attacks, arson and sabotage on the mainland. The most notorious were the blowing up of Clerkenwell Prison – with the death of twelve innocent people – and the daring rescue of Fenian activists Thomas Kelly and Timothy Deasy from a Manchester police van in September 1867. Unfortunately, Sergeant Charles Brett was killed in the struggle and, in the following days, police swooped on five suspected Fenians who were then swiftly convicted of his murder.

All other things being equal, this was exactly the kind of self-defeating terrorism which Marx and Engels abhorred: an insurrectionary vanguard getting ahead of the material conditions and consequently endangering the broader social revolution. But that was to ignore the influence of Lizzy, who had already shifted Engels's thinking on the non-historic question. She was, as Engels later described her, 'a revolutionary Irishwoman' and active partisan of the Fenian movement. Marx's son-in-law, Paul Lafargue, described her being 'in continual touch with the many Irishmen in Manchester and always well informed of their conspiracies'. He even suggested that 'more than one Fenian found hospitality in Engels's house and it was thanks to his wife that the leader in the attempt to free the condemned Sinn Feiners [Kelly and Deasy] on their way to the scaffold was able to evade the police'.[156] It was a story repeated by Max Beer, who described Engels's house 'as the safest refuge of the Fenian fugitives from justice; the police had no inkling of their hiding-place'.[157] There is little supporting evidence to suggest Lizzy was involved in the 1867 prison-van break, but their house on Hyde Road was tantilizingly close to the railway arch where, as Engels had it, 'the great Fenian liberation battle was enacted'. Maybe, just maybe, Lizzy and Engels helped some of the forty-strong Fenian mob slip away.

As a hapless terrorist outfit built around romantic nationalism, what the Irish Republican Brotherhood needed above all was a martyrology, and the subsequent execution of three of the five convicted Fenians – William Allen, Michael Larkin and Michael O'Brien – provided just that. Engels correctly predicted it would 'transform the liberation of Kelly and Deasy into an act of heroism, such as will now be sung at the cradle of every Irish child in Ireland, England and America. The Irish women will see to that as surely as did the Polish womenfolk.'[158] Despite the much needed self-righteous halo it promised, the hanging of the three 'Manchester martyrs' sent Lizzy, Tussy and Jenny into collective mourning. 'Jenny goes in black since the Manchester execution, and wears her Polish cross on a *green* ribbon,' Marx reported. 'I need hardly tell you that black and green are the prevailing colours in my house, too,' Engels slightly wearily replied.[159]

The response of the Manchester working class to the cause of Irish liberation was very different from that of the emotional Marx daughters. Rather than uniting with the IRB and realizing their common cause against an exploitative ruling class, the Manchester proletariat responded to the Fenian 'atrocities' with a wave of anti-Irish sentiment which had been building since Irish immigration into

Lancashire had peaked in the early 1860s. When this combined with a broader distaste for the city's liberal millocracy in the wake of their parsimonious response to the cotton famine, it delivered an extraordinary Tory revival just in time for the newly enfranchised urban working class to cast their vote in the 1868 elections. For Engels, this was the final indignity: the promise of Manchester – the citadel of proletarian revolution – had vanished for ever. 'What do you say about these elections in the factory districts?' he asked Marx indignantly. 'The proletariat has once again made an awful fool of itself. Manchester and Salford return 3 Tories against 2 Liberals . . . Everywhere the proletariat are the rag, tag and bobtail of the official parties, and if any party has gained strength from the new voters, it is the Tories . . .' The raw psephology of the situation was appalling: 'it cannot be denied that the increase in working-class votes has brought the Tories more than their simple percentage, and has improved their relative position'. Ireland, and the Irish question, had emboldened not eviscerated the English class structure.[160]

In 1868 such setbacks could be swallowed since the years of storm, stress and accursed commerce had finally revealed their fruit. 'The day that manuscript is sent off, I shall drink myself to kingdom come,' Engels had promised Marx in 1865.[161] Inevitably, it would take another couple of years before the first volume of *Das Kapital* – 'this economy shit' – was ready for the printers. But when it appeared, the relief was tangible. The sacrifice, the boredom, the barren frustration of the Manchester years had been worth it. 'I am exceedingly gratified by this whole turn of events, firstly, for its own sake, secondly, for your sake in particular and your wife's, and thirdly, because it really is time things looked up,' Engels wrote in a heartfelt letter to Marx. 'There is nothing I long for so much as for release from this vile commerce, which is completely demoralizing me with all the time it is wasting. For as long as I am in it, I am good for nothing else . . .' 'Without you, I would never have been able to bring the work to a conclusion,' Marx wrote back with a guilty air to his steadfast funder in May 1867, 'and I can assure you it always weighed like a nightmare on my conscience that you were allowing your fine energies to be squandered and to rust in commerce, chiefly for my sake, and into the bargain, you had to share all my *petites misères* as well.'[162] But he chose not to dedicate the work to Engels. Instead, Marx gave that honour to Wilhelm Wolff, who had died in 1864 and left him a very welcome £843.

Engels's contribution to Marx's masterwork had been above and beyond the monetary. He had provided many of the book's core insights into the actual workings of capital and labour (to which Marx added a generous plundering of Blue Book material and official reports) as well as its essential philosophy. And now Engels set to work with his blue pencil on the gargantuan German manuscript which arrived in the summer of 1867. He suggested a barrage of edits, clarifications and rewrites. 'The train of thought is continually interrupted by illustrations and the illustrated point never resumes at the end of the illustration, so that one always leaps from the illustration of one point straight into the exposition of another point. That is dreadfully tiring and even confusing if one is not very attentive,' he rightly noted of Marx's often inchoate style.[163] At times it felt too rushed – 'the piece you have inserted on Ireland was done in the most fearful haste, and the material is not properly knocked into shape at all'[164] – and in other passages too angry, 'Sheet two in particular has the marks of your carbuncles rather firmly stamped upon it . . .'[165] Luckily, Engels was one of the *very* few people from whom Marx was willing to accept criticism.

The result though was a triumph: the foundation text of scientific socialism and one of the classics of Western political thought. Marx combined in *Das Kapital*, in the apposite summary of Robert Skidelsky,

a dialectical theory of historical stages, a materialist theory of history (in which the struggle of classes replaces Hegel's struggle of ideas in humanity's ascent), an economic and moral critique of capitalist civilization (embodied in the exploitation and alienation theses), an economic demonstration that capitalism was bound to collapse (because of its contradictions), a call to revolutionary action, and a prediction (perhaps more an assurance) that communism would be the next—and final—historical stage.[166]

At the intellectual crux of *Das Kapital* was the theory of surplus value (which Engels regarded as Marx's second monumental discovery after historical materialism) which was the alchemist's equation for explaining precisely how class exploitation occurs in a capitalist economy. For Marx, the enforced sale of the worker's labour-power for less than the exchange-value of the commodities produced by his labour-power was the ratchet by which the bourgeoisie were progressively enriched and the proletariat steadily alienated from its own labour and humanity. In essence, Marx argued that, if in six hours the worker was producing enough output that could be exchanged to cover his subsistence needs, then the remaining six hours' output, of a twelve-hour day, was being expropriated by the capitalist for his profit. This exploitative mode of production – the necessary result of systems of private property – was unnatural, historically transient and violently inequitable. The great hope of liberation promised by *Das Kapital* was that this form of capitalist iniquity would be destroyed by a class-conscious proletariat.

Along with the constant diminishing number of the magnates of capital, who usurp and monopolize all advantages of this process of transformation grows the mass of misery, oppression, slavery, degradation, exploitation; but with this too grows the revolt of the working class, a class always increasing in numbers and disciplined, united, organized by the very mechanism of the process of capitalist production itself. The monopoly of capital becomes a fetter upon the mode of production, which has sprung up and flourished along with and under it. Centralization of the means of production and socialization of labour at last reach a point where they become incompatible with their capitalist integument. This integument is burst asunder. The knell of capitalist private property sounds. The expropriators are expropriated.

But the dry theory of surplus value was never going to be enough to popularize the communist cause, so Marx embellished the book with all the hellish detail of Victorian factory life which Engels had provided. 'They mutilate the labourer into a fragment of man, degrade him to the level of an appendage of a machine, destroy every remnant of charm in his work and turn it into a hated toil,' was how he described the industrial process of 'Capitalist Accumulation'; '. . . they transform his life-time into working-time, and drag his wife and child beneath the wheels of the Juggernaut of capital'.[167] And yet one always had to remember that the funds which kept Marx afloat through

Das Kapital's long literary gestation, the money that powered this excoriating prose, came ultimately from the very same exploited labour-power – the mill-hands of Ermen & Engels, that juggernaut of capital.

Since its first appearance, this vast tome has been subject to numerous different readings by different audiences – as a work of economics, political science, satire, literary Gothic, sociology and all or none of the above. That tradition of multiple interpretations begins with Engels. Having sacrificed seventeen years of his life for this opus he was determined to ensure it did not succumb to the usual conspiracy of silence. 'I am convinced that the book will create a real stir from the moment it appears,' he wrote to Marx in 1867, 'but it will be very necessary to help the enthusiasm of the scientifically-inclined burghers and officials on to its feet and not to despise petty stratagems . . .' Engels was always keen on petty stratagems and, with all the cunning of a seasoned PR, he opened up his contact book to generate some decent coverage. 'I hope you will be able to bring Karl Marx's book to the attention of the German-American press and of the workers,' he wrote to his fellow 1848 veteran Hermann Meyer then involved in the American communist movement. 'The German press is still observing complete silence in respect of *Capital*, and it really is of the greatest importance that something should be said,' he complained to Ludwig Kugelmann in Hanover. 'We have a moral obligation to damned well get these articles into the papers, and as near simultaneously as possible, especially the European ones, and that includes the reactionary ones.'[168]

In the end, he realized he would have to do it himself. 'Do you think I should attack the thing from the bourgeois point of view, to get things under way?' he asked Marx.[169] Both men agreed that the best thing to attract attention was 'to get the book denounced' and create a journalistic firestorm. All the modern panoply of media manipulation and literary salesmanship was put to work by Marx's most gifted publicist as Engels churned out review after review for the English, American and European press. For *Die Zukunft*, he assumed a lofty academic tone – 'we acknowledge that we regard the new introduced category of surplus-value as an advance'; for the *Staats-Anzeiger für Württemberg*, a more commercial slant – 'German businessmen . . . will here find a copious source of instruction and will thank us for having directed their attention to it'; for the *Beobachter*, a suitably patriotic interpretation – 'we may say that it is one of those achievements which do honour to the German spirit'; and for the *Demokratisches Wochenblatt*, his own true voice – 'As long as there have been capitalists and workers on earth no book has appeared which is of as much importance for the workers as the one before us. The relation between capital and labour, the axis on which our entire present system of society turns, is here treated scientifically for the first time.'[170]

Engels's contract with Gottfried Ermen was due to expire in June 1869. Both men wanted this uncomfortable partnership to end. The question was, at what price? Characteristically, Engels's first thoughts were for Marx's family finances and the current state of his debts. 'Can you manage with £350 for your *usual* regular needs for a year,' he asked his friend as he opened severance negotiations with Ermen. The aim was to reach a settlement which would secure himself a suitable *rentier* income and the Marx family a healthy annual subsidy. As usual, it was a stressful, 'murky business' trying to pin down shifty Gottfried Ermen, and Engels was forced to walk away with a less than optimal settlement. 'If I had wished to drive things with G. Ermen to extremes, that is, risk a breach, and had then had to start something else, I think I could have squeezed out about £750 more,' he explained to his brother Hermann. 'But I had absolutely no interest in being tied to jolly old commerce for about another ten years.'[171] Ermen knew his reluctant business partner was never going to set up a competitor firm and so drove a miserly bargain, leaving Engels, in the end, with a lump sum of £12,500 (something approaching £1.2 million in today's terms). For a partnership in such a successful, multinational business it was not a large amount. But, as Gottfried predicted, Engels would take any price. 'I was with Engels when he reached the end of his forced labour and I saw what he must have gone through all those years,' Tussy wrote of Engels's last day at work,

I shall never forget the triumph with which he exclaimed 'for the last time!' as he put on his boots in the morning to go to his office. A few hours later we were standing at the gate waiting for him. We saw him coming over the little field opposite the house where he lived. He was swinging his stick in the air and singing, his face beaming. Then we set the table for a celebration and drank champagne and were happy.[172]

Engels was indeed delighted. 'Hurrah! Today *doux commerce* is at an end, and I am a free man ... Tussy and I celebrated my first free day this morning with a long walk in the fields.'[173]

Shedding the misery of commercial life – with all the personal and ideological compromises it had entailed – saw Engels reborn at the age of forty-nine. 'Today is the first day of my freedom,' the still dutiful son wrote to his mother. 'This morning, instead of going into the gloomy city, I walked in this wonderful weather for a few hours in the fields; and at my desk, in a comfortably furnished room in which you can open the windows without the smoke making black stains everywhere, with flowers on the windowsills and trees in front of the house one can work quite differently than in my gloomy room in the warehouse, looking out on to the courtyard of an ale-house.'[174] With his newly recovered liberty, Engels was even starting to enjoy his Manchester life as he worked in his study, perused the newspapers at his club, and walked the Cheshire countryside with Lizzy and the dogs. However, if Gottfried Ermen was not sorry to see the back of his troublesome partner, there were some colleagues disappointed at the departure. A little note in the Amsterdam archives from Henry Bayley, an Ermen & Engels clerk, reveals that Engels was not always the bullying ogre of office lore. 'I sincerely regret the loss of your kindness amongst us and my inability to show you my appreciation of the same,' Mr Bayley wrote to his erstwhile employer. 'I cannot help trespassing further to say how much I feel indebted to you for the many acts of kindness shown to me while working under you.'[175]

The leisured pursuits of a retired mill owner in the Manchester suburbs were never going to sustain Engels for long. After Lizzy had one too many rows with what remained of her family, the couple decided to move to London in late summer 1870. 'In the last eighteen years, I have been able to do as good as nothing *directly* for our cause, and have had to devote myself to bourgeois activities,' Engels had earlier apologized to his fellow '48 veteran Friedrich Lessner. All that was now set to change. Having endured the political abstinence of his wilderness years, Engels was hungry to return to Marx's side on the ideological barricades. 'It will always be a pleasure for me to bash the same enemy on the same battlefield together with an old comrade like you,' he promised Lessner.[176] Engels the political street-brawler was once again ready for action.

7

'The Grand Lama of the Regent's Park Road'

Acclimatizing to London life was not easy for Engels. 'One accustoms oneself only with difficulty to the gloomy atmosphere and the mostly melancholy people, to the seclusion, the class divisions in social affairs, to the life in closed rooms that the climate prescribes.' What is more, 'one has to tone down somewhat the spirit of life brought over from the Continent, to let the barometer of zest for life drop from 760 to 750 millimetres until one gradually begins to feel at home'. Yet this low-skied, pea-souped capital had its benefits, as 'one finds oneself slowly blending in and discovers that it has its good side, that the people generally are more straightforward and trustworthy than else-where, that for scholarly work no city is so suitable as London, and that the absence of annoyances from the police compensates for a great deal'.[1]

In fact, London proved a perfect home for Engels as he settled back into his favoured role as Marx's adviser and all-purpose propagandist. Immediately elected on to the General Council of the International Working Men's Association (commonly known as the International), Engels got to work behind the scenes enforcing the doctrine of *Das Kapital* and stamping out ideological deviation. As the International's corresponding secretary for Belgium, then Italy, Spain, Portugal and Denmark, Engels was placed in *de facto* charge of co-ordinating the proletarian struggle across the continent. His passion for low politics, dark skills at organization and rapid ability to churn out a barbed polemic made him the ideal choice to keep the European Left's war-ring factions in order. In the words of the Austrian communist Victor Adler, he proved himself the 'greatest tactician' of international socialism.

What was more, he masterminded this messy, hydra-headed machine all from his study at No. 122 Regent's Park Road, in the now exceptionally expensive north London village of Primrose Hill. It had all been arranged for Engels by Jenny Marx. Sounding a little like Margaret Schlegel on first encountering Howards End, an excited Mrs Marx had written to Engels in Manchester in July 1870, 'I have now found a house, which charms all of us because of its wonderful open situation.' She knew exactly what Engels would need for his move south: four, ideally five bedrooms; a study; two living rooms; a kitchen; and nothing on too steep a gradient given Lizzy's asthma. 'It is next to Primrose Hill, so all the front rooms have the finest and openest view and air. And round about, in the side streets, there are shops of all sorts, so your wife will be able to buy everything herself.' The interior of the house boasted an impressive kitchen and a 'very spacious bathroom with large bathtub'. Jenny, who had clearly not yet abandoned her bourgeois predilection for property, thought it best 'if your wife came with you right away and saw for herself. You know we shall be very happy to have her with us.'[2]

Ensconced in Regent's Park Road, Engels was back where he wanted to be, openly living with Lizzy (now that the social mores of bourgeois Manchester were of no concern) and a good ten-minute walk from Marx and his family. Close, but not too close. Above all, Engels had returned to the political firmament, side by side with his lifelong collaborator fighting for the communist cause. As their ideas circulated through the rapidly industrializing regions of Europe and socialist parties formed where the authorities allowed, the opinions of 'the old Londoners' or 'the two spiritual fathers', as they became known, proved ever more influential.

'Every day, every post, brought to his house newspapers and letters in every European language,' recalled Paul Lafargue, 'and it was astonishing how he found time, with all his other work, to look through, keep in order, and remember the chief contents of them all.' Engels's extraordinary linguistic ability – from Russian to Portuguese to Romanian (as well as regional dialects such as Provençal and Catalan) – meant that as corresponding secretary of the International he made it a point of honour to reply in the tongue in which he had been addressed. In addition, Engels was in charge of editing and

authorizing the official imprints of the Marxian canon. 'When anything of his writings, or of Marx's writings, was to be translated into
other languages, the translator always sent the translations to him for
supervision and correction . . .' Alongside the correspondence came
the familiar flotsam and jetsam of émigrés, exiles, chancers and acolytes to whom Engels unfailing opened his door. 'It was like a little
Tower of Babel business,' according to Tussy's lover Edward Aveling.
'For not only those of us that were really of his family were present,
but the Socialists from other countries made 122 Regent's Park Road
their Mecca.'[3]

Primrose Hill had been subject during the preceding thirty years to
exactly the kind of class-based urban planning Engels had chronicled
in *The Condition of the Working Class in England*. Previously a
secluded district of cottages and farms on the edges of London, it had
gained a rough, seedy reputation thanks to its proximity to Chalk
Farm Tavern – a notorious heavy drinking, whoring and fighting
shop. But gentrification called in the mid-nineteenth century as Lord
Southampton and the Eton College estate started to lay out a model
village, transforming open fields into a descending array of detached
and semi-detached villas followed by a series of terraced streets. Plans
to build to the top of Primrose Hill itself were only foiled when the
Crown Estate purchased the plot and transformed it from an open
grazing pasture to an ordered, paved and planted space for respectable
middle-class recreation. With blue-chip developers and a well-tended
park (where the primroses still bloomed), it was no wonder the area
quickly became 'a pleasantly leafy, prosperous but not ostentatious,
middle-class district'.[4]

Alongside the developers, the railway had also been at work shaping
Engels's new neighbourhood. In Manchester, it had been the land
grab of the Leeds–Liverpool line which dictated the contours of the
city; in Primrose Hill it was London–Birmingham. The track from
Euston station (named after a Suffolk village on one of Lord Southampton's estates) to Birmingham New Street created a northern and
eastern boundary which was complemented on the south by the
Regent's Canal. Behind the streets' fashionable, neo-Regency veneer
was a London suburb hammered into shape by the messy, dirty forces

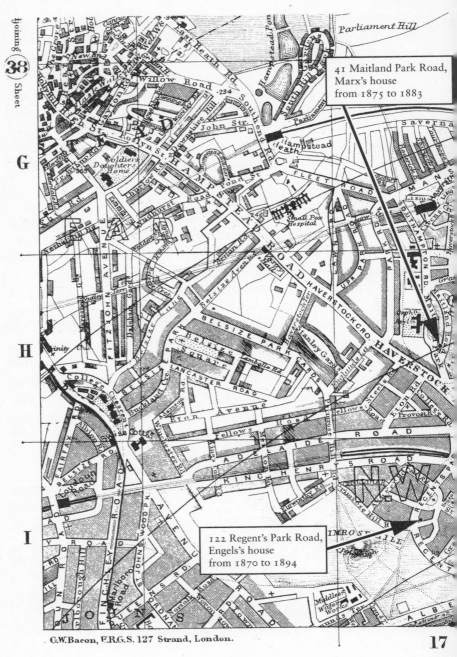

41 Maitland Park Road, Marx's house from 1875 to 1883

122 Regent's Park Road, Engels's house from 1870 to 1894

G.W.Bacon, F.R.G.S. 127 Strand, London.

17

Marx and Engel's north London milieu, from an A–Z of 1888.

Junction Rd.

Mercers

GH

TUFNELL PARK

Gospel Oak

RD

Highgate Rd.

KENTISH

FORTESS ROAD

KNOCK

CARLETON ROAD

Hillrop Road

crescent

Crescent

Ospringe Rd.

Countess Rd.

TOWN

LEIGHTON ROAD

162

HUNGER

Peckw'r St.

Islip St.

Lady Margaret Rd.

Prince of Wales

GRA

S

Fortess Rd.

Gaisford St.

Osney

Busby

Patshull Rd.

Bartholomew Road

Clarence Road

CAMD

Lawford Rd.

Bartholomew Rd.

Camden

Rousden

Park

KENTISH TOWN ROAD

ROCHESTER RD.

Camden Square

PRINCE OF WALES

VICTORIA ROAD

East Rd.

Prince

Clarence Rd.

CHALK FARM RD

SAINT PAULS RD

Brecknock

Bonny St.

Wrotham Rd.

CAMD

EN

MIDLAND

RAILWAY

GREAT

RAILWAY DEPOT

James

Union

Gloucester

Wellington

CAMDEN

TOWN

HIGH

Georges St.

Hamilton St.

ST.

KING'S

CROSS

ROAD

Albert St.

HAM

ROAD

St Pancras

of industrialization. And the men and women behind those industries wafted, like the filthy smog and steam from the Midlands trains, across the tracks and into the neighbourhood itself. Bordering the railway lines, along the edge of the terraced streets, were vast railway sheds for stoking, refuelling and cleaning the trains. Nearby stood the iconic Round House at Chalk Farm for major engineering works. This was a noisy, stinking, eye-watering environment where 'flakes of soot often an inch across, like black gossamer lace, constantly floated about, settling everywhere'. With the trains came hundreds of engineers, signalmen, lamp men, porters, shunters and cleaners who provided tenants for the subdivided houses and thirsty custom for the plentiful pubs (which Engels, with his predilection for bottled Pilsener, tended to avoid).[5]

Today, Engels's four-storey, terraced home still stands at 122 Regent's Park Road opposite the Queens pub and diagonally across the entrance to Primrose Hill. Thanks to the efforts of local resident Jenny Hutt (daughter of leading Communist Party activist Allen Hutt) a 1971 blue plaque from the Greater London Council marks the spot describing Engels rather anodynely as a 'political philosopher'. The house itself was converted into flats during the 1960s, but walking around it one can still get a feel of how it worked in the 1870s, with the kitchen and bathroom in the basement, a morning room and dining room on the ground floor separated off by double doors. The first floor – which most Victorians would have used as their drawing room – was converted into Engels's vast study: an airy, well-lit studio with a polished Norwegian pine floor, ceiling-high bookcases, a magisterial fireplace and tall French windows looking out on to the noisy bustle of Regent's Park Road and beyond to Primrose Hill. Engels was characteristically fastidious about his study. 'The rooms were more like reception rooms than a scholar's study,' according to one visitor.[6] The succeeding two floors were given up to bedrooms for himself, Lizzy, maidservants, Pumps the niece and any passing houseguest. One such guest was the German Social Democrat Eduard Bernstein, who was to become a regular at Regent's Park Road during the 1880s. 'Upstairs we soon began a political conversation, which often assumed a very lively character,' he recalled of a rumbustious evening at No. 122. 'Engels' stormy temperament, which concealed such a truly noble character, and many good qualities, revealed itself to us as unreservedly as the joyous conception of life peculiar to the Rhineland. "Drink, young man!" And with these words, in the midst of a violent dispute, he kept on refilling my glass with Bordeaux, which he always had in the house.'[7]

Despite his bohemian inclinations, Engels could never quite shake off his Calvinist work ethic. Breakfast would be followed by a couple of hours of study and correspondence before the highlight of the day: his visit to Marx in Maitland Villas. 'Engels came to see my father every day,' Tussy remembered. 'They sometimes went for a walk together but just as often they remained in my father's room, walking up and down, each on his side of the room, boring holes with his heel as he turned on it in his corner ... Frequently they walked up and down side by side in silence. Or again, each would talk about what was then mainly occupying him until they stood face to face and laughed aloud, admitting that they had been weighing opposite plans for the last half hour.'[8] When they did go for a walk, it was a brisk, discursive hike of 'one and a half German miles' up and around Hampstead Heath where the Rhinelanders breathed in 'more ozone than in the whole of Hanover'. Engels would then return to Primrose Hill to send off any remaining letters by the 5.30 p.m. post before having an early evening dinner with Lizzy at 7 p.m., then more reading, drinking and chatting after which a late 'supper' and bed around 2 a.m.

This regimented week-day existence all changed of a Sunday. 'On Sundays, Engels would throw open his house. On those puritanical days when no merry men can bear life in London Engels's house was open to all, and no one left before 2 or 3 in the morning,' recalled the communist exile August Bebel. All and sundry – 'socialists, critics and writers. Anybody who wanted to see Engels could just go' – were welcome at No. 122 for an afternoon of wine-fuelled discussion, stomach lined by 'a fairly "liberal" helping of meat and salad'. The house speciality was a springtime bowl of *Maitrank* – a May wine flavoured with woodruff. There would be German folk songs round the piano or Engels reciting his favourite poem, *The Vicar of Bray* (which he later translated into German for the Social Democrat songbook *Vorwärts*), while the cream of European socialism – from Karl

Kautsky to William Morris to Wilhelm Liebknecht to Keir Hardie – paid court to the man whom the British Marxist Henry Hyndman called the 'Grand Lama of the Regent's Park Road'. It was just about as far as you could get from the seedy image of émigré, anarchist nihilism – of dirty pubs, furtive meetings and Soho porn shops – which Joseph Conrad conjured up in *The Secret Agent*. The lights were on, the shutters open, and the Pilsener flowing. Election nights to the German Reichstag were a particularly riotous affair. 'Then Engels laid in a huge cask of special German beer, laid on a special supper, invited his very intimates. Then, as the telegrams came pouring in from all parts of Germany far into the night, every telegram was torn open, its contents read aloud by the General, and if it was victory we drank, and if it was defeat we drank.'[9] But the social pinnacle of the year was Christmas, which Engels the noted atheist celebrated with Prince Albert-like ardour. 'Christmas was kept by Engels after the English fashion, as Charles Dickens had so delightfully described it in *The Pickwick Papers*,' according to Bernstein's memoirs.

The room is decorated with green boughs of every kind, between which, in suitable places, the perfidious mistletoe peeps forth, which gives every man the right to kiss any person of the opposite sex who is standing beneath it or whom he can catch in passing. At table the principal dish is a mighty turkey, and if the exchequer will run to it this is supplemented by a great cooked ham. A few additional attractions – one of which, a sweet known as tipsy-cake, is, as the name denotes, prepared with brandy or sherry – make way for the dish of honour, the plum-pudding, which is served up, the room having been darkened, with burning rum. Each guest must receive his helping of pudding, liberally christened with good spirits, before the flame dies out. This lays a foundation which may well prove hazardous to those who do not measure their consumption of the accompanying wines.[10]

Given such an extensive roster of communist visitors, it is no surprise Engels was watched by an array of security forces. A January 1874 report to the Préfecture de Police in Paris describes Engels as '*l'ami et protégé de Karl Marx*' and '*un homme de lettres*'. The police spy, codenamed 'Blatford', placed opposite No. 122, was clearly concerned by Engels's activities and reported in August that '*Engels est très occupé*', spending his days with '*beaucoup d'étrangers*'. Over the coming years, according to the files, Engels flits in and out of the French government's concerns as 'Jack' replaces 'Blatford' and discovers a copy of the subversive magazine *Le Socialiste* in Engels's post.[11] In the shadows, nudging up alongside the Parisian spooks, the Metropolitan Police also took an interest. For Engels, who otherwise valued the lack of British state harassment, these hapless officers were a source of amusement rather than annoyance. 'We have every evening a bobby promenading before the house,' he noted in 1883 as he and Carl Schorlemmer hid giggling behind the shutters. 'The imbeciles evidently think we are manufacturing dynamite, when in reality we are discussing whisky.'[12]

In 1916 it was said you could hear the guns of the Somme from the top of Primrose Hill. In 1871 the low thud of Otto von Bismarck's troops shelling Paris was indiscernible, but the wider reverberations of the Paris Commune were certainly felt along Regent's Park Road. At the outbreak of the Franco-Prussian war, Marx and Engels had been surreptitiously inclined to back the Prussians on the grounds that 'Bismarck is doing a bit of our work, in *his own* way and without meaning to, but all the same he is doing it.' Their loathing for Bonaparte was such that any means to dislodge him from power were deemed worthy of support. Then they discovered that your enemy's enemy can turn out to be your enemy as well. 'Due to the unexpected victories chauvinism has gone horribly to the heads of German philistines,' Engels noted after Bismarck had decapitated the French army at Sedan in September 1870. As the Bonapartist Empire collapsed and a new, more peaceable French Government of National Defence was sworn in, the Prussian army did not simply amble back to their barracks as the Primrose Hill communists had hoped they would. Instead, Bismarck demanded a massive indemnity, the cession of Alsace-Lorraine, and a march through the Champs-Élysées (pretty much the entire package of pre-World War I resentment). 'The fact is that you cannot see beyond the end of your noses,' Engels wrote to his jingoistic brother Rudolf back in Engelskirchen. 'You have made sure that for many years to come France (which after all lies on your border) will remain your enemy.'[13] Bismarck's punitive post-war demands served only to galvanize the French as tens of thousands signed up for a *levée en masse* to resume the fight against the Prussians. But they were no match for the well-trained, well-armed Prussian troops who steadily ground down the French patriots until the struggle culminated with a battle for the capital, where the Paris National Guard stood fast. But rather than storming the city, the Prussians decided to dig in, hoping to starve the 2.2 million inhabitants into surrender. Under siege for weeks and then months, the stoical Parisians famously held out by expanding their dietary repertoire to include rats, horses, dogs, cats and then the entire contents of the city zoo – kangaroos and all. As the Prussian noose tightened around Paris, a political chasm opened between France's moderate republican politicians and the revolutionaries inside the capital, with the former urging an armistice and the latter a death-or-glory counter-attack. As privations worsened and the Prussians unleashed an indiscriminate bombardment of the city, the moderate Adolphe Thiers moved to negotiate a surrender. On 1 March 1871 the Prussians had their hubristic march-past – preceded two months earlier by the proclamation of a new German Empire in the Versailles Hall of Mirrors – and then left a weakened, hungry, angry Paris to its own bloody devices.

On 18 March 1871 a contingent of French government troops marched up Montmartre to reclaim a set of cannons from the Paris National Guard. Thiers and his fellow moderates in the National Assembly – now sitting at Versailles – had been increasingly concerned at the radical sentiments infecting the Parisian soldiery and their representative body, the Republican National Guard Federation ('Fédérés'), and wanted them swiftly disarmed after the Prussian departure. But at Montmartre, when the government troops were confronted by the Fédérés, intermingled with the working-class neighbourhood's women and children, they opted to lay down their guns and join forces with the republican soldiers. This symbolic moment of military obeisance was the single spark Paris needed. Despite all Baron Haussmann's urban improvements of the previous decades – the barrier-proof boulevards, the dispersal of working-class neighbourhoods, the easy transport for the movement of troops – Paris was still the city of revolution: the barricades went up, the remaining government troops scurried back to Versailles, and a new city council was announced with the title of 'Paris Commune' consciously evoking the revolutionary Commune of 1792. 'What resilience, what historical initiative, what a capacity for sacrifice in these Parisians,' gushed Marx. 'However that may be, the present rising in Paris – even if it be crushed by the wolves, swine and vile curs of the old society – is the most glorious deed of our Party since the June [1848] insurrection in Paris.'[14] Early events seemed to confirm his optimism. On 19 April the Commune produced its 'Declaration to the French People', which established the right of permanent involvement by citizens in communal affairs, open accountability of officers and magistrates (whose salaries were capped), the replacement of army and police by the National Guard, liberty of conscience and the transferral of redundant workshops or factories to 'the co-operative association of the workers who were employed in them'.[15] 'As almost only workers, or recognized representatives of the workers, sat in the Commune, its decisions bore a decidedly proletarian character,' according to an admiring Engels.[16] Indeed, these brief, glorious weeks represented an exemplary 'dictatorship of the proletariat' (understood more in the classical Roman rather than the continental twentieth-century sense) and, as such, a model for all aspirant social revolutionaries.

Yet inside the Hôtel de Ville, the class imperative was never quite so pure since the Commune's conscious proletarian element was balanced by a strong contingent of skilled manual and white-collar workers. To add to the mongrel make-up of 1871, there was also a range of deviant political philosophies at play on the ground. Proudhonist sentiments had always found a warm reception amongst the artisans and petty-tradesmen of Paris, and the Commune's plan for worker co-operatives was obviously indebted to this socialist lineage. At the same time, the Commune's most militant revolutionaries were Jacobins and Blanquists rather than Marxists – although many were simultaneously members of the International. In addition, there was a strongly civic republican edge to the Communards' thinking: an organic commitment to building a 'democratic and social' republic for Paris by Parisians without interference from those external, political powers which had historically corrupted their city.

In fact, this promiscuity of thought proved a relief for Marx and Engels: when it all went wrong, there was someone else to blame.

Thanks to the absence of a properly organized revolutionary workers' party, they later claimed, the Communards failed to launch an assault on the reactionary government forces at Versailles and were hopelessly reticent about seizing the Bank of France. Instead, they bunkered down for another siege, which in the event lasted barely a month before government troops bludgeoned their way into the capital. Against this 120,000-strong force, the Communards – even with their barricades and guerrilla tactics – never stood a chance, and so, on 21 May 1871, began the *semaine sanglante* which saw an estimated 10,000 Communards liquidated. 'The breechloaders could no longer kill fast enough; the vanquished were shot down in hundreds by *mitrailleuse* fire,' in Engels's dramatic account. 'The "Wall of the Fédérés" at the Père Lachaise cemetery, where the final mass murder was consummated, is still standing today, a mute but eloquent testimony to the frenzy of which the ruling class is capable as soon as the working-class dares to stand up for its rights.'[17] One of the more unpredictable consequences of this bloodbath was a rare falling out between Engels and his conservative mother, who naturally took the side of the National Government when it came to crushing the Commune. 'If I have not written to you for so very long, it was because I wanted to answer your latest comments on my political activity in a way that would not give you offence,' Engels replied gingerly before accusing his mother of forgetting 'the 40,000 men, women and children whom the Versailles troops massacred with machinery after people disarmed'. Beyond Engels's exaggeration of the casualty figures, what is historically noteworthy is that Mrs Engels clearly thought Marx himself responsible for the entire dreadful episode and was furious that he had dragged her beautiful, innocent son into it. Engels, who always put friend before family, cleared Marx of any responsibility for the atrocities (if not the Commune itself). 'If Marx were not here or did not even exist, nothing about the situation would have altered. Hence it is very unjust to blame him for this, and I cheerfully recall that a long time ago Marx's relations maintained that *I* had corrupted him.'[18] Yet by the end of the letter, Engels had reverted to his loving, filial self, recounting for Elise tales of his Ramsgate holiday, trips to the Viennese beer hall in the Strand, and offering supportive words to her in her ongoing struggle to unite him with his warring brothers. It was one of his final letters to his mother who, without much warning, died in the autumn of 1873 and, in the process, extinguished Engels's last truly affectionate connection to his family on the continent.

Elise Engels had not been alone in blaming Karl Marx for the bloody events of 1871. Despite his lack of practical influence over the Communards and the relatively minor role played by the International in the struggle, Marx became intimately connected with the Commune thanks to his polemical defence of 1871, *The Civil War in France*. Translated and sold in multiple editions across the continent, the pamphlet cemented the idea that the sinister, shady, illusive International was directing the worldwide working-class movement. 'Little as we saw or heard openly of the influence of the "International", it was in fact the real motive force whose hidden hand guided, with a mysterious and dreaded power, the whole machine of the Revolution,' was the judgement of the conservative *Fraser's Magazine*. The Catholic weekly *The Tablet* branded it 'a society whose behests are obeyed by countless thousands from Moscow to Madrid, and in the New World as in the Old, whose disciples have already waged desperate war against one government, and whose proclamations pledge it to wage war against every government'.[19] Needless to say, Marx was delighted by this belated celebrity. 'I have the honour to be at this moment the most calumniated and the most menaced man in London,' he wrote to Ludwig Kugelmann. 'That really does one good after a tedious twenty years' idyll in the backwoods.'[20]

So what was the International, this terrifying subterranean force able to tumble governments? Marx generally played down its conspiratorial aura, describing it as 'nothing but the international bond between the most advanced working men in the various countries of the civilised world'.[21] Established in 1864 at St Martin's Hall, in central London, on the back of the Polish insurrection and a growing feeling of international solidarity amongst the British labour aristocracy, the International Working Men's Association was a predominantly European workers' movement uniting Proudhonists, trade unionists, revolutionary Blanquists, Utopian socialists and a few Marxist adherents in the broader class struggle. In London, the body was initially closely associated with the Italian nationalist leader Mazzini as well as with workers in the London building trade. Marx had reluctantly gone along to the first meeting as an observer but ended the evening with a seat on the General Council and responsibility for composing the inaugural address. Engels was sceptical of this new talking shop from the outset, thinking the International both an unwanted distraction from Marx's work on *Das Kapital* and highly susceptible to the fruitless, faction fighting so endemic on the Left. 'I suspect that there will very soon be a split in this new association between those who are bourgeois in their thinking and those who are proletarian, the moment the issues become a little more specific.' And he was downright frosty about starting up a chapter in Manchester. 'As for the suggestion that I should form a branch of the International Association here, it's quite out of the question.'[22] Co-ordinating political activities with local radicals would seriously imperil his position at Ermen & Engels, not to mention at the next meet of the Cheshire Hounds.

As the International grew in stature – with an estimated 800,000 regular members by the end of the 1860s and strategic alliances across a range of trade unions – Engels's hostility eased, not least because he had always believed passionately in the internationalism of the proletarian cause. 'No working man in England – nor in France either, by-the-bye – ever treated me as a foreigner,' he wrote pointedly in his introduction to *The Condition of the Working Class*. 'With the greatest pleasure I observed you [the working men of England] to be free from that blasting curse, national prejudice and national pride, which after all means nothing but *wholesale selfishness* . . .'[23] More importantly, Marx desperately needed some political assistance: through the late 1860s he had fought an exhaustive turf war against a powerful Proudhonist faction in an attempt to make Marxism the International's official creed. But Marx was now facing an altogether more tenacious opponent.

It was as if Michael Bakunin had been genetically engineered to infuriate Marx and Engels: of high birth, raffishly charismatic, romantic, impetuous and, worst of all, Russian, he was an intellectual heavyweight with sharp organizational abilities. Unsurprisingly, he has earned the affection of twentieth-century historians and intellectuals – from E. H. Carr to Isaiah Berlin to Tom Stoppard (who is notably generous towards him and fellow Russian exile Alexander Herzen in *The Coast of Utopia* trilogy) – all bewitched by his fairy-tale life story. Engels had last met Bakunin in the lecture halls of 1840 Berlin where they both sat, with the other Young Hegelians, hectoring poor old Schelling. He was in Paris in 1848 and then Dresden in 1849, manning the barricades alongside Richard Wagner as they attempted to install a revolutionary government. However, Bakunin failed to flee in time when the Saxon troops turned up: arrested in Chemnitz, he was held in jail before being handed over to the Austrian authorities (who wanted him for inciting the Czechs) who chained him to the wall of Olmütz fortress before handing him on to the Russians. His next place of rest was St Petersburg's notoriously barbaric Peter and Paul fortress – where his health deteriorated sharply – until a change of Tsar and entreaties from his well-connected family secured him exile for life in Siberia. But the dozy officialdom of northern Siberia was no match for Bakunin: by the spring of 1861 he was away to the mouth of the Amur River and thence, from ship to ship, to Yokohama and San Francisco. Having diddled an English clergyman out of $300, Bakunin made swift passage across America and, by December 1861, he was back in London knocking on Herzen's door.[24]

Bakunin's extended incarceration meant that he had avoided all the reactionary fervour of post-1848 politics and returned to political life with his revolutionary zeal undimmed. However, he was now more sceptical of the national bourgeois revolutions which had characterized 1848–9 and, like many in communist circles, concluded that the next stage of the struggle would have to be international in character. He established, first of all, a League of Peace and Freedom and then his own International Alliance of Socialist Democracy, but his mind's eye was always set on infiltrating the International Working Men's Association itself. If Bakunin had been nothing more than a magnetic personality, he could have been swiftly despatched; what was lethal was the strength of his ideas. His doctrine of anarchism was oriented around a highly attractive notion of total individual freedom (but not Stirner-like egoism): ' "life", in Bakunin's sense, is an endless, indefatigable, endeavour towards freedom for every individual, every community, and the whole human race'.[25] He predicted in Marx and Engels's communism the prospect of a state authoritarianism as suffocating and dictatorial as the existing bourgeois iniquities. 'I am not a communist, because communism concentrates and swallows up in itself for the benefit of the State all the forces of society,' Bakunin wrote, 'because it inevitably leads to the concentration of property in the hands of the State, whereas I want the abolition of the State, the final eradication of the principle of authority and patronage proper to the State, which under the pretext of moralizing and civilizing men, has hitherto only enslaved, persecuted, exploited, and corrupted them.'[26] His constituency was the industrial age's social residuum – the paupers, peasantry and lumpenproletariat – who would never be served well by the centralized logic of scientific socialism. Instead, Bakunin's anarchist vision was of a society organized into small autonomous communes with absolute freedom amongst the members. What that signified, in transitional terms, was a commitment immediately to abolishing the authority of the capitalist state – whereas Marx and Engels thought the state would dissolve of itself ('wither away') *following* the social revolution and temporary 'dictatorship of the proletariat'. With typically Russian bravado, Bakunin was making the putschist mistake of wanting impractical political change when the material, socio-economic pre-conditions were not yet ripe.

Nevertheless, his dreamy promise of human freedom – which, just to add to Engels's fury, also encompassed the pan-Slav peoples – had its admirers. As his Alliance of Socialist Democracy picked up followers in Switzerland, Spain and Italy, he grandiosely proposed a merger with the far more powerful International. Engels the party organizer instantly spied the scam: 'It is clear as daylight that the International cannot get involved in this fraud. There would be two General Councils and even two Congresses: this would be a state within the state and right from the start, conflict would break out . . .' But he warned Marx to play his hand carefully, since 'if you violently oppose this Russian intrigue, you will unnecessarily arouse the very numerous – particularly in Switzerland – political philistines among the journeymen, and harm the International. With a Russian . . . one must never lose one's TEMPER.' That was not to suggest that Engels was ever soft on the man he called 'that fat Bakunin'. 'If this damned Russian really thinks of intriguing his way to the top of the workers' movement, then the time has come to give him once and for all what he deserves.'[27]

From his move down to London and election on to the General Council, Engels – who always liked to lead a hunt – propelled himself to the forefront of the struggle against Bakuninism and its attempts to undermine the International as a centralized, policy-making organization. The anarchists' ambition was to run it on purposefully anti-authoritarian lines as 'a simple office for correspondence and statistics'. To the military-minded Engels, a man whose sense of discipline crossed imperceptibly from personal to party matters, this self-regarding idealism threatened to undo the entire communist cause. Moreover, he regarded Bakunin's counter-vision as a direct affront to Marx's authority and an alternative power base that had to be smothered at birth. So from his elegant, marble and pine study at No. 122, with its handily placed pillar-box over the road, Engels became the global hub for every manner of Machiavellian procedural manoeuvre against the anarchists. All the tricks he had learned running the Paris Communist League were now deployed against the Bakuninist insurgency in Spain and Italy. In a celebrated essay for the Italian paper *Almanacco Republicano*, 'On Authority' (which Lenin much admired), he confronted the anarchist farrago by reminding his readers of the principle which he and Marx had first outlined in *The German Ideology*, that class struggle was an arduous, ruthless task requiring tight discipline and organization in the face of the ruling elite. Revolution, he now announced, was 'certainly the most authoritarian thing there is; it is the act whereby one part of the population imposes its will upon the other part by means of rifles, bayonets and cannon – authoritarian means, if such there be at all'.[28] To Paul Lafargue in Madrid, where Marx's son-in-law was serving his apprenticeship at the Spanish International, he wrote that 'I should very much like to know whether the good Bakunin would entrust his portly frame to a railway carriage if that railway were administered on the principle that no one need be at his post unless he chose to submit to the authority of the regulations . . . Just try abolishing "all authority, even by consent," among sailors on board a ship!'[29] In the wake of the Commune's disintegration, where the terrible absence of an organized workers' party had doomed the revolution to failure, this anarchist self-indulgence was shortsighted and politically dangerous. 'Just now, when we have to defend ourselves with all the means at our disposal, the proletariat is told to organize not in accordance with requirements of the struggle it is daily and hourly compelled to wage, but according to the vague notions of a future society entertained by some dreamers.'[30]

The animosity came to a head at the 1872 Hague Congress where Marx and Engels used foul means and fair to purge Bakunin and his Swiss followers. With the support of Paul Lafargue, Engels led the prosecution of Bakunin as both a terrorist *provocateur*, happy to use the services of Russian gangsters, and as the member of a wider political conspiracy 'got up to hamper the proletarian movement'. On the last day of the congress a vote was called. 'Then I saw Engels,' the German social democrat Theodor Cuno wrote. 'He was sitting to the left of the presiding officer, smoking, writing, and eagerly listening to the speakers. When I introduced myself to him he looked up from his paper, and seizing my hands he joyfully said: "Everything goes well, we have a big majority."'[31] By twenty-seven votes to seven, Bakunin was out. But it was a Pyrrhic victory since Marx and Engels had already stunned the congress by announcing the evacuation of the International's General Council to New York City (where it petered out four years later). Marx claimed he was exhausted by the endless European politicking; Engels played up the prospect of a fresh start in a virgin political landscape full of proletarian promise. In truth, it was an admission of unexpected political defeat: the cancer of anarchism had eaten into the body politic of the International and the entire organization needed to be dissolved and founded again from first principles. Marx and Engels were never quite such successful political operators as they thought.

Fat Bakunin was not the only charismatic ideologue Marx and Engels had to face down: the exotic figure of Ferdinand Lassalle proved a further rival for the hearts and minds of the European workers' movement. Another product of the Young Hegelian stud at Berlin, Lassalle was a philosopher and activist given over to flamboyant displays of chivalry – such as his decade-long advocacy of the divorce case of Countess von Hatzfeldt. Unlike Engels, this son of a self-made

Jewish tailor had never quite got the romance of 'Young Germany' out of his system. After the failure of '48, from his box at the Berlin opera Lassalle was involved with various proletarian parties before establishing in 1863 the General Association of German Workers (Allgemeiner Deutscher Arbeiterverein). Never a man over-burdened by crises of confidence, allegations of misappropriated funds and dictatorial treatment of colleagues dogged Lassalle wherever he pitched his political tent. 'It would be a pity about the fellow because of his great ability, but these goings-on are really too bad,' Engels wrote to Marx in 1856 after the Düsseldorf communists complained about Lassalle's high-handed manner. 'He was always a man one had to keep a devilish sharp eye on and as a real Jew from the Slav border was always [willing] to exploit anyone for his own private ends on party pretexts.'[32] Marx was inclined to be lenient since Lassalle was helping him to find a publisher for Das Kapital, but Engels fell out permanently with him over the 1859 Franco-Austrian war: whereas Engels placed the struggle against Bonaparte above all else, Lassalle feared an Austrian victory would only accelerate nationalistic reaction in Germany.

Lassalle did not remain long in Marx's good graces either. In 1861 Marx had travelled to Prussia in an attempt to reclaim his citizenship and, while awaiting the (negative) decision, enjoyed a high-society summer with Lassalle and his Berlin fast set. The following year Lassalle returned the favour, residing at the impoverished Marxes in London for three weeks and, in the process, sending their precarious family finances into free-fall. The great philosopher was furious with this spendthrift, vainglorious popinjay, and a personal breakdown in relations opened up all their political differences: Lassalle's notion of a Malthusian-derived 'iron law of wages' (which were naturally kept low as more working-class children entered the labour market) led him to argue for a Proudhonian future of producer co-operatives set up by the state. Indeed, Lassalle always retained a romantic, almost Hegelian belief in the state as the highest form of human organization and thus the best potential agent of working-class emancipation. He even entered secret talks with Chancellor Bismarck in the hope of crafting this ideal state on the back of a grand electoral pact between the working class and Junker aristocracy united against the exploitative bourgeoisie (whom Bismarck also despised). But before Lassalle could realize this political masterplan, his Don Juan inclinations got the better of him when in 1864 he took a bullet in the stomach from the enraged fiancé of a young girl he had been courting. Suddenly, Engels rather admired the man. 'Whatever Lassalle may have been in other respects as a person, writer, scholar – he was, as a politician, undoubtedly one of the most significant men in Germany,' he wrote on hearing of the bizarre death. 'But what an extraordinary way to lose one's life . . . Such a thing could only happen to Lassalle, with his strange and altogether unique mixture of frivolity and sentimentality, Jewishness and chivalresquerie.'[33] But as soon as he was informed about Lassalle's secret alliance with Bismarck, it was straight back to the insults against 'Baron Izzy', 'Lazarus', 'Smart Ephraim' or, in pointed reference to his dark features, 'the Jewish nigger'.

Such personalized attacks were stock in trade for Marx and Engels with the physical deformities, sexual peccadilloes and personal habits of their political opponents all subject to merciless ridicule. Yet their particular focus on ethnicity (and this was not an isolated case of saloon-bar boorishness on Engels's behalf: he complained about the number of Jews at the Schiller Anstalt in Manchester, was affectionately obsessed by Paul Lafargue's Creole heritage, and repeatedly used the term 'nigger' even when it was thought prejudicial in a nineteenth-century context) does briefly raise the rather ahistorical question as to whether Engels was a racist. Of course, he was a man of his time and politically committed to proletariat universalism, but when one combines his elemental outbursts with harsher strictures on the Slavs and other non-historic people there are palpably racist inclinations. Such sentiments emerge only fitfully into the historical light – as in 1866 when he and Marx discussed a new book by Pierre Tremaux, *The Origin and Transformation of Man and Other Beings*, which attempted to prove that geology and soil were instrumental in the development of racial characteristics. Initially, Engels was dismissive about Tremaux and his thesis. 'Perhaps the man will demonstrate in the 2nd volume how he explains that we Rhinelanders on our Devonian transitional massif . . . did not become idiots and niggers ages ago, or else he will assert that we are really niggers.' But Marx continued to think there was something in Tremaux's work forcing

Engels to backtrack a little: 'the man deserves credit for having emphasized the effect of the "soil" on the evolution of races' – pointing to
his basic belief in a graduated hierarchy of races and cultures.[34] Like
many of his milieu, he certainly thought western Europeans were more
civilized, advanced and cultured than Africans, Slavs, Arabs and the
slaves of the American South. Yet when it came to the raw politics of
race, Engels was always on the right side: he supported the North
against the South in the Civil War and, as we have seen, was appalled
by the butchery unleashed on the Jamaican rebels by Governor Eyre
during the 1865 Morant Bay rebellion. And, despite his own cultural
reflex towards anti-Semitism, he consistently condemned Jewish persecution when it re-emerged – amongst both socialists and conservatives – in late 1870s Germany. Indeed, he used an entire essay on the
issue to condemn anti-Semitism as backward and noxious – 'nothing
but the reaction of the medieval, decadent strata of society against
modern society . . . [it] only serves reactionary ends'. Engels wanted
the socialists to make the struggle against anti-Semitism their struggle
and he outlined just how indebted the movement was to Jews, beginning with Heine and Börne via Marx, Victor Adler and the leading
German social democrat Eduard Bernstein. And, like Marx, he
believed that anti-Semitism would ultimately die out with capitalism.[35]
Yet when it came to the Jews Engels could never fully shake off his
own Prussian reflexes.

Whether it was down to his 'Jewish cunning' or not, Lassalle's
intellectual legacy certainly had a significant impact on German
working-class politics. 'Izzy has given the movement a Tory-Chartist
character, which it will be difficult to get rid of,' Engels regretfully
noted after his death.[36] This was especially dangerous given the direction the German state was heading: Bismarck, it seemed, had learned
much from his old opponent Napoleon III and was now successfully
imitating the Bonapartist template of populist authoritarianism, managed elections and a political equilibrium which allowed 'the real
governmental authority' to lie 'in the hands of a special caste of army
officers and state officials'.[37] Bismarck's reverence for state absolutism
was now camouflaged under public opinion and an extended suffrage
– a trap which Lassalle and his followers seemed content to blunder
straight into.

Thankfully, Marx and Engels thought they had their own party to counter Lassalle's Bismarckian appeasement. Germany had come late to the Industrial Revolution but, during the second half of the nineteenth century, its now unified economy did all it could to catch up. Huge rail, road and naval infrastructure projects along with major advances in the chemical, metal and electrical industries saw an unprecedented expansion in the urban working class. This was the age of the booming Ruhr valley: of factory production lines, vast foundries, cartels and joint-stock companies backed by the big four banks – Deutsche, Dresdner, Darmstädter and Disconto-Gesellschaft. With mass industrialization and urbanization came new support for radical politics in the labourers' overcrowded quarters of Berlin, Munich, Hamburg and Frankfurt. In 1869 these constituencies gained a voice in the Social-Democratic Workers' Party founded at Eisenach by August Bebel and Wilhelm Liebknecht. As still patriotic Germans, Marx and Engels were enormously proud of the Eisenach party, regarding it as the most authentic, practical realization of the International ideal. Unlike the sloth of the English working-class movement, the confusion of Proudhonism amongst the French and Belgians, and the Bakuninist plague which infected Spain and Italy, the Germans held true to scientific socialism. Yet the founding fathers were never slow to point out where they thought the Eisenachers were going wrong – and they tended to give Liebknecht a particularly hard time for the various compromises which the management of a democratic party entailed. Their criticisms reached a climax in 1875 when, at a meeting in Gotha, Liebknecht took the Eisenachers into alliance with Lassalle's General Association of German Workers under the banner of the Socialist Workers' Party of Germany (Sozialistiche Arbeiterpartei Deutschland).

In Regent's Park Road Engels was incredulous. While Marx penned his withering *Critique of the Gotha Programme* highlighting all the Lassallean fallacies which the Eisenachers had fallen for, Engels castigated Bebel for dropping the commitment to trade unionism, accepting the flawed notion of an 'iron law of wages' and signing up to the Utopian nonsense of eliminating social and political inequality. Engels, the bohemian aficionado of the high life, was never a Leveller: 'living conditions will always evince a certain inequality which may be reduced to a minimum but never wholly eliminated. The living conditions of Alpine dwellers will always be different from those of the plainsmen. The concept of a socialist society as a realm of equality is a one-sided French concept...' With this wretched kowtowing to Lassallean doctrine, Liebknecht had shown signs of ideological freelancing and Engels pompously warned Bebel that 'Marx and I could never recognise a new party set up on that basis and shall have to consider most seriously what attitude – public as well as private – we should adopt towards it. Remember that abroad we are held responsible for any and every statement and action of the German Social-Democratic Workers' Party.'[38] Once again, they directed most of their ire towards Liebknecht for his failure to consult beforehand and desperate 'anxiety to achieve unity and pay *any* price for it'.[39]

Bismarck was far more perturbed by this spectre of organized, unified socialism, and two hapless attempts on the life of the Emperor Wilhelm I provided just the excuse he needed in 1878 to introduce the illiberal *Sozialistengesetz* prohibiting all organizations 'that seek by means of Social Democratic, Socialistic, or Communistic activities to overthrow the existing political and social order'. While individual social democrats were free to stand for election, the anti-socialist law prohibited all assemblies and publications, outlawed trade unions, saw party members summarily dismissed from jobs and declared the SAPD organization illegal. Inevitably, this torrent of state persecution served both to radicalize party members and engender a highly effective underground organization. While Engels expressed deep sympathy for the jailed leadership and their families (whom he supported financially), he was delighted by the political consequences of this excessive clampdown, which he hoped would move the party leftward from its Gotha compromises. 'Mr Bismarck who, for seven years, has been working for us as if he was in our pay, now appears incapable of moderating his offers to speed up the advent of socialism,' he wrote to his Russian correspondent Pyotr Lavrov.[40] To Engels's mind, Bismarck had entered the zone of *Zugzwang* – the situation in chess where any move only hastens the player's own demise. 'In Germany we have fortunately reached the stage when every action of our adversaries is advantageous to us,' he told Bebel, 'when all historical forces are playing into our hands, when nothing, absolutely nothing, can

happen without our deriving advantage from it . . . Bismarck is working for us like a real Trojan.' The first fruits fell at the October 1881
elections when the socialists secured 312,000 votes in predominantly
urban areas, translating into twelve Reichstag seats. 'Never has a
proletariat conducted itself so magnificently,' declared Engels. 'In
Germany, after three years of unprecedented persecution and unrelenting pressure, during which any form of public organization and
even communication was a sheer impossibility, our lads have returned,
not only in all their former strength, but actually stronger than before.'[41]
Gratifyingly, the German working class had finally reclaimed the
proletarian leadership from the French and English.

But even this stunning advance had its risks as electoral success
allowed political power to gravitate upwards from the militant
grassroots to a legitimized, often middle-class parliamentary leadership dangerously susceptible to reformist ideas. Engels, who always
contended that 'the masses in Germany have been far better than their
leaders', now combed every announcement from the Reichstag group
for signs of weak-willed opportunism. Issuing from the Regent's Park
Road presidium came sometimes daily instructions about how to vote
on individual bills (from protective tariffs to the minutiae of the
Schleswig-Holstein canal – which Engels decreed too shallow at nine
metres) or what political stance to take on any given controversy. It
was extreme micro-management as Engels remained ever alert to 'the
voices of the representatives of the petit-bourgeois, terrified lest the
proletariat, impelled by its revolutionary situation, should "go too
far"'. With half an eye to covering his own bourgeois tracks, Engels
was adamant that class struggle had to remain fundamental to the
movement: 'The emancipation of the working class must be achieved
by the working class itself.'[42] And so he and Marx were greatly relieved
when, at a clandestine 1880 Congress of Social Democracy in Wyden
Castle in Switzerland, the SAPD rowed back from its Reichstag
reformism and recommitted itself to the revolutionary struggle 'with
all means'.

Engels spent a large part of the 1870s concerned with his other means:
the liquid cash and stock capital he had taken out of Ermen & Engels
on retirement. In the process, he metamorphosed into one of the

stock villains of vulgar Marxism – the *rentier*. He did so at a highly propitious time as the British economy mirrored Engels's move from north to south with the City of London and its financial services sector beginning to assert themselves from under the industrial canopy. Economic historians have come to call the last third of the nineteenth century 'the Great Depression', as agriculture suffered and prices fell. But for those with a regular income, it was boom time. 'We here are now in the full swing of prosperity and thriving business,' Engels wrote in *Der Volkstaat* in 1871. 'There is a surplus of capital on the market and it is looking everywhere for a profitable home; bogus companies, set up for the happiness of mankind and the enrichment of the entrepreneurs, are shooting up out of the ground like mushrooms. Mines, asphalt quarries, horse-drawn tramways for big cities, and iron works seem to be the most favoured at the moment . . .'[43] Engels was living in the louche London of Trollope's coruscating novel *The Way We Live Now* – the London of joint-stock capitalism, a roaring exchange, Mansion House and a cast of international financiers beautifully embodied in the baroque crook Augustus Melmotte, who 'could make or mar any company by buying or selling stock, and could make money dear or cheap as he pleased'. It was the London of an army of black-coated clerks populating the endless offices of commerce, banking, shipping, insurance and real estate. In Marxian terms, the British economy was on its way towards a more concentrated form of monopoly capitalism. ' "Floating" – transforming large private concerns into limited companies – has been the order of the day for the last ten years and more,' Engels reported in 1881. 'From the large Manchester warehouses of the City to the ironworks and coalpits of Wales and the North and the factories of Lancashire, everything has been, or is being, floated.'[44] And this surplus capital was soon at work around the world. Imperial London became 'the clearing house of the world', funding railways in Peru, trams in Lisbon, mining in New South Wales and tea plantations in India. Between 1870 and 1914 the United Kingdom was responsible for 44 per cent of global foreign investment (compared with 19.9 per cent by France and 12.8 per cent by Germany) with an ever-increasing proportion heading to major infrastructure projects and extractive industries in the Empire. 'Britain was becoming a parasitic rather than a competitive economy,' in the words of Eric Hobsbawm, 'living off the remains of world monopoly, the underdeveloped world, her past accumulations of wealth and the advance of her rivals ... The prophets already – and not incorrectly – predicted the decline and fall of an economy symbolized now by the country house in the stockbrokers' belt of Surrey and Sussex and no longer by hard-faced men in smoke-filled provincial towns.'[45]

Primrose Hill was some way from Surrey, but Engels was a part of this colonial-capitalist, stockbroking nexus. The contradictions had not ended with his last day at the mill. 'I, too, have stocks and shares, buying and selling from time to time,' Engels told Eduard Bernstein, entering the rather surreal debate as to whether the German social democrats' paper in exile, *Der Sozialdemokrat*, should run a finance page. Engels, like Marx, preferred to peruse the *Economist*. 'I am not so simple as to look to the socialist press for advice on these operations. Anyone who does so will burn his fingers, and serve him right!' Engels's own portfolio of shares was lucrative and extensive: his probate at death revealed a stockholding valued at £22,600 (some £2.2 million in today's money) with shares in the London and Northern Railway Company, the South Metropolitan Gas Company, the Channel Tunnel Corporation Ltd, and even some imperial investments – notably the Foreign and Colonial Government Trust Company.[46] Luckily, investment in the stock exchange was deemed ideologically sound. 'You are right in describing the outcry against the stock exchange as petit-bourgeois,' he informed Bebel in language approaching a Papal bull. 'The stock exchange simply adjusts the distribution of the surplus value already stolen from the workers...' In fact, as the stock exchange tends to centralize and concentrate capital, it serves an essentially revolutionary purpose, 'so that even the most stupid can see where the present economy is taking them'. One had to look beyond its obvious rascality to realize that there was no shame in living indirectly on the exploitation of others: 'one can perfectly well be at one and the same time a stock exchange man and a socialist and therefore detest and despise the class of stock exchange men'. As we know, it was a contradictory existence with which Engels had long been familiar. 'Would it ever occur to me to apologise for the fact that I myself was once a partner in a firm of manufacturers? There's a fine reception waiting for anyone who tries to throw that in my teeth!'[47]

As ever, the question was what one did with the profits after tax (and 'we poor *rentiers* are made to bleed' he once complained of the Treasury take). Engels remained faultlessly generous to party causes and personal cases alike. In addition to the minimum annual subsidy to Marx of £350, Engels paid for the education of the children of Eugene Dupont, a Manchester factory foreman he knew; the funeral expenses for various impoverished Soho socialists; and regularly supported party newspapers and émigré charities. Sadly, Engels's philanthropic spirit was ritually abused by those he loved best. His weak spot had always been the Marx daughters and their various renegade partners knew it all too well. By far the worst offender was Laura Marx's husband, the doctor turned Proudhonist turned member of the International General Council, Paul Lafargue. Having assisted Engels in the struggle against Bakuninism in Spain, he returned to London and, as future author of the idler tract 'The Right to Be Lazy', practised what he preached. A half-hearted attempt to establish a photolithography workshop soon collapsed due to lack of investors and so Lafargue naturally turned to Uncle Engels. 'I am ashamed of pestering you again when you have just advanced me several large amounts; but to settle my debts and be able to back my invention, it is imperative for me to have the sum of £60,' he wrote peremptorily to Engels in June 1875. Luckily for him, Engels had a decent admiration for Lafargue's intellect and advocacy skills as well as a growing affection for this wilful, sensuous, cocky young man. In turn, Lafargue enjoyed the company of the more risqué Engels as an avuncular counterweight to his censorious father-in-law. 'To the great beheader of champagne bottles, fathomless swallower of ale and other adulterated trash, secretary to the Spaniards: Greetings and may the god of good carousals watch over you,' opened a typically banterish letter from Lafargue, before going on to ask, 'Does Mrs Burns take baths in the "*baignoire*" [bath-tub] I brought you from Bordeaux that you might extinguish the fire residing in your bowels?'

More often than not, these letters would then end, 'I shall need another £50 to pay my landlord.' And so it went on with demands for rent, rates, utility expenses and even underwear. 'Your bank-note arrived like manna in the midst of the desert,' Lafargue wrote (in a vein very similar to Karl Marx) from Paris in 1882 where he had returned to socialist politics, 'unfortunately we have not been able to make it last forever; I would beg you to send me some money, as I need to buy some underclothes for Laura.' But he was certainly pushing his luck in 1888 when he 'forgot to tell you [Engels] to send me a cheque for £15 to fill the gap left by the wine'.[48] Yet Engels could rarely say no to the Marx *filles*: he even went to watch Tussy's ill-fated adventures on the stage. 'The girl showed a great deal of self possession and looked quite charming,' he reported proudly back to Marx. 'If she really wants to make her mark in public she must unquestionably strike out a line of her own, and she'll do that all right'.[49] However, what Engels really enjoyed doing with his money was paying for family holidays with himself, Lizzy and the Marx clan heading out to the English seaside. Renting a summer house stocked with plenty of Pilsener at Ramsgate, Eastbourne, New Brighton, Bridlington Quay, Great Yarmouth, Worthing or the Isle of Wight was Engels's idea of heaven. 'After being fortified by me at the station with a glass of port,' Engels reported to the absent Marx in the summer of 1876 of goings-on at Ramsgate, 'she [Jenny Marx] and Lizzy are loafing about on the sands and rejoicing at not having to write any letters.'[50]

Taking the sea air was as much for medicinal purposes as holiday relaxation. Lizzy had a frail constitution at the best of times, and by the late 1870s her fifty-year-old frame was suffering badly from asthma, sciatica and an aggressive tumour of the bladder. In the summer of 1878 Engels feared he wouldn't even be able to get her down to the seaside. 'Last week she scarcely ever left her bed. The thing is exceedingly grave and might turn out very badly.'[51] During these darkening declining years, Engels the legendary Lothario proved himself a surprisingly attentive carer, seeing to Lizzy's modest needs and helping out with household chores. But he was fighting the inevitable and by the evening of 11 September 1878 Lizzy was entering her wolf hours. At which point something unexpected and rather touching occurs – a quintessentially Victorian moment of death-bed melodrama. Engels the great materialist, atheist and scourge of bourgeois family values rushes round the corner to St Mark's Church, Regent's Park, to collect the Reverend W. B. Galloway. Despite years of being popularly acknowledged as 'Mrs Engels', Lizzy the Irish Catholic wanted as her final wish to have her fifteen-year relationship sanctified in the eyes of God before she met her maker. As she lay dying in her bed upstairs at Regent's Park Road, she and Engels were married by special licence according to the rites of the Church of England. It was a very rare, very loving moment as Engels placed the needs of Lizzy before ideological purity. His dearly beloved wife then died at 1.30 a.m. and was buried as 'Lydia' – complete with a Celtic cross on the gravestone – at the Roman Catholic cemetery of St Mary's, next door to Kensal Green in north-west London. Her death was altogether less sudden than Mary's collapse and Engels appeared far more stoical about the loss. And perhaps because they had, finally, officially married and perhaps because his own, censorious mother was no longer around, he felt able to send out the official bereavement notice he had omitted to do after Mary's death. 'I herewith notify my friends in Germany that in the course of last night death deprived me of my wife, *Lydia*, nee *Burns*.'[52]

This time, in public at least, Marx behaved himself when it came to his friend's grief. But, in private, he was snidely poking fun at Engels and his illiterate Irish love in a letter sent to Jenny just a couple of days after Lizzy's death.

When Tussy, Mrs Renshaw and Pumps . . . were sorting out the dead woman's odds and ends, Mrs Renshaw [Lizzy and Engels's friend] found, amongst other things, a small packet of letters and made as if to hand them to Mr Chitty [Engels], who was present at the operation. 'No,' said he, 'burn them! I need not see her letters. I know she was unable to deceive me.' Could Figaro (I mean the real one of Beaumarchais) have *trouve cela*? As Mrs Renshaw remarked later to Tussy: 'Of course, as he had to write her letters, and to read to her the letters she received, he might feel quite sure that these letters contained no secrets for him – but they might do so, for her.'[53]

However, the real object of Marx's mirth was Pumps. Mary Ellen Burns enters stage left into Engels's life like some Shakespearean jester – Macbeth's porter or Hamlet's gravediggers – ostensibly providing light relief but, in reality, a source of intense annoyance to all around. Everything Engels thought Hegel had proffered about history as tragedy and farce is embodied in the character of 'the drunken enchanter', 'the amiable tippler' Pumps. The eldest of ten poor children, this niece of the Burnses was originally taken on by Lizzy to help with the household sometime during the mid-1860s. A pretty, flirtatious, temperamental creature, she accompanied them in the move south before being sent to Heidelberg in 1875 (at Engels's expense) to attend finishing school. The arrangement worked well until a very much more self-aware Pumps returned to London in 1877, refused to assist the ailing Lizzy in running the household and harrumphed back to her parents in Manchester. The sweaty, smelly reality of work in her brother's fish shop soon led her to re-examine her options and she slunk back south in the spring of 1878.[54]

For a girl on the make, the death of Lizzy gave Pumps the chance to seize control of Regent's Park Road. She 'has already put on quite the air, not to say behaviour, of a *"princesse regnante"*, along with the five guinea mourning gown', Marx noted waspishly four days after Lizzy's demise; 'this last, however, has only served to increase her ill-conceived "glee"'.[55] Now *in situ* as housekeeper, she was for Marx a perennial, irksome presence. However, he was at least grateful to her for a steady stream of gossip since it seemed few of the socialists passing through No. 122 could escape her buxom charms. 'There is little going on in "our circle",' Marx wrote to his daughter Jenny Longuet in 1881, 'Pumps still awaits "news" from [Friedrich] Beust [of the Cologne Workers Association]; has in the meanwhile thrown an eye upon [Karl] "Kautsky" who, however, did not yet "declare"; and she will always feel grateful to [Carl] Hirsch for having not only virtually "declared", but, after a refusal, renewed his "declaration", just before his trip to Paris.' Two months later a new suitor was sniffing around. 'Hartmann [a socialist émigré] has on Friday last left for New York and I am glad that he is out of harm's way,' Marx updated Jenny. 'But foolishly, a few days before his departure, he *asked the hand of Pumps from Engels* – and this was by writing, telling him at the same time that he believed he committed no mistake in doing so, *alias*, he (Hartmann) believed in his (Hartmann's) acceptance on the part of Pumps – the which girl had indeed rather flirted with him, but only to stir Kautsky.'[56]

For all the tiresome marriage proposals and histrionics, Pumps was a pretty young girl and her feminine attractions probably outweighed the nonsense which Engels otherwise had to put up with. Through her there was a living connection with the Burns sisters and his Manchester past. Unfortunately, she was also a little too giving with her love and allowed herself to be seduced by a City spiv named Percy Rosher. Despite his much vaunted ideological distaste for the bourgeois hypocrisy of marriage, Engels the pragmatist made Rosher do the decent thing and marry the girl, but over the coming years he was the one who had to foot the bill. Rosher, a failing chartered accountant, was a wretched case who gained a strong conviction, like the other hapless sons-in-law who surrounded Marx and Engels, that he was owed a living by his elders. In 1881 he took Pumps off Engels's hands but the quarrelling couple remained a regular Sunday presence, perennial holiday companions (which, at least, allowed a delighted Engels to play the role of grandfather to her growing brood) and were frequently to be found back in Regent's Park Road on extended stays. Nonetheless, Pumps's boisterous, girlish behaviour helped ease Engels out of his post-Lizzy depression. By the summer of 1879 the raffish Engels was back on form suggestively asking Marx whether he thought it a good idea if they were, 'to shake-off the Eternal-Feminine for once and go at being BACHELORS somewhere or other for a week or two?'[57]

Engels's return to rude health thrust him back into his position as communist comptroller – unearthing the last redoubts of Bakuninist and Lassallean heresy, overseeing the activities of Liebknecht and Bebel – as well as turning his mind to one of the more practical dilemmas of Marxist politics. From their pioneering days together in 1840s Paris, Marx and Engels had regarded the proletarian revolution as contingent upon a certain level of industrial and economic progress bringing in its train class consciousness, class struggle and all the other precursors of change. Yet, as every writer on Marxism has pointed out, it was in markedly underdeveloped Tsarist Russia – that reactionary, feudal autarky towards which Marx and Engels were so personally and perennially hostile – that a proletarian revolution of sorts first achieved regime change.[58] That is not to suggest that Marx and Engels would have been surprised by the events of 1917. Ever the optimist, in 1874 Engels regarded the Russian revolution as 'far closer than it would appear on the surface', 'in the offing' a year later, and 'bound to break out some time or other; it may break out any day' by 1885.[59] The question which bedevilled them and the entire Russian Marxist movement was what form the revolution would take. In the later decades of the nineteenth century there were two schools of thought: the first, under the Emancipation of Labour Group headed by Georgi Plekhanov, argued along orthodox Marxist lines that Russia would have to follow the western European course of progressive industrialization, working-class immiseration and the development of class consciousness before a proletarian revolution could occur (which would, in the event, be assisted by the mass of Russian peasantry). The second approach was adopted by the narodniki or 'Populists' who, inspired by the writings of Nikolai Chernyshevski, suggested that Russia's unique heritage of primitive village communes meant that it could follow a different road to socialism. Rather than enduring the horrors of Western capitalist transition, it could – following a few terrorist outrages – take an accelerated path to a communist future based on its heritage of joint land ownership (obschina), communal relations of production and primitive agrarian socialism. Alexander Herzen and Peter Tkachov went so far as to suggest that the Russian peasants were, in fact, the chosen people of socialism, born communists, destined to take the mantle from the slovenly Europeans.

Previously, Marx and Engels had been highly dismissive of primitive forms of communal life. In their writings on India, Asia and even Ireland, they had condemned the village commune as the backward adjunct of 'oriental despotism' and an anachronistic drag on the global march towards socialism. In the 1870s, though, as the prospect of revolution in western Europe receded, and as both men became more and more interested in early human history (the era of gens, tribes and communal living they read about in Lewis H. Morgan's influential study of 1877, *Ancient Society or Researches in the Lines of Human Progress from Savagery, Through Barbarism to Civilization*), they looked again at the political possibilities of primitive communism. Dropping his innate anti-Slav prejudice, Engels suddenly thought the Russian model should no longer be dismissed: 'the possibility undeniably exists of raising this form of society to a higher one,' he wrote in his 1875 essay 'On Social Relations in Russia', '. . . without it being necessary for the Russian peasants to go through the intermediate stages of bourgeois small holdings'. There was one coda. 'This, however, can only happen if, before the complete break-up of communal ownership, a proletarian revolution is successfully carried out in Western Europe, creating for the Russian peasant the precondition requisite for such a transition.'[60] Marx and Engels further revised this sequence in their 1882 preface to the second Russian edition of the *Communist Manifesto* – 'if the Russian Revolution becomes a signal for a proletarian revolution in the West, so that both complement each other, the present Russian common ownership of land may serve as the starting point for a communist development.' Marx made the point again in an endlessly rewritten and suspiciously unsent letter to the Russian socialist Vera Zasulich.

Theoretically speaking, then, the Russian 'rural commune' can preserve itself by developing its basis, the common ownership of land, and by eliminating the principle of private property which it also implies; it can become a direct point of departure for the economic system towards which modern society tends; it can turn over a new leaf without beginning by committing suicide; it can gain possession of the fruits with which capitalist production has enriched mankind, without passing through the capitalist regime, a regime which, considered solely from the point of view of its possible duration hardly counts in the life of society.[61]

From this it is clear that towards the end of his days Marx had started to relent on the issue of a uniform process of socio-economic capitalist advance applicable to all nations: with the help of the European proletariat, he now intimated that Russia could pursue its own primitive path to socialism.

Engels, however, was regretting this rethinking and, in one of the few clear examples of philosophical divergence between the two men, reverted to the original Marxist paradigm. Against his better judgement, he had once been attracted by the charisma of the *narodniki* and regarded Tsarist Russia as such a reactionary despotism that even Blanquist terrorism might be justified to get the revolution going. But by the 1890s his disagreements with Marx were obvious: the now steadily industrializing Russian society was no different, he suggested, from England, Germany or America and would have to undergo exactly the same wretched process of economic development. 'I am afraid we shall have to treat the [Commune] as a dream of the past, and reckon, in future, with a capitalist Russia,' he gloomily told Nikolai Danielson, the Russian translator of *Das Kapital*.[62] The truth was that the Russian commune had existed for hundreds of years, was showing little sign of positive development and now, in fact, acted as a 'fetter' on the progress of the peasantry. What was more, he now dismissed as 'childish' the suggestion that the communist revolution might 'spring not from the struggles of the west European proletariat but from the innermost interior of the Russian peasant'. The Marxist schema was such that it was 'an historical impossibility that a lower stage of economic development should solve the enigmas and conflicts which did not arise, and could not arise, until a far higher stage'.[63]

To help the Russian Marxists understand their historical conundrum, he drew a parallel with the experience of the early Utopian socialist Robert Owen. The workmen Owen employed in his factory at New Lanark in the 1820s had, like the Russian peasantry of the *obschina*, been 'raised on the institutions and customs of a decaying communistic gentile society, the Celtic-Scottish clan', but they showed absolutely no understanding of socialist principles.[64] The uncomfortable reality was that Russia would just have to accept there was no short-cut to socialism via the Commune and buckle under to the slow, painful march of history. In one of Engels's horribly prescient predictions he forecast that, in Russia, 'the process of replacing some 500,000 landowners and some 80 million peasants by a new class of bourgeois landed proprietors cannot be carried out but under fearful sufferings and convulsions. But history is about the most cruel of all goddesses, and she leads her triumphal car over heaps of corpses, not only in war, but also in "peaceful" economic development.'[65]

Neither Marx nor Engels lived long enough to witness Russia's savage convulsions of 1917 and beyond. As they entered their seventh decade, death stalked the old Londoners. By the summer of 1881 Jenny Marx was visibly weakening under the weight of her cancer and on 2 December she succumbed. The last three weeks of her life were spent cruelly separated from her 'wild black boar', her 'wicked knave', her 'Moor', as Marx's racking bronchitis and pleurisy kept him cordoned off from her. He couldn't even attend her funeral, in an unconsecrated corner of Highgate cemetery, north London. It was left up to Engels to give a generous eulogy celebrating her 'full conviction' in 'atheist Materialism' and declaring that 'we shall often miss her bold and prudent counsels, bold without brag, prudent without sacrifice of honour'.[66]

Marx was not slow to follow her to the grave. The second half of the 1870s had seen him increasingly disabled by a range of ailments from headaches to carbuncles to insomnia, kidney and liver trouble and, finally, an unshakeable catarrh. Certainly, these were serious physical afflictions, but there might also have been a return of his psychosomatic condition. Marx never finished volumes two and three of *Das Kapital* and, as with his earlier form, the less he wrote and the more distracted he became by other topics (such as years spent researching the primitive Asian commune), the faster his body deteriorated. Whether it was because the economics of *Das Kapital* no longer appeared credible or the political possibilities of communism realistic, Marx seemed to be stealthily retreating from his philosophical *grand projet*. There followed numerous trips to Carlsbad to take the waters for his liver troubles and Ventnor in the Isle of Wight for the mild, ion-rich sea air. After Jenny's death, the search for a healthy resort became all the more urgent as a warm, dry climate was desperately needed to placate his bronchitis. As a sure sign of his illness, he was now for the first time finding Engels uncomfortable company. 'Engels's excitement in fact has upset me,' he wrote to his daughter Jenny. 'I felt I could no longer stand it; hence my impatience to get from London away on any condition whatever!'[67] He trudged from Algiers to Monte Carlo to France to Switzerland – and, at every location, he brought the bad weather with him. The bronchitis became chronic and then, in January 1883, another hammer blow fell, with the death of his daughter Jenny Longuet from cancer of the bladder. Marx returned home to die.

In the miserable winter of early 1883, every afternoon saw Engels take a brief walk from Regent's Park Road to Maitland Park Road to visit his lifelong companion. At 2.30 p.m. on the 14 March 1883 he 'arrived to find the house in tears'.

It seemed that the end was near. I asked what had happened, tried to get to the bottom of the matter, to offer comfort. There had been only a slight haemorrhage but suddenly he had begun to sink rapidly. Our good old Lenchen, who had looked after him better than a mother cares for her child, went upstairs to him and then came down. He was half asleep, she said, I might come in. When we entered the room he lay there asleep, but never to wake again. His pulse and breathing had stopped. In those two minutes he had passed away, peacefully and without pain.[68]

With Marx went Western philosophy's greatest intellectual partner-ship and Engels's dearest friend. 'Yours is not an ordinary, or a family, loss,' Engels's old Chartist ally Julian Harney wrote to him. 'Your friendship and devotion, his affection and trust, made the fraternal connection of Karl Marx and Friedrich Engels something beyond anything I have known of other men. That there was between you a tie "passing the love of woman," is but the truth. I seek in vain in words to express my sense of your bereavement; and my profound sympathy for and with your sorrow.'[69]

Shattered by the loss, Engels nonetheless thought Marx's end had been a becoming death for such a great man. In a bullish letter to their mutual American friend Friedrich Sorge, he paid tribute to Marx's personal bravery, 'Medical skill might have been able to give him a few more years of vegetative existence, the life of a helpless being, dying – to the triumph of the doctors' art – not suddenly, but inch by inch. But our Marx could never have borne that.'[70] And now, only hours after he had seen his friend's final features 'rigid in death', Engels looked to cement the magnitude of his genius. 'We all of us are what we are because of him; and the movement is what it is today because of his theoretical and practical activities; but for him we should still be in a welter of confusion,' he told Liebknecht, generous to the end.[71] In Marx's absence, the challenge now was to see it through. 'What else are we here for?' Having given so many years of his own life to their philosophical struggle, Engels would not let Marx's ideas die with him.

8

Marx's Bulldog

'An immeasurable loss has been sustained both by the militant proletariat of Europe and America, and by historical science, in the death of this man,' was Engels's sombre judgement over the cold body of Karl Marx on the morning of 17 March 1883. There were only eleven mourners present in Highgate's steep eastern cemetery when Marx was laid to rest alongside his wife, Jenny. Today, the Gothic catacombs and meandering wooded paths of this sprawling 'Victorian Valhalla' enjoy a steady traffic of tourists and ideologues drawn to Marx's bombastic 1950s shrine. Overlooked by unbecoming hospital accommodation, the cemetery's edge has blossomed into a communist redoubt with Iraqi, South African and Jewish socialists all buried in the shadow of their first prophet. In 1883 it was a much lonelier affair as Tussy, sons-in-law Paul Lafargue and Charles Longuet, alongside scientists E. Ray Lankester and Carl Schorlemmer, as well as old communist hands Wilhelm Liebknecht and Friedrich Lessner, huddled together by the graveside. Telegrams came from France, Spain and Russia together with wreaths from *Der Sozialdemokrat* and the Communist Workers' Education Society. But it was Engels's short, secular eulogy which dominated the proceedings.

Wasting little time on Marx's marriage, children, or even their forty-year friendship, Engels moved quickly to codify exactly what Marxism meant. It was a speech intended more for the European communist diaspora than his fellow mourners and sentiment had no place when it came to laying down an ideological legend. 'Just as Darwin discovered the law of development of organic nature, so Marx discovered the law of development of human history ... But that is not all. Marx also discovered the special law of motion governing the present-day capitalist mode of production and the bourgeois society that this mode of production has created.' 'Such was the man of science,' Engels declaimed. He would miss him terribly. 'And he died beloved, revered and mourned by millions of revolutionary fellow-workers – from the mines of Siberia to California, in all parts of Europe and America – and I make bold to say that though he may have had many opponents he had hardly one personal enemy. His name will endure through the ages, and so also will his work!'[1]

This posthumous sanctification of Marx's legacy didn't end on the paths of Highgate cemetery. A few weeks later Engels could be found denouncing in the most strident terms an Italian communist, Achille Loria, for daring to misinterpret Marx's work and traduce his reputation. 'What you are not entitled to do, and what I shall never permit anyone to do, is slander the character of my departed friend,' Engels declared before signing off to Loria 'with all the sentiments you deserve'.[2] 'When Marx died nothing concerned him [Engels] so much as the defence of his memory,' as Harold Laski put it; 'few men have ever been so eager to prove the greatness of a colleague at the expense of his own eminence'.[3]

In death as in life, Engels embraced his role as Marx's bulldog driven at all costs to guard his friend's political bequest. And yet, during the twentieth century, a crucial question mark emerged over the years following the funeral with suggestions that Engels consciously reworked the meaning of his collaborator's oeuvre. The graveside comparison with Darwin's evolutionary biology and Newton's laws of motion hints at the scientistic turn within which Engels tried to enfold Marx. As a result, Engels has been accused of falsely remoulding Marxism: of letting his scientific enthusiasms anaesthetize the humanistic impulse of the authentic, original Marx and replace it, in his friend's absence, with a mechanistic politics devoid of the inspiring, fulfilling promise of socialism.

In turn, it is intimated, Engels was responsible for the official ideology of Stalin's Soviet Union and the horrors of Marxism-Leninism. It is a convenient charge to make – helpfully exculpating Marx from the 'crimes' of Marxism – but one which misreads the nature of the Marx-Engels collaboration. What is certainly true is that Engels, one of the most voracious intellects of his day, was mesmerized by the

BURIALS in the LONDON CEMETERY COMPANY's North London or Kentish Town and Highgate Cemetery of SAINT JAMES, in Swain's Lane, in the Parish of ST. PANCRAS, in the County of Middlesex, next Highgate, in the Year 1883

Name.	Abode.	When Buried.	Age.	By whom the Ceremony was performed.	
Walter Samuel Smith No. 6161	5 Tavistock Terrace Holloway Road	14th March 1883	65 years	Robert Pittman	✗ 24093
Mary Haycraft No. 6162	8 Canonbury Park South Islington	15th March 1883	77 years	Kerr Allen	✗ 7159
Hannah Goodwin No. 6163	60 St George's Road Regents Park St Pancras	16th March 1883	64 years	Bevill Allen	✗ 17255
Karl Marx No. 6164	41 Maitland Park Road – St Pancras	17th March 1883	64 years	Fredk Engels	✗ 24748
Mary Belinda Hill No. 6165	10 Elsworthy Terrace Primrose Hill South Hampstead	19th March 1883	28 years	E. W. Frecketton	✗ 25497
Salome Stammers Izard No. 6166	10 Hazelville Road Hornsey Lane Islington	20th March 1883	90 years	Alfred Rowland	✗ 17784
Mary Ann Blackhouse No. 6167	43 Sussex Road Holloway	20th March 1883	73 years	C D Maynard	✗ 5137
John Smith No. 6168	92 Carleton Road Tufnell Park Islington	20th March 1883	63 years	R L Tofet	✗ 16147

Cemetery record of Karl Marx's burial, with Friedrich Engels as the officiating minister.

scientific advances of the nineteenth century and sought, alongside Marx, to position their socialism within this scientific epoch of change. As such, he helped to systematize his friend's ideological canon into a popular and codified doctrine which would help shift European social democracy in a fundamentally Marxist direction. Marxism as a mass political movement begins not with *Das Kapital* or the ill-fated First International, but with Engels's voluminous pamphlets and propaganda of the 1880s. His great gift to his departed comrade was to transform Marxism into one of the most persuasive and influential political philosophies in human history. He did so in Marx's name and with Marx's blessing, remaining true to the ideology they had developed together.

'A great city, whose image dwells in the memory of man, is the type of some great idea,' Benjamin Disraeli wrote in his 1844 novel *Coningsby*. 'Rome represents Conquest; Faith hovers over the towers of Jerusalem; and Athens embodies the pre-eminent quality of the antique world – Art.' But the world was changing, Disraeli thought, and a new civilization approaching. 'What Art was to the ancient world, Science is to the modern; the distinctive faculty. In the minds of men the useful has succeeded to the beautiful. Instead of the city of the Violet Crown, a Lancashire village has expanded into a mighty region of factories and warehouses. Yet rightly understood, Manchester is as great a human exploit as Athens.'[4]

Engels's early years were spent in the emotional grip of the romantics; his middle age was given over to science, technology and useful knowledge. There were few better places to pursue such studies than Manchester, the city where science stood out as Disraeli's 'distinctive faculty'. In fact, across northern Europe the nineteenth century had witnessed a series of paradigm shifts in the natural and physical sciences. In chemistry, the French aristocrat Antoine Laurent Lavoisier had opened up the field of quantitative chemistry which Justus von Liebig then took into the realm of organic compounds. In biology, the German botanist Matthias Schleiden made a series of advances in cellular theory which his friend the physiologist Theodor Schwann extended to encompass the animal world. In physics, William Robert Grove was carrying out pioneering work with the first fuel cell and anticipating the conservation of energy theory, while James Clerk Maxwell was taking Faraday's work on electricity towards a unified theory of electromagnetism.

Manchester was the setting for much of this scientific revolution. It was the chemist John Dalton, a lecturer at Manchester New College and stalwart of the city's Literary and Philosophical Society (where many of his experiments were carried out), who developed Lavoisier's quantitative work to establish modern atomic theory and the framework for the periodic table. He was a civic hero whose body lay in state at the town hall on his death in 1844 as 40,000 Mancunians turned up to pay their respects in a single day. His pupil James Joule was almost as remarkable. The wealthy scion of a brewing family, through his painstaking experiments he investigated the controversial question – which Grove had been struggling with – as to whether energy could be conserved. Drawing on trials with his beer-making technology, he demonstrated how the total amount of 'energy' can remain the same whilst being transferred from one source to another, in his case the mechanical energy of stirring transferred into heat (i.e. measuring how heat is created by work). William Thomson, the future Lord Kelvin, and the German scientist Rudolf Clausius took Joule's results to establish the two laws of thermodynamics, defining the idea of energy and describing how energy and ultimately information evolves. Manchester's municipal leaders were understandably proud of Joule's scientific contribution and connected his life to the identity of the city by placing a meditative statue of him, opposite that of Dalton, in the town hall's tessellated portico. The meaning could not have been clearer: in Manchester, science and commerce marched hand in hand.

The democracy of science, its pursuit by everyday technicians and businessmen, was an essential part of Manchester's provincial, dissenting self-image. In the city's Literary and Philosophical Society, Geological Society and Natural History Society, it was revered as a purposefully meritocratic discipline in which Manchester's unfashionable middling sort could succeed just as much as the elites of London and Oxbridge. Indeed, more so: the city's combination of technology, industry and commercial practicality endowed it with an intellectual advantage absent from ivory tower university towns. As a result, a rich intellectual exchange in scientific and technological expertise existed between the industrializing communities of north-west England and Rhenish Germany – with German chemists being in particular demand (thereby establishing Lancashire and Cheshire's regional excellence in industrial chemistry which much later led ICI to create its major plant at Northwich). Scientific debate and discovery were alive in the mills, workshops and laboratories as well as the city's athenaeums, lyceums and debating societies. In her novel *Mary Barton* (1848), Elizabeth Gaskell elegiacally described how, 'in the neighbourhood of Oldham there are weavers, common hand-loom weavers, who throw the shuttle with unceasing sound, though Newton's "Principia" lies open on the loom, to be snatched at in work hours, but revelled over in meal times, or at night'. And she went on to characterize Manchester's factory-hand botanists – 'equally familiar with either the Linnaean or the Natural system' – and entomologists, 'who may be seen with a rude looking net, ready to catch any winged insect'.[5] To cater for the expanding scientific interest, the mid-1860s saw the inauguration of Penny Science Lectures with thousands of Manchester mechanics and artisans crammed into Hulme Town Hall or Free Trade Hall to hear the likes of T. H. Huxley on 'The Circulation of the Blood', W. B. Carpenter on 'The Unconscious Action of the Brain', John Tyndall on 'Crystalline Molecular Forces' and William Spottiswoode on 'The Polarisation of Light'.

From his earliest days in Salford attending public experiments at the Owenite Hall of Science, Engels embraced this scientifically minded milieu. 'I must now go to the Schiller Institute to chair the *Comite*,' he wrote to Marx in 1865. 'By the by, one of the fellows there, a chemist, has recently explained [John] Tyndall's experiment with sunlight to me. It is really capital.'[6] His most obvious entrée to the world of science was through his friend the chemistry professor and socialist Carl Schorlemmer – rechristened 'Jollymeier' in the Marx-Engels vernacular – who tutored him in the fundamentals of chemistry and scientific method. Author of *The Rise and Development of Organic Chemistry* (1879), Schorlemmer was an expert on hydrocarbons and alcohol radicals. For thirty years he worked in the Owens College laboratories as private assistant to the self-promoting scientist and politician Sir Henry Roscoe – who thought Schorlemmer's knowledge 'of both branches of chemistry was wide and accurate, whilst his sustained power of work, whether literary or experimental, was truly Teutonic'.[7] Others within Engels's scientific circle included the English geologist John Roche Dakyns and another German chemist, Philipp Pauli, who worked for an alkali company in St Helens and later housed Pumps during her time at finishing school in Rheinau. As another intellectual balm to the boredom of Ermen & Engels office life, Engels immersed himself in the scientific controversies of the day. He read the geologist Charles Lyell and evolutionary theorist T. H. Huxley ('both very interesting and pretty good'); Grove on physics and von Liebig's pupil August Wilhelm von Hofmann on chemistry ('for all its faults, the latest chemical theory does represent a great advance on the old atomistic theory'); and was an early advocate of the French practice of vivisection as a means of understanding nerve functions.[8] Ever the rationalist, Engels also developed a macabre scientific interest in the terminal ailments of his friends. 'Anyone who has but once examined the lung tissue under the microscope, realises how great is the danger of a blood vessel being broken if the lung is purulent,' he wrote to Adolph Sorge of Marx's condition two days before his friend died.[9] He was equally clinical in a letter to Carl Schorlemmer's brother during Jollymeier's final hours, '. . . in the past week or so he has been found beyond doubt to have developed a carcinogenic tumour of the right lung extending pretty much over the whole of the upper third of the organ'.[10]

Like so many Victorians, Engels was fascinated by Charles Darwin's *On the Origin of Species* (1859) and the theory of evolution by natural selection. 'Darwin, by the way, whom I'm reading just now, is absolutely splendid,' Engels wrote to Marx in December 1859. 'Never before has so grandiose an attempt been made to demonstrate historical evolution in Nature, and certainly never to such good effect. One does, of course, have to put up with the crude English method.'[11] Marx, who thought the work a telling reflection of mid-Victorian capitalist savagery and identified with Darwin's notion of evolutionary progress based on conflict and struggle, needed no encouragement. 'It is remarkable how Darwin rediscovers, among the beasts and plants, the society of England with its division of labour, competition, opening up of new markets, "inventions" and Malthusian "struggle for existence"',' Marx wrote back some years later whilst going over the work of Ricardo and Darwin in preparation for *Das Kapital*.[12] Indeed, Marx was so enamoured of Darwin's work that he later sent an edition of *Das Kapital* to the great evolutionist at Downe House – where, sadly for Marx, its pages remained for the most part uncut. Darwin himself thought the Germanic notion of a connection 'between Socialism and Evolution through the natural sciences' quite simply 'a foolish idea'.[13]

By then Engels himself was having doubts about Darwin. Or, rather, he was less convinced by the school of 'social Darwinism' which was forming around the work of the philosopher Herbert Spencer. In contrast to Marx, he was far more sceptical of any simplistic parallel between the evolutionary theory of the animal world and human society. Stretching back to *The Condition of the Working Class* – with its harrowing accounts of the bestiality of Manchester's proletariat – it had always been Engels's contention that capitalism's great crime was to reduce man to the state of animality. 'All that the Darwinian theory of the struggle for existence boils down to is an extrapolation from society to animate nature of Hobbes' theory of *bellum omnium contra omnes* and of the bourgeois-economic doctrine of competition together with Malthus's theory of population.' For Engels, what the social Darwinists didn't realize was that the outcome of the struggle for existence in human society was not an *individual* 'survival of the fittest', but rather the natural dominance of an entire class: 'the producing class [the proletariat] takes over the management of production and distribution from the class that was hitherto entrusted with it [the bourgeoisie] but has now become incompetent to handle it, and there you have the socialist revolution'.[14] However, Engels's most significant scientific contribution went beyond this vulgar communist take on Darwinist theory. Instead, it was to connect the extraordinary scientific advances of the mid-nineteenth century – in atomic theory, cell biology and physical energy – with the philosophy of the man who had first ushered Marx and Engels towards communist enlightenment.

In July 1858 a bored Engels had asked to borrow Marx's copy of Hegel's *Philosophy of Nature*. 'I am presently doing a little physiology which I shall combine with comparative anatomy,' he wrote of his extracurricular endeavours (to which Marx wondered whether 'it [was] on Mary you're studying physiology, or elsewhere?'). 'Here one comes upon highly speculative things, all of which, however, have only recently been discovered; I am exceedingly curious to see whether the old man may not already have had some inkling of them,' continued Engels. He was particularly keen to see whether anything in Hegel's philosophical writings had forecast the recent breakthroughs in physics and chemistry. For properly understood, Engels suggested, 'the cell is Hegelian "being in itself" and its development follows the Hegelian process step by step right up to the final emergence of the "Idea" – i.e. each completed organism'.[15] From his earliest days reading Hegel, with a glass of punch in his Barmen bedroom, Engels had always admired the methodology of the dialectic: the critical process by which, through each progressive, contradictory stage of thought, Spirit was eventually self-realized. Previously, Marx and Engels had applied Hegel's dialectic to the realm of history, economics and the state. In *The Poverty of Philosophy* (1847), Marx had criticized Proudhon for failing to understand how the roots of modern capitalism were embedded in pre-existing economic systems – 'that competition was engendered by feudal monopoly' – and used Hegel's method for revealing as much:

Thesis: Feudal monopoly, before competition.
Antithesis: Competition.
Synthesis: Modern monopoly, which is the negation of feudal monopoly in so far as it implies the system of competition, and the negation of competition insofar as it is monopoly.
Thus modern monopoly, bourgeois monopoly, is synthetic monopoly, the negation of the negation, the unity of opposites . . .[16]

Similarly, with the historic transition of the social structure – from feudalism to the bourgeois age and thence the proletarian revolution – the dialectic was a helpful explainer. Now Engels thought he had also discovered signs of the Hegelian method in the newly revealed processes of the natural and physical sciences. As a materialist and atheist, Engels had as his scientific starting point the presence of matter existing independently of and prior to human consciousness. In contrast to the mechanical materialists of the eighteenth century (with their static view of nature and humanity), Engels regarded this matter as being in a constant, Hegelian state of change and transformation. 'Motion is the mode of existence of matter,' he wrote in an essay on natural philosophy. 'Never anywhere has there been matter without motion, nor can there be.'[17] This was where the genius of Hegel's dialectical method came in, as its rhythms of contradiction and progress offered a perfect intellectual explanation for the transformation of things in themselves which the nineteenth-century scientific revolution was now revealing – energy from heat, man from ape, repeated cell division. 'The modern scientific theory of the interaction of natural forces (Grove's *Correlation of Forces*, which I think appeared in 1838) is, however, only another expression or rather the positive proof of Hegel's argument about cause, effect, interaction, force, etc.,' he wrote in a letter in 1865 to the German philosopher Friedrich Lange, explicitly linking advances in physics to Hegel's philosophy.[18] Again and again Engels returned to 'old man Hegel' as an ancient prophet whose theories unknowingly forecast the new terrain of evolutionary biology and atomic theory. 'I am deeply immersed in the doctrine of essence,' he explained to Marx in 1874 after reading some recent speeches by the physicist John Tyndall and Darwin popularizer T. H. Huxley. 'This brought me back again . . . to the theme of dialectics,' which Engels thought 'goes much more nearly to the heart of the matter' than the empirically minded English scientific community could possibly appreciate.[19]

Clearly, there was a book in all this. 'This morning in bed the following dialectical points about the natural sciences came into my head,' Engels wrote lackadaisically to Marx in 1873 before expounding ad nauseam on Newtonian matter in motion, the mathematics of trajectories, and the chemical nature of animate and inanimate bodies.[20] A distracted Marx, far more concerned about the poor marital prospects of his daughters, failed to reply to most of the points. Undeterred, Engels ploughed on, happy to use his Primrose Hill retirement to pursue these questions of fundamental science. 'When I retired from business and transferred my home to London,' he later reflected, 'I went through as complete a "moulting", as [Justus von] Liebig calls it, in maths and the natural sciences, as was possible for me, and spent the best part of eight years on it.'[21]

17. 'Composed of the first gentlemen in that aristocratic county'. A meet of the Cheshire Hounds, by Henry Calvert.

18. 'What Art was to the ancient world, Science is to the modern; the distinctive faculty.' Physicist James Joule (*left*) and chemist John Dalton face each other across the impressive entrance to Manchester Town Hall.

19. Engels as the second father and the giver of good things. 'The General' with Marx and his daughters – (*left to right*) Laura, Eleanor, Jenny – on holiday in 1864.

20. The much indulged Laura Marx.

21. Lizzy Burns, the only Mrs Friedrich Engels – of 'genuine Irish proletarian blood' with 'passionate feelings for her class'.

22. Eleanor Marx, the beloved and doomed 'Tussy'.

23. 'The Grand Lama of the Regent's Park Road' in 1891.

24. The Mecca of international socialism. Engels's study at No. 122 Regent's Park Road as it looks today.

25. Hampstead Heath – 'London's Chimborazo' – Marx and Engels's favourite walking and family picnic spot.

26. 'Look at the Paris Commune. That was the dictatorship of the proletariat.' Barricade at the Faubourg Saint-Antoine during the Commune, 18 March 1871.

27. A panorama of the fires in Paris during the Commune, May 1871.

28. 'The greatest event to have taken place in England since the last Reform Bills'. Striking dockers march through the London streets in 1889.

29. Engels thought the dockers' political cohesion and proletarian class consciousness heralded 'the beginning of a complete revolution in the East End'. Posing for a photograph, with float, 1889.

30. The global reach of Friedrich Engels. A poster in Havana, Cuba, commemorating the 130th anniversary of the Communist Manifesto, *c*.1978.

31. An icon of colonial resistance. Engels, alongside Marx and Lenin, on a war-torn mural in Addis Ababa, Ethiopia, 1991.

From these investigations emerged the jumbled reams of notes and short essays which became the symbolically titled *Dialectics of Nature*. Or, rather, it didn't emerge until 1927 when the Marx-Engels Institute in Moscow published it after Eduard Bernstein, one of Engels's literary executors, passed the manuscripts to Albert Einstein, who thought the science confused (especially the mathematics and physics) but the overall work of such historical note as to be worthy of a broader readership.[22] Composed between 1872 and 1883, the *Dialectics* is a mélange of German, French and English notations on the scientific and technological developments of the day. 'Wenn Coulomb von particles of electricity spricht, which repel each other inversely as the square of the distance, so nimmt Thomson das ruhig hin als bewiesen,' reads a typical sentence. Just as he had earlier attempted with military history, Engels sought to explain the scientific advances emerging out of industrial England, France and Germany as responses to the changing mode of production. His lifetime in the cotton industry meant he knew only too well the natural symbiosis between economic necessity and technical breakthroughs in such fields as dyeing, weaving, metallurgy and milling.

The *Dialectics*' grander ambition was to explain the nineteenth century's seemingly disparate scientific discoveries as the logical, tangible fulfilment of Hegelian dialectics. Whereas Hegel's philosophy had been limited to the ethereal world of Spirit, Engels's concern was to connect theory with practice (praxis) just as he and Marx had done earlier by inverting Hegelian idealism into a materialist theory that could explain the history and progress of social and economic formations. 'In nature, amid the welter of innumerable changes, the same dialectical laws of motion impose themselves as those which in history govern the apparent fortuitousness of events,' he announced, linking the Hegelian idea of the 'cunning of reason' in history to the logic behind the apparent randomness of events in the laboratory.[23] The great merit of the Hegelian system was, Engels argued, that 'for the first time the whole world, natural, historical, intellectual, is represented as a process – i.e., as in constant motion, change, transformation, development; and the attempt is made to trace out the internal connection that makes a continuous whole of all this movement and development'.[24] By turning Hegel the right way up – by regarding ideas as the product of nature and history – one could show how the apparent randomness of the natural and physical world was eminently explicable. 'If we turn the thing round, then everything becomes simple, and the dialectical laws that look so extremely mysterious in idealist philosophy at once become simple and clear as noonday.'[25]

Leaning heavily on new discoveries in the conservation of energy, cellular structure and Darwinian evolution, Engels followed Newton in proposing three laws of what would later become known as dialectical materialism (although Engels himself would use only the term 'materialist dialectic'). The first law, 'of the transformation of quantity into quality and vice versa', proposed that *qualitative* change in the natural world is the result of *quantitative* change following an accumulation of stresses. For instance, an increased number of atoms in a molecule would produce substantive, qualitative change (say, ozone instead of oxygen); an increase or decrease in temperature could transform H_2O from solid to liquid to gas (ice to water to steam). Secondly, 'the law of the interpenetration of opposites' stated in faithful Hegelian fashion that 'the two poles of antithesis, like positive and negative, are just as inseparable from each other as they are opposed, and despite all their opposition they mutually penetrate each other'.[26] In other words, contradictions inherent within natural phenomena were the key to their progressive development. A contention buttressed by Engels's third and final dialectic, 'the law of the negation of the negation', in which the internal contradictions of a phenomenon give rise to another system, an opposite, which is then, in turn, itself negated as part of a teleological process leading to a higher plane of development. In the same thesis–antithesis–synthesis format which Marx had employed in *The Poverty of Philosophy*, Engels offered in *Dialectics of Nature* a totalizing vision of the natural and physical world which then he illustrated with a series of test cases. 'Butterflies, for example, spring from the egg by a negation of the egg, pass through certain transformations until they reach sexual maturity, pair andare in turn negated, dying as soon as the pairing process has been completed and the female has laid its numerous eggs.' Similarly, 'the whole of geology is a series of negated negations, a series in which old rock formations are successively shattered and new ones deposited'.[27]

In the shadow of Darwin, Engels put his dialectics to the test with a materialist account of man's early evolution in a chapter entitled 'The Part played by Labour in the transition from Ape to Man' – an essay the late evolutionary biologist Stephen Jay Gould always regarded as one of the more impressive side alleys of Darwinian thought in the nineteenth century.[28] As ever, Engels had his aim trained on the Idealist tradition which, in this case, meant the false doctrine by which homo sapiens was primarily identified in terms of his brain power. Matter not mind was still this Young Hegelian's mantra. Focusing on three essential features of human evolution – speech, a large brain and upright posture – Engels sought to prove how 'labour created man himself'. This was in contrast to Darwin's more cerebral template, which assumed that the growth in brain size and intellect occurred *prior* to the development of two-legged walking. It also reaffirmed Engels's hostility to any transfer from the animal kingdom to human society since labour was 'an exclusively human characteristic' marking it out from the bestial world.

When man came down from the trees and 'adopted a more and more erect posture', according to Engels, he freed his hands for using tools. 'Mastery over nature began with the development of the hand, with labour, and widened man's horizon at every advance.' The demands of labour slowly brought communities together, nurtured systems of mutual support and created the context in which speech and other intellectual acts could then occur. In the long chronology of human evolution, the material demands of labour came first followed only later by speech – and, in turn, the move from a vegetable to meat diet and, with it, the nourishment of larger brains together with the domestic use of fire and animal husbandry.[29] In the midst of this intriguing if rambling essay, Engels observes that one of the early differences between the animal world and human society was the latter's ability to manipulate the natural environment to its advantage.[30] By contrast, animals were limited to utilizing their accumulated sensory knowledge of the environment for safety and food. That said, this animal instinct was an impressive natural capacity which Engels had seen at work on numerous occasions from his Cheshire mount. 'While fox-hunting in England one can daily observe how unerringly the fox makes use of its excellent knowledge of the locality in order to elude its pursuers, and how well it knows and turns to account all favourable features of the ground that cause the scent to be lost.'[31] Yet another solid socialist reason for riding to hounds.

Engels's contribution to mathematical theory was less noteworthy. Always strong on arithmetic, from the 1870s he started to develop an interest in calculus, geometry, applied maths and theoretical physics. For mathematics had undergone an equally significant process of intellectual evolution during the nineteenth century which both Marx and Engels followed closely. Calculus had been rethought by Karl Weierstrass, a new understanding of algebraic integers developed by Richard Dedekind, and there had been advances in differential equations and linear algebra. As with his researches into biology, physics and chemistry, Engels thought a dialectical method and an appreciation of materialist fundamentals was an essential explainer to all developments in the discipline. 'It is not at all true that in pure mathematics the mind deals only with its own creations and imaginations,' he confidently asserted. 'The concepts of number and form have been derived from no source other than the world of reality.'[32] To Engels's mind, there was nothing in maths which wasn't already in nature; mathematics was simply an explanatory reflection of the physical world. As a result, he attempted to crowbar all sorts of mathematical models into his triadic system of dialectics. 'Let us take an arbitrary algebraic magnitude, name a,' begins one passage in *Dialectics of Nature*. 'Let us negate it, then we have $-a$ (minus a). Let us negate this negation by multiplying $-a$ by $-a$, then we have $+a$, that is the original positive magnitude, but to a higher degree, namely to the second power.'[33] As the Trotskyist scholar Jean Van Heijenoort has pointed out, this is all horribly confused whereby 'negation' in Engels's terms can mean any number of differing mathematical operations to achieve the final result.[34] Worse was to come as Engels, playing the reductive philistine, dismissed complex numbers and theoretical mathematics – those parts of theoretical science which went beyond a reflection of natural phenomena – as akin to witchcraft. 'When one has once become accustomed to ascribe to the [square root of] -1 or to the fourth dimension some kind of reality outside of our own heads, it is not a matter of much importance if one goes a step further and also accepts the spirit world of the mediums.'[35]

Despite the obvious limitations of Engels's scientific modelling, it proved in the twentieth century among his most durable and damaging legacies. For generations of communists, Engels's writings on the natural and physical sciences offered a guide to research in and out of the laboratory. Eric Hobsbawm remembers scientists of the 1930s earnestly hoping their bench work would fit within Engels's template.[36] In the Soviet Union and communist bloc, this aspiration became government policy as the official practice of science took place within the strict paradigm of dialectical materialism with any research suspected of subjectivism or idealism summarily dismissed as 'bourgeois science'. In a celebrated 1931 paper, for example, the Soviet physicist Boris Hessen reinterpreted Isaac Newton's work on gravitational attraction as the inevitable product of a decaying feudal and rising mercantile, capitalist society. Similarly, a 1972 biography of Engels produced in the GDR could straight-facedly explain twentieth-century scientific advances entirely in light of *Dialectics of Nature*: 'the discoveries in the field of quantum theory [have] proved the dialectical thesis of the unity of the continuity and discontinuity of matter; in the field of physics, Einstein's theory of relativity concretized the philosophical ideas of Engels about matter, motion, space and time, and the theory of the elementary particles confirmed the views of Engels and Lenin on the inexhaustibility of atoms and electrons'.[37]

Scientific research amongst British communists was also carried out against the backdrop of Engels's system. In 1940 an English edition of *Dialectics of Nature* was published with a preface by the British geneticist and communist J. B. S. Haldane helpfully explaining how dialectics 'can be applied to problems of "pure" science as well as to the social relations of science'.[38] The cult intensified after the war with the establishment of the Engels Society by the philosopher Maurice Cornforth (author of *Dialectical Materialism: An Introductory Course*) and a small band of Communist Party scientists. Intended to be open to 'all science workers who are concerned with approaching and developing the problems of their science from the standpoint of Marxism-Leninism', its aim was to combat reactionary tendencies in science, counter 'misuse' of scientific knowledge by the West and to take a stand 'against very long-term objectives, divorced from contemporary problems of practice' and to oppose 'agnosticism and impotence, which are characteristic of decaying capitalism'. Discussion groups in London, Birmingham, Manchester and Merseyside were set up alongside chemistry, physics, psychology and even astronomy subgroups. A taste of the society's debates is given by the 1950 edition of the 'Transactions of the Engels Society', which ran a paper headed 'Against Idealist Cosmology'. The authors gleefully reported how 'modern bourgeois astronomy finds itself in a condition of chronic ideological crisis' whereas Soviet astronomy was in rude health thanks to its being 'firmly based on the materialist conception of the infinity of the universe'.

As the Engels Society had to convene in the Music Room of the Society for Cultural Relations with the USSR at 14 Kensington Square, London, its members were also unable to escape the fallout from the campaign of academic repression launched by 'comrade-scientist' Stalin and his megalomaniac science tsar, Academician Trofim Denisovich Lysenko. Engels, who in his later years consistently warned of the dangers of reading Marx in a rigid, doctrinal fashion, was now summoned in aid to justify the most terrible assaults on intellectual freedom. In philosophy, linguistics, physiology, physics and most especially biology, Stalin demanded that scientific enquiry coalesce with the 'correct' party line, with new discoveries liable to be discounted on purely ideological grounds. What this signalled in the biological sciences was a total disavowal of heredity in genetics (a bourgeois invention with obvious affinities to Nazi eugenics) and, in its place, Lysenko revived the early twentieth-century, neo-Lamarckian ideas of the agriculturalist Ivan Michurin and his conviction in environmental determinism. At the 1948 Congress of the All-Union Agricultural Academy the genetic theories of Mendel and Morgan were denounced as 'unscientific' and 'reactionary' – their leading advocate, the geneticist Nikolai Vavilov, having already been worked to death in the labour camps – and woe betide anyone who fell on the wrong side of this decree.[39] In the Engels Society archives there is a terrifying example of a free-thinking, free-speaking Soviet academic, Youri Zhdanov, who did just that. With the typed endorsement that this letter is 'of great interest', Zhdanov's fearful self-denunciation to the Central Committee of the CPSU (B) – cc'd to Comrade Stalin himself – was reprinted in full.

In my contribution to discussion at the Lecturers' Training College on the disputed question of Modern Darwinism, I undoubtedly committed a number of grave errors ... In this, the 'university habit' of giving my point of view without reflection in various scientific discussions, made its appearance ... I consider it my duty to assure you, Comrade Stalin, and through you to the C.C. of the C.P.S.U. (B), that I was and remain a convinced follower of Michurin. My faults result from my not having studied sufficiently the historical side of the problem, so as to organise a struggle for the defence of Michurinism. All this is the result of inexperience and lack of maturity. I will correct my faults by action.[40]

To their credit, the Engels Society chose to criticize the Lysenko purges, make a principled plea for intellectual pluralism and, in the process, remain far truer to Engels's original beliefs in scientific debate and research than the academic thuggery of the Politburo.

Part of the reason the *Dialectics* was published only posthumously was that Engels interrupted his studies to indulge his and Marx's favourite pastime of ideological knockabout. 'It is all very well for you to talk,' he wrote to Marx in 1876 with an air of mock-indignation. 'You can lie warm in bed and study ground rent in general and Russian agrarian conditions in particular with nothing to disturb you – but I am to sit on the hard bench, swill cold wine, suddenly interrupt everything again and break a lance with the tedious Dühring.'[41]

Eugen Dühring, the object of their ire, was a blind philosophy lecturer at the University of Berlin whose brand of socialism was beginning to make significant inroads into German social democracy. Amongst his early acolytes was Eduard Bernstein. Like Bakunin and Proudhon before him, Dühring criticized the centralism and economic determinism of Marx and Engels and proposed instead a gradualist political programme which would secure more immediately obvious material gains for the working class. Dühring's 'force theory' stressed the efficacy of strikes, collective action, and even violence, in leading the proletariat towards his ideal social system of *Wirtschaftscommunen* – autonomous communes of working people.[42] It was a pragmatic political manifesto which numerous leading German socialists were more willing to embrace than what seemed the arcane and unrealizable philosophies of Marx. All of which infuriated Engels. 'Never before has anyone written such arrant rubbish,' he wrote to Marx from his Ramsgate summer cottage in July 1876. 'Windy platitudes – nothing more, interspersed with utter drivel, but the whole thing dressed up, not without skill, for a public with which the author is thoroughly familiar – a public that wants by means of beggar's soup and little effort to lay down the law about everything.'[43] More worrisomely, Dühring was just as aggressive an ideological combatant as the old Londoners. He dismissed Marx as a 'scientific figure of fun' but saved his real spleen for Engels, the 'Siamese twin', who 'only had to look into himself' to come up with his exploitative portrait of the manufacturer in The Condition of the Working Class. Dühring aimed direct for Engels's Achilles heel. 'Rich in capital, but poor in insight about that capital, he is one of those who are – in accordance with a time-honoured theory once established in Jerusalem – commonly compared to a rope or a camel that cannot pass through the eye of a needle.'[44]

Encouraged by Wilhelm Liebknecht and putting aside some initial qualms about attacking a blind man ('the chap's colossal arrogance precludes my taking that into account'), Engels launched a sustained denunciation of Dühring and all his works through the pages of Germany's leading socialist newspaper, Vorwärts.[45] Although Engels dismissed Dühring's arguments as no more than 'mental incompetence due to megalomania', the text went beyond the usual Marx-Engels invective into a broader definition and defence 'of the dialectical method and of the communist world outlook'.[46] The philosophy of dialectical materialism which Engels had been plugging away at in his Dialectics notebook was now refined, polished and served up in book form as Herr Eugen Dühring's Revolution in Science – which would become more popularly known as Anti-Dühring (1878). All of Engels's great gifts as a propagandist and popularizer were on display as he countered the allure of Dühring with a pacey, engaging and comprehensible explanation of the science of Marxism. For after his sustained immersion in modern maths, biology, physics and chemistry, Engels had begun to regard his and Marx's socialism within the same intellectual template as the scientific paradigm shifts of the nineteenth century.

To help the readers of *Anti-Dühring* appreciate the context, he transported them back to the 1840s to reacquaint them with the founding moment of Marxism: the move from Hegelian idealism to Marxist materialism via the philosophy of Feuerbach. Marx's genius, as Engels originally pointed out in an 1859 essay, was to turn Hegel right way up, take his head out of the sky and replace his idealism with material realities. Whereas Hegel had charted the march of Spirit towards the Idea, Marx was concerned with the trajectory of material circumstances. 'Marx was and is the only one who could undertake the work of extracting from the Hegelian logic the kernel containing Hegel's real discoveries in this field, and of establishing the dialectical method, divested of its idealist wrappings, in the simple form in which it becomes the only correct mode of the development of thought.'[47] As Marx himself put it in an 1873 afterword to *Das Kapital*, 'The mystification which dialectic suffers in Hegel's hands, by no means prevents him from being the first to present its general form of working in a comprehensive and conscious manner. With him it is standing on its head. It must be turned right side up again, if you would discover the rational kernel within the mystical shell.'[48] After years of playing down its importance, Engels was now forthright about recording his and Marx's debt to the Hegelian tradition. 'Marx and I were pretty well the only people to salvage conscious dialectics from German idealist philosophy for the materialist conception of nature and history,' was how he inelegantly put it in the preface to *Anti-Dühring*.[49] The metaphysical clutter of idealist philosophy was stripped away to leave the pristine dialectical method ready to explain science, history and even modern class antagonism.

However, Engels's real achievement in *Anti-Dühring* was to apply dialectical materialism, richly informed by his immersion in the natural sciences, to capitalism. Engels's three laws – the transformation of quantitative change into qualitative, the struggle of opposites and the negation of the negation – could now explain not only biology, chemistry and evolution but existing tensions within bourgeois society. 'Both the productive forces engendered by the modern capitalist mode of production and the system of distribution of goods established by it have come into crying contradiction with that mode of production itself,' he proclaimed in full dialectical flow, 'so much so that if the whole of modern society is not to perish, a revolution in the mode of production and distribution must take place, a revolution which will put an end to all class distinctions'.[50] The opposites had to be opposed, the negation negated and, just as the butterfly springs from the chrysalis, a new society would emerge from the inherent contradictions of the old. This critical tool for reading society's endlessly shifting contradictions and readiness for revolution was Marx's definitive contribution to Western thought.

The point of philosophy was always to change, rather than just interpret the world. And the political implications of dialectical materialism were also spelt out in a section of *Anti-Dühring* rewritten by Engels and then published separately as *Socialism: Utopian and Scientific* (1880; 1882). The idea for this more focused primer in scientific socialism came from Marx's son-in-law Paul Lafargue, who faced in France similar difficulties to Liebknecht in Germany when it came to cementing Marxism as the dominant socialist faith. The French communist movement was split between the so-called 'Collectivists' (centred on Jules Guesde and Lafargue) and the Possibilists (led by Benoît Malon), who advocated a reformist agenda little different from the municipal socialism developing in various British cities. While Marx and Engels criticized Guesde's 'revolutionary phrasemongering' – inviting Marx's famous quip, 'All I know is that I am not a Marxist!' – they supported the Collectivists' philosophical stance and Engels's pamphlet was designed to bolster their ideological backbone.

The three chapters which comprised *Socialism: Utopian and Scientific* underlined the effects of Engels's immersion in the natural sciences as he distinguished the scientific rigour of Marxism from the lofty nostrums of the early Utopian socialists (for whom the Possibilists still had a soft spot). The early pages were taken up with a clinical dismemberment of the 'pure phantasies' and Utopian dreams of Saint-Simon, Robert Owen and Charles Fourier. Yet the language was not nearly as harsh as it had been in the early 1840s. Instead, the mature Engels found much of worth in Fourier's critique of sexual relations in bourgeois society; he expressed admiration (as a former factory employer himself) for Owen's industrial paternalism; and he saluted Saint-Simon's analysis of the way that economic realities dictate political forms. Nonetheless, the Utopians' core failure remained a misguided vision of socialism as some kind of eternal truth which had simply to be discovered and explained for its demands to be implemented. By contrast, Engels presented socialism as a science which 'had first to be placed upon a real basis'.[51] And it was Marx who did just that with his explanation of capitalist production (through the theory of surplus value) and the realities of class struggle (through the materialist conception of history). While Marx's method exposed the class-based, capitalist nature of bourgeois society, the genius of his dialectical system was to chart a future course.

After an accumulating series of stresses, Engels explained, quantitative change would become qualitative. Just as steam comes from water and butterflies from caterpillars, 'The capitalist relation is not done away with. It is, rather, brought to a head.'[52] Tensions inherent within capitalist society, the disjuncture between the economic base and the political superstructure, reach a tipping point and a workers' revolution ensues. What then? The proletariat must seize political power, Engels announced, and transform the means of production into state property. 'But, in doing this, it abolishes itself as proletariat, abolishes all class distinction and class antagonisms, abolishes also the State as State.'[53] Here was the great political miracle of communism as startling in its way as the conservation of energy or the biology of the cell. 'State interference in social relations becomes, in one domain after another, superfluous, and then dies out of itself; the government of persons is replaced by the administration of things, and by the conduct of processes of production.' Just as Saint-Simon first predicted, future socialist rule would dissolve traditional politics and become a question of rational, technocratic management. Or, in the more obviously biological terminology of Engels, 'the state is not abolished. It withers away.'[54] At last exploitation is no more and the Darwinian struggle for survival is over as 'anarchy in social production is replaced by systematic, definite organization'. Under the leadership of the proletariat, humanity achieves true freedom liberated from its animal instincts. 'It is the ascent of man from the kingdom of necessity to the kingdom of freedom.'[55] This was the epic, political endpoint for all Engels's lofty speculation on Hegelian idealism, atomic theory, Darwinian evolution and the negation of the negation. Here was where Marx's dialectical materialism led: the proletariat revolution, emerging from the chrysalis of bourgeois society, and the coming communist dawn.

Far in excess of *The Condition of the Working Class in England* or *The Peasant War in Germany* or even his military writings, *Socialism: Utopian and Scientific* was Engels's bestseller. He proudly described it making 'a regular revolution' and 'tremendous impression' in France. 'Most people are too lazy to read stout tomes such as *Das Kapital* and hence a slim little pamphlet like this has a much more rapid effect,' he boasted to his American friend Friedrich Sorge.[56] Lafargue, who commissioned the work, was equally pleased to see it having 'a decisive effect on the direction of the socialist movement in its beginnings'.[57] Neither man exaggerated its impact. Combined with *Anti-Dühring*, Engels's *Socialism: Utopian and Scientific* was instrumental in shaping the direction of continental communism as social democrats in France, Germany, Austria, Italy and England finally had a comprehensible guide to Marxism. According to the Soviet scholar and first director of the Marx-Engels Institute, David Ryazanov, *Anti-Dühring* 'was epoch-making in the history of Marxism. It was from this book that the younger generation which began its activity during the second half of the 1870s learned what was scientific socialism, what were its philosophic premises, what was its method . . . For the dissemination of Marxism as a special method and a special system, no book except *Capital* itself, has done as much as *Anti-Dühring*. All the young Marxists who entered the public arena in the early eighties were brought up on this book.'[58] Together with the likes of August Bebel, Georgi Plekhanov, Victor Adler and Eduard Bernstein (who recanted and converted to Marxism after reading *Anti-Dühring*), Karl Kautsky was one member of that generation entering the public arena who came fully to understand scientific socialism only under Engels's pupillage. 'Judging by the influence that *Anti-Dühring* had upon me,' he wrote towards the end of his life, 'no other book can have contributed so much to the understanding of Marxism. Marx's *Capital* is the more powerful work, certainly. But it was only through *Anti-Dühring* that we learnt to understand *Capital* and read it properly.'[59]

Yet from the Western Marxist scholar György Lukács onwards, via Jean-Paul Sartre and Louis Althusser, a recurring criticism has been that what Engels codified in the 1880s was never really Marxism. It was *his* materialism, *his* dialectics, *his* scientism and *his* false conjunction of Marx with Hegel. 'The misunderstanding that arises from Engels's account of dialectics can in the main be put down to the fact that Engels – following Hegel's mistaken lead – extended the method to apply also to nature,' according to Lukács. 'However, the crucial determinants of dialectics – the interaction of subject and object, the unity of theory and practice, the historical change in the reality underlying the categories as the root cause of changes in thought, etc. – are absent from our knowledge of nature.'[60] Marxism as it appeared in *Anti-Dühring* and *Socialism: Utopian and Scientific* was thus 'Engelsian inversion' or 'Engelsian fallacy' which represented a grotesque misinterpretation of Marx's thinking. In the harsh strictures of Norman Levine, 'The first deviant from Marxism was Engels. And thus it was Engelsism which laid the basis for the future dogmatism, the future materialistic idealism of Stalin.'[61] As for evidence, these 'true Marxists' point to a series of silences in the Marx-Engels correspondence which suggests that Marx never approved of Engels's later writings and sought subtly to distance himself without hurting his friend's feelings.

Whatever mechanical revisions happened to Marxism in the twentieth century, it is a misreading of the Marx-Engels relationship to suggest either that Engels knowingly corrupted Marxian theory or that Marx had such a fragile friendship with him that he (Karl Marx!) could not bear to express a disagreement. There is no evidence that Marx was ashamed or concerned about the nature of Engels's popularization of Marxism. Indeed, he was the prime mover behind *Anti-Dühring*, had the entire manuscript read to him, contributed a small section on economics and in 1878 recommended the book as 'very important for a true appreciation of German Socialism'.[62] The reality is that Marx, like Engels, had been energized by the scientific progress of the day. 'Especially on the field of natural science,' as Wilhelm Liebknecht recalled,

– including physics and chemistry – and of history Marx closely followed every new appearance, every progress; and Moleschott, Liebig, Huxley, – whose 'Popular Lectures' we attended conscientiously – were names mentioned in our circle as often as Ricardo, Adam Smith, McCulloch and the Scotch and Irish economists. And when Darwin drew the consequences of his investigations and presented them to the public we spoke for months of nothing else but Darwin and the revolutionizing power of his scientific conquests.[63]

Equally, Marx had been drawn back to the work of Hegel in the 1870s and was the first to make the claim that the dialectical law applied to both nature and society. Like it or not, *Anti-Dühring*'s grand theoretical system was the expression of authentic, mature Marxist opinion. For the previous thirty years Engels had given himself up to explaining and popularizing the work of his 'first fiddle' and there seems little reason why he would suddenly start in the 1870s, under Marx's watch, to invert, falsify or deviate from his master's voice.[64] In the ensuing decades, as we shall see, others reinterpreted Engels's interpretation, but that is a misdemeanour for which he cannot be held intellectually culpable.

In the meantime, Engels had to break off from his scientific work to get on with the Herculean task of ordering Marx's literary estate. 'Quotations from sources in no kind of order, piles of them jumbled together, collected simply with a view to future selection. Besides that there is the handwriting which certainly cannot be deciphered by anyone but me, and then only with difficulty,' he wrote despairingly to August Bebel after wading through the Maitland Park Road archives.[65] Knowing his lifelong devotion to Marx and inevitable loneliness without him, Bebel, Kautsky and Liebknecht all urged Engels to leave London after Marx's funeral and join them on the continent. Engels, who had grown affectionately accustomed to England's low barometer life, refused point blank. 'I shall not go to any country from which one can be expelled. But that is something one can only be safe from in England and America,' he told his young disciples. Moreover, 'only here does one have the peace one needs if one is to go on with one's theoretical work'.[66] Primrose Hill had evolved into the organizational hub of global communism and, to honour his friend's memory, Engels was determined to keep intact 'the many threads from all over the world which spontaneously converged on Marx's study'.[67]

Engels now also had to play paterfamilias both to the international

Marxist movement and to the leaderless Marx clan. Happily that meant taking on as housekeeper the Marx family retainer, Helene Demuth or Nim, at 122 Regent's Park Road (where the two of them nostalgically sifted through Marx's correspondence and enjoyed a mid-morning tipple), and unhappily dealing with the two grieving, warring Marx daughters. 'I requested you, the other day, to inform me (which, as you had made a public declaration, I had a right to do) whether Mohr had told *you* that he wished Tussy to be his literary executrix,' wrote an angry Laura Lafargue from Paris to Engels in June 1883, fearful that she was being carved out of Marx's intellectual inheritance.[68] She had assumed that she, rather than Samuel Moore, would be translating *Das Kapital* and was furious that London-based Engels and Tussy were unilaterally commandeering her father's legacy. 'You know very well there is on my part no other desire but to consider your wishes as much as possible and in every respect,' Engels wrote back soothingly. 'What we all of us are desirous of seeing carried out, is a befitting monument to the memory of Mohr, the first portion of which will and must be the publication of his posthumous works.'[69]

But that was no simple matter. 'Had I known,' Engels lamented to Bebel, 'I should have pestered him day and night until it was all finished and printed.'[70] To his horror and indignation, what Engels discovered when he entered Marx's study and started leafing through his papers was that the much anticipated Volume II of *Das Kapital* had succumbed to Marx's weakness for prevarication, evidential avarice and immersion in tangential topics. Whether deliberately or not, Marx had scuttled his masterwork. 'Had it not been for the mass of American and Russian material (there are over two cubic metres of books of Russian statistics alone), Volume II would have long since been printed. These detailed studies held him up for years.'[71] So in addition to overseeing translations of Marx's work into English, Italian, Danish and French ('Try to be more faithful to the original,' Engels berated Lafargue struggling with *The Poverty of Philosophy*, 'Marx isn't a man with whom one can afford to take liberties'), Engels also set about supervising the German publication of Volumes II and III of *Das Kapital*.[72]

In his study at Regent's Park Road, from the summer of 1883 to the spring of 1885, he worked feverishly to collate and decipher the myriad revisions, statistical charts, discontinued lines of thought and incomprehensible jottings which would become the first German edition of *Das Kapital* Volume II, 'The Process of Circulation of Capital'. It was an arduous, frustrating task, and yet Engels revelled in the sensation that 'I can truly say that while I work at this book, I am living in communion with him [Marx].'[73] Enjoyable as it was to be conversing with his old comrade, the line by line editing of Marx's impenetrable, cramped handwriting was endangering Engels's health. And the manuscripts, according to Paul Lafargue, were in a terrible state: 'they contain abbreviations which have to be guessed at, crossings-out and innumerable corrections which have to be deciphered; it is as difficult to read as a Greek palimpsest with ligatures'.[74] By the mid-1880s Engels's eyes were weakening under the strain as he showed signs of conjunctivitis and myopia. To ease the strain, he was forced to initiate a new generation – 'two competent gentlemen', Karl Kautsky and Eduard Bernstein – into the hieroglyphic mysteries of Marx's handwriting before then employing a German socialist typesetter, Oskar Eisengarten, to take dictation. But Engels still had to check Marx's manuscript over and by 1887 he had developed chronic ophthalmia which was severely constricting his ability to read with anything other than natural light. Thankfully, after much trial and error the scientifically minded Engels found a remedy. 'Last year and up till August I used cocaine and, as this grew less effective (on account of habituation), went on to $ZnCl_2$, which works very well,' he informed his physician friend Ludwig Kugelmann.[75] But when it came to his progressively ageing body, his real worry was a doctor's warning that 'I'm unlikely to be able to mount a horse again – hence unfit for active service, dammit!'[76]

True to his conscientious nature, Engels released Volume II of *Das Kapital* in May 1885 barely two years after Marx's death. Its publication allowed Engels to continue the battle against the usual range of bourgeois critics – notably, the German economist Johann Karl Rodbertus who had accused Marx of plagiarism – and once again position Marxism and the theory of surplus value as part of the nineteenth century's scientific paradigm-shift. 'Marx stands in the same relation to his predecessors in the theory of surplus value as

Lavoisier stood to Priestley and Scheele,' Engels's introduction declared, using one of his favourite chemistry analogies. 'The existence of that part of the value of products which we now call surplus value had been ascertained long before Marx . . . But they did not get any further . . . He saw that this was a case neither of dephlogisticated air nor of fire-air, but of oxygen . . .'[77] However, what Volume II didn't solve was the problem which Engels had first identified in 1867 and Marx had promised to answer at a later stage, namely the question of whether constant capital (machinery) was able to generate profits through surplus value and, given the different ratios of variable to constant capital (of labour to machinery), how could profit rates be equal across different capitals? In other words, in Meghnad Desai's formulation, 'was (non-labour) capital relevant to profitability or not?' Rather than solving the conundrum, Engels weakly threw the issue back at Marx's critics: 'If they can show how an equal average rate of profit can and must come about, not only without a violation of the law of value, but rather on the very basis of it, we are willing to discuss the matter further with them.'[78]

Even with the publication in 1894 of the third and final volume of *Das Kapital*, the problems remained unresolved. Engels was not overly exercised. He regarded the third volume of Marx's masterwork as even more influential and significant than the first. 'Our theory is thereby provided for the first time with an unassailable basis while we ourselves are enabled to hold our own successfully on all fronts,' he wrote confidently to August Bebel. 'As soon as this [volume] appears, the philistines in the party will again be dealt a blow that will give them something to think about.'[79] However, the book was in an even worse shape than the previous editions, with a dizzying paper trail of notes, drafts, paraphrasing and equations jumbled together. But in contrast to his frustrations with the editing of Volume I, Engels at last, in the absence of Marx, had the freedom to mould the text as he saw fit, filleting the illustrations and eliminating the literary carbuncles. 'As this crowning volume is such a splendid and totally unanswerable work, I consider myself bound to bring it out in a shape in which the whole line of argument stands forth clearly and in bold relief,' he told Nikolai Danielson.[80]

However, since the publication in 1993 of Marx's Volume III

manuscript of 1864–5, it has become clear just how liberal this editorial initiative was. In order to get the line of argument clear, Engels markedly changed Marx's original intent on numerous occasions by integrating footnotes into the text, amalgamating sections, adding subdivisions and inserting his own thoughts. This was most obviously the case when it came to the much debated Part III, 'The Law of the Tendency of the Rate of Profit to Fall', in which Marx outlined how profits tend to decline under capitalism as labour-saving technology progressively reduces the scope for extracting surplus value from living labour. Marx then connected this falling tendency of profitability within companies to the probability of the survival of capitalism itself.[81] The question was, at what rate? Whereas Marx's original manuscript spoke of the 'shaking' of capitalist production, perhaps with an eye to the quantitative–qualitative shifts explored in *Anti-Dühring*, Engels spoke more definitively – in terms reminiscent of the youthful *Communist Manifesto* – of the 'collapse' of capitalism. A small change, but one with far-reaching consequences for twentieth-century Marxists who repeatedly looked for a systemic 'crisis' or 'breakdown' of capitalism to usher in the communist dawn. Momentarily, Marx's bulldog had slipped the leash, but it was all for the greater good of the cause. 'Engels wanted to be not just editor, but curator of Marx's legacy and editor all in one,' in the words of a recent study. 'Engels produced a readable version of Marx's manuscript for the users for whom it was meant, a group that ranged from theoretically aware workers to philologically interested academics.'[82] And, with the publication of Volume III, he felt at last the job was done, Marx's memory honoured. 'I am glad your long voyage with Marx's *Capital* is nearly ended,' Engels's old Chartist friend Julian Harney wrote to him in 1893. 'Never, I think, at least in modern times, has any man found so faithful, so devoted a friend and champion, as Marx has found in you.'[83]

Engels's fragile health had not been the only obstacle to the speedy publication of Marx's papers. The unshakeable presence of the leeching, tragicomic Roshers was another drain on Engels's emotions. To no one's great surprise, Pumps's slow-witted and increasingly deaf husband, Percy Rosher, was not proving a great success as a chartered accountant. So as Engels wrestled with dialectical materialism, new editions of *Das Kapital*, and marshalling the forces of international socialism, he also had to deal with the Roshers' family finances. By December 1888 Engels was warning the other recidivist sponger on his books, Paul Lafargue, that Percy's affairs were 'going rather badly' and it could shape up to be a tight financial year. As feared, the following autumn saw the hapless Percy 'completely smashed up' and it was left to Engels to negotiate on Percy's behalf with his brother and father to avoid an outright bankruptcy. 'However it may end,' Engels sagely predicted, 'it's sure to cost me a lot of money.'[84] And so it did as Pumps and Percy never ceased touching kind Uncle Engels for cash – much to the annoyance of the Lafargues. 'I am sorry to come pestering you just when you have so many worries and troubles over Percy's affairs, but I am compelled to do so, for we have exhausted our means,' Paul Lafargue wrote to Engels in November 1889 as he saw worrying signs of Engels's resources being diverted.[85]

Over the next five years Engels, the most revered Marxist theoretician and communist strategist of his day, was dragged ever deeper into the farcical world of the Roshers and their various schemes for making money – from 'The Rainbow Engineering Company' to 'The Rosher System for Swimming Baths'. The worst of it was having to deal with Percy's father, Charles Rosher, and his demands for loans and 'investments' in various business projects couched in a series of brazen letters. 'No one with whom he [Percy] is connected has a deeper sense of your kindness and generosity to Percy – than I have,' began one ludicrous correspondence. 'Personally I have to be very careful . . . to make ends meet . . . I venture to say that Percy with his allowance from you, plus salary is [having] more income than I am.' Charles Rosher went on to intimate in very clear language that he would only pay Percy a salary if Engels agreed to bankroll the company. 'So far as I have had opportunity of judging it will be a long time before he will be worth much in my business,' Charles shamefacedly concluded of his son's singularly unimpressive abilities.[86] And when Engels demurred at providing Rosher with more resources, Percy was duly sacked.

It was no better with brother Howard, for whom Percy then went to work in a cement, builders' and gardeners' materials company on the Isle of Wight. Demands for bridging loans, cash injections and even commercial advice appeared to arrive with every post by the early 1890s. 'My dear Mr Engels, I much regret having to ask if you could kindly oblige us again with an exchange cheque,' was a familiar request from Howard Rosher.[87] Engels knew his good nature was being abused by a bunch of chancers, yet he stoically put up with it so he could enjoy the beery company of Pumps, the memory of the Burnses and seaside holidays with her and the children in their house at Ryde. 'He *does* love the tipsy Pumps,' Tussy explained to her sister. 'He rages against Pumps – and loves her.'[88] But by 1894 his patience had finally snapped after Percy junked his job, 'spent a lot of money (not his own)', gave Engels's name in surety for a loan and turned up destitute on his doorstep at Primrose Hill. 'After all I have done for them, I am not going to quietly submit to such treatment, and did not receive them very heartily,' he told Laura Lafargue. 'What Percy is going to do and how this is to end, is more than I know.'[89] And that, thankfully, is the last we hear of Percy Rosher.*

Amidst the piles of letters, jottings and unfinished essays which Engels brought over to Regent's Park Road from Marx's study was one set of notes which particularly sparked his interest. Out from the morass of Russian statistical tables was an inspiring collection of thoughts on the nature of prehistoric society. In the early 1880s Marx had drawn up a detailed synopsis of a voguish work by the American anthropologist Lewis Henry Morgan, entitled *Ancient Society or Researches in the Lines of Human Progress from Savagery, Through Barbarism to Civilization* (1877). A hybrid mixture of Darwinism and materialism, Morgan's book sought to trace the evolution of human society from the primitive state of social organization to modern civilization. With much of his primary research drawn from the habits of the Iroquois confederacy of tribes in northern New York state, Morgan charted the impact of technological development and changing conceptions of property rights on the tribal and then family form. In terms of

---

* There is, in truth, one final glorious twist: Percy Rosher had persuaded Engels to take out a life insurance policy for him (so as to secure the future of Pumps's children). With no sense of irony, following Engels's death, Percy threatened to sue the Engels Estate for £87 in unpaid prospective contributions.

family structure, Morgan thought progress from savagery to civilization meant the inexorable move from consanguineous tribes to a
patriarchal-based, 'monogamian' (or nuclear) family household.

As Marx's extensive 'Ethnological Notebooks' have since revealed,
this was a topic of wide-ranging dialogue between him and Engels
who now added anthropology to his broadening range of scientific
enthusiasms. In the mid-1860s the two had disagreed over the significance of Pierre Tremaux's *The Origin and Transformation of Man
and Other Beings*, with its cack-handed causational theory about the
function of geology and soil in the formation of race. In early 1882,
as Marx was fighting off his chest infection in the Isle of Wight, Engels
had written to him, 'in order finally to get clear about the parallel
between the Germans of Tacitus and the American Redskins'.[90] This
followed the publication of Hubert Howe Bancroft's *The Native Races
of the Pacific States of North America* (1875), which seemed to stress
less the means of production and more the role of blood bonds in
shaping early American primitive communities.

On the eve of Marx's death, in February 1883, an essay by Karl
Kautsky on early sexual relations – which anachronistically applied
notions of sexual jealousy to 'primitive' societies and failed to connect
ancient patterns of shared land with the practice of shared wives –
revived Engels's interest in the topic. The discovery of Marx's notes
on Morgan then convinced him of the need to write something in
order to ward off further ideological deviation. When Bernstein stayed
at Regent's Park Road in early 1884, Engels 'read to me, night after
night, until the small hours of the morning, passages from Marx's
manuscripts, and the synopsis of a book with which he connected
Marx's extracts from the American writer Lewis Morgan's *Ancient
Society*'.[91] The project was, Engels hoped, to be the 'fulfilment of a
behest': to connect Morgan's researches with Marx's materialist reading of history. And, in the process, extend some of his own biological
insights from the world of butterflies and insects to womanhood and
gender relations. Somewhat unexpectedly, the womanizing Engels
ended up authoring the foundation text of socialist feminism.

*The Origin of the Family, Private Property and the State, in Light
of the Researches by Lewis H. Morgan* (1884) began with what Engels
clearly regarded as a progressive feminist principle: 'According to the

materialistic conception, the determining factor in history is, in the final instance, the production and reproduction of immediate life.'[92] At a stroke, he placed female production of human life on the same theoretical plane as the production of the means of existence – of which, in the communist canon, there was no higher virtue. His next move was, in Hegelian fashion, to historicize the family form by showing its fluid nature over the preceding epochs and point to its future incarnation under communist governance. Just as the proletariat had to understand capitalism was a transitory state, so women could rejoice that current gender inequalities were a passing interlude.

Engels did this by unpicking the materialist foundations of Morgan's chronology: the progression from a promiscuous, tribal system of living common amongst the Iroquois (sharing sexual partners and property) to the modern form of the 'pairing family' was intimately connected to the advances in the mode of production. Bluntly, the modern family and all its failings were the product of private property. However, what made Engels's interpretation especially noteworthy was how his account of family life was explored through the gaze of women and, with it, their history of social emasculation as society moved from matrilineal to patrilineal kinship patterns. 'The more the old traditional sexual relations lost their naive, primeval character, as a result of the development of the economic conditions of life . . . the more degrading and oppressive they must have appeared to the women . . .'[93] For, as Morgan had outlined, the early consanguineous system of group marriage and polygamy was far more egalitarian and autonomous than the 'brothel-tainted imagination' of modern philistine prejudice might suggest. 'Woman occupied not only a free but also a highly respected position among all the savages and all barbarians of the lower and middle stages and partly even of the upper stage.'[94] In the savage tribe, women were far freer than under liberal-bourgeois society.

The fall from grace came with the introduction of individual family property rights (as distinct from broader clan or tribe rights) and, accompanying them, the practice of inheritance through the male line. Individual ownership and private property signalled the overthrow of the mother right and 'the world historic defeat of the female sex'. From that point on, the patriarchal family form was unstoppable as the husband seized the reins and the woman was 'degraded, enthralled, became the slave of the man's lust, a mere instrument for breeding children'.[95] Just as private property instigated the modern class system, so gender relations became another element of the social divide: women now joined the ranks of those oppressed by the capitalist mode of production. 'The first class opposition that appears in history coincides with the development of the antagonism between man and woman in monogamous marriage, and the first class oppression coincides with that of the female sex by the male,' Engels declared.[96] In the family, the husband was the bourgeois and the wife the proletariat, with predictably brutal and often murderous outcomes.

It was the high-bourgeois, mid-Victorian family Engels had particularly in mind: behind that veneer of evangelical virtue festered hypocrisy, prostitution and abuse. 'This Protestant monogamy leads merely, if we take the average of the best cases, to a wedded life of leaden boredom, which is described as domestic bliss,' he wrote with the authority of one who had lived for two decades amongst the Dissenting elites of northern England; '. . . the wife . . . differs from the ordinary courtesan only in that she does not hire out her body, like a wage worker, on a piecework, but sells it into slavery once and for all'.[97] The inevitable accompaniment of monogamy – in dialectical terms, the inherent contradiction in the form – was prostitution and hetaerism. For whereas in primitive communities sexual licence was unashamedly enjoyed by both genders, in the private property family 'the right of conjugal infidelity' is solely the prerogative of the male. Sex love, as Engels clumsily put it, was possible only amongst a proletariat devoid of both private property and Christian bourgeois norms. As such, he romantically if mistakenly believed, proletarian marriages lacked the abusive practices of their bourgeois counterparts.

Having set out the transience of various family forms over the preceding stages of human society, Engels now advocated a further revolution in sexual relations. It was a theme he had first touched upon in *The Condition of the Working Class in England* when he charted the effects on the family unit of female employment in Manchester's mills and factories. The new industrial reality of working women and unemployed men had served only to desex both parties: 'The wife supports the family, the husband sits at home, tends the children, sweeps the room and cooks.' Engels reported the experience of a friend of his visiting a former workmate in St Helen's, Lancashire, who 'sat and mended his wife's stocking with his bodkin'. '"No, I know this is not my work, but my poor missus is i' th' factory . . . so I have to do everything for her what I can, for I have no work, nor had any for more nor three years, and I shall never have any more work while I live"; and then he wept a big tear.'[98] Yet the conclusion which the precocious 24-year-old Engels drew from this was not that women should be prevented from working (indeed, industrialization promised them a new era of liberation free from domestic servitude), but rather, 'if the reign of the wife over the husband, as inevitably brought about by the factory system, is inhuman, the pristine rule of the husband over the wife must have been inhuman too'.[99] The domestic upset produced by mass female employment graphically exposed how it was only private interests rather than human affection which was holding the modern family together and that was no basis for a fulfilling equality of the sexes. Industrialization had ripped away the veneer of 'natural' patriarchy and he optimistically believed that with the spread of female wage earners, 'no basis for any kind of male supremacy is left in the proletarian household, except, perhaps, for something of the brutality toward women that has spread since the introduction of monogamy'.[100]

On the surface it might well seem that capitalism and its demands for female labour offered the surest route to sexual equality, but the exploitation of modern family life could be fully solved only by the transition to communism. Once inheritable wealth was turned back into a shared pool of social property then the narrow, economic foundations of the 'pairing' family would disintegrate. As Engels put it in a letter of 1885, 'True equality between men and women can, or so I am convinced, become a reality only when the exploitation of both by capital has been abolished, and private work in the home been transformed into a public industry.'[101] Women could emerge from under the patriarchal cosh only once the family ceased to exist as an economic unit, private housekeeping became a socialized event, and – most radically of all – 'the care and upbringing of children becomes a public affair'.[102] Private property, wealth and even children all had to be passed over as shared goods to the wider community.

With almost Fourierist verve, Engels then laid out the Utopian promise offered by this sexual revolution: women marrying for love rather than money (which would lead to 'a gradual rise of more unrestrained sexual intercourse' and, with it, 'a laxer public opinion regarding virginal honour and female shame'); wives no longer having to tolerate their husband's infidelities for fear of losing their property; and marriages built on mutual affection and respect together with people being spared 'the useless mire of divorce proceedings'.[103] Not quite Fourier's free-love phalanstery, but not far off.

One sexual freedom which Engels was not willing to sanction was homosexuality. In 1869 Karl Marx had sent him a copy of the German lawyer Karl Ulrich's book *Argonauticus*, which argued that same-sex desire was inborn, that masculinity and femininity should be regarded as a continuum, and coined the term 'Urning' to describe homosexual and lesbian attraction. Engels, revealing all of his Prussian Calvinist upbringing, was appalled by such 'unnatural revelations'. 'The paederasts are beginning to count themselves, and discover that they are a power in the state,' he wrote back to Marx in a hyperbolic, homophobic rant. '*Guerre aux cons, paix aux trous-de-cul* ["War on the cunts, peace to the arse-holes"] will now be the slogan. It is a bit of luck that we, personally, are too old to have to fear that, when this party wins, we shall have to pay physical tribute to the victors . . . just wait until the new North German Penal Code recognizes the *droits du cul* [rights of the arse-hole]; then he will operate quite differently. Then things will go badly enough for poor frontside people like us, with our childish penchant for females.'[104] By way of contrast, the English socialist Edward Carpenter, in his privately circulated essay *Homogenic Love* (1893), took Engels's critique of the bourgeois family to a different conclusion by arguing for the virtue of non-procreative sex and, with it, the cultural and legal acceptance of homosexuality as part of a broader process of socialist emancipation.[105] Carpenter's Platonic vision of 'Comradeship' offered an altogether different socialism from Engels's fecund Utopia of free-love and communal child-rearing.

Never as pervasive a theory as dialectical materialism, Engels's writings on the family nonetheless proved a significant contribution to socialist theory in the twentieth century. Indeed, an entire generation of Marxist feminists was brought up on his work. The feminist and activist Kate Millett recorded in her 1970 book, *Sexual Politics*, how Engels's treatment of marriage and the family as historical institutions, 'subject to the same processes of evolution as other social phenomena . . . laid the sacred open to serious criticism, analysis, even to possible drastic reorganization'.[106] Similarly, Shulamith Firestone's *The Dialectic of Sex: A Case for Feminist Revolution* (1970) drew on Engels's writings to make the case for a post-patriarchal settlement and communal living. What many feminists admired about Engels's approach was his treatment of gender differences as economically produced rather than biologically determined: patriarchy was another function of bourgeois class society and both needed to be undone.[107]

More recently Engels's work has been criticized, principally by anthropologists, for its failure to acknowledge male domination in primitive societies (even, at one point, seeming to sanction the tribal habits of *ius primae noctis*) and by his vision of the division of labour as innate rather than socially constructed. In addition, a new wave of feminists has criticized Engels for failing to appreciate female sexual desires as distinct from the reproductive process, for depicting women as naturally yearning for permanent marriage and, more significantly, a reductive failure to 'attend seriously to questions of sexuality, ideology, domesticity or the division of labour and power between women and men generally'.[108] Leaving aside these often anachronistic criticisms, what is surely of greater interest is how on earth these feminist ideas came from Engels – the great Lothario, slave to Paris's finest *grisettes*, and rough seducer of Mrs Moses Hess. The truth was that the views of Engels in his sixties had profoundly matured from his raffish days in the boudoirs and brothels of the 1840s. Engels even endorsed plans in the German Reichstag for outlawing prostitution – whilst warning of the repercussions which could hit sex workers if the experience of England's Contagious Diseases Act was anything to go by. 'It is my belief that, in dealing with this matter, we should above all consider the interests of the girls themselves as victims of the present social order, and protect them as far as possible from ending up in the gutter,' the reformed one-time client told August Bebel.[109]

There is also a powerful case for suggesting that for much of his adult life Engels lived out his beliefs. Although contradictions of Hegelian proportions enveloped much of Engels's professional existence, when it came to his personal affairs he refused to submit to bourgeois norms; it was only on Lizzy's death-bed that he finally wed his partner to soothe her religious qualms. Cynics might suggest that this had more to do with inheritance rights and shares in Ermen & Engels, but to my mind it was a principled objection to what he regarded as the hypocrisy of marriage. Engels was also acutely aware of the fragile social position of women in the bourgeois family system when it came to the collapse of relationships. Sentiments he expressed not only when it came to enforcing the Roshers' marriage, but also in typically forthright manner in October 1888 when Karl Kautsky announced he was leaving his wife, Louise, for a girl he had met in Salzburg (who, in turn, swiftly exchanged him for his brother, Hans). Engels, who always admired Louise Kautsky, upbraided Karl for having dealt 'the most terrible blow a woman can possibly receive'. At great length, he spelt out the consequences of divorce in contemporary society: while no social stigma attached itself to the husband, 'the wife loses her status altogether; she has got to begin all over again and do so under more difficult circumstances'. Engels urged him to reflect very carefully on the matter and then, if there was no other option, proceed 'only in the most considerate manner possible'.[110]

Such admirable appreciation of the difficulties faced by divorcees in nineteenth-century Europe are all alas overshadowed by Engels's personal response to the women's movement of the day. As we have seen, part of the reason he fell for Mary and then Lizzy was their earthy, illiterate contrast to the 'priggishness and sophistry of the "heddicated" and "sensitive" daughters of the bourgeoisie' and there are numerous references in Engels's letters extolling his innate abhorrence for 'affected, "eddicated" Berlin ladies'.[111] In fact, purposeful, intelligent women who were neither pretty nor named Marx were the subject of instinctive misogynistic abuse by Engels. He particularly disliked middle-aged female intellectuals: so, the secularist feminist and theosophist Annie Besant was 'Mother Besant'; the journalist and war correspondent Emily Crawford, 'Mother Crawford'; the activist and sexual health campaigner Gertrud Guillaume-Schack, 'Mother Schack'. Needless to say, he was highly dismissive of the campaign for female suffrage – 'these little madams, who clamour for women's rights' – and regarded their cause as a distraction behind which class rule would flourish.[112] 'Those Englishwomen who championed a women's formal right to allow themselves to be as thoroughly exploited by capitalists as men are, have, for the most part, a direct or indirect interest in the capitalist exploitation of both sexes,' he wrote to 'Mother Schack', explaining how he was more focused on the coming generation than on formal equality amongst the existing one.[113] Yet when, in 1876, a female candidate bounced up the steps of No. 122 Regent's Park Road seeking Engels's vote for the London School Board elections (for which women were eligible to stand following the 1870 Education Act), he couldn't help but give her all his seven votes – as a result, 'she had more votes than any of the other seven candidates for election. Incidentally, the ladies who sit on school boards here are notable for the fact that they do very little talking and a great deal of working – as much on average as three men.'[114]

Finally, after his arduous years of dialectical materialism and hand-to-hand combat with Marx's manuscripts, with his eyes fading and his rheumatic legs going, Engels rewarded himself with a holiday. Even as an ageing man, he always enjoyed the prospect of travel: new people, ideas and places were the secret to Engels's preternatural youthfulness. In 1888 the United States of America promised all three. What was more, an American edition of *The Condition of the Working Class in England* had appeared in 1886 and, after decades of egregious exploitation, the US working class seemed to be evolving towards class consciousness. 'At this very moment I am receiving the American papers with accounts of the great strike of 12,000 Pennsylvanian coal-miners in the Connellsville district,' Engels wrote in the appendix to the American edition of the *Condition*, 'and I seem but to read my own description of the North of England colliers' strike of 1844.'[115]

Mark Twain famously christened this period of unfathomable prosperity and poverty 'The Gilded Age': an epoch of robber barons and intensifying inequality; the industrial might of the Vanderbilts, Morgans, Dukes and Carnegies (who would become such champions of Herbert Spencer's 'social Darwinism') alongside workplace unrest and the first red shoots of socialism. In 1886, the year of the 'great upheaval', over 700,000 workers either went out on strike or faced employer lockouts as disputes over wage cuts, mechanization and de-skilling intensified.[116] In Chicago, some 90,000 workers marched through the streets on the first May Day rally called by the Federation of Organized Trades and Labor Unions – a show of strength which spiralled tragically out of control three days later with the Haymarket Square massacre (in which police opened fire on demonstrators after an anarchist bomb was thrown). Engels was highly encouraged by the 'American vigour' of the US labour movement, in contrast to Britain's still quiescent working class, eking out the last embers of the mid-Victorian boom. 'The last Bourgeois Paradise on earth is fast changing into a Purgatory, and can only be prevented from becoming, like Europe, an Inferno by the go-ahead pace at which the development of the newly fledged proletariat of America will take place,' he wrote to his US translator, Florence Kelley-Wischnewetzky (who, in time, inevitably metamorphosed into 'Mother Wischnewetzky'), 'I only wish Marx could have lived to see it!'[117]

Of course, there were problems with the US situation – not least an unfortunate lack of ideological rigour. 'Theoretical ignorance is an attribute of all young nations,' Engels sagely observed. However, with youth also came a welcome absence of the cultural and intellectual detritus which made European socialism so sclerotic. America was notable for its 'purely bourgeois institutions unleavened by feudal remnants or monarchical traditions, and without a permanent and hereditary proletariat'.[118] As such, it offered a clean sheet in which bourgeois hegemony could quickly be followed by a fast-track proletarian revolution. On this 'more favoured soil', the organized working class was achieving in months the sort of political and electoral advances their European counterparts took years to master. Frustratingly, such progress risked being undone by the all-too-familiar party split within the progressive movement. After the May Day riots, the Federation of Organized Trades and Labor Unions retreated towards 'business' unionism, narrowly guarding the interests of its members rather than opposing the Gilded Age capitalist settlement. Those workers who were politically active were divided between a Socialist Labor Party, controlled for the most part by German émigrés, and the Noble and Holy Order of the Knights of Labor. Founded in 1869 by Philadelphia garment workers, it was a guild-like fraternal order open to all 'producers' (excluding barmen and lawyers) from trade unionists to socialists to unskilled labourers. In an earlier period of his life, Engels would have dismissed the Knights as dreamy, Proudhonist and petit-bourgeois – with their plans for co-operatives, working-class mutuals and an emotional sanctification of labour as against the Darwinian evils of capitalism – but the politically astute communist elder now thought them 'the unavoidable starting point' for US proletarian politics. By contrast, the Socialist Labor Party, though highly orthodox in its Marxian philosophy, displayed all the classic faults of an over-intellectualized émigré circle: too much idealist philosophy and not enough practical politics.

But Engels wanted to see it for himself. On 8 August 1888 he set sail for New York aboard the *City of Berlin*, together with Carl Schorlemmer, Eleanor Marx and her lover, Edward Aveling. Tussy recalled the 68-year-old Engels in high spirits on the steamer, 'always ready in any weather to go for a walk on deck and have a glass of lager. It seemed to be one of his unshakeable principles never to go round an obstacle but always to jump or climb over it.'[119] Yet when they reached America, Engels had no desire to address socialist congresses, rally the proletarian troops, tour Pittsburgh railroads or visit Pennsylvanian steel mills. Instead, in an echo of his 1849 walking tour, Engels opted to act the tourist, incognito, with a month-long itinerary which took him from New York to Boston, on to Niagara Falls and then to Canada and Lake Ontario.

In his journal of the trip there is the familiar European refrain about the speed and bustle of US life – 'an American cannot bear the idea of anyone walking in front of him in the street, he must push and brush past him' – but also a rather surprised tone at the aesthetics of late nineteenth-century America. 'Don't you believe that America is a new country – it is the most old-fashioned place in the world,' he reported back to Laura Lafargue.[120] The cabs and carriages they endured along the eastern seaboard were worthy of the seventeenth century, while the decor of the houses and hotel rooms they stayed in was remarkable for its faux Old World vogue – 'everywhere, the chairs, tables and cupboards mostly look like the heirlooms of past generations'.[121]

The people were a different matter. Maybe because of his own background in trade, maybe because he had spent so much of his life in thrusting, bartering, entrepreneurial Manchester, Engels could not help but admire the unapologetic vitality and social mobility of the US immigrant ethos. And no one better embodied this aspiration than his nephew, Pumps's brother Willie Burns, starting out on a new life in Boston after emigrating from Lancashire. In contrast to the hopeless Percy, Burns was 'a wonderful fellow, bright, energetic and with his heart and soul in the movement. He is doing well, works for the Boston & Providence Railroad (now the Old Colony), gets $12 a week, has a nice wife (whom he brought with him from Manchester) and three children.' In the land of the free, unencumbered by class prejudice and feudal remnants, 'nothing would induce him to return to England; he's just the lad for a country like America', predicted Engels the unlikely apostle of the American dream.[122]

For Engels the urbanist, the high point of his tour was not 'very pretty' Cambridge, MA, or 'beautiful, elegant' Concord (where he enjoyed a prison visit), but the 'grandest site for the capital of Capitalist Production you can see', New York City. As so many Marxists who would follow his lead in the twentieth century, Engels found in America the *ne plus ultra*, the hyper-reality, of the late capitalist form. While Horkheimer, Adorno and Marcuse would discover it along the inter-war freeways of Los Angeles and campuses of southern California, in the 1880s it was the East Coast which represented the crystal ball of capitalism's future.[123] 'We got into New York after dark and I thought I got into a chapter of Dante's *Inferno*,' Engels began his account to Laura Lafargue somewhat predictably before describing his wonderment at the 'elevated railways thundering over your head, tram-cars by the hundred with rattling bells, awful noises on all sides'. In 1840s Manchester, it was the mills, manu-factories and Oxford Road slums which testified to the capitalist urban form; in 1880s New York, it was the manipulated mass culture and *son et lumière*, technological spectacle of the modern city. Manhattan was, in the later idiom of Walter Benjamin, a fairground or dream-world of high-bourgeois consumer commodification. 'Naked electric arc-lights over every ship,' Engels noted, 'not to light you but to attract you as an advertisement, and consequently blinding you and confusing everything before you.' New York was, in short, 'a town worthy to be inhabited by the most vile-looking crowd in the world, they all look like discharged croupiers from Monte Carlo'.[124]

Despite these revealingly English reservations about the vulgarity of the New Yorkers, Engels enormously enjoyed his trip across the Atlantic. The high altitude, the go-ahead Yankees, the first-rate food and the widespread availability of German beer convinced him he would return. 'The voyage has done me a tremendous amount of good,' he wrote to his brother Herman on the steamer back as he cracked into his supply of California Riesling; 'I feel at least five years younger, all my little infirmities have faded into the background, even my eyes have improved . . .'[125] He returned to London physically invigorated and politically exhilarated about the prospects of proletarian revolution. Back with Nim in Regent's Park Road, he was now ready to put aside the science and philosophy of the last decade and embrace the dirty business of politics and making Marx's ideas matter on the street. In 1890 the seventy-year-old Engels returned full time to the workers' struggle – which, to his great joy, now finally encompassed the British proletariat. Some fifty years after crossing the Channel to sniff out the scent of revolution, he sensed England was at last ready to rise.

9

First Fiddle

'On 4 May, 1890, the English proletariat, rousing itself from forty years of hibernation, rejoined the movement of its class.'[1] On its inaugural May Day march, an event later to be subsumed into the Soviet calendar of military parades and Red Square hardware, London witnessed a bravura display of socialist prowess with workers and activists gathering from first light along the Victoria Embankment. Leading the procession were the dock labourers and gas workers of the East End, followed by the ranks of the Women's Trade Union League, the Bloomsbury Socialist Society, the North Camberwell Progressive Club, the East Finsbury Radical Club, the West Newington Reform Club and myriad trade unions. Accompanying them on their progression through the streets of commercial London – along Holborn and Oxford Street to Marble Arch – were councillors, parliamentarians, school board members and such stars of the socialist firmament as Fabian playwright George Bernard Shaw, the socialist MP Robert Cunninghame Graham, the gas workers' leader Will Thorne, the Marx sons-in-law Paul Lafargue and Edward Aveling, a young George Lansbury and Engels himself. For a brief, delirious day the heart of Empire fell under the sway of the radical Left.

By the time the procession entered Hyde Park – the once fashionable parade ground of London high society transformed during the nineteenth century into 'the Park of the People' – numbers had swelled to over 200,000 with radical banners and placards dotting the horizon. 'I was on platform 4 (a heavy goods wagon),' Engels recalled, 'and could only see part – a fifth, say, or an eighth – of the crowd, but it was one vast sea of faces, as far as the eye could reach.' Inevitably, there were the usual personal rivalries, factional disputes and precious

321

little fraternal feeling within the socialist hierarchy. But for Engels the rally heralded a symbolic shedding of liberal confusion from the English working classes who, after the collapse of the mid-Victorian boom, had finally rediscovered their Chartist, socialist inheritance. 'What wouldn't I give for Marx to have witnessed this awakening, he who, on this self-same English soil, was alive to the minutest symptom!' he wrote wistfully to August Bebel. For the first time in almost half a century, Engels the resident Anglophile had heard the voice of the British proletariat ring out once more – and it did him a power of good. 'I carried my head a couple of inches higher as I climbed down from the old goods wagon.'[2]

Just as remarkable as the crowds was Engels's presence at Hyde Park. The steely operator who had functioned so long in the shadows of Marx, who had not really adopted a public profile since 1840s Paris, was re-emerging in his own right. 'Only now did he, who so far, to use his own words, had been second fiddle, show all he was capable of,' recalled Wilhelm Liebknecht. As an adviser, exhorter and mentor in the struggles of the international working-class movement, 'he showed that he could play first fiddle too'. 'At every difficulty that we who work in the vineyard of our master, the people, come across, we go to Engels,' wrote his devoted Tussy in 1890. 'And never do we appeal to him in vain. The work this single man has done in recent years would have been too much for a dozen ordinary men.'[3] As May Days were commemorated across the continent and Marxism was adopted as the official ideology of an ever greater swathe of socialist parties – from Austria to Spain, Russia to America and now, gratifyingly, England – Engels's decrees could prove decisive. Often muttering the lament 'if only Marx was alive today', the Grand Lama of the Regent's Park Road spent his final, energetic years mulling over the emerging intellectual and organizational issues confronting socialism: from the continued vitality of capitalism to the political challenge of welfarist social democracy to the suffrage strategy of mass workers' parties. In the face of rapidly shifting political terrain, Engels the great doctrinaire revealed himself a surprisingly supple tactician rarely ashamed to rethink strategy or question sacred tenets.

From the practical to the philosophical, in his ebbing days 'the General' always stood ready to assist the cause. What kept him steadfast was his unrelenting love for life and a preternatural conviction that history was on his side, that the forward march of socialism was more realizable than ever before. With it came a gut determination to last just a few years longer, to 'take a peek into the new century' and witness the Marxist triumph he had made his life's work.

'We are all socialists now,' was the insouciant response of liberal statesman Sir William Harcourt to the changing political weather of late 1880s Britain. The once unshakeable ideological tenets of the mid-Victorian era – individualism, *laissez-faire*, self-help, evangelical certitude – were starting to crumble in the face of a growing desire for ameliorative state action. In Birmingham, Glasgow and London local councils were experimenting with radical programmes of municipal socialism; in Oxford, the English Idealist philosopher T. H. Green was reviving Hegel to offer a new philosophy of progressive state intervention and, with it, the intellectual foundations of New Liberalism; Henry George's seminal text, *Progress and Poverty* (1879), with its powerful demand for land reform, was making waves across England and Ireland; and in Bloomsbury drawing rooms, Sheffield Halls of Science and East End radical clubs, socialist ideas of humanity, equity and class consciousness were being debated with enthusiasm for the first time in forty years. For Engels, these stirrings in the nation that had given birth to the Industrial Revolution and suckled the first proletariat were long overdue.

Ten years earlier, at the start of the 1880s, he had optimistically thought socialism was on the verge of revival and agreed to contribute to the trade unionist paper the *Labour Standard*. Through the summer of 1881 Engels slogged away encouraging the trade unions to mobilize their members, drop their parochial, guild-like mentality and confront en masse the exploitative capitalist class. 'There are plenty of symptoms that the working class of this country is awakening to the consciousness that it has for some time been moving in the wrong groove,' he wrote, urging the union barons to forgo demands for higher wages and shorter hours and concentrate on 'the wages systems itself'.[4] But it did no good: 'I do not see any progress,' he complained in a resignation letter to the paper's editor George Shipton in August 1881.[5] To Engels's frustration, the ingrained pusillanimity of the English proletariat was proving more intractable than ever. 'For five whole months I tried, through *The Labour Standard*, for which I wrote leading articles, to pick up the threads of the old Chartist movement and disseminate our ideas so as to see whether this might evoke some response,' he explained to his '48 comrade Johann Phillip Becker. The result? 'Absolutely nothing.'[6] The unfortunate truth, Engels concluded, was that as long as the English working class continued to share in the fruits of the British Empire's industrial monopoly there was no hope of socialism. They were getting rich off colonial hegemony and, seeing little reason to upset such a profitable arrangement, had auctioned themselves off to the Liberal Party. Only the demise of Britain's commercial advantage in the face of American competition and a sustained period of impoverishment could possibly spur the workers to action. 'On no account whatever allow yourself to be bamboozled into believing that a real proletarian movement is afoot here,' Engels complained to Bebel in 1883. 'Participation in the domination of the world market was and is the economic basis of the English workers' political nullity.'[7]

So, the annoyance was all the greater for the avidly proletarian Engels that when English socialism *did* revive it was not the result of a grand socio-economic climacteric – on the contrary, it was highly intellectual, even spiritual in origin and led by annoyingly middle-class *penseurs*. 'Needless to say that today there is indeed "Socialism again in England", and plenty of it,' Engels wrote in 1892 in a new introduction to *The Condition of the Working Class in England*. 'Socialism of all shades; Socialism conscious and unconscious, Socialism prosaic and poetic, Socialism of the working class and of the middle class, for, verily, that abomination of abominations, Socialism, has not only become respectable, but has actually donned evening dress and lounges lazily on drawing-room *causeuses*.'[8] Henry Hyndman's account of a day of socialist action makes clear just how apt such criticisms were. 'It was a curious scene, Morris in his soft hat and blue suit, Champion, Frost and Joynes in the morning garments of the well-to-do, several working-men comrades, and I myself wearing the frock-coat in which Shaw said I was born, with a tall hat and good gloves, all earnestly engaged in selling a penny Socialist paper during the busiest time of the day in London's busiest thoroughfare.'[9] For the pioneers of English socialism were a class apart from those they hoped to emancipate: there was the Christian or 'Sacramental Socialist' grouping centred around Stewart Headlam's Guild of St Matthew; Edward Carpenter's Millthorpe commune of New Lifers, manly comradeship and Eastern mysticism; Thomas Davidson's vaguely Owenite Fellowship of the New Life (which would, in turn, sprout the Fabian Society); and an eclectic range of other societies from the East End-based Labour Emancipation League to the Land Reform Union to the National Secular Society. What drew these bohemian radicals and angst-ridden bourgeois towards socialism was, according to the Fabian ideologue Beatrice Webb, 'a consciousness of sin . . . a growing uneasiness, amounting to conviction, that the industrial organisation, which had yielded rent, interest, and profits on a stupendous scale, had failed to provide a decent livelihood and tolerable conditions for a majority of the inhabitants of Great Britain'.[10] For numerous other English socialists, it was a spiritual conveyor belt from Nonconformity to secularism and then to a religion of humanity built upon an ethical notion of socialism and fellowship. Few had read *Das Kapital*, their political connections with continental communism were minimal and their grasp of dialectical materialism abysmal. There was only one amongst the English socialists who could honestly count himself a conviction Marxist: the top-hatted Hyndman, founder of the most influential socialist sect in 1880s London, the Social Democratic Federation (SDF). The only problem was Engels couldn't stand him.

Henry Mayers Hyndman, the son of a West India merchant, trained for the Bar, tried his hand at journalism and, in the end, married well. His epiphany came in 1880 when he read *Das Kapital* in French and introduced himself to Karl Marx, 'the Aristotle of the nineteenth century', becoming in the process a persistent and tiresome presence at Maitland Park Road. Hyndman always claimed it was his intimate friendship with Marx which antagonized the resentful Engels, driving him 'to break down what he thought might be a rival influence to his own'. As was so often the case with the upper reaches of socialist politics, an awful lot of it came down to personalities. Hyndman dismissed the Marx-Engels relationship as built around the financial dependence of the former on the latter with the 'exacting, suspicious, jealous' Engels demanding (with a well-turned play on *Das Kapital*) 'the exchange value of his ready cash' in friendship. 'Mrs Marx could not bear to think of it,' wrote Hyndman in his autobiography. 'She spoke of him [Engels] to my wife more than once as Karl Marx's "evil genius" and wished that she could relieve her husband from any dependence upon this able and loyal but scarcely sympathetic coadjutor.'[11] And Hyndman didn't reserve these views for posterity. He repeatedly used his SDF paper, *Justice*, to attack the lofty, detached Engels and his 'Marxist clique' for failing to support him, the SDF and a unified socialist party in Britain. 'Engels has a perfect genius for overthrowing good understanding and for setting men by the ears,' he railed. 'If there were nobody else to intrigue and plot against, he would intrigue and plot against himself.'[12]

While Engels did guard his friendships rather proprietarily, what infuriated both him and Marx was Hyndman's shameless plagiarism of *Das Kapital* for his communist credo, *England for All* (1881), with no acknowledgement of the author. More than that, Engels thought that behind Hyndman's socialist veneer there lurked an old-fashioned Tory chauvinist (an accurate analysis given Hyndman's later acceptance of 'Tory Gold' to fund his election campaigns). 'Hyndman is shrewd and a good business man, but superficial and STOCK-JOHN-BULL,' Engels confided to Kautsky. 'Moreover his ambition far outruns his talents and achievements.'[13] Never entirely at one with the working class, Hyndman ran the SDF with a combination of high-handed imperiousness and rigid Marxist orthodoxy. Indeed, the philosophical strictures he imposed were too much even for Engels. 'The SDF is in fact a sect pure and simple,' the increasingly pluralist Engels told Kautsky. 'It has ossified Marxism into a hard and fast dogma' and was in danger of repelling prospective supporters.[14] Worse than all that was Hyndman's demagogic vanity – which Engels thought dangerously on display in February 1886 when Hyndman, John Burns and his wealthy backer H. H. Champion led a rally through Pall Mall and Piccadilly which sparked an afternoon of rioting by 8,000 unemployed East Enders happy to tear up the West End for the day. 'What has been achieved is to equate socialism with looting in the minds of the bourgeois public and, while this may not have made matters much worse, it has certainly got us no further,' was Engels's sour judgement on 'Bloody Monday'.[15] It all pointed to the fundamental problem with the SDF and its executive of socialist charlatans who were 'determined to conjure up overnight a movement which, here as elsewhere, necessarily calls for years of work'.[16] No one seemed capable in Britain of the kind of steady organizational and ideological slog which Liebknecht and Kautsky were undertaking in Germany or Lafargue and Guesde in France.

So Engels was delighted when, in 1884, Edward Aveling and William Morris split from the SDF to establish a rival Socialist League. He instantly summoned them to Regent's Park Road for a quick tutorial on party management, discipline and propaganda – the result of which was the creation of Morris's elegant journal, *Commonweal*, and a network of Socialist League branches siphoning off disgruntled SDF members. However, the relationship between Morris and Engels was never going to be easy. The aethereal, ethical, Arts and Crafts Morris rarely disguised his lack of interest in the rational, technical precepts of scientific socialism. 'To speak frankly, I do not know what Marx's Theory of Value is, and I'm damned if I want to know,' he explained to one public meeting. 'It is enough political economy for me to know that the idle rich class is rich and the working-class is poor, and that the rich are rich because they rob the poor.'[17] His Utopian tract, *News from Nowhere*, advocated a revolutionary return to the pre-industrial past with medieval garb, craft guilds, the Houses of Parliament turned into a dung-heap and a London rid of industry – a vision diametrically opposed to Engels's belief that socialism depended on the kind of technological advances and prosperity unleashed by the industrial revolution. Unsurprisingly, Engels was wont initially to dismiss Morris as 'a very rich but politically inept art lover', but after the split from the SDF and the discovery of a shared interest in Old Norse mythology the friendship warmed. Not for long: as soon as Morris started to flirt with anarchism, Engels excommunicated him as 'a sentimental dreamer pure and simple'. Engels feared it would take an exhaustive course of bi-weekly seminars to teach Morris about socialism, 'but who has the time to do it, and if you drop him for a month, he is sure to lose himself again. And is he worth all that trouble even if one had the time?'[18] And so Engels shortsightedly turned his back on potentially the most inspiring and magnetic figures within the British socialist pantheon.

But at least Morris, in his own misguided way, was pulling in the right direction, unlike the Fabians. George Bernard Shaw, Sidney Webb, Sydney Olivier, Annie Besant, Frank Podmore and the rest of this consciously intellectual ginger group committed two cardinal sins in Engels's eyes: they dared to criticize Marx's economics and were suspiciously 'eddicated, middle-class types. 'A dilettante lot of egregiously conceited mutual admirers who soar above such ignorant people as Marx,' as he petulantly put it to Laura Lafargue.[19] And while he was willing to give the Fabian Society some credit for their socialist redirection of the London County Council, he regarded them in the main as an unhelpful wing of the welfarist, Liberal Party whose slowly-slowly strategy of political permeation constituted an exercise in class futility. But such high-handed dismissiveness, along with the abuse meted out to Hyndman and Morris, would have been more credible if Engels had had his own candidate, someone of skill and industry with a popular following, ready to lead the socialist movement. He didn't. In fact, out of a foolishly misplaced sense of loyalty to the Marx clan, Engels decided to back one of the most reviled and distrusted characters in British socialism.

'I must give you some other news . . . You must have known, I fancy, for some time that I am very fond of Edward Aveling – and he says he is fond of me – so we are going to "set up" together . . . I need not say that this resolution has been an easy one for me to arrive at. But I think it is for the best . . . Do not misjudge us – He is very good – and you must not think too badly of either of us. Engels, as always, is all that is good,' so Tussy informed her sister, Laura, of her 'marriage' to Edward Bibbins Aveling in 1884.[20] The fourth son of a Congregationalist minister, Aveling had enjoyed a stellar career as a scientist, with a Fellowship at University College London and lectureship in Comparative Anatomy, until his vocal secularism cost him his tenure. As a result, in the early 1880s he relaunched himself as 'the people's Darwin' and used the public platform of the National Secular Society to bring a mass, often working-class audience to atheism and Darwinian philosophy. He then transcribed his lectures and courses into a series of popular, easily understandable penny tracts such as 'The Student's Darwin' and 'Darwin Made Easy'.[21] Aveling's subsequent journey towards Marxism began in 1884 after he encountered Hyndman and the SDF through his growing involvement with London school board politics. In the ensuing months Aveling became a gifted, intelligent, industrious and conscientious servant to the socialist cause; unfortunately, he was also a shit. Hyndman thought him 'a man of very bad character'; Kautsky, 'an evil creature'; and even the generous Bernstein, 'a despicable rogue'.[22] 'One of the several models who sat unconsciously for Dubedat,' George Bernard Shaw recalled of Aveling's role in crafting the unattractive anti-hero for his play *The Doctor's Dilemma*, that he 'was morbidly scrupulous as to his religious and political convictions and would have gone to the gallows sooner than recant a syllable of them. But he had absolutely no conscience about money and women.'[23] This was obvious in his relations with Tussy with whom he eloped in 1884 despite being still legally wed to a Miss Isabel Campbell Frank, daughter of a highly prosperous poulterer, whom he never officially divorced. For Engels, such bourgeois foibles were of no concern. 'The fact is that Aveling has a lawful wife whom he cannot get rid of *de jure* although he has for years been rid of her *de facto*,' he briskly explained to the sceptical Bernstein, having blessed the union and given the happy couple £50 for a honeymoon in the Peak District.[24] But Aveling did not have nearly so kind a heart as Engels and, in successive years, he would torment Tussy with serial infidelities, humiliate her with a *de jure* marriage to an actress after Campbell Frank's death in 1892, and ultimately have a knowing hand in her suicide. That said, there was *some* good in Aveling and, in the early years, he encouraged Tussy in her political activism, supported her writing, and gave her a level of emotional fulfilment which she had been lacking since the death of her father.

In the meantime, both Tussy and Engels had to put up with his accumulating debts and embarrassing financial irregularities. Charles Bradlaugh, Aveling's old boss at the National Secular Society, was the first to accuse him of misappropriating funds following his departure from the organization in 1884. Whilst this allegation could just about be put down to political rivalry, the next set of charges was altogether more damaging. 'Aveling's Unpaid Labour: The Socialists Are Disgusted and Say So about His Exorbitant Bill' was the *New*

York Herald splash following the Socialist Labor Party's (SLP) investigation of the near $1,600 expenses Aveling and Tussy had run up during their 1886 US speaking tour. 'The enterprising socialist lecturers went to study poverty at a first class hotel in Baltimore, and patronized the wine cellar so liberally that their bill for two days amounted to $42,' the paper went on in a well-sourced demolition job.[25] The nub of the case was that Aveling tried to put Tussy's trip through the books when the SLP had agreed to pay only for his expenses. In fact, the allegations and salacious media leaks (which the British press gleefully recycled) pointed to deeper ideological divisions within the US socialist movement fought out over the arrival of the Avelings. And Engels was having none of it. In a trenchant letter to his American translator and prominent SLP apparatchik, Florence Kelley-Wischnewetzky, he spoke from the heart when he warned, 'woe be to the man who, being of bourgeois origin or superior education, goes into the movement and is rash enough to enter into money relations with the working-class element'. He then laid out a line of reasoning which he would maintain over the coming years: 'I have inherited from Marx the obligation to stand by his children as he would have done himself, and to see, so far as lies in my power, that they are not wronged.'[26] Aveling was now a protected member of the family firm, repeatedly shielded by a grievously indulgent Engels. When money went missing or a cheque bounced or a contract was reneged on (as they invariably were), Engels would airily dismiss it as 'the slapdash literary Bohemian in Aveling'.[27] Marx would most likely have cut Aveling free as an embarrassment to the cause, but Engels stuck with him both from clan loyalty and a secret admiration for his rakish, arrogant demeanour. He described him affectionately to Sorge as a 'very talented and serviceable sort of chap and thoroughly honest, but gushing as a flapper, with a perpetual itch to do something silly. Well, I can still recall the time when I was much the same kind of idiot.'[28]

Above all, Engels endorsed Aveling's ideological outlook and political strategy. Although Aveling did a terrible job of helping Sam Moore with the translation of *Das Kapital*, Engels respected him as an effective and appropriately scientific popularizer of Marxism for the English market. To Aveling's mind, Marx and Darwin not only shared similar character traits – 'the physical presence of each was commanding . . . in moral character the two men were alike . . . the nature of each was beautiful, kindling affection in, and giving affection to, all that was worthy' – but also methodology. 'That which Darwin did for Biology, Marx has done for Economics. Each of them by long and patient observation, experiment, recordal, reflection, arrived at an immense generalisation, – a generalisation the likes of which their particular branch of science had never seen.' In language that Engels could only have admired, he outlined in 'The Student's Marx' the profundity of Marx's *scientific* breakthrough. 'Electricity now has its ohms, its farads, its amperes; chemistry had its periodic law; the physiologists are reducing the bodily functions to equations; and the fact that Marx could express many of his generalisations in Political Economy in mathematical terms is so much evidence that he had carried that science further than his predecessors.'[29]

Equally attractively, there was more to Aveling than just talk. With his background in the street propaganda of the National Secular Society, he got to work with Tussy trying to build up an independent, properly proletarian workers' party beginning in the godless pastures of 'outcast London'. East of Aldgate Pump, a long way from Primrose Hill, in the alleys and rookeries of Whitechapel, Bethnal Green, Mile End and Hoxton, the hidden poverty of Victorian London lay: a landscape peopled in the popular imagination by a residuum of Jews, dockers, negresses and 'rough' ne'er-do-wells who came to be codified in the unnatural crimes of Jack the Ripper. Here was where immorality, drunkenness and dark acts took place; a eugenic bog, rising up from the Hackney marshes, best sealed and written off from the rest of the capital. But to Tussy, the poverty evident on these cold, hungry streets was replete with political promise. It came alive on 13 November 1887 when, once again, the hunger-stricken East End marched on the plutocratic West End and endured a 'Bloody Sunday' for their efforts as London's Metropolitan Commissioner, Sir Charles Warren, unleashed his troops on William Morris, Annie Besant, John Burns, Edward Carpenter, Tussy, Aveling and others amongst the 100,000 demonstrators. Tussy turned up at Regent's Park Road afterwards, as Engels relayed it to Paul Lafargue, 'her coat in tatters, her hat crushed and torn by a blow from a staff, having been arrested by bobbies but released on the orders of an inspector'. Although Engels had some tactical criticisms of confronting mounted police in Trafalgar Square ('being the place most favourable to the government . . . with barracks close by and with St James's Park – in which to muster reserves of troops – a stone's throw away from the field of battle'), the day's unwarranted violence suddenly energized the East End where for months the socialists had been fruitlessly preaching in radical clubs and pubs.[30] What kept the political momentum going was the unexpected, long overdue but very welcome intervention of organized labour.

In spring 1889 Will Thorne, a socialist stoker at the Beckton gasworks, started to unite his fellow workers into a National Union of Gasworkers and General Labourers – with a constitution drawn up with the help of Tussy and Aveling – in an attempt to improve the site's appalling terms and conditions. Within four months, the union had some 20,000 members and Thorne had secured a cut in the basic working day from twelve hours to eight. In the tightly knit communities of working-class East London, there was a long tradition of gasworkers doubling as dock labourers, and Thorne's success in winning concessions from the gas works increased the pressure on the reactionary dock corporations to follow suit. In the 1890s ten miles of docklands – from West India Docks to St Katherine's Dock to Millwall Dock to Victoria Dock – stretched along the wide eastern estuary of the Thames employing near 30,000 men in a vast complex of warehouses, wharves, basins and jetties which secured London's status as 'earth's emporium'. Conditions there were amongst the most brutal in Britain, as the great London chronicler Henry Mayhew discovered one October morning: 'Then begins the scuffling and scrambling, and stretching forth of countless hands high in the air, to catch the eye of him whose voice may give them work . . . it is a sight to sadden the most callous, to see *thousands* of men struggling for only one day's hire, the scuffle being made the fiercer by the knowledge that hundreds out of the number there assembled must be left to idle the day out in want.'[31] On 12 August 1889 Ben Tillett, the secretary of the small Tea Operatives' Union, found himself besieged by men insisting he follow Thorne's lead and confront the dock owners. But his demands for an increase in wages from 4d to 6d an hour, with 8d for overtime and a minimum employment period of half a day, were rejected out of hand by dock bosses, who remained confident that the East End's vast reserve army of labour would always undermine worker solidarity. Together with the socialist activists Tom Mann and John Burns (with Aveling and Tussy beavering away in the background), Tillett proved them wrong by founding the Dock, Wharf, Riverside and General Labourers' Union of Great Britain and Ireland. Not only that, the dock labourers' leaders managed a disciplined, month-long strike of almost 60,000 men and a powerful public relations offensive with open-air meetings in Tower Hill, dignified marches through the City of London, and a well-run relief fund. Whether it was this spectre of politicized labour, or the calming intervention of Cardinal Manning, or the arrival of £30,000 from the Australian dockers, in the end the wharf bosses caved in to Burns's demand for 'the full round orb of the docker's tanner'.

Reading the reports of the strike in the London papers, Engels was ecstatic. 'The dock strike has been won. It's the greatest event to have taken place in England since the last Reform Bills and marks the beginning of a complete revolution in the East End,' he wrote to Karl Kautsky in September 1889.[32] 'Hitherto the East End had been in a state of poverty-stricken stagnation, its hallmark being the apathy of men whose spirit had been broken by hunger, and who had abandoned all hope ... Then, last year, there came the victorious strike of the [Bryant & May] match-girls. And now, this gigantic strike of the most demoralized elements of the lot, the dock labourers . . .', he told Bernstein.[33] This was the point: what was so encouraging about the dock labourers' protest, he explained in the *Labour Leader*, was that even the lumpenproletariat now appeared ready to rise. 'If Marx had lived to witness this! If these poor down-trodden men, the dregs of the proletariat, these odds and ends of all trades, fighting every morning at the dock gates for an engagement, if they can combine, and terrify by their resolution the mighty Dock Companies, truly then we need not despair of any section of the working class.'[34] The dock labourers' and gasworkers' trade unions were symbolic of a tectonic shift in labour politics: the challenge by a new generation of trade unions, with their belief in class solidarity and socialist ideology, to the guild-like conservatism of the old craft unions. 'These new trade unions of unskilled men and women are totally different from the old organizations of the working-class aristocracy and cannot fall into the same conservative ways,' he told Laura before recounting with almost paternal pride Tussy's role in radicalizing the East End.[35] These then were Engels's people: not the SDF demagogues or the Fabian beard-strokers, but the East End activists, trade unionists and socialists whom he hoped would form a British socialist workers' party and, as a public signal of approbation, he invited them into his home at Regent's Park Road. 'Of the English, William Thorne was the most welcome visitor of those outside the family circle,' remembered Edward Aveling. 'For him Engels had the very greatest admiration, respect, and affection; of his character, and his value to the movement, the very highest opinion.'[36] Engels also compared John Burns favourably with Oliver Cromwell. They, in turn, honoured Engels, the grand old man of European socialism, with pride of place on their May Day platform.

In the event, leadership of the British labour movement fell not to Aveling, Thorne or Burns, but to the prickly, teetotal, Nonconformist ex-miner Keir Hardie. Hardie was consciously opposed to 'the State Socialists of the German type', and his socialism was, in the words of his biographer Kenneth O. Morgan, 'fundamentally ethical, a vision of justice and equality' which owed more to the Puritan 'good old cause' than Marxian communism. His vehicle was the Independent Labour Party (ILP) which emerged from the Trades Union Congress in the early 1890s and, from the outset, had a far more Liberal–Labour feel to it than any outwardly socialist intent. Nonetheless, it seemed the only credible, national political grouping dedicated to workers' interests and Engels gave it the benefit of the doubt. 'Since the *bulk* of its members are undoubtedly first class, since its centre of gravity lies in the provinces rather than in that hive of intrigue, London, and its programme is substantially the same as our own, Aveling did right in joining it and in accepting a position on the Executive,' Engels told Sorge in January 1893.[37] But within only a matter of weeks Aveling had managed to poison Engels's mind against Hardie whom Engels, in turn, started to accuse of demagogic ambitions, collaboration with the Tories, and financial irregularities. By January 1895 Engels had grown impatient of the ILP and was dismissing Hardie as 'a cunning, crafty Scot, a Pecksniff and arch-intriguer, but too cunning, perhaps, and too vain'.[38] Hardie himself was oblivious to this withdrawal of favour and, after Engels's death, wrote warmly of his Regent's Park Road chats and remained adamant that both Engels and Marx would have endorsed the political development of the ILP.[39] The truth is that, by this time, Engels was out of touch with much that was going on in British socialism thanks to his continuing dependence on Aveling. It is difficult to overemphasize the widespread distrust, even loathing, which so many in the British socialist camp felt towards Aveling – whom they regarded as an ambitious man on the make with highly immoral personal attributes damaging to their political cause and offensive to their working-class Puritan morality. Resentful at Engels's attempts to 'foist' the distrusted and deviant Aveling 'as a leader upon the English Socialist and Labour movement', activists started to shun Regent's Park Road, and Engels's personal influence over the political direction and ideology of English socialism markedly diminished.[40] 'Why was there no Marxism in Great Britain?' has been a long-standing academic conundrum and, if by no means the determining reason, Engels's misguided allegiance to Aveling certainly contributed to the lack of a unified Marxist party.[41] It was a rare political misjudgement, driven by a characteristic loyalty to the Marx clan.

When it came to the continental socialist movement, Engels faced a different set of problems. 'I have to follow the movement in 5 large and a lot of small European countries and the U.S. America,' he grumbled to Laura Lafargue in 1894. 'For that purpose I receive 3 German, 2 English, 1 Italian dailies and from January 1 the Vienna daily, 7 in all. Of weeklies I receive 2 from Germany, 7 Austria, 1 France, 3 America (2 English, 1 German), 2 Italian, and 1 each in Polish, Bulgarian, Spanish and Bohemian, 3 of which in languages I am still gradually acquiring.'[42] In addition, there was an endless postbag of international correspondence and 'calls of the most varied sorts of people'. Well into the 1890s Regent's Park Road remained the Mecca of international socialism with a growing intake of exiles, Russian disciples and, in 1893, the hosting of an Anglo-Franco-German social-ist summit of August Bebel, Paul Lafargue and John Burns. The

Primrose Hill comings and goings had accelerated from mid-1888 when the editorial team of *Der Sozialdemokrat* – Eduard Bernstein, Julius Motteller, Leonard Tauscher and Herman Schluter – moved en masse from Zurich to London and settled on the other side of the tracks in Kentish Town and Tufnell Park. Naturally, every Sunday they trekked across north London to join Engels for an afternoon of Pilsener, political scandal and scientific socialism. Presiding over it all was Marx's old housemaid, Nim, who ordered Engels's life with a loving decorum: hiring and firing staff, sitting at the head of the Sunday table and giving Engels the domestic freedom to pursue his political and philosophical projects. A lovely insight into Engels's world at the tail end of the 1880s is given by his account of New Year's Eve 1888. 'We got into it in a very queer way,' he recounted to Laura Lafargue,

we went as usual to Pumps' in a cab, the fog was thickening . . . after a full hour's drive in the dark and cold we arrived at Pumps' where we found Sam Moore, Tussy and the Schluters (Edward never turned up) and also Tauscher . . . Well, it got blacker and blacker, and when the New Year came, the air was as thick as pea-soup. No chance of getting away; our cabman, ordered for one o'clock, never arrived, and so the whole lot had to stop where they were. So we went on drinking, singing, card-playing and laughing till half-past five, when Sam and Tussy were escorted by Percy to the station and caught the first train; about 7 the others left, and it cleared up a little; Nim slept with Pumps, Schorlemmer and I in the spare bed, Percy in the nursery (it was after seven when we went to sleep) and got up again at about 12 or 1 to return to Pilsener etc. . . . The others drank coffee about half past four, but I stuck to claret till seven.[43]

Sadly, this happy cohabitation between Engels and Nim – with its nostalgic mix of Marx memories, mid-morning sharpeners and shared weakness for Party gossip – came to an abrupt end in 1890 when Nim collapsed with a suspected uterine tumour. As with the end of Lizzy, Engels provided an excellent hospice for the dying Helene, caring for her as his own kith and kin. 'My good, dear, loyal Lenchen fell peacefully asleep yesterday afternoon after a short and for the most part painless illness,' Engels wrote sadly to Sorge on 5 November 1890. 'We had spent seven happy years together in this house. We were the only two left of the old guard of the days before 1848. Now here I am, once again on my own.'[44] He followed this letter with a note to Adolf Riefer, one of Nim's few known relatives, announcing the death of his aunt, Helene Demuth, and plans for her estate. For there still remained one living, breathing lie – Nim and Marx's illegitimate son, Freddy Demuth – which the discreet, loyal Engels had to tidy up. 'The deceased made a will in which she named as her sole heir Frederick Lewis, the son of a deceased friend, whom she had adopted when he was still quite small and whom she gradually brought up to be a good and industrious mechanic.' Dissembling still further, Engels explained to Riefer how Freddy, 'out of gratitude and with her permission', had decided to assume the name Demuth and, as such, was named in the will.[45] Thus was one of the last pieces of subterfuge on Engels's part enacted: another posthumous defence of Marx's reputation, covering up once more his ignominious philandering. The ill-treated Freddy Demuth, of 25 Gransden Avenue, Hackney, East London, rightly received Helene's entire estate valued at £40. To the disinherited Riefer, this extraordinary act of generosity to the adult son of an old friend might just have seemed a little bit odd.

Engels sank into a deep depression after burying Helene alongside Karl and Jenny Marx at the family plot in Highgate. With her death, another intimate connection to the Marxes, to his generation and their lifetimes' struggle, was lost, as well as the kind of doting, jokey, female company he relished. In his low funk, he replied to a condolence telegram from Louise Kautsky, Karl Kautsky's former wife, whom he had defended so chivalrously during her divorce. 'What I have been through these many days, how terribly bleak and desolate life has seemed and still seems to me, I need not tell you,' he moaned. 'And then came the question – what now? Whereupon, my dear Louise, an image, alive and comforting, appeared before my eyes, to remain there night and day, and that image was you.'[46] Engels's unexpected solution to his lonely state was for Louise, a struggling Viennese midwife, to take up Nim's former position in Regent's Park Road: there would, of course, be no 'manual services', just a supervisory role of the household staff and a total freedom to pursue other interests.

Louise jumped at the chance to move to London and the delighted Engels soon had a new woman in his life and with her, as he put it, 'a little sunshine has returned'. In Engels's final years the two of them enjoyed a highly productive, supportive and affectionate relationship, with the younger Louise acting, far more than Nim, as a secretarial assistant taking care of correspondence, organizing papers, monitoring the international press and even proofreading his articles. Engels's letters to his global circle of correspondents became inundated with mentions of her; soon she started adding her own notes to the letters, signing herself as 'The Witch'. Did Engels the ageing Lothario take more than just a professional interest in the witty, pretty, thirty-year-old Louise? Most probably, but 'the difference in our ages precludes marital no less than extra-marital relations, so that nothing remains but that self-same housewifeliness'.[47] Over time, these sentiments developed into paternal affection as Engels grew to regard Louise 'as I do Pumps, Tussy or Laura, just as though she were my own child'.[48]

But there was a jealous child in this loving brood: the dreaded, drunken Pumps was far from happy with Louise's arrival. Whereas she had coexisted easily enough with the unthreatening Nim, playing the flirtish, doltish girl to Nim's staid matron, she rightly sensed the entrance of stylish, attractive Louise into Regent's Park Road would undermine her lucrative relationship with Engels. Ever her father's daughter, Tussy Marx watched the unfolding family dynamic with unrestrained glee. 'Finally Louise arrived,' she reported back to Laura. 'Meantime the General had screwed his courage to the sticking point and Pumps had been informed that on my (!!) invitation Louise was coming over, and must be properly treated . . .' But the threats didn't work: Pumps repeatedly humiliated Louise with all sorts of petty etiquette tricks and drunken behaviour until it all came to a head at Engels's seventieth. 'On the General's birthday Pumps getting more drunk than usual confided to Louise that she "knew she had to behave to her, or she'd get cut out of the Will"!'[49] In the end, Engels had to give Pumps a proper talking to – 'my lecture and a few hints' – so she clearly understood 'that her position in my house depends very much upon her own behaviour'.[50] Revealing something of her true mettle, Louise held her nerve against the shameless niece and Pumps was forced to accept that the days of her Primrose Hill primacy were firmly over.

In comparison to such highly strung domestic diplomacy, dealing with the factional infighting of European socialism was relatively straightforward. Most of Engels's time in 1888–9 was taken up by preparations for the Paris Congress scheduled for July 1889, the hundredth anniversary of the storming of the Bastille. The problem was there were two competing events: one organized by the renegade French Possibilists in conjunction with Hyndman's SDF and various English trade unions (The International Workers' Congress); the other the official Marxist jamboree co-ordinated by Lafargue, Guesde and their French Workers' Party (The International Socialist Labour Congress). Engels's task was to ensure the latter eclipsed the former by securing the involvement of the German and Austrian Marxist parties, who had a rather tetchy relationship with Lafargue and the French socialists. In the early months of 1889 an increasingly ill-tempered correspondence bounced back and forth from Primrose Hill to Berlin, Vienna and Paris. 'One thing I do know,' Engels exploded to Wilhelm Liebknecht after one sulky impasse too many, 'you can arrange the next congress yourselves; I shall wash my hands of it.'[51] Yet the reality was that Engels was the only figure capable of bringing the European communist parties together; he alone, as acting 'first fiddle', enjoyed the stature and authority to coalesce the inherently fissiparous movement. In the event, the congress just about worked, with nearly 400 delegates representing the worker and socialist parties of twenty nations converging on the French capital. 'You can congratulate yourself on having saved the congress,' Lafargue wrote to Engels (who personally declined to join the throng), 'but for you and Bernstein, the Germans would have left us and deserted to the Possibilists.'[52] Held under the shadow of the 'hideous' Eiffel Tower and amidst the vulgar commercial-imperial bustle of the 1889 World's Fair, the congress witnessed the launch of what became the Second Socialist International. 'The capitalists have invited the rich and powerful to the *Exposition universelle* to observe and admire the product of the toil of workers forced to live in poverty in the midst of the greatest wealth human society has ever produced,' as Paul Lafargue put it, in language so redolent of his late father-in-law. 'We, socialists, have invited the producers to join us in Paris on 14 July. Our aim is the emancipation of the workers, the abolition of wage-labour and the creation of a society in which all women and men irrespective of sex or nationality will enjoy the wealth produced by the work of all workers.'[53] Despite an often reformist and compromising tone prevalent in some of the debates, Engels was delighted with the outcome. 'Our Congress is in session and proving a brilliant success,' he reported back to Sorge.[54] After the ignominious end of the First International, Engels felt Paris showed the global socialist struggle gaining a far more secure footing with an end to anarchist influence, a welcome settlement between socialist theory and workers' activism as well as clear policy commitments on political engagement, sexual equality, trade union rights and the establishment of May Day as International Labour Day.

While Paris might have been the venue for the founding of the Second International, the driving force behind late nineteenth-century socialism was located firmly in Berlin and Vienna. To his incredulity, Bismarck's anti-socialist law had served only to swell the left-wing ranks of what became in 1890 the Sozialdemokratische Partei Deutschlands (SPD). Alarmed, the German chancellor changed tack, seeking to neutralize the socialist challenge through a programme of progressive welfare reforms. But despite the introduction of health insurance, accident insurance and old age and disability pensions the SPD vote jumped from 7.5 per cent in 1878 to 19.7 per cent in 1890. 'Since last Thursday evening when the telegrams announcing victory came raining in here thick and fast, we are in a constant intoxication of triumph,' was Engels's response from Regent's Park Road to the astonishing million and a half votes for the socialists translating to thirty-five deputies in the 1890 Reichstag poll. 'The old stability is gone forever.'[55]

With an expanded franchise, the prospect of real political power was now in the offing and Engels felt it was more important than ever that the SPD adopted a correct ideological line devoid of any remaining Lassallean traits. In the wake of their electoral success, a congress was set for Erfurt in October 1891, and in the run-up to it Engels deployed all his political cunning to ensure Marx's posthumous influence over the direction of German socialism. He mischievously

reprinted Marx's 'Marginal Notes' on the reviled 1875 Gotha programme, in which he had so heavily castigated Liebknecht and Bebel
for succumbing to Lassallean socialism, and reissued Marx's *Civil
War in France*, with its defence of the Commune's dictatorship of the
proletariat. Engels then heavily edited the first draft of the Erfurt social-
democratic programme, urging the SPD not to avoid a confrontation
with the feudal, semi-absolutist German state even as he revived his
conviction in the need for a democratic way-stage to communism. 'If
one thing is certain it is that our party and the working class can only
come to power under the form of a democratic republic.'[56]

As it turned out, his fears of ideological back-sliding were unwarranted. Although in terms of party positioning Erfurt adopted a series
of highly practical, reformist policies (universal suffrage, free school-
ing, progressive income tax, medical care and legal aid), to the European socialist movement as a whole the SPD Congress signalled the
ideological triumph of Marxism with a philosophical programme
slavishly echoing *Das Kapital*. 'We have had the satisfaction of seeing
Marx's critique win all along the line,' Engels wrote to Sorge with the
intense personal satisfaction of having honoured Marx's legacy in the
country of his birth. 'Even the last traces of Lassalleanism have been
eliminated.'[57] After Erfurt and the SPD's official conversion, Marxism
took comprehensive control of the Second International. As Leszek
Kolakowski has described it, 'Marxism seemed to be at the height of
its intellectual impetus. It was not the religion of an isolated sect, but
the ideology of a powerful political movement.'[58]

However, the SPD's commitment to suffrage, municipal socialism,
even the proportional representation voting system, highlighted a
broader political shift which the trimming, older and wiser Engels was
coming to terms with. The hero of the '48 revolution, the stalwart of
the Barmen barricades who wanted to deliver the socialist revolution
by bloody force, was tapering his political strategy to an age of mass
democracy. With Europe's economies somehow managing the transition from industrial revolution to monopoly capitalism – with its
underpinnings of state cartels, colonial exploitation and high finance
– the strength and mutability of capitalism was shown to be far
sturdier than previously imagined. If the capitalist system was not
likely to be brought to a juddering halt by an immediate economic

crisis, then the way to proletarian triumph had to involve the sort of democratic party politics which Marx and Engels had first supported in 1848. But the stark difference in 1891 was that Engels thought democratic socialist parties could now move straight to power, via the ballot box, without having to endure the intermission of radical-bourgeois rule which had seemed necessary in the reactionary, feudal days of 1848.[59] There was the real possibility, Engels concluded, of a direct transition to socialism under a proletarian government which had been voted into power by the newly enfranchised working class – as the SPD seemed likely to be in Germany. For given the growing working-class vote, 'the possibility of our coming to power is merely a calculation of probability in accordance with mathematical laws'.[60] It was a prospect of ultimate, inevitable, peaceable socialist triumph which Engels relished. 'This very lack of undue haste, this measured but nonetheless inexorable advance, has about it something tremendously impressive which cannot but arouse in the rulers the same sense of dread as was experienced by the prisoners of the state inquisition in that room in Venice where the walls moved inwards an inch each day . . .' he mused to August Bebel's wife, Julie.[61]

Of course, democracy was slower and less romantic than the call to revolution, but Engels now regarded universal suffrage as a respectable weapon in the socialist armoury. Like a democratic ingénue, Engels described how elections allowed socialists to reveal their strength every three years, enable the party leadership to stay in touch with the workers, and offer either a platform for socialist advocacy in Parliament or even the opportunity of power. Never afraid to adopt a new political strategy in the face of changing circumstances, Engels, the self-styled Montagnard who once caricatured himself nursing a guillotine, now announced that 'the time of surprise attacks, of revolutions carried through by small conscious minorities at the head of the masses lacking consciousness is past'.[62] What was more, thanks to the overwhelming force which state armies could mobilize, rebellion in the 1848 style, 'the era of barricades and street fighting has gone for good'.[63] Contrary to Lenin's later assertions, Engels was no vanguardist. He even opposed plans for a general strike in response to the potential outbreak of a European war as unnecessarily provocative to bourgeois authorities itching to impose a military clampdown. 'We, the "revolutionaries", the "overthrowers" – we are thriving far better on legal methods than on illegal methods and overthrow. The parties of order, as they call themselves, are perishing under the legal conditions created by themselves . . .'[64]

In coming to terms with this new electoral landscape thrown up by an expanding suffrage, Engels reached for an unexpected analogy. In the early 1880s his voracious reading had alighted on the history of the early Christian Church under the late Roman Empire. Drawing on his Young Hegelian heritage of biblical criticism, he had penned a small article on the Book of Revelation and, in the process, recounted 'how Christianity got hold of the masses, exactly as modern socialism does'.[65] We hear no more of this thought until, a decade on, Engels again was struck by the comparison between the inexorable march of socialism across Europe and the unstoppable spread of Christianity within the Empire. The aggressive atheist and teenage baiter of the good Christian Graeber brothers was, in his old age, altogether more willing to give greater credence to the social gospel of Jesus. 'The history of early Christianity has notable points of resemblance with the modern working-class movement,' Engels wrote in a historical essay on the early Church. 'Like the latter, Christianity was originally a movement of oppressed people; it first appeared as the religion of slaves and freedmen, of poor people deprived of all rights, of peoples subjugated or dispersed by Rome.' And even if the one promised salvation in the afterlife and the other societal transformation here on earth, they both shared an unquenchable eagerness for struggle and a bloody heritage of martyrdom. 'Both are persecuted and subjected to harassment . . . And in spite of all persecution, nay, even spurred on by it, they forge victoriously, irresistibly ahead.'[66]

But in contrast to the Christians, he and Marx were never inclined, as Engels put it, 'like good Quakers, to turn the other cheek'.[67] For all Engels's talk of an end to the barricades and the futility of armed insurrection, he adamantly refused 'to subscribe heart and soul to absolute legality' and was always careful to defend the socialist's moral right to force. Legality was a political tactic relevant for the SPD in the current German political climate rather than any kind of ethical absolute. 'But I preach those tactics only for the Germany of today and even then with many reservations,' he explained in a letter to Paul Lafargue after some within the SPD hierarchy had misinterpreted Engels's views as a blanket commitment to peaceable means. 'For France, Belgium, Italy, Austria, such tactics could not be followed as a whole and for Germany, they could become inapplicable tomorrow.'[68] To Engels's frustration, these caveats were overlooked and, thanks to the ensuing revisionism of Eduard Bernstein, in future years he would also be blamed (in addition to the militant excesses of Marxism-Leninism) for the crimes of SPD reformism with its commitment to political gradualism. Engels was never a Fabian: if a mass workers' party, elected into office, was the swiftest way to socialism, then so be it. Otherwise, the retired Cheshire huntsman was still raring to join the cavalry charge.

As Second International socialism surged across the European continent, Engels wanted to witness it first hand. His opportunity was an International Workers' Congress set for Zurich in August 1893 to which he excitedly set off (with Louise) via Cologne, the Rhineland, Mainz and Strasbourg. Meeting the new generation of socialist leaders face to face – Filipo Turati from Italy, Pavel Axelrod from Russia, Stanislaw Mendelson from Poland, as well as old friends such as August Bebel and Victor Adler – Engels announced himself highly impressed with the commitment of the activists. But what really took his breath away was the beauty of the female delegates. 'The women were splendidly represented,' he reported back to Laura Lafargue. 'Besides Louise, Austria sent little [Adelheid] Dworzak, a charming little girl in every respect; I fell quite in love with her ... These *Viennoises sont des Parisiennes nées, mais des Parisiennes d'il y a cinquante ans*. Regular *grisettes*. Then the Russian women, there were 4 or 5 with wonderfully beautiful *leuchtende Augen* [shining eyes], and there were besides Vera Zasulich and Anna Kulischoff.'[69] But he found the socialist nitty-gritty of the Zurich debates deeply tedious and, excusing himself from the composite motions, sped off to the Canton of Graubunden to visit his brother Hermann – the former commander of counter-revolutionary forces in 1848, but with whom Engels had entered into an increasingly affectionate brotherly correspondence over the previous decade, exchanging letters on illnesses, tax rates and ailing lustful thoughts.

On 12 August, Engels returned to Zurich to give the congress closing speech. 'We wanted to close the meeting: the last votes were taken in feverish haste,' recalled the young Belgian socialist party leader, Van-der-Velde, of the last day. 'One name was on every lip. Friedrich Engels entered the hall: among storms of cheering he came to the platform.'[70] This was surely Engels's moment, stepping out from the shadow of Marx and imprinting his own character on the socialist movement which he had done so much to found, nurture and fund. But, even then, he wouldn't claim the credit. 'I could not but experience deep emotion at the unexpectedly splendid reception which you have given me, accepting it not for myself personally but as a collaborator of the great man whose portrait hangs up there,' he explained to the 400 delegates, pointing upwards to a picture of Marx. Some fifty years since he and Marx first began publishing their tracts in the *Deutsche-Französische Jahrbücher*, 'socialism has developed from small sects to a mighty party which makes the whole official world quail. Marx is dead, but were he still alive there would be not one man in Europe or America who could look back with such justified pride over his life's work.' He then made a principled plea for freedom of debate within the movement, 'in order not to become a sect', before leaving the hall to huge acclamation and a highly vocal rendition of the 'Marseillaise'.[71]

It was a message of humility and pride which Engels repeated time and again as his continental trip turned into something of a victory lap. In Vienna – where 'the women especially are charming and enthusiastic' – he addressed rapturous crowds of 6,000. 'When you come from England with this distracted and disunited working class, when you have heard for years nothing but bickering and squabbles from France, from Italy, from America, and then go amongst these people . . . and see the unity of purpose, the splendid organization, the enthusiasm . . . you cannot help being carried away and saying: this is the centre of gravity of the working-class movement,' he reflected to Laura.[72] His journey culminated in Berlin, the city of his officer training and which Marx and Engels had reviled above all others, where he was welcomed back by the socialist newspaper *Vorwärts*. 'When Friedrich Engels, with his 73 years, today looks out on the capital city of the Reich, it may give him a joyful and elevating feeling that out of the calcified and pedantic royal residence of the king of Prussia of the year 1842 has developed the powerful proletarian native city which today greets him as – *Social Democratic Berlin.*'[73] Some 3,000 socialists packed into the Concordia Hall to hear Liebknecht recount Engels's history of service and sacrifice to the party. 'You know that I am not an orator or a parliamentarian; I work in a different field, chiefly in the study and with the pen,' Engels modestly replied before revealing his delight at the transformation of Berlin from Junker playpen to socialist powerhouse.[74] He went on to pay tribute to the disciplined electoral success of the SPD which he felt sure, given steady industrialization and proletarianization, was set to enjoy further triumphs. For what the 1893 continental excursion – with its vast crowds, glowing newspaper coverage and motivated activists – had convinced Engels of was the rightness of the suffrage strategy: the workers' vote was growing with irreversible vigour allowing the socialists to make an ever greater series of political demands until the necessary confrontation with the bourgeois state occurred. All they had to do was hold their nerve, avoid provocation and stay the course.

There was only one pitfall he truly feared. 'I would consider a European war to be a disaster; this time it would prove frightfully serious and inflame chauvinism everywhere for years to come, since all peoples would be fighting for their own existence,' Engels had written to Bebel in 1882. 'Such a war would, I believe, retard the revolution by ten years, at the end of which, however, the upheaval would doubtless be all the more drastic.'[75] This fear of the anti-revolutionary effects of a European conflagration marked another reversal of thinking. Until the early 1870s both Marx and Engels were adamant that war on the continent would naturally advance the socialist cause since it would eliminate the great reactionary obstacle of Tsarist Russia. Just as the French wars of the 1790s intensified revolutionary sentiment, so the communists assumed another Great Powers conflict would unite and radicalize the European working class. But after Bismarck's annexation of Alsace-Lorraine and the growing nationalist antagonism between France and Germany, Engels concluded that war might in fact derail those country's workers' movements amidst an unedifying upsurge of chauvinism. 'It is precisely because everything's going so marvelously,' he wrote to Bebel, 'that I wouldn't exactly wish for a world war.'[76] Even if a workers' revolution arose from the ashes of a world war, modern technological advances and the transformation of European armies into industrialized killing machines meant this route to communism would entail too high a body count. 'Eight to ten million soldiers will strangle one another, and in the process will eat all Europe more bare than any swarm of locusts,' he wrote presciently in 1887 of a coming conflagration. 'The devastation of the Thirty Years War, comprised into three or four years and extended over the whole continent: famine, pestilence, general barbarization of armies and peoples alike through extreme want.'[77]

The way to avoid war and salvage the prospect of a less gory revolution was, Engels believed, to transfer the political strategy the party was pursuing in the electoral to the military sphere. In the wake of SPD success in the 1877 Reichstag elections, Engels mused how 'at least half if not more of these men of 25 (the minimum age) who voted for us spent two to three years in uniform and they know perfectly well how to handle a needle gun and a rifled cannon'.[78] As socialism attracted ever greater popular support, it was essential that its philosophy made its way into the barracks and battalions of the Prussian regiments – where, in turn, soldiers would soon begin to question the orders of their reactionary, bellicose commanders. 'When every able-bodied man serves in the army, this army increasingly reflects popular feelings and ideas, and this army, the great means of repression, is becoming less secure day by day: already the heads of all the big states foresee with terror the day when soldiers under arms will refuse to butcher their fathers and brothers.'[79] Engels, the once steadfast sceptic of the militia system, now urged mass conscription as an even more effective democratic tool than the franchise. The unstoppable mathematics of socialist advance would take the army in its wake, and once the armed forces turned socialist, the sort of jingoistic wars being adumbrated by the leaders of France, Russia and Germany would prove impossible just as the troops' traditional, counter-revolutionary function (so bloodily on display in the Paris Commune) would be neutered. 'I have more than once heard him say,' the SDF activist Ernest Belfort Bax recalled, 'that as soon as one man in three, i.e., one-third, of the German army actually in service could be relied on by the Party leaders, revolutionary action ought to be taken.'[80]

This then was Engels aged seventy-three – advancing the Marxist cause, inspiring the faithful, delivering the latest volumes of *Das Kapital*, providing analyses on Sino-Russian relations, the German peasant question and Russian *obschina* (an urgent issue in light of the 1891–2 great famine), the ILP and SPD. He remained that same restless, inquisitive, productive and passionate architect of scientific socialism who first emerged in the 1840s. Avoiding both dogma and platitude, Engels's political interventions remained neither overly prescriptive nor unhelpfully vague. As always he was never afraid of telling his socialist colleagues, in the bluntest language, where they went wrong. His health remained good and he continued to celebrate his birthdays in characteristically robust style. 'We kept it up till half past three in the morning,' Engels boasted of his seventieth birthday to Laura Lafargue, 'and drank, besides claret, 16 bottles of champagne – the morning we had had 12 dozen oysters. So you see I did my best to show that I was still alive and kicking.'[81] One visitor to Regent's Park Road in 1891 described meeting 'a tall bearded, vigorous, bright-eyed and genial septuagenarian' who proved 'a generous and delightful host'.[82] Tussy called him, 'the youngest man I know. As far as I can remember he has not grown any older in the last 20 years.'[83] He continued to take his daily walks on Hampstead Heath ('London's Chimborazo'), but his recurring groin trouble from a fox-hunting fall had now forced him to give up smoking and reduce his Pilsener intake, whilst he was beginning to suffer from ever more aggressive bouts of bronchitis, stomach aches and rheumatism of the legs. Yet what really seemed to worry him was the spectre of 'encroaching baldness'.

At home, with Pumps banished to the Isle of Wight, Louise Kautsky governed the domestic setting. 'You know the General is always under the thumb of the "lady of the house",' Tussy wrote to Laura. 'When Pumps was with him, lo, she was good in his sight; now Pumps is dethroned and Louise is the queen who can do no wrong.' Tussy was less amused by Louise's introduction of a foreign body into Engels's household: her new live-in husband, the Austrian physician and member of the National Liberal Club, Ludwig Freyberger. Tussy thought him an anti-Semite and a creep with dubious political affiliations who had changed 122 Regent's Park Road from a laughter-filled socialist redoubt for the greater Marx clan into an uneasy Viennese *ménage à trois*. 'I would not trust a fly to his tender mercies,' she wrote angrily to Laura in March 1894 with a litany of complaints about Freyberger's various manipulations, 'he is an adventurer pure and simple, and I am heartily sorry for Louise.'[84] She was even more upset when, in autumn 1894, the Freybergers persuaded the 74-year-old Engels to move out of his own home.

A child had followed the marriage of Ludwig to Louise and it was decided that No. 122 was too cramped for their familial needs. So for another £25 p.a. rent, the quartet marched 500 paces down the road to No. 41. On the face of it, Engels didn't seem to mind this minor change of residence. 'Downstairs we have our communal living-rooms, on the first floor my study and bedroom, on the second Louise, her husband, the baby daughter,' as Engels described the layout for Sorge, '. . . on the third floor the two housemaids, lumber-room and visitor's room. My study is at the front, has three windows and is so big that I can accommodate nearly all my books in it and yet, despite its size, very nice and easy to heat. In short, we are a lot better off.'[85] Engels, who doted on all of Pumps, Laura and Jenny's children like a grandfather, had no problem sharing the house with an infant, remained devoted to Louise and even appreciated Freyberger's 'draconian medical supervision' of his various physical ailments. But for the fragile, emotional Tussy, who was contending with her own multiple Aveling crises, it seemed 'the General' had been taken from her: increasingly she depicted him as an infantilized, bullied and frightened old man held against his will in the evil clutches of the Freybergers. 'I don't think the poor old General even fully realizes what he is made to do, he has come to the condition where he is a mere child in the hands of the monstrous pair,' she complained to Laura. 'If you knew how they bully and frighten him by constantly reminding him he is too old for this and too old for that . . . and saw how utterly depressed, and lonely, and miserable he is . . .'[86] Tussy was particularly concerned about the fate of her father's manuscripts, which were at risk of falling into the Freybergers' hands – this despite Engels's repeated affirmations (as evinced in his will) that all Marx's papers would be handed over, on his death, straight to Tussy.

The struggle between Tussy and Louise – with the former blaming the latter for spreading rumours about her and Aveling and generally interfering in the London Marxist circle – must have been an unwelcome source of angst to the ageing Engels. In Tussy's defence, it does seem that the acquisitive Freybergers were unnecessarily controlling about access to Engels by his Sunday afternoon crowd and had half an eye on their landlord's estate. But given that both the Lafargues and the Avelings had over the previous years ignored numerous heartfelt invitations from the lonely Engels to join him either for Christmas or a summer holiday, Tussy's fury was about more than living conditions at No. 41. Her exaggerated accounts of Engels's confusion and her own paranoia about the Marx manuscripts – which led to a blazing row between Engels and the Avelings over Christmas 1894 – was a displacement vehicle for her much deeper fear of losing 'Uncle Angel' and, with him, that deep, abiding connection to her late, adored Mohr. Maybe Tussy had sensed what Dr Freyberger had so far missed, that Engels was dying.

Friedrich Engels had begun his remarkable life in the furnace of Germany's Industrial Revolution, amongst the yarn bleacheries and textile works of the Wupper valley; he concluded it amidst the Victorian elegance of the Duke of Devonshire's fastidiously English seaside retreat, Eastbourne. By the 1880s this gentlemanly resort had become his favoured holidaying spot, where he liked to take a well-positioned house along Cavendish Place hosting Nim, Schorlemmer, Pumps and her brood – as well as Laura or Tussy if he was lucky. There Engels sat, the lover of the good things and happy times in life, with Pumps's children crawling round his knees, an open bottle of Pilsener, a letter on the go and a stoical resolve in the face of the August mist and rain. In the summer of 1894 he appears to have suffered a small stroke while on holiday and began to fear he might not make that longed-for peek into the new century. 'Between ourselves, my 75th year doesn't hold out quite so much promise as previous ones,' he wrote mordantly to Sorge.[87] By the following spring an unwelcome complication had arisen. 'Sometime ago I got a swelling on the right side of the neck, which after some time resolved itself into a bunch of deep-seated glands infiltrated by some cause or other,' he wrote to Laura in the matter-of-fact tone he liked to adopt on medical issues. 'The pains arose from direct pressure of that lump on the nerve and will of course only give way when that pressure disappears.'[88] To aid the healing process, Engels departed for Eastbourne earlier than usual in June 1895, where he planned to get to work on a new edition of his *Peasant War in Germany* and tidy up some of Kautsky's forthcoming *History of Socialism*.

What Engels the keen physiologist didn't realize was that he was already suffering from an aggressive cancer of the oesophagus and larynx which Freyberger had finally detected in early March 1895 and had then shared his diagnosis with the Austrian medic and socialist Victor Adler. Being doctors, they naturally thought it best to keep their patient in the dark and so the ensuing weeks see a heartrending correspondence as Engels latches on to every false dawn of returning health. 'Thank you for your letter – there is some improvement but, in accordance with the principles of dialectics, the positive and the negative aspects are both showing a cumulative tendency,' he joked in a suitably scientistic vein to Eduard Bernstein in early July 1895. 'I am stronger, eat more and with a better appetite and look very well, or so I am told; thus my general condition has improved.' He was already having trouble swallowing, but on the other hand, 'I have found out several weak sides of my capricious appetite and take *lait de poule* [egg-nog] with brandy, custards with stewed fruits, oysters up to nine a day etc.'[89] However, by 21 July his condition had become extremely grave. Sam Moore, his old friend from Manchester days, met Ludwig Freyberger off the train from Eastbourne and reported back to Tussy. 'I am sorry to say that his report is anything but cheering; he says that the disease has attained such a hold that, considering the General's age, his state is precarious. Apart from the diseased glands of the neck there is danger either from weakness of the heart or from pneumonia – and in either of these two cases the end would be sudden.'[90] With his health rapidly deteriorating, Engels was evacuated from Eastbourne back to London. 'Tomorrow we return,' he wrote to Laura who was waiting for him at Regent's Park Road. 'There seems to be at last a crisis approaching in my potato field on my neck, so that the swellings may be opened and relief secured. At last! So there is hope of this long lane coming to a turning.' He then went on, in his last known letter, to ridicule both the SDF and ILP for their poor showing in the recent general election, before signing off in vintage Engels fashion, 'Here's your good health in a bumper of *lait de poule* fortified by a dose of *cognac vieux*.'[91]

Despite the *bonhomie*, Engels sensed his mortality looming and chose to add a late codicil to his 1893 will. As would be expected of the man, both documents were businesslike, pragmatic and extraordinarily generous to the loving clique who surrounded him. His estate was to be divided into eight parts with three parts for Laura Lafargue, three parts for Tussy and the remaining two parts for Louise Freyberger. With the estate valued at £20,378 after death duties, this worked out at a very lucrative £5,000 each for Tussy and Laura (after subtracting one third for Jenny Marx Longuet's children) and almost £5,100 for Louise.* Tussy, Laura and Jenny's children were also to receive any continuing royalties from the sales of *Das Kapital*. Pumps was left £2,230 (with which she emigrated to the United States), Ludwig Freyberger £210 for medical assistance, and Louise the rights to the lease on Regent's Park Road as well as the household effects. Meanwhile, all loans to Pumps and Percy, Laura and Paul Lafargue, and Edward Aveling were expunged. Most importantly of all, Engels acceded to the wishes of the Marx daughters when it came to their father's papers: not only were all his manuscripts and family letters to be given to Tussy as literary executor, he now commanded that *all* letters to Marx were to be handed over to her. His own letters from known correspondents were to be returned to them with the rest passed to his literary executors, August Bebel and Eduard Bernstein. In addition, he allocated a further £1,000 to Bebel and Paul Singer as an election fighting fund for helping SPD candidates. The Party, Pumps, Louise, Marx's daughters and his old friend's ideological bequest were all painstakingly taken care of. His blood brother, Hermann, was handed back an oil painting of their father.

---

* Engels also left £227 worth of 'wine and other liquors' in his cellar. In addition, his wine merchants, Twigg & Brett, had 142 dozen bottles in their cellars as the property of Friedrich Engels. These included 77 dozen bottles of claret, 48 dozen bottles of port and 13 dozen bottles of champagne.

The reading of the will wasn't long in coming. By early August the once Herculean General could take nourishment only in fluid forms, was drifting in and out of consciousness and had lost the power of speech. Bebel visited him and found he could still 'make bad jokes on his writing board'.[92] He could also chalk out, in these dying days, the identity of Freddy Demuth's true father to a distraught Tussy and so exculpate himself from that particular misdemeanour. Soon after 10 p.m. on 5 August 1895 Louise Freyberger briefly left his side to change for night-duty. When she came back, 'all was over'.[93] After suffering 'broncho-pneumonia' for the previous two days, Engels died alone in his bed. 'So he was laid low,' Wilhelm Liebknecht lamented,

that titanic mind who together with Marx laid the foundations of scientific socialism and taught the tactics of socialism, who at the early age of 24 wrote the classical work *Condition of the Working Class*, the co-author of the *Communist Manifesto*, Karl Marx's alter ego who helped him to call to life the International Working Men's Association, the author of *Anti-Dühring*, that encyclopaedia of science of crystal transparency accessible to anybody who can think, the author of *The Origin of the Family* and so many other works, essays and newspaper articles, the friend, the adviser, the leader and the fighter – he was dead.[94]

The funeral was not as Engels would have wished. Instead of an intimate, private gathering of mourners for an unpublicized cremation, word of the gathering spread and near eighty people crammed into the rooms of the Necropolis Company at the Westminster Bridge Road station of London and South Western Railway. In addition to the Avelings, Lafargues, Roshers, Longuet children, Freybergers and some Engels cousins, from the SPD came Liebknecht, Singer, Kautsky, Lessner and Bernstein; for the Austrians, August Bebel; for the Russians, Vera Zasulich; and the admired Will Thorne from the Socialist League. There were wreaths from the Belgian, Italian, Dutch, Bulgarian and French Socialist parties and speeches from amongst others Engels's nephew, Gustav Schlechtendahl, and Samuel Moore. After some secular valedictions, the train bearing Engels's body eased out of London heading along a single track to the Woking crematorium.

*

MEMORIAL NOTICE

Frederick Engels, the life-long friend of Carl Marx and the most conspicuous figure in the international Socialist movement since the death of Marx, died on Monday night at his residence in London.

The *Manchester Guardian* (7 August 1895) quietly notes
Friedrich Engels's passing.

'To the west of Eastbourne the cliffs along the coast gradually rise until they form the great chalky headland of Beachy Head, nearly six hundred feet in height. Overgrown with grass on the top, it slopes gently at first, and then suddenly falls steeply to the water, while down below it exhibits all manner of recesses and outlying masses.' It was to this quintessentially English setting, 'on a very rough day in autumn', that Eduard Bernstein travelled together with Tussy, Aveling and Friedrich Lessner. These four rough-hewn socialists – an incongruous quartet in genteel Eastbourne – hired a small boat and started to row steadily out into the English Channel. 'About five or six miles off Beachy Head,' they turned to face the dramatic shoreline of the South Downs and then, following the clear dictates of his will, cast the urn and ashes of Friedrich Engels into the sea. In death as in life there was nothing to detract from the glory of Marx: no Highgate headstone or family tomb, no public memorial for Engels the man of such attractive contradiction and limitless sacrifice. After his brief, final years as first fiddle, Engels had returned to the orchestra.[95]

Epilogue

Let us return to the city of Engels on the banks of the river Volga. Given its everyday, grisly modernity, it is easy to forget the town's remarkable origins in the reign of Catherine the Great during the mid-eighteenth century. As the European-born Empress of Russia, Catherine II had been determined to inject some Western culture into Russia's bloodstream, raise the country's economic productivity and populate the lawless Volga region with dependable, industrious settlers. This meant enticing thousands of German farmers, labourers and tradesmen to leave their Hessian towns and villages for the fertile plains of southern Russia. And, over the course of the 1760s, some 30,000 Germans were induced to choose a new life in colonies stretching over 200 miles up and down the Volga valley.[1] One of the most popular destinations was around Saratov, where the soils were known to be especially fecund, and, on the other side of the river, the small settlement of Pokrovskaia, which grew as a lucrative trading and storage hub on the salt transportation routes. Through generations of grafting, the Volga Germans transformed their region into some of the most prosperous and peaceable lands in the Russian Empire. And in 1914 the unincorporated Pokrovskaia was officially christened Pokrovsk in honour of the Holy Blessed Virgin (after *pokrov*, a protective shroud or veil) and, following the 1917 Russian Revolution, it joined Saratov as a patriotic member of the Autonomous Soviet Socialist Republic of Volga Germans.

In 1931 the name was changed again under less consensual circumstances. For the Soviet regime was not gentle to the Volga republic. During the early 1920s, in the aftermath of the Russian civil war, military requisitioning and failed harvests, the region had suffered a devastating famine with grass, roots, bark, hides and straw all becoming staple ingredients in this once well-fed district. The population plummeted by nearly one third in the wake of rocketing mortality rates and mass emigration. But just as the soil started to recover and harvests revive, the Fifteenth Congress of the Communist Party began its 1927 session. Its outcome was General Secretary Joseph Stalin's butcherous peasant policy: to secure the industrial transformation of the Soviet economy, Stalin demanded the transfer of food supplies into the cities, a clampdown on rural grain hoarding, and the mass collectivization of agriculture. To deliver this agro-industrial revolution, he unleashed an unrelenting war against the counter-revolutionary kulak class – those rural small-holders eking out an existence a little above the average with perhaps half a dozen acres of land, some livestock and hired labour. 'We have gone from a policy of *restricting* the exploiting proclivities of the kulaks to the policy of *eliminating* the kulaks as a class,' Stalin boasted in a 1929 speech to agricultural students.[2] Penal taxation, demands for grain 'contributions' and forcible reallocation of land were then followed by the night-time knock of the secret police as the Gulags started to fill up. By 1930 nearly 80 per cent of the private holdings in the Volga region had been compulsorily integrated into local collectives, while almost half a million colonists from the Volga, Caucasus and South Russia were deported during the anti-kulak terror.

But the economic gains of Stalin's Five-Year Plan were also evident. Saratov and Pokrovsk underwent rapid industrialization with the construction of railway repair depots, brickworks, bread-baking plants, glue factories and the beginnings of an aircraft assembly line. Shock brigades at the bone-processing plants and Stakhanovite workers at the railway junctions pledged themselves to struggle ever harder to meet Moscow's 'productional-financial plan'. And it was to celebrate precisely such progress, as well as to commemorate the Volga's proud Germanic heritage, that the presidium of the Central Executive Committee of the USSR decided in October 1931 to rename Pokrovsk in honour of Prussia's second greatest socialist, Engels (the nearby town of Ekaterinenstadt having already taken Marksstadt). The name of Pokrovsk, according to one official statement, 'was yellowed and dried out like her mother – the fairy tale about the

"Virgin Mary".' In this scientific, Soviet era, it was an embarrassing hangover from feudal and superstitious times, recalling 'the atrocious period of Tsarist rule, which used national religion as a smokescreen for the egregious enslavement of the working masses'.[3]

More than that, the prospect of renaming offered a further official chance for connecting the great strides of the Soviet Union with one of modern Marxism's founding fathers. For were not Stalin's policies – crushing the kulaks, Mensheviks and 'bourgeois nationalists'; collectivizing the farms; rationalizing production; taking the 'giant steps' towards a modern, industrial future – being dutifully carried out in the name of Friedrich Engels? The Soviet propaganda machine had no doubt: Engels was a name, one Volga newspaper asserted, 'worthy of what we have accomplished and will accomplish in the socialist reformation of agriculture based upon consolidated collectivization and the liquidation of kulakism as a class'.[4] 'The city of Engels, the centre of the first national republic of consolidated collectivization, the centre which with its industrial development has become the forge of mighty national proletarian cadres,' as a different editorial had it, 'will take its place among the proletarian centres of the country of socialist development worthy of the name of Karl Marx's fellow combatant and friend.'[5]

This prestigious title did not come without responsibilities. 'It demands of us the tireless fulfilment of all of the tasks we face in building the socialist system. Our Volga-German Komsomol [party youth organization] must meet them by carrying out a veritable assault to fulfil and over fulfil the grain supply . . . to solve the socialist stock-breeding problem . . . to tirelessly liquidate illiteracy in time for the anniversary of the October Revolution.' Such selfless industry could be the only correct response to the inspirational life of their new patron saint. For 'Marx's victory was only possible thanks to Engels's great willingness to sacrifice himself . . . he stuck to "damned commerce" in order to earn enough to allow Marx to dedicate himself to his great life's work uninterrupted.' The residents of Engels would strive to follow such a lofty example of socialist sacrifice. 'To work, Komsomol! Show that we are worthy of transferring the name of this revolutionary, who accomplished so astoundingly much for the international proletariat, to the centre of our Volga-German

Republic! Once upon a time, there was Pokrovsk – watch out: here's Engels!'[6]

Ten years later, however, such ideological devotion secured no clemency in the face of a paranoid Stalin confronting the spectre of total war with Nazi Germany. On 28 August 1941 the Soviet Presidium issued another decree, 'Pertaining to the Resettlement of the Germans in the Volga District'. 'According to trustworthy information received by the military authorities,' the edict began ominously,

there are, among the German population living in the Volga area, thousands and tens of thousands of diversionists and spies who, on a signal being given from Germany, are to carry out sabotage in the area inhabited by the Germans of the Volga ... [However] none of the Germans of the Volga area have reported to the Soviet authorities the existence of such a large number of diversionists and spies among the Volga Germans; consequently the German population of the Volga area conceals enemies of the Soviet people and of Soviet authority in its midst.

Operation Barbarossa, Adolf Hitler's audacious invasion of Russia in June 1941, was set to hit the residents of Engels hard. As the Wehrmacht scythed their way through the Ukraine, the Crimea and southern Russia, Stalin ordered the region's loyal, industrious Volga Germans rounded up en masse. In textbook Soviet logic, since they had failed to offer up the presumed Nazi traitors in their midst, all were guilty and all had to suffer. 'In case of diversionary acts which would be carried out by German diversionists and spies in the Volga province upon a signal from Germany, the Soviet government, in accordance with wartime laws, will be compelled to take punitive measures against the entire German population of the Volga province.'[7] After surviving the horrors of collectivization, the Great Famine and the Great Terror there now came wholesale removal as the autonomous Volga province was officially wiped from Soviet geography. Catherine the Great's 200-year-old German communities joined Stalin's growing list of undesirables – rightists, Trotskyists, saboteurs, wreckers, collaborators and 'fifth columnists' – raised at dead of night by the secret police and dispersed to the eastern edges of Siberia. And just as the protection of the Holy Blessed Virgin had failed to save the inhabitants of Pokrovsk from previous Soviet cruelties, so now the communist halo of Engels offered no cover to its German inhabitants. In their tens of thousands the Volga Germans became another statisti- cal testament to the industrial inhumanity of Stalin's Marxist-Leninist state.

For any biographer, the question must surely be whether Engels the man was in some form responsible for the fate of Engels the city. Did his philosophy, as the Volga propaganda sheets claimed, help to shape the contours of Stalin's Soviet Union? For ideological opponents of Marx and Engels, the usual method of invalidating their philosophy has long been the rush to the Gulag: a quick reference to the dictator- ship of the proletariat and force as the midwife of every old society pregnant with a new one and the reader is on his way to the Krasnoy- arsk camps. 'In his own idiosyncratic ways, indeed, he [Lenin] could not have been more loyal to the doctrines and doings of Marx and Engels,' as a recent history of communism by Robert Service puts it. 'The co-founders of Marxism had approved of violent revolution, dictatorship and terror ... Many assumptions of Leninism sprang directly from the Marxism of the mid-nineteenth century.'[8] What is more, many of the political leaders of the Soviet Union, the Eastern bloc and then the anti-imperial communist movement came to their Marxism specifically through the works of Engels. His writings – Anti-Dühring, and the abridged Socialism: Utopian and Scientific; Ludwig Feuerbach and the End of Classical German Philosophy – provided an easily accessible conduit to the complexities behind Das Kapital. And nowhere more so than in Russia.

As we have seen, Marx and Engels were always circumspect about the prospect or even the desirability of a proletarian revolution taking place in Russia. Endless tergiversations about the role of the obschina, concerns over the Oriental habit for despotism, debates about the speed of industrialization and the role of the peasantry led Marx to conclude that there could be a Russian road to socialism only if it occurred concurrently with a complementary proletarian revolution in the advanced West. Engels would not even admit to this: in his final years he remained adamant that the still feudal Tsarist state would have to pass through all the intermediate stages of mass industrialization, working-class immiseration and bourgeois rule before any prospect of revolution would be in the offing.

But history arrived early for Russia and, in 1917, Lenin's Bolsheviks successfully diverted a popular revolution into their extraordinary ideological experiment. The first chair of the Council of the People's Commissars certainly knew his Marx, but he often seemed to prefer his Engels. Indeed, Lenin thought it 'impossible to understand Marxism and to propound it fully without taking into account the entire work of Engels'.[9] Lenin's earliest and arguably most influential instructor in the Marxist doctrine was the exiled Russian leader of the Emancipation of Labour group, Georgi Plekhanov. From his Geneva outpost, Plekhanov had turned time and again to Engels for philosophical and strategic advice as to the most efficacious way of implementing Marxism in Russia. 'First of all, please spare me "mentor" – my name is simply Engels,' the 'Grand Lama' replied to one particularly fulsome Plekhanov enquiry.[10]

What Plekhanov took from his reading of Engels was a belief in Marxism as a complete theoretical system capable of explaining history, natural science, economics and, most importantly of all, political action. For Plekhanov was the first to bestow Marxism with the title 'dialectical materialism', by which he meant a totalizing, philosophical worldview based on Marx and Engels's application of Hegelian dialectics to the natural and physical sciences and then societal change itself. With its step-by-step account of contradictions, qualitative and quantitative change, and the negation of the negation, dialectical materialism seemed to provide an unbreachable political route map for Russia's revolutionaries. However, Plekhanov always retained an intellectual's purity and never swayed from Engels's conviction that socialism in Russia could not be imposed overnight, but had to follow a period of bourgeois-democratic rule and sustained industrial growth. These were both the preconditions and contradictions of capitalist society which would provide the chrysalis for a communist transformation; he was deeply hostile to any kind of Leninist insurrection which would see a vanguard elite instigate a top-down socialist revolution from inside the walls of the Kremlin. The result of such a febrile putsch in Russian society, Plekhanov rightly feared, would be 'a political abortion after the manner of the ancient Chinese or Persian empires – a renewal of Tsarist despotism on a communist basis'.[11]

While the power-hungry Lenin ignored such reservations, he certainly imbibed from Plekhanov (before their political split) his *interpretation* of Engel's *codification* of Marx. In the process, the science of Engels's Marxism – with all its provisional humility and capacity for revision – metamorphosed into an irreproachable dogma. In what resembled a philosophical version of Chinese whispers, Lenin swallowed Plekhanov's version of dialectical materialism whole. 'Dialectics IS the theory of knowledge of (Hegel and) Marxism,' Lenin declared.[12] As such, Marxism for Lenin was a complete body of theory akin to 'a single piece of steel, [from which] you cannot eliminate even one basic premise, one essential part, without departing from objective truth, without falling a prey to bourgeois-reactionary falsehood'.[13] The unalterable natural laws of the dialectic explained the inevitable, scientific ascent of socialism; the fluid, destructive process of contradiction; and, rightfully understood, offered a complete programme for communist governance. 'This insistence on the integrality of Marxism was inherited from Plekhanov by Lenin, and became part of the ideology of the Soviet state,' in the judgement of Leszek Kolakowski.[14] And what the dialectic gave Lenin the revolutionary was a profound intellectual self-confidence and an awesome degree of ideological rigour. In a purple passage from *The Teaching of Karl Marx*, Lenin favourably compared the inspiring mystery of dialectical materialism to Darwinian evolution:

A development that repeats, as it were, the stages already passed, but repeats them in a different way, on a higher plane ('the negation of negation'); a development, so to speak, in spirals, not in a straight line; a development in leaps and bounds, catastrophes, revolutions; 'intervals of gradualness'; transformation of quantity into quality, inner impulses for development, imparted by the contradiction, the conflict of different forces and tendencies reacting on a given body or inside a given phenomenon or within a given society; interdependence, and the closest, indissoluble connection between all sides of every phenomenon (history disclosing ever new sides), a connection that provides the one world-process of motion proceeding according to law

– such are some of the features of dialectics as a doctrine of evolution more full of meaning than the current one.[15]

Joseph Stalin took the practical implementation of dialectical materialism to even greater heights. For as the Soviet regime appeared to depart ever more violently from Marx and Engels's ideals, its official rhetoric became ever more fulsome in its claims to orthodoxy. 'Marxism is not only the theory of Socialism; it is an integral world outlook, a philosophical system, from which Marx's proletarian socialism logically follows,' Comrade General-Secretary Stalin declared. 'This philosophical system is called dialectical materialism.'[16] He went on to outline precisely what he meant in a personal contribution to one of the most important publications in official Soviet literature, the *Short Course: History of the Communist Party of the Soviet Union (Bolsheviks)* (1938). Stalin's chapter, 'Dialectical and Historical Materialism', which set out the Marxist fundamentals of the Soviet system, opened with the rigid authority of a commissar's edict: 'Dialectical materialism is the world outlook of the Marxist-Leninist Party.' He then illustrated this truth with various laws of science – water to steam, effects of heat on platinum wire, oxygen to ozone – lifted straight from Engels's *Dialectics of Nature*. Stalin explained how these sharp shifts in form confirmed Engels's assertion that nature was a connected and integrated whole in which no phenomenon could be understood on its own, that it was in a state of continuous movement with change occurring rapidly and abruptly, and that driving its development were the internal contradictions inherent to all natural phenomena. Yet with much greater precision than either Engels or Lenin, Stalin then spelled out the political ramifications of dialectical materialism in a direct challenge to any reformist or social-democratic interpretation. 'If the passing of slow quantitative changes into rapid and abrupt changes is a law of development,' he reasoned, 'then it is clear that revolutions made by oppressed classes are a quite natural and inevitable phenomenon.' As a result, 'the transition from capitalism to Socialism and the liberation of the working class from the yoke of capitalism cannot be effected by slow changes, by reforms, but only by a qualitative change of the capitalist system, by revolution'.[17]

Making a play for total ideological legitimacy, Stalin tied the actions of the Soviet state inextricably to the scientific principles of Marxism-Leninism. 'The bond between science and practical activity, between theory and practice, their unity, should be the guiding star of the party of the proletariat.'[18] And since the Communist Party, which to all intents and purposes meant the will of Stalin, necessarily embodied the true interests of the proletariat, every policy it pursued logically enjoyed the ideological imprimatur of Marxist sanctity. Cornelius Castoriadis explains the Soviet rationale best: 'If there is a true theory of history, if there is a rationality at work in things, then it is clear that the direction this development takes should be left to the specialists of this theory, to the technicians of this rationality. The Party's absolute power has a philosophical status ... If this conception is true, this power *must* be absolute.'[19] The iron cage of the Soviet system was such that what the party decreed instantly became scientific truth.

Against a backdrop of intimidation and liquidation, the Stalinist state transformed the nuances and complexities of Marxist philosophy into a rigid, totalizing orthodoxy which infected almost every element of Russia's cultural, scientific, political and even private life.[20] While Engels had compared the growth of socialism to the early Christian Church, in the USSR it was akin to the worst form of heresy-hunting, medieval Catholicism with liturgies, rituals and a choir of communist saints. There were no doubts; only salvation in this faith which provided the way, the truth, the life. And Stalin's *Short Course* was its sacred text: an indisputable explication of Marxism-Leninism which stipulated the correct party line on all matters of socialist thought. 'It was published and taught everywhere without ceasing,' Kolakowski recalls. 'In the upper forms of secondary schools, in all places of higher learning, party courses etc., wherever anything was taught, the *Short Course* was the Soviet citizen's main intellectual pabulum.'[21]

As the Soviet Union's geopolitical sphere of influence extended, so the *Short Course* made its way round the world in tens of millions of copies with smart covers and high-quality Moscow print. The effect was to make dialectical materialism one of the most influential philosophies of the twentieth century, memorized and recited in communist circles from Phnom Penh to Paris to St Pancras, north London, where a young historian named Raphael Samuel wallowed in its icy certainties. 'As a science of society, it offered itself as an all-embracing determinism, in which accidents were revealed as necessities, and causes inexorably followed by effects,' he later wrote in a memoir of his upbringing in the providential London milieu of the Communist Party of Great Britain. 'As a mode of reasoning, it provided us with *a priori* understandings and universal rules – laws of thought which were both a guide to action and a source of prophetical authority.' But the point of Marxist philosophy still remained to change the world. 'Stalin's dictum: "Theory without Practice is Barren; Practice without Theory is Blind", became as familiar to generations of Communists as Engels's boiling kettle [exemplifying the shift from water to steam as a quantitative to qualitative shift] was in classes on dialectics.'[22] Stalin's *Short Course* quoted extensively from *Anti-Dühring* and Plekhanov and Lenin often turned more readily to Engels's literature than Marx's, while it was dialectical materialism – far more so than the theory of surplus value – which provided the driving philosophy for the Soviet-directed global communist movement. 'It is the *Dialectics of Nature* which has become the constantly quoted authoritative source for the exposition of the dialectic in Soviet Marxism,' reported Herbert Marcuse in the 1950s.[23]

So – to repeat – was Engels responsible for the terrible misdeeds carried out under the banner of Marxism-Leninism? Even in our modern age of historical apologies, the answer has to be no. In no intelligible sense can Engels or Marx bear culpability for the crimes of these historical actors carried out generations later, even if the policies were offered up in their honour. Just as Adam Smith is not to blame for the inequalities of the free-market West or Martin Luther for the nature of modern Protestant evangelicalism or the Prophet Muhammad for the atrocities of Osama bin Laden, so the millions of souls which Stalinism despatched (or those who died in Mao's China, Pol Pot's Cambodia or Mengistu's Ethiopia) do not rest on the account of two nineteenth-century London philosophers – and not just because of the simple anachronism of the charge.

In stark contrast to the way in which communist parties seized power in the twentieth century, from 1848 onwards Engels was highly sceptical of vanguard-led, top-down revolutions. He always believed in a workers' party led by the working class itself (rather than intellectuals and professional revolutionaries) and remained adamant that

the proletariat would arrive at socialism through the contradictions of the capitalist system and the development of political
self-consciousness rather than having it imposed upon them by a
self-selecting communist junta. 'The Social Democratic Federation
over here and your German-American Socialists share the distinction
of being the only parties that have contrived to reduce Marx's theory
of development to a rigid orthodoxy which the working man is not
expected to arrive at by virtue of his own class consciousness; rather
it is to be promptly and without preparation rammed down his throat
as an article of faith,' he complained pointedly to Friedrich Sorge in
May 1894.[24] The emancipation of the masses could never be the
product of an external agent, a political *deus ex machina*, even if it
came in the form of V. I. Lenin. Moreover, as his guidance to the
German SPD suggested, Engels was inclined towards the end of his
life to advocate the peaceable, democratic road to socialism through
the ballot-box rather than the barricade (whilst always retaining the
moral right to insurgency). In the specific Russian context, it is most
likely that Plekhanov's post-1917, now 'Menshevik', demands for a
period of bourgeois rule and capitalist development before any effective transition to a socialist state would have been more in tune with
Engels's thinking than the Bolshevik will to power.

Despite the easy caricature from both anti-communists and Marx
apologists alike, Engels was never that narrow-minded, mechanistic
architect of dialectical materialism which twentieth-century Soviet
ideology so exalted. There lies an unconscionable philosophical chasm
between Engelsism and Stalinism: between an open, critical and
humane vision of scientific socialism and a scientistic socialism so
horribly devoid of any ethical precepts. As John O'Neill has argued,
Engels's socialism has no necessary connection with twentieth-century
state Marxism since the link depends on Engels adhering to a dogmatic
conception of science committed to 'methodological certainty' and
'doctrinal orthodoxy' – both of which Engels rejected when it came
to scientific enquiry and historical materialism.[25] The closed logic of
Stalin's *Short Course* would have been anathema to the perpetually
inquisitive Engels: behind his barracking demeanour, he was interested
in challenging ideas, following new trends and often rethinking his
own positions. 'So-called "socialist society" is not, in my view, to

be regarded as something that remains crystallized for all time, but rather as being in process of constant change and transformation like all other social conditions,' he wrote in 1890. 'I see absolutely no difficulty in carrying out this revolution over a period, i.e. gradually.'[26] In many ways Engels's thinking was far more heuristic and less ossified than Marx's. In *Anti-Dühring*, he concluded that the most valuable result of his scientific investigations was to 'make us extremely distrustful of our present knowledge, in as much as in all probability we are just about at the beginning of human history'.[27] And he adopted something of a proto-Popperian stance on questions of scientific fallibility. 'The knowledge which has an unconditional claim to truth is realized in a series of relative errors; neither the one nor the other can be fully realized except through the unending duration of human existence.'[28] When it came to historical materialism, he similarly pleaded with one correspondent not to 'take every word I have said above for gospel' and told another that 'our view of history is first and foremost a guide to study, not a tool for constructing objects after the Hegelian model'.[29]

A few months before the end of his life, Engels told the German political economist Werner Sombart in very clear terms how 'Marx's whole way of thinking is not so much a doctrine as a method. It provides, not so much ready-made dogmas, as aids to further investigation and the method for such investigation.'[30] This is not the language of a closed, totalizing political philosopher yearning to construct a new Leviathan. What is more, Engels directly and repeatedly criticized those Marxist parties – like Hyndman's SDF, the *Jungen* faction of the SPD or the German Socialist Labor Party in the US – who attempted hermetically to seal off Marxism from further debate, 'turning our theory into the rigid dogma of an orthodox sect'.[31] Engels, like Marx, only rarely thought himself a Marxist in a narrow, partisan sense. Instead, he approached Marxism as an altogether grander truth that did not require the kind of paranoiac, protective genuflection which some party apparatchiks were already beginning to practise.

But the most crucial difference between Engels and his illegitimate acolytes in the Soviet Union and elsewhere was their respective starting points. He and Marx came to a scientific appreciation of their political philosophy during the 1860s and 70s as part of an attempt to redefine historical materialism in light of Darwinism and other advances in the natural and physical sciences. Much of their intellectual framework, stretching back to their earliest readings of Hegel, was fully formed by the time they sought to connect their ideas with the emergent, scientific vogue. By contrast, the next generation of socialists came to their Marxism along a very different ideological trajectory: in the words of Kautsky, 'they had started from Hegel, I started from Darwin'.[32] The likes of Kautsky, Bernstein, Adler, Aveling, Plekhanov, Lenin and the political leadership of the Second International – whose ideological awakening began with an immersion in the works of Charles Darwin, Herbert Spencer and the positivist Auguste Comte – read Marx and Engels from a more obviously organic, evolutionary perspective.[33] The Italian communist Enrico Ferri's *Socialism and Positive Science* (1894), Ludwig Woltmann's *Darwinian Theory and Socialism* (1899), Karl Kautsky's highly influential *Ethics and Historical Materialism* (1906) and the above extract from Lenin (who thought 'the idea of development, of evolution, has almost completely penetrated social consciousness') were just a few of the contributions to a burgeoning communist literature explicitly linking Darwinism and Marxism. This was the vital intellectual bridge, constructed after Engels's death, from late nineteenth-century Marxism to the dialectical materialism of Soviet orthodoxy. How Engels was read by a different generation nurtured on a different set of philosophical and scientific premises is a separate issue from the author's original intent and one for which he cannot be held responsible.

Just as importantly, the essential characteristics of Engels the man – which surface only fitfully in his texts – were sharply at odds with the brazen inhumanity of Marxism-Leninism. He was more than just good to his dogs. For all his scientific enthusiasms, belief in rational progress and fervour for technological advance, Engels retained elements of both the Utopian socialist tradition (against which he had so self-consciously defined his and Marx's approach) and the Protestant eschatological inheritance he had abjured as a teenager. His *telos* was a dialectical culmination of the global class struggle: the withering away of the state, the liberation of mankind and a workers' paradise of human fulfilment and sexual possibility – in sum, a leap from the kingdom of necessity to the kingdom of freedom. Neither a Leveller nor a statist, this great lover of the good life, passionate advocate of individuality and believer in the open battle of ideas in literature, culture, art and music could never have acceded to the Soviet communism of the twentieth century despite all the Stalinist claims of his paternity.

But neither could he have accepted the current settlement. If we can now strip away the accretions of twentieth-century Marxism-Leninism, the 'dictatorial deviation' which so poisoned the well of social justice, and return to the authentic Engels of nineteenth-century Europe, then a very different, strikingly contemporary voice re-emerges. From his eyrie in the Manchester cotton industry, Engels understood as few other socialists did the true face of rampant capitalism. And as our post-1989 liberal Utopia of free trade and Western democracy totters under the strain of both religious orthodoxy and free-market fundamentalism, his critique speaks down the ages: the cosy collusion of government and capital; the corporate flight for cheap labour and low skills; the restructuring of family life around the proclivities of the market; the inevitable retreat of tradition in the face of modernity, and the vital interstices of colonialism and capitalism; the military as a component of the industrial complex; and even the design of our cities as dictated by the demands of capital. But it is recent events in the world's stock markets and banking sector which bring Engels's criticisms so readily to the fore. 'The present world financial crisis ... dramatises the failure of the theology of the uncontrolled global free market, and forces even the United States government to consider taking public actions forgotten since the 1930s,' commented Eric Hobsbawm in 2008. It seemed that Engels's emphasis on the dangers of monopoly capitalism and concentrated finance, as well as judicious editing of Volume III of *Das Kapital*, with his stress on the tendency towards 'collapse', might at last have borne fruit. In Hobsbawm's verdict, a revival of Marxist thought in the current climate means a return to an 'analysis of the central instability of capitalist development, which proceeds through self-generated periodic economic crises, with political and social dimensions'.[34]

Engels's relentless denunciation of the devastating processes of capitalism is particularly apposite when it comes to the unregulated global market. 'The cheap prices of its commodities are the heavy artillery with which it batters down all Chinese walls,' explained the *Communist Manifesto*. 'It compels all nations, on pain of extinction, to adopt the bourgeois mode of production; it compels them to introduce what it calls civilization into their midst, i.e., to become bourgeois themselves.' While Marx and Engels would have regarded today's opposition to globalization *per se* as being illogical, Engels's critique of the human costs of capitalism is at its most resonant in those countries at the sharp end of the world economy – most notably, the emerging 'BRIC' markets of Brazil, Russia, India and China. For here all the horrors of break-neck industrialization – of capitalism red in tooth and claw transforming social relations, destroying old customs and habits, turning villages into cities and workshops into factories – are on show with the same savagery previously displayed in nineteenth-century Europe. With China now claiming the mantle of 'Workshop of the World', the pollution, ill-health, political resistance and social unrest prevalent in the Special Economic Zones of Guangdong Province and Shanghai appear eerily reminiscent of Engels's accounts of Manchester and Glasgow. Compare and contrast, as the scholar Ching Kwan Lee has done, Engels's description of employment conditions in an 1840s cotton mill:

In the cotton and flax spinning mills there are many rooms in which the air is filled with fluff and dust . . . The operative of course had no choice in the matter . . . The usual consequences of inhaling factory dust are the spitting of blood, heavy, noisy breathing, pains in the chest, coughing and sleeplessness . . . Accidents occur to operatives who work in rooms crammed full of machinery . . . The most common injury is the loss of a joint of the finger . . . In Manchester one sees not only numerous cripples, but also plenty of workers who have lost the whole or part of an arm, leg or foot.

with the testimony of a Chinese migrant worker in Shenzhen in 2000:

There is no fixed work schedule. A twelve-hour workday is minimum. With rush orders, we have to work continuously for thirty hours or more. Day and night . . . the longest shift we had worked non-stop lasted for forty hours . . . It's very exhausting because we have to stand all the time, to straighten the denim cloth by pulling. Our legs are always hurting. There is no place to sit on the shop floor. The machines do not stop during our lunch breaks. Three workers in a group will just take turns eating, one at a time ... The shop floor is filled with thick dust. Our bodies become black working day and night indoors. When I get off from work and spit, it's all black.[35]

The awful added irony is that such unleavened exploitation is actively sanctioned by the Communist Party of China.

This was never Engels's vision of society. From his teenage years amidst the riches and poverty, the misery and degradation of the Barmen bleacheries, he was convinced there was a more dignified place for humanity in the modern age. For him and Marx, the welcome abundance offered by capitalism deserved to be distributed through a more equitable system. For millions of people around the world that hope still holds. Today, some two decades after the fall of the Berlin Wall and the global collapse of state communism, Friedrich Engels, that eminent Victorian of sacrifice and contradiction, would once more be predicting the negation of the negation and the fulfilment of his good friend Karl Marx's promise.

Notes

Preface

1. *Reminiscences of Marx and Engels* (Moscow, 1958), p. 185
2. Heinrich Gemkow et al., *Frederick Engels: A Biography* (Dresden, 1972), p. 9
3. Paul Lewis, 'Marx's Stock Resurges on a 150-Year Tip', *New York Times*, 27 June 1998
4. *The Times*, 20 October 2008
5. Meghnad Desai, *Marx's Revenge: The Resurgence of Capitalism and the Death of Statist Socialism* (London, 2002)
6. Karl Marx, Frederick Engels: *Collected Works* (New York, 1976), Vol. 6, pp. 486–7 [henceforth, MECW]
7. Jacques Attali, *Karl Marx ou l'esprit du monde* (Paris, 2005)
8. 'Marx after Communism', *The Economist*, Vol. 265, No. 8304, 21 December 2002
9. Francis Wheen, *Karl Marx* (London, 1999)
10. See Gustav Mayer, *Friedrich Engels: Eine Biographie* (The Hague, 1934) and *Friedrich Engels* (London, 1936); Grace Carlton, *Friedrich Engels: The Shadow Prophet* (London, 1965); Gemkow et al., *Engels: A Biography*; W. O. Henderson, *The Life of Friedrich Engels* (London, 1976); David McLellan, *Engels* (Sussex, 1977); Terrell Carver, *Engels* (Oxford, 1981) and *Friedrich Engels: His Life and Thought* (London, 1991); J. D. Hunley, *The Life and Thought of Friedrich Engels* (London, 1991).
11. E. P. Thompson, *The Poverty of Theory and Other Essays* (London, 1978), p. 261
12. Richard N. Hunt, *The Political Ideas of Marx and Engels* (Pennsylvania, 1974), p. 93
13. Norman Levine, 'Marxism and Engelsism', *Journal of the History of the Behavioural Sciences*, 11, 3 (1973), p. 239

14. MECW, Vol. 26, p. 382
15. Tony Judt, *Reappraisals: Reflections on the Forgotten Twentieth Century* (London, 2008), p. 125
16. MECW, Vol. 26, p. 387

Chapter 1: Siegfried in Zion

1. MECW, Vol. 2, pp. 578–9
2. *Reminiscences of Marx and Engels* (Moscow, 1958), p. 183
3. Quoted in M. Knieriem, *Die Herkunft des Friedrich Engels: Briefe aus der Verwandtschaft* (Trier, 1991), pp. 39–40
4. See Heinrich Gemkow et al., *Frederick Engels: A Biography* (Dresden, 1972), p. 16
5. T. C. Banfield, *Industry of the Rhine* (1846), (New York, 1969), pp. 122–3
6. MECW, Vol. 2, p. 8
7. Banfield, *Industry of the Rhine*, p. 142
8. Christopher Clark, *Iron Kingdom: The Rise and Downfall of Prussia, 1600–1947* (London, 2006), p. 125
9. *Die Herkunft des Friedrich Engels*, pp. 555, 600
10. Hughes Oliphant Old, *The Reading and Preaching of the Scriptures in the Worship of the Christian Church* (Cambridge, 1998), Vol. 5, p. 104
11. MECW, Vol. 2, p. 555
12. Knieriem, *Die Herkunft des Friedrich Engels*, p. 21
13. See Gustav Mayer, *Friedrich Engels: Eine Biographie* (The Hague, 1934), Vol. I, p. 7
14. Quoted in Manfred Kliem, *Friedrich Engels: Dokumente seines Lebens* (Leipzig, 1977), p. 37
15. MECW, Vol. 44, p. 394
16. Ibid., Vol. 2, p. 14
17. Knieriem, *Die Herkunft des Friedrich Engels*, p. 463
18. See James J. Sheehan, *German History, 1770–1866* (Oxford, 1989)
19. Knieriem, *Die Herkunft des Friedrich Engels*, pp. 463, 464, 470
20. MECW, Vol. 6, p. 259
21. Ibid., Vol. 2, p. 553
22. Ibid., Vol. 38, p. 30
23. Ibid., Vol. 2, p. 582
24. Ibid., pp. 20, 585. See also Volkmar Wittmütz, 'Friedrich Engels in der Barmer Stadtschule 1829–1834', in *Nachrichten aus dem Engels-Haus*, 3 (1980)

25. See Isaiah Berlin, 'The Counter-Enlightenment', in *Against the Current* (London, 1997)

26. Edmund Burke, *Reflections on the Revolution in France* (Harmondsworth, 1986), p. 170

27. Hugh Trevor-Roper, *The Romantic Movement and the Study of History* (London, 1969), p. 2

28. See Celia Applegate, 'Culture and the Arts', in Jonathan Sperber (ed.), *Germany 1800–1870* (Oxford, 2004)

29. M. de Stäel, *Germany* (London, 1813), p. 8

30. See 'The Growth of Participatory Politics' in Sheehan, *German History*

31. Jack Zipes, *The Brothers Grimm* (London, 2002), p. 26

32. See Clark, *Iron Kingdom*, p. 385

33. MECW, Vol. 2, p. 33

34. Ibid., p. 95

35. Ibid., p. 585

36. Ibid., p. 399

37. Quoted in *Reminiscences*, p. 193

38. MECW, Vol. 2, p. 117

39. Ibid., pp. 499, 503

40. Ibid., p. 528

41. Quoted in *Reminiscences*, pp. 192, 174

42. Ibid., p. 94

43. MECW, Vol. 2, p. 511

44. Ibid., p. 530

45. Quoted in Sheehan, *German History*, p. 573

46. MECW, Vol. 2, p. 421

47. Friedrich Engels, *The Condition of the Working Class in England* (Harmondsworth, 1987), p. 245

48. See Richard Holmes, *Shelley: The Pursuit* (London, 1987)

49. See James M. Brophy, 'The Public Sphere', in Jonathan Sperber (ed.), *Germany 1800–1870* (Oxford, 2004)

50. MECW, Vol. 2, p. 558

51. Quoted in Paul Foot, *Red Shelley* (London, 1984), p. 228. Eleanor Marx would later take up the Shelley baton, together with her lover Edward Aveling, in their joint work *Shelley and Socialism* (1888)

52. Heinrich Heine, *Sämmtliche Werke* (Hamburg, 1867), XII, p. 83

53. MECW, Vol. 2, p. 422

54. Mayer, *Eine Biographie*, I, p. 17

55. MECW, Vol. 2, p. 392

56. Ibid., p. 135

57. See Sheehan, *German History*, pp. 646–7
58. MECW, Vol. 2, p. 9
59. Ibid., Vol. 24, p. 114
60. Gemkow et al., *Frederick Engels. A Biography*, p. 30
61. MECW, Vol. 2, p. 25
62. Ibid., p. 426
63. Ibid., p. 454
64. Quoted in David McLellan, *The Young Hegelians and Karl Marx* (London, 1969), p. 3
65. MECW, Vol. 2, pp. 426, 454, 461–2
66. Ibid., p. 471
67. Ibid., p. 528
68. Ibid., p. 486
69. See William J. Brazill, *The Young Hegelians* (London, 1970)
70. MECW, Vol. 16, p. 474
71. See J. E. Toews, *Hegelianism: The Path Toward Dialectical Humanism, 1805–1841* (Cambridge, 1980), pp. 65–6
72. MECW, Vol. 2, p. 489
73. See Gareth Stedman Jones, 'Engels and the History of Marxism', in Eric Hobsbawm (ed.), *The History of Marxism* (Brighton, 1982), I, p. 301
74. MECW, Vol. 2, pp. 99, 169

Chapter 2: The Dragon's Seed

1. MECW, Vol. 2, p. 181
2. E. H. Carr, *Michael Bakunin* (London, 1975), p. 95; Alastair Hannay, *Kierkegaard: A Biography* (Cambridge, 2001), pp. 162–3
3. MECW, Vol. 2, p. 187
4. Ibid., Vol. 26, p. 123
5. See Anthony Read and David Fisher, *Berlin* (London, 1994); Robert J. Hellman, *Berlin: The Red Room and White Beer* (Washington, DC, 1990); Alexandra Richie, *Faust's Metropolis* (London, 1999)
6. Heinrich Heine, *Sämmtliche Werke* (Hamburg, 1867), I, p. 240
7. MECW, Vol. 3, p. 515
8. Ibid., Vol. 26, p. 357
9. G. W. F. Hegel, *Philosophy of Right*, translated with notes by T. M. Knox (Oxford, 1942), p. 10
10. Quoted in Peter Singer, *Hegel* (Oxford, 1983), p. 32
11. Hegel, *Philosophy of Right*, p. 160

12. Leszek Kolakowski, *Main Currents of Marxism* (London, 2005), p. 61

13. J. E. Toews, *Hegelianism: The Path Toward Dialectical Humanism, 1805–1841* (Cambridge, 1980), p. 60

14. Christopher Clark, *Iron Kingdom: The Rise and Downfall of Prussia, 1600–1947* (London, 2006), p. 434

15. MECW, Vol. 26, p. 363

16. Ibid., Vol. 6, pp. 162–3

17. Ibid., Vol. 6, pp. 359–60

18. Ibid., Vol. 2, p. 197

19. Ibid., Vol. 26, p. 364

20. William J. Brazill, *The Young Hegelians* (London, 1970), p. 146; MECW, Vol. 3, pp. 462–3; quoted in David McLellan, *The Young Hegelians and Karl Marx* (London, 1969), p. 88

21. Ludwig Feuerbach, *Provisional Theses for the Reformation of Philosophy*, quoted in Lawrence S. Stepelevich (ed.), *The Young Hegelians* (Cambridge, 1983), p. 156

22. Ibid., p. 167

23. MECW, Vol. 2, p. 537

24. Ibid., p. 550

25. Ibid., Vol. 48, pp. 393–4

26. See Brazill, *The Young Hegelians*; Hellman, *Berlin*

27. Stephan Born, *Erinnerungen eines Achtundvierzigers* (Leipzig, 1898), pp. 26–7

28. See Engels's essay, 'Alexander Jung: Lectures on Modern German Literature', in the *Rheinische Zeitung*, No. 160, 7 July 1842 for evidence of his clear break with Young Germany.

29. Quoted in Hellman, *Berlin*, p. 73

30. For those who are unfamiliar:

> I'm very well acquainted, too, with matters mathematical
> I understand equations, both the simple and quadratical
> About binomial theorem I'm teeming with a lot o' news
> With many cheerful facts about the square of the hypotenuse
>
> I'm very good at integral and differential calculus
> I know the scientific names of beings animalculous
> In short, in matters vegetable, animal, and mineral
> I am the very model of a modern Major-General.

31. MECW, Vol. 2, pp. 321, 322, 335, 336

32. Much of the following account of Marx's early life is drawn from David

McLellan, *Karl Marx: His Life and Thought* (London, 1983), pp. 1–104; Francis Wheen, *Karl Marx* (London, 1999), pp. 7–59; and Eric Hobsbawm's essay in the *Dictionary of National Biography*

33. Born, *Erinnerungen*, p. 68

34. 'Ink in his blood', *Times Literary Supplement*, 23 March 2007, p. 14

35. MECW, Vol. 50, p. 503

36. Marx-Engels Archives, International Institute of Social History, Amsterdam, M4 (M2/1)

37. MECW, Vol. 2, p. 586

38. See Eric Hobsbawm, 'Marx, Engels and Pre-Marxian Socialism', in Eric Hobsbawm (ed.), *The History of Marxism*, I (Brighton, 1982). Or, as Kolakowski puts it, 'At the time when Marx came into the field as a theoretician of the proletariat revolution, socialist ideas already had a long life behind them.' L. Kolakowski, *Main Currents of Marxism*, p. 150

39. For a good example of this tradition, see Tony Benn, *Arguments for Socialism* (London, 1979), pp. 21–44

40. Henri de Saint-Simon, *Letters from an Inhabitant of Geneva*, in Ghita Ionescu (ed.), *The Political Thought of Saint-Simon* (Oxford, 1976), p. 78

41. Ibid., p. 10

42. Quoted in F. A. von Hayek, *The Counter-Revolution of Science* (Illinois, 1952), p. 121

43. Henri de Saint-Simon, *The New Christianity* in Ionescu (ed.), *The Political Thought of Saint-Simon*, p. 210

44. *Œuvres complètes de Charles Fourier* (Paris, 1966–8), Vol. VI, p. 397, quoted in J. Beecher and R. Bienvenu, *The Utopian Vision of Charles Fourier* (London, 1975), p. 119

45. See Gareth Stedman Jones, 'Introduction' in Charles Fourier, *The Theory of the Four Movements* (Cambridge, 1996)

46. Quoted in Beecher and Bienvenu, *Fourier*, pp. 116–17

47. Frank Manuel implies that the frigid banality of Fourier's own life inspired some of his loftier visions. 'Fourier the bachelor lived alone in a garret and ate *table d'hote* in the poorer Lyons restaurants, disliked children and spiders, loved flowers and cats ... From all accounts he was a queer duck ... One sometimes wonders whether this inventor of the system of passionate attraction ever experienced one.' Frank E. Manuel, *The Prophets of Paris* (Harvard, 1962), p. 198

48. MECW, Vol. 24, p. 290

49. Ibid., Vol. 4, p. 643

50. Ibid., Vol. 24, p. 290. Engels's view of the Utopian socialists waxed and waned over the years. By 1875 he was notably more generous about their

contribution to communism and suggested that 'German theoretical socialism will never forget that it rests on the shoulders of Saint-Simon, Fourier and Owen – three men who, in spite of all their fantastic notions and all their utopianism, stand among the most eminent thinkers of all time and whose genius anticipated innumerable things the correctness of which is now being scientifically proved by us . . .' MECW, Vol. 23, pp. 630–31

51. Isaiah Berlin, 'The Life and Opinions of Moses Hess', in *Against the Current* (London, 1997), p. 214

52. Moses Hess, *Rom und Jerusalem* (Leipzig, 1899), p. 16

53. Quoted in Shlomo Avineri, *Moses Hess* (London, 1968), p. 11

54. Berlin, *Against the Current*, p. 219

55. See Andre Liebich (ed.), *Selected Writings of August Cieszkowski* (Cambridge, 1979)

56. Quoted in McLellan, *The Young Hegelians*, p. 10

57. 'Über die sozialistische Bewegung in Deutschland,' in Moses Hess, *Philosophische und sozialistische Schriften 1837–1850* (Liechtenstein, 1980), p. 293

58. See Gareth Stedman Jones, 'Introduction', *The Communist Manifesto* (London, 2002)

59. Quoted in Avineri, *Moses Hess*, p. 61

60. Ibid., p. 84

61. MECW, Vol. 3, p. 406

62. 'Die Europaische Triarchie', in Hess, *Philosophische und sozialistische Schriften*, ed. Cornu and Mönke, p. 117

63. Moses Hess, *Briefwechsel* (Amsterdam, 1959), p. 103

Chapter 3: Manchester in Black and White

1. *Manchester Guardian*, 27 August 1842

2. *Manchester Times*, 7 July 1842

3. Friedrich Engels, *The Condition of the Working Class in England* (Harmondsworth, 1987), p. 239

4. See Alan Kidd, *Manchester* (Keele, 1996)

5. Thomas Cooper, *The Life of Thomas Cooper, written by Himself* (London, 1873), p. 207

6. Engels, *Condition of the Working Class*, pp. 82, 156

7. MECW, Vol. 3, p. 392

8. Ibid., Vol. 26, p. 317

9. *Reasoner*, V, p. 92

10. See Kidd, *Manchester*; W. D. Rubinstein, 'The Victorian Middle Classes: Wealth, Occupation, and Geography', *The Economic History Review*, 30, 4 (1977)

11. Alexis de Tocqueville, *Journeys to England and Ireland* (1835) (London, 1958), pp. 94, 107

12. Quoted in L. D. Bradshaw, *Visitors to Manchester* (Manchester, 1987), p. 25

13. Léon Faucher, *Manchester in 1844* (Manchester, 1844), p. 16

14. Thomas Carlyle, 'Chartism', in *Selected Writings* (Harmondsworth, 1986), p. 211

15. Robert Southey, *Letters from England by Don Manuel Alvarez Espriella* (London, 1808), p. 83

16. Quoted in Bradshaw, *Visitors to Manchester*, p. 54

17. Hippolyte Taine, *Notes on England* (1872) (London, 1957), p. 219

18. J. P. Kay, *The Moral and Physical Condition of the Working Classes Employed in the Cotton Manufacture in Manchester* (1832) (Manchester, 1969), p. 8

19. E. Chadwick, *Report on the Sanitary Conditions of the Labouring Population of Great Britain* (1842) (Edinburgh, 1965), p. 78

20. Ibid., p. 111

21. Wilmot Henry Jones (Geoffrey Gimcrack), *Gimcrackiana, or Fugitive Pieces on Manchester Men and Manners* (Manchester, 1833), pp. 156–7

22. *Manchester Guardian*, 6 May 1857

23. Quoted in Bradshaw, *Visitors to Manchester*, p. 28

24. R. Parkinson, *On the Present Condition of the Labouring Poor in Manchester* (Manchester, 1841), p. 85

25. Faucher, *Manchester*, p. 69

26. Benjamin Disraeli, *Sybil, or the Two Nations* (London, 1981), p. 66

27. MECW, Vol. 2, p. 370

28. Engels, *Condition of the Working Class*, p. 68

29. MECW, Vol. 2, pp. 370, 373, 378

30. Engels, *Condition of the Working Class*, p. 182

31. F. R. Johnston, *Eccles* (Eccles, 1967), p. 88

32. In November 2007 the *Salford Star* went to interview the residents of Engels House to ask their thoughts on the man who gave his name to their tower block. Resident Gordon Langlands was having terrible problems with the damp. 'The Council just seem to be deafing me on it, they're just a bunch of comedians. But it's getting beyond a joke now. Someone told me to move out but I've built this place up. This Engels, he would have sorted it.' See the *Salford Star*, 6 November 2007

33. My thanks to Colin Farlow for this information. More broadly on Ermen and Engels see J. B. Smethhurst, 'Ermen and Engels', *Marx Memorial Library Quarterly Bulletin*, No. 41 (1967); Roy Whitfield, *Frederick Engels in Manchester: The Search for a Shadow* (Salford, 1988); W. O. Henderson, *The Life of Friedrich Engels* (London, 1976)

34. MECW, Vol. 38, p. 20. The factory referred to in this letter is actually the Engelskirchen one. The sentiment remains the same.

35. Engels, *Condition of the Working Class*, p. 27

36. MECW, Vol. 4, p. 226

37. Faucher, *Manchester*, p. 25

38. Engels, *Condition of the Working Class*, p. 245

39. MECW, Vol. 3, pp. 387, 380

40. Ibid., Vol. 3, pp. 380, 387, 388

41. Ibid., Vol. 25, pp. 346–7

42. John Watts, *The Facts and Fictions of Political Economists* (Manchester, 1842), pp. 28, 35, 36, 13

43. *Manchester Guardian*, 26 September 1838

44. Engels, *Condition of the Working Class*, p. 241; MECW, Vol. 2, p. 375

45. See G. D. H. Cole, 'George Julian Harney', in *Chartist Portraits* (London, 1941)

46. *Reminiscences of Marx and Engels* (Moscow, 1958), p. 192

47. F. G. Black and R. M. Black (eds.), *The Harney Papers* (Assen, 1969), p. 260

48. Engels, *Condition of the Working Class*, p. 160

49. Anon., *Stubborn Facts from the Factories by a Manchester Operative* (London, 1844), p. 40

50. MECW, Vol. 6, p. 486

51. Engels, *Condition of the Working Class*, p. 242; MECW Vol. 3, p. 450

52. Thomas Carlyle, 'Sign of the Times', in *Selected Writings*, p. 77

53. Thomas Carlyle, *Past and Present* (1843), (New York, 1965), p. 148

54. MECW, Vol. 3, p. 463

55. Ibid., Vol. 10, p. 302

56. Engels, *Condition of the Working Class*, p. 276

57. George Weerth, *Sämmtliche Werke* (Berlin, 1957), Vol. 5, pp. 111, 128. This is, perhaps, a little unfair. The more civic-minded J. B. Priestley would later describe pre-war Bradford as 'at once one of the most provincial and yet one of the most cosmopolitan of English provincial cities' celebrated for its foreign residents. 'I can remember when one of the best-known clubs in Bradford was the *Schillerverein*. And in those days a Londoner was a stranger

sight than a German ... A dash of the Rhine and the Oder found its way into our grim runnel – "t' mucky beck".' See J. B. Priestley, *English Journey* (London, 1933; 1993), pp. 123–4

58. Eleanor Marx-Aveling to Karl Kautsky, 15 March 1898, Karl Kautsky Papers (Amsterdam), DXVI, 489

59. See Whitfield, *Engels in Manchester*, p. 70

60. Edmund Wilson, *To the Finland Station* (London, 1991), p. 159. W. O. Henderson concurs. He describes Mary as 'an Irish millhand who lived in Ancoats at 18 Cotton Street, off George Leigh Street, in the factory district'. See W. O. Henderson, *Marx and Engels and the English Workers* (London, 1989), p. 45

61. Max Beer, *Fifty Years of International Socialism* (London, 1935), p. 77

62. Heinrich Gemkow, 'Fünf Frauen an Engels' Seite', *Beiträge zur Geschichte der Arbeiterbewegung*, 37, 4 (1995), p. 48

63. Engels, *Condition of the Working Class*, p. 182

64. Edmund and Ruth Frow, *The New Moral World: Robert Owen and Owenism in Manchester and Salford* (Salford, 1986)

65. Weerth, *Sämmtliche Werke*, Vol. I, p. 208

66. Engels, *Condition of the Working Class*, p. 170

67. Whitfield, *Engels in Manchester*, p. 21

68. Ibid., p. 30

69. MECW, Vol. 3, pp. 418, 423, 441

70. Ibid., Vol. 3, p. 440

71. Ibid., Vol. 3, p. 399

72. MECW, Vol. 4, p. 32

73. Ibid., pp. 431, 424. See also, Gregory Claeys, 'Engels' *Outlines of a Critique of Political Economy* (1843) and the Origins of the Marxist Critique of Capitalism', *History of Political Economy*, 16, 2 (1984)

74. Many of the ideas within Engels's 'Outlines' would reappear in Marx's *Economic and Philosophical Manuscripts*, where, along with Hess, it is described as 'the only *original* German work[s] of any interest in this field'. See Karl Marx, *Early Writings* (Harmondsworth, 1992), p. 281. Crucially, Marx then extended the notion of alienation to the activity of labour itself.

75. Karl Marx to Friedrich Engels, 9 April 1863, MECW, Vol. 41, p. 466

76. MECW, Vol. 38, p. 10

77. Engels, *Condition of the Working Class*, p. 31

78. *Reminiscences*, p. 137

79. MECW, Vol. 38, p. 13

80. Engels, *Condition of the Working Class*, p. 31

81. MECW, Vol. 38, pp. 10–11

82. Engels, *Condition of the Working Class*, p. 30
83. Ibid., pp. 89, 92
84. Ibid., p. 98
85. MECW, Vol. 3, p. 390
86. Engels, *Condition of the Working Class*, p. 125
87. Ibid., pp. 193–4
88. Ibid., p. 184
89. Ibid., pp. 31, 174, 216, 69
90. Ibid., p. 275
91. Ibid., p. 86
92. Ibid., p. 87
93. MECW, Vol. 23, p. 365
94. See Ira Katznelson, *Marxism and the City* (Oxford, 1992); Aruna Krishna-murthy, ' "More Than Abstract Knowledge": Friedrich Engels in Industrial Manchester', *Victorian Literature and Culture* (2000), 28, 2, pp. 427–48. Today, one of the finest practitioners of this fashionable academic trope is the Californian-based writer Mike Davis, whose 2006 essay, *Planet of Slums*, is a similarly Engelsian, 'black and white' approach to the class structure of the twenty-first century, global city. In a searing update of the *Condition*, Davis recounts with equal vituperation the sanitary state of the modern mass conurbations ('Today's poor megacities – Nairobi, Lagos, Bombay, Dhaka, and so on – are stinking mountains of shit that would appal even the most hardened Victorians'), but also points to the power relationships under-pinning the spatial inequality of the city. A chapter entitled 'Haussmann in the Tropics', investigating squatter and working-class clearances in contem-porary Africa, China and Central America, is pure Engels. 'Urban segregation is not a frozen status quo, but rather a ceaseless social war in which the state intervenes regularly in the name of "progress," "beautification", and even "social justice for the poor" to redraw spatial boundaries to the advantage of landowners, foreign investors, elite homeowners, and middle-class com-muters. As in 1860s Paris under the fanatical reign of Baron Haussmann, urban redevelopment still strives to simultaneously maximize private profit and social control.'
95. Steven Marcus, *Engels, Manchester and the Working Class* (London, 1974), p. 145
96. Simon Gunn, *The Public Culture of the Victorian Middle Class* (Man-chester, 2000), p. 36. See also Marc Eli Blanchard, *In Search of the City* (Stanford, 1985), p. 21
97. *Guardian*, 4 February 2006. See also Asa Briggs's comment that, 'If Engels had lived not in Manchester but in Birmingham his conception of

"class" and his theories of the role of class history might have been very different,' in Asa Briggs, *Victorian Cities* (London, 1990), p. 116. By contrast, W. O. Henderson described Engels's motives as follows: 'he was a young man in a bad temper who vented his spleen in a passionate denunciation of the factory system ... the unrestrained violence of his language and his complete failure to understand any point of view different from his own ... may be explained by the fact ... Engels was suffering from an overwhelming sense of frustration'. See W. O. Henderson and W. H. Chaloner (eds.), *The Condition of the Working Class in England* (Oxford, 1958), p. xxx

98. Engels, *Condition of the Working Class*, p. 61

99. Ibid., pp. 143–4. For Lenin, this was the book's signal achievement: it revealed that the proletariat was not just 'a suffering class' but that, 'in fact, the disgraceful economic condition of the proletariat was driving it irresistibly forward and compelling it to fight for its ultimate emancipation'. See *Reminiscences of Marx and Engels*, pp. 61–2

100. Ibid., p. 52

101. Gareth Stedman Jones, 'The First Industrial City? Engels' Account of Manchester in 1844', unpublished paper, p. 7. See also Gareth Stedman Jones, 'Engels and the Industrial Revolution', in Douglas Moggach (ed.), *The New Hegelians: Politics and Philosophy in the Hegelian School* (Cambridge, 2006)

102. Engels, *Condition of the Working Class*, p. 100

103. Alexis de Tocqueville, *Journeys to England and Ireland* (1835) (London, 1958), p. 108

104. Engels, *Condition of the Working Class*, p. 64

105. Ibid., p. 243

106. Ibid., p. 291

107. MECW, Vol. 23, p. 347

108. Friedrich Engels, *Anti-Dühring* (Peking, 1976), pp. 385–6

109. MECW, Vol. 23, p. 389

110. *Der Bund der Kommunisten*, documents and materials, Vol. 1, Berlin (GDR), p. 343, quoted in Michael Knierim (ed.), *Über Friedrich Engels: Privates, Öffentliches und Amtliches Aussagen und Zeugnisse von Zeitgenossen* (Wuppertal, 1986), p. 27

111. Jurgen Kuczynski, *Die Geschichte der Lage der Arbeiter unter dem Kapitalismus* (Berlin, 1960), Band 8, pp. 168–9

112. Karl Marx, *Capital*, Vol. I (Harmondsworth, 1990), p. 349

113. For a proper appreciation of the work's significance see S. H. Rigby, *Engels and the Formation of Marxism* (Manchester, 1992), p. 63

Chapter 4: 'A Little Patience and Some Terrorism'

1. Honoré de Balzac, *Old Goriot* (1834) (Harmondsworth, 1951), pp. 304, 37–8. Engels, like Marx, was a great fan of Balzac preferring him even over Zola. '*La Comédie humaine* gives us a most wonderfully realistic history of French "Society", especially of *le monde parisien*, describing, chronicle-fashion, almost year by year from 1816–1848 the progressive inroads of the rising bourgeois upon the society of nobles, that reconstituted itself after 1815 and set up again, as far as it could, the standard of *la vieille politesse française*. He describes how the last remnants of this, to him, model society gradually succumbed before the intrusion of the vulgar moneyed upstart, or were corrupted by him,' Engels wrote to his correspondent Margaret Harkness in 1888. MECW, Vol. 48, p. 168

2. Quoted in David McLellan, *Karl Marx: His Life and Thought* (London, 1983), p. 57

3. Quoted in David McLellan (ed.), *Karl Marx: Interviews and Recollections* (London, 1981), p. 8

4. Quoted in Shlomo Avineri, *The Social and Political Thought of Karl Marx* (Cambridge, 1968), pp. 140–41

5. Isaiah Berlin, *Karl Marx: His Life and Environment* (Oxford, 1978), p. 60

6. Karl Marx, 'Paris Manuscripts', in *The Early Texts* (Oxford, 1971), p. 148

7. MECW, Vol. 26, p. 317

8. Quoted in *Reminiscences of Marx and Engels* (Moscow, 1958), p. 64

9. Gustav Mayer, *Friedrich Engels: Eine Biographie* (The Hague, 1934) I, p.175

10. Quoted in *Reminiscences*, p. 92

11. Ibid., p. 91

12. MECW, Vol. 26, p. 382

13. Ibid., Vol. 47, p. 202

14. Ibid., Vol. 46, p. 147

15. Ibid., Vol. 29, p. 264; Vol. 26, p. 382

16. Ibid., Vol. 4, p. 241

17. Ibid., Vol. 4, p. 7

18. Ibid., Vol. 4, pp. 7, 93

19. Ibid., Vol. 38, p. 6

20. Ibid., Vol. 38, pp. 18, 28, 17–18, 25

21. Ibid., Vol. 38, pp. 29, 3

22. Ibid., Vol. 38, pp. 3, 4

23. Ibid., Vol. 4, pp. 230–31

24. Ibid., Vol. 38, p. 4

25. Ibid., p. 232

26. Ibid., p. 23

27. Quoted in Mayer, *Eine Biographie*, pp. 215–17

28. MECW, Vol. 4, p. 243

29. Ibid., p. 252

30. Ibid., p. 255

31. Ibid., p. 263

32. Quoted in Manfred Kliem, *Friedrich Engels: Dokumente seines Lebens* (Leipzig, 1977), p. 142

33. MECW, Vol. 38, p. 572

34. Heidelberg University Library, manuscripts, no. 2560 (Cod. Heid. 378 XXX), quoted in Michael Knierim (ed.), *Über Friedrich Engels: Privates, Öffentliches und Amtliches Aussagen und Zeugnisse von Zeitgenossen* (Wuppertal, 1986), p. 8

35. MECW, Vol. 38, p. 39

36. Quoted in *Reminiscences*, p. 194

37. MECW, Vol. 38, pp. 29, 33

38. Ibid., Vol. 43, p. 518

39. *Guardian*, 4 February 2006

40. F. G. Black and R. M. Black (eds.), *The Harney Papers* (Assen, 1969), p. 239

41. Quoted in E. H. Carr, *Michael Bakunin* (London, 1975), p. 146

42. Stephan Born, *Erinnerungen eines Achtundvierzigers* (Leipzig, 1898), p. 74

43. Max Beer, *Fifty Years of International Socialism* (London, 1935), p. 78

44. Born, *Erinnerungen*, p. 73

45. Eleanor Marx-Aveling to Karl Kautsky, 15 March 1898, Karl Kautsky Papers (Amsterdam), DXVI, 489

46. Max Stirner, *The Ego and Its Own* (Cambridge, 1995), p. 323. See also Lawrence S. Stepelevich, 'The Revival of Max Stirner', *Journal of the History of Ideas*, 35, 2 (1974)

47. MECW, Vol. 38, p. 12

48. Ibid., Vol. 6, p. 166

49. Ibid., Vol. 5, pp. 90, 36–7

50. Quoted in *The Writings of the Young Marx*, translated and edited by Lloyd D. Easton and Kurt H. Guddat (New York, 1967), p. 431

51. Ibid., p. 47

52. MECW, Vol. 26, pp. 313–14

53. Ibid., Vol. 6, p. 5

54. Born, *Erinnerungen*, p. 72

55. MECW, Vol. 6, p. 79

56. Ibid., Vol. 6, p. 56

57. Ibid., Vol. 6, p. 529

58. Ibid., Vol. 26, p. 320

59. Quoted in *Reminiscences*, p. 270

60. MECW, Vol. 26, p.319

61. Ibid., Vol. 38, pp. 39–40

62. P. J. Proudhon, *Confessions d'un révolutionnaire* (Paris, 1849), quoted in Francis Wheen, *Karl Marx* (London, 1999), p. 107

63. MECW, Vol. 6, p. 512

64. Born, *Erinnerungen*, p. 47

65. Eugène Sue, *The Mysteries of Paris* (Cambridgeshire, 1989), p. 9

66. Quoted in Colin Jones, *Paris: Biography of a City* (London, 2004), p. 349

67. Balzac, *Old Goriot*, p. 133

68. See David H. Pinkney, *Decisive Years in France 1840–1847* (Princeton, 1986); Philip Mansel, *Paris between Empires* (London, 2001)

69. MECW, Vol. 38, pp. 80–83

70. Ibid., p. 91

71. Ibid., p. 16

72. Born, *Erinnerungen*, pp. 51–2

73. MECW, Vol. 38, p. 115

74. Isaiah Berlin, *Against the Current* (London, 1997), p. 219

75. MECW, Vol. 38, pp. 56, 65, 108, 153

76. Marx-Aveling to Kautsky, 15 March 1898, Karl Kautsky Papers (Amsterdam), DXVI, 489. To add to the confusion, Stephan Born writes of Engels having to leave Paris after chivalrously intervening with a French count who had dumped his mistress without providing for her. The count then contacted some amenable government ministers who had Engels deported. See Born, *Erinnerungen*, p. 71

77. Born, *Erinnerungen*, p. 49

78. MECW, Vol. 6, p. 98

79. Ibid., Vol. 6, p. 102

80. Ibid., Vol. 38, p. 139

81. Ibid., Vol. 6, pp. 345, 348, 351, 354

82. Quoted in *Reminiscences*, p. 153

83. MECW, Vol. 26, p. 322

84. Wilhelm Liebknecht, *Karl Marx: Biographical Memoirs* (New York, 1968), p. 26

85. For an analysis of the textual and intellectual interstices between *The*

Condition of the Working Class in England and *The Communist Manifesto*, see Terrell Carver, *Friedrich Engels: His Life and Thought* (London, 1991)
86. For a full account of the intellectual genealogy of the *Manifesto*, see Gareth Stedman Jones, Introduction, in Karl Marx and Friedrich Engels, *The Communist Manifesto* (Harmondsworth, 2002)
87. MECW, Vol. 6, p. 487
88. Ibid., p. 558

Chapter 5: The Infinitely Rich '48 Harvest

1. MECW, Vol. 6, p. 559
2. Ibid., Vol. 6, p. 647
3. Ibid., Vol. 38, p. 169
4. Ibid., pp. 159–60
5. See Christopher Clark, *Iron Kingdom: The Rise and Downfall of Prussia, 1600–1947* (London, 2006); James J. Sheehan, *German History, 1770–1866* (Oxford, 1989), p. 658
6. See David E. Barclay, 'Political Trends and Movements, 1830–50', in Jonathan Sperber (ed.), *Germany 1800–1870* (Oxford, 2004)
7. MECW, Vol. 26, p. 123
8. Quoted in P. H. Noyes, *Organization and Revolution: Working-Class Associations in the German Revolution of 1848–49* (Princeton, 1966), pp. 286–7
9. See Jonathan Sperber, *Rhineland Radicals* (Princeton, 1991)
10. See Oscar J. Hammen, *The Red '48ers* (New York, 1969)
11. MECW, Vol. 26, p. 122
12. Ibid., Vol. 38, pp. 171, 173
13. Ibid., Vol. 26, p. 123
14. Ibid., Vol. 11, p. 40
15. See Philip Mansel, *Paris between Empires* (London, 2001); Hammen, *The Red '48ers*
16. MECW Vol. 7, pp. 124, 130, 128
17. Ibid., Vol. 7, pp. 131–2
18. Ibid., Vol. 7, p. 587
19. Ibid., Vol. 38, p. 541
20. Ibid., Vol. 7, p. 460
21. *Neue Rheinische Zeitung*, 7 November 1848, quoted in David McLellan, *Karl Marx: His Life and Thought* (London, 1983), p. 189
22. MECW, Vol. 7, p. 514

23. Ibid., pp. 518, 519

24. Ibid., pp. 526–9

25. See Istvan Deak, *The Lawful Revolution: Louis Kossuth and the Hungarians* (New York, 1979); Ian Cummins, *Marx, Engels and National Movements* (London, 1980)

26. MECW, Vol. 7, p. 423

27. Quoted in Roman Rosdolsky, *Engels and the 'Nonhistoric' Peoples: The National Question in the Revolution of 1848* (Glasgow, 1986), p. 135

28. MECW, Vol. 8, p. 234

29. Ibid., Vol. 8, p. 366

30. Ibid., Vol. 46, pp. 206–7

31. Ibid., Vol. 8, p.238

32. Ibid., Vol. 26, p. 128

33. Ibid., Vol. 8, p. 439

34. Ibid., Vol. 9, p. 171

35. Sheehan, *German History, 1770–1866*, p. 691

36. MECW, Vol. 9, p. 399

37. Ibid., p. 447

38. See Sperber, *Rhineland Radicals*

39. C. H. A. Pagenstecher, *Lebenserinnerungen von Dr med. C. H. Alexander Pagenstecher* (Leipzig, 1913), Vol. III, p. 63

40. MECW, Vol. 9, p. 448

41. Ibid., Vol. 10, pp. 602–3

42. Pagenstecher, *Lebenserinnerungen*, p. 66

43. Carl Hecker, *Der Aufstand in Elberfeld im Mai 1849 und mein Verhaltniss zu demselben* (Elberfeld, 1849), p. 38

44. *Elberfelder Zeitung*, 3 June 1849, No. 130

45. The story originates from a very brief account by the Barmen manufacturer's son Ernst von Eynern held in the Wuppertal archives, *Friedrich von Eynern. Ein bergisches Lebensbild. Zeitschrift des Bergischen Geschichtsvereins*, Bd. 35, 1900/01, S. 1–103.

46. Pagenstecher, *Lebenserinnerungen*, p. 66

47. H. J. M. Körner, *Lebenskämpfe in der Alten und Neues Welt* (Zurich, 1866), II, p. 137

48. MECW, Vol. 9, p. 448

49. Ibid., p. 449

50. Quoted in Manfred Kliem, *Friedrich Engels: Dokumente seines Lebens* (Leipzig, 1977), p. 280

51. MECW, Vol. 10, p. 172

52. Ibid., Vol. 10, pp. 172, 193, 202

53. Ibid. Vol. 38, p. 204
54. Ibid., Vol. 38, p. 203
55. Ibid., Vol. 10, p. 211
56. Ibid., Vol. 10, p. 224
57. Ibid., Vol. 38, p. 203
58. See M. Berger, *Engels, Armies and Revolution* (Connecticut, 1977), p. 37
59. MECW, Vol. 10, p. 237
60. Ibid., Vol. 38, p. 203
61. Ibid., Vol. 38, p. 207
62. Ibid., Vol. 10, pp. 150–51
63. Ibid., Vol. 38, p. 213

Chapter 6: Manchester in Shades of Grey

1. MECW, Vol. 40, p. 236
2. Ibid., Vol. 38, p. 250
3. Ibid., Vol. 42, p. 172
4. Alexander Herzen, *My Past and Thoughts* (London, 1968), Vol. 3, p. 1045
5. MECW, Vol. 10, p. 381
6. Ibid., Vol. 38, p. 222
7. Ibid., Vol. 24, p. 12
8. Ibid., Vol. 10, p. 24
9. Ibid., Vol. 10, p. 283
10. Ibid., Vol. 38, p. 289
11. Jenny Marx, 'A Short Sketch of an Eventful Life', in Robert Payne (ed.), *The Unknown Karl Marx* (London, 1972), p. 125
12. Letter from Jenny Marx to Joseph Weydemeyer, 20 May 1850, quoted in Francis Wheen, *Karl Marx* (London, 1999), p. 158
13. MECW, Vol. 38, p. 241
14. Quoted in W. O. Henderson, *Marx and Engels and the English Workers* (London, 1989), p. 20
15. Quoted in Gustav Mayer, *Friedrich Engels* (London, 1936), p. 130
16. MECW, Vol. 38, p. 379
17. A. J. P. Taylor, 'Manchester', *Encounter* (1957), 8, 3, p. 9
18. *Manchester Guardian*, 11 October 1851
19. MECW, Vol. 38, p. 255
20. Ibid., p. 281
21. Thomas Cooper, *The Life of Thomas Cooper, written by Himself* (London, 1873), p. 393

22. MECW, Vol. 40, p. 344
23. Ibid., Vol. 38, p. 264
24. Ibid., Vol. 41, p. 465
25. Manfred Kliem, *Friedrich Engels: Dokumente seines Lebens* (Leipzig, 1977), p. 114
26. MECW, Vol. 38, p. 250
27. Ibid., p. 302
28. Quoted in Gustav Mayer, *Friedrich Engels: Eine Biographie* (The Hague, 1934), Vol. II, p. 12
29. MECW, Vol. 38, p. 379
30. Ibid., Vol. 38, pp. 383, 401
31. Ibid., Vol. 42, p. 88
32. Wuppertal archives, *Friedrich von Eynern. Ein bergisches Lebensbild. Zeitschrift des Bergischen Geschichtsvereins* Bd. 35, 1900/01, S. 1–103.
33. MECW, Vol. 42, pp. 192, 195
34. Quoted in J. B. Smethhurst, 'Ermen and Engels', *Marx Memorial Library Quarterly Bulletin*, No. 41 (1967), p. 10
35. See Harold Perkin, *Origins of Modern English Society* (London, 1991)
36. Heinrich Gemkow et al., *Frederick Engels: A Biography* (Dresden, 1972), p. 332
37. MECW, Vol. 42, p. 172
38. Ibid., Vol. 41, p. 332
39. Ibid., Vol. 39, p. 581
40. David McLellan, *Karl Marx: A Biography* (London, 1995), p. 264
41. MECW, Vol. 42, p. 172
42. Jenny Marx, 'A Short Sketch of an Eventful Life', pp. 130–31
43. MECW, Vol. 39, p. 590
44. Francis Wheen, *Karl Marx* (1999), p. 84
45. *Reminiscences of Marx and Engels* (Moscow, 1958), p. 185
46. MECW, Vol. 38, pp. 321, 395, 451
47. Ibid., Vol. 39, p. 58
48. Ibid., Vol. 41, pp. 74, 197, 203, 230
49. Ibid., p. 141
50. Ibid., p. 423
51. R. Arthur Arnold, *The History of the Cotton Famine* (London, 1864), p. 113
52. Quoted in W. O. Henderson, *The Lancashire Cotton Famine* (Manchester, 1969), p. 107
53. See John Watts, *The Facts of the Cotton Famine* (London, 1866)
54. MECW, Vol. 38, p. 409

55. Ibid., p. 419
56. Quoted in McLellan, *Karl Marx*, p. 284
57. MECW, Vol. 39, p. 391
58. Ibid., Vol. 39, p. 164
59. Ibid., Vol. 39, p. 212; Vol. 40, pp. 451–2
60. Ibid., Vol. 38, p. 494
61. Ibid., Vol. 41, p. 14
62. Ibid., Vol. 40, p. 256, 283
63. Ibid., Vol. 41, p. 351
64. Ibid., Vol. 43, p. 160
65. Ibid., Vol. 42, p. 388. See Meghnad Desai, *Marx's Revenge: The Resurgence of Capitalism and the Death of Statist Socialism* (London, 2002), pp. 60–61
66. MECW, Vol. 42, p. 390
67. Ibid., Vol. 41, pp. 394, 411, 414
68. Jenny Marx, 'A Short Sketch of an Eventful Life', p. 126
69. For a fuller account of this story, and the historiographical debates surrounding it, see McLellan, *Karl Marx*, pp. 264–274; Wheen, *Karl Marx*, pp. 170–75; Terrell Carver, *Friedrich Engels: His Life and Thought* (London, 1991), pp. 166–9; Yvonne Kapp, *Eleanor Marx* (London, 1976), Vol. II, pp. 430–40; Yvonne Kapp, 'Frederick Demuth: New Evidence from Old Sources', *Socialist History*, 6 (1994)
70. See Kliem, *Friedrich Engels*, p. 488
71. See Roy Whitfield, *Frederick Engels in Manchester: The Search for a Shadow* (Salford, 1988)
72. MECW, Vol. 39, p. 443
73. In the archives of the Working Class Movement Library, Salford is a 1970 letter from John Millar, City Planning Officer, in response to Ruth Frow's request for a plaque to be placed on the house. In light of the demolition, he felt there would be 'little point'. See 'Engels in M/CR' box.
74. MECW, Vol. 41, pp. 344, 427
75. Ibid., Vol. 24, p. 170
76. Ibid., Vol. 27, p. 305. For a full life of Schorlemmer, see Karl Heinig, *Carl Schorlemmer: Chemiker und Kommunist Ersten Ranges* (Leipzig, 1974)
77. See W. O. Henderson, 'Friends in Exile', in *The Life of Friedrich Engels* (London, 1976)
78. MECW, Vol. 40, p. 490
79. See Ralph Greaves, *Foxhunting in Cheshire* (Kent, 1964); Gordon Fergusson, *The Green Collars: The Tarpoley Hunt Club and Cheshire Hunting History* (London, 1993)

80. Marx-Engels Archives, International Institute of Social History, Amsterdam (R49)

81. MECW, Vol. 40, p. 97

82. *Reminiscences*, p. 88

83. Hansard, Vol. 665, No. 133 (12 October 2004), Col. 174

84. MECW, Vol. 14, p. 422

85. Ibid., Vol. 40, p. 236

86. *Reminiscences*, p. 88

87. MECW, Vol. 40, pp. 264–5

88. Ibid., p. 131

89. See Alan Kidd, *Manchester* (Keele, 1996)

90. MECW, Vol. 19, p. 360

91. Marx-Engels Archives, International Institute of Social History, Amsterdam (M17)

92. MECW, Vol. 42, p. 560

93. See *The Sphinx*, Vol. II, No. 38, 1 May 1869

94. MECW, Vol. 39, p. 479

95. Ibid., p. 249. But there is an irony in Engels's embrace of Manchester's civil society. According to the critical theorist Jürgen Habermas, the voluntary societies of the nineteenth-century European city provided the 'theatrical scaffolding' for what he terms 'the bourgeois drama'. Through the social leadership of clubs such as the Albert, the Brazenose and Schiller Anstalt, the middle classes established a cultural hegemony within the public sphere of the urban world which both codified inter-class relations and underpinned the mid-Victorian stability Engels so abhorred. The myriad middle-class civil associations which honeycombed Manchester helped to construct, in the words of historian Martin Hewitt, a 'moral imperialism' which subtly but effectively kept the working classes in their place. Collectively, they constituted a strategy of social control and cultural de-proletarianization: rather than realizing class consciousness and seeing the bourgeoisie as their class enemy, the working class started to ape the middle-class ethic of rational recreation and useful knowledge. Bourgeois notions of leisure and sociability – in concert halls, gentleman's clubs, charities and educational institutes – subtly helped to unpick the radical ambition of the Manchester proletariat. Whether he realized it or not, Engels was a part of the cultural hegemony transforming Manchester from the crucible of physical force Chartism to the scene of placid Hallé soirées.

96. MECW, Vol. 40, pp. 82, 104, 105

97. Ibid., pp. 131, 149

98. Ibid., p. 151

99. MECW, Vol. 42, pp. 231, 225

100. Ibid., Vol. 40, p. 202

101. Ibid., Vol. 47, p. 229

102. Ibid., Vol. 41, p. 138

103. Ibid., Vol. 41, pp. 260, 267, 266

104. Ibid., Vol. 24, p. 192

105. Ibid., Vol. 29, p. 263

106. Ibid., Vol. 11, p. 103. It might also be worth noting that Marx's celebrated introduction to *The Eighteenth Brumaire* – 'Hegel remarks somewhere that all great, world-historical facts and personages occur, as it were, twice. He has forgotten to add: the first time as tragedy, the second as farce' – was most likely inspired by a letter Marx received from Engels in December 1851 as he was composing the work. 'But, after what we saw yesterday, there can be no counting in the *peuple*, and it really seems as though old Hegel, in the guise of the World Spirit, were directing history from the grave and, with the greatest conscientiousness, causing everything to be re-enacted twice over, once as grand tragedy and the second time as rotten farce,' was Engels's response to Bonaparte's coup. See MECW, Vol. 38, p. 505

107. MECW, Vol. 50, p. 266

108. Ibid., Vol. 49, pp. 34–6

109. Ibid., Vol. 21, p. 94

110. Ibid., Vol. 10, p. 399

111. Ibid., Vol. 10, p. 412

112. Ibid., Vol. 10, p. 422

113. Ibid., Vol. 10, p. 469

114. Ibid., Vol. 38, p. 370

115. Ibid., Vol. 10, p. 332

116. Ibid., Vol. 39, pp. 423–5, 434–6

117. Ibid., Vol. 13, p. 524

118. Ibid., Vol. 40, p. 400

119. Ibid., Vol. 41, p. 280

120. See W. O. Henderson and W. H. Chaloner (eds.), *Engels as Military Critic* (Manchester, 1959)

121. MECW, Vol. 11, p. 204

122. Ibid., Vol. 17, p. 437

123. Ibid., Vol. 18, p. 540

124. Ibid., Vol. 42, p. 399

125. See Stephen Bull, *'Volunteer!' The Lancashire Rifle Volunteers 1859–1885* (Lancashire, 1993)

126. For a good example of a different contemporary approach to the

volunteer corps, see *The Sack; or, Volunteers' Testimonial to the Militia* (London, 1862)

127. MECW, Vol. 44, pp. 7, 17, 32
128. Ibid., Vol. 11, pp. 85–6
129. Ibid., Vol. 25, pp. 154–5
130. Friedrich Engels, *Anti-Dühring* (Peking, 1976), p. 221
131. MECW, Vol. 14, p. 416
132. Ibid., Vol. 14, p. 545
133. Ibid., Vol. 6, p. 472
134. Karl Marx and Friedrich Engels, *On Colonialism* (Moscow, 1968), pp. 81–2
135. MECW, Vol. 39, p. 82
136. Marx and Engels, *On Colonialism*, p. 152
137. MECW, Vol. 24, p. 11
138. Ibid., Vol. 42, p. 205; Vol. 47, p. 192
139. Ibid., Vol. 18, p. 67
140. Ibid., Vol. 46, p. 322
141. D. A. Farnie, *The English Cotton Industry and the World Market 1815–1896* (Oxford, 1979), p. 105
142. MECW, Vol. 46, p. 322
143. Ibid., Vol. 41, pp. 441–7
144. Karl Kautsky Papers (Amsterdam), DXVI, p. 489
145. MECW, Vol. 49, p. 378
146. Kapp, *Eleanor Marx*, Vol. I, p. 107
147. MECW, Vol. 43, p. 311
148. Quoted in *The Daughters of Karl Marx: Family Correspondence, 1866–1898* (London, 1982), p. 51
149. MECW, Vol. 43, p. 541
150. Ibid., p. 311
151. Karl Marx and Friedrich Engels, *On Ireland* (London, 1971), p. 14. Extracts from Engels's 'Unpublished History of Ireland' were later serialized by *The Irish Democrat* newspaper. See, *The Irish Democrat*, New Series, No. 71 and 72, (November–December 1950)
152. MECW, Vol. 40, pp. 49–50
153. Ibid., Vol. 40, p. 49
154. Ibid., Vol. 43, pp. 473–4
155. R. F. Foster, *Modern Ireland* (London, 1989), p. 391
156. *Reminiscences*, p. 88
157. Max Beer, *Fifty Years of International Socialism* (London, 1935), p. 78
158. MECW, Vol. 42, p. 474

159. Ibid., Vol. 42, p. 483
160. Ibid., Vol. 43, p. 163
161. Ibid., Vol. 42, p. 178
162. Ibid., Vol. 42, p. 371
163. Ibid., Vol. 42, p. 406
164. Ibid., Vol. 43, p. 160
165. Ibid., Vol. 42, p. 381
166. Robert Skidelsky, 'What's Left of Marx', *New York Review of Books* (47), 18 (2000)
167. Karl Marx, *Capital* (Moscow, 1954), p. 645
168. MECW, Vol. 42, pp. 363, 451, 467–8
169. Ibid., Vol. 42, p. 426
170. Ibid., Vol. 20, pp. 208, 227, 224, 231
171. Ibid., Vol. 38, pp. 170, 187, 194
172. *Reminiscences*, p. 185
173. MECW, Vol. 43, p. 299
174. Ibid., pp. 299, 302–3
175. Marx-Engels Archives, International Institute of Social History, Amsterdam (L167)
176. MECW, Vol. 43, p. 252

Chapter 7: 'The Grand Lama of the Regent's Park Road'

1. MECW, Vol. 47, p. 355
2. Ibid., Vol. 43, p. 561; Vol. 44, p. 142
3. *Reminiscences of Marx and Engels* (Moscow, 1958), pp. 310–11
4. See Donald J. Olsen, *The Growth of Victorian London* (London, 1976), p. 246
5. See A. D. Webster, *The Regent's Park and Primrose Hill* (London, 1911); Friends of Chalk Farm Library, *Primrose Hill Remembered* (London, 2001)
6. *Reminiscences*, p. 94
7. Eduard Bernstein, *My Years of Exile: Reminiscences of a Socialist* (London, 1921), p. 153
8. *Reminiscences*, p. 186
9. Ibid., pp. 335, 316
10. Bernstein, *My Years of Exile*, p. 197
11. Marx-Engels Archives, International Institute of Social History, Amsterdam (M33)
12. MECW, Vol. 47, p. 5

13. Ibid., Vol. 44, pp. 47, 66, 120

14. Ibid., p. 131

15. See Robert Tombs, *The Paris Commune* (London, 1999)

16. MECW, Vol. 27, p. 185

17. Ibid., Vol. 47, p. 186

18. Ibid., Vol. 44, pp. 228–9

19. Quoted in Francis Wheen, *Karl Marx* (London, 1999), p. 333

20. MECW, Vol. 44, p. 157

21. Ibid., Vol. 22, p. 355

22. Ibid., Vol. 42, pp. 20, 157

23. Friedrich Engels, *The Condition of the Working Class in England* (London, 1987), p. 28

24. See Edmund Wilson, *To the Finland Station* (London, 1991), pp. 264–8

25. Leszek Kolakowski, *Main Currents of Marxism* (London, 2005), p. 205

26. Quoted in E. H. Carr, *Michael Bakunin* (London, 1975), p. 341

27. MECW, Vol. 43, pp. 191, 193, 336

28. Ibid., Vol. 23, p. 425

29. Ibid., Vol. 44, pp. 295, 286

30. Ibid., Vol. 23, p. 66

31. *Reminiscences*, p. 209

32. MECW, Vol. 40, p. 27

33. Ibid., Vol. 41, p. 558

34. Ibid., Vol. 42, pp. 320, 323. See also, Diane Paul, ' "In the Interests of Civilization": Marxist Views of Race and Culture in the Nineteenth Century', *Journal of the History of Ideas* (42), 1 (1981)

35. MECW, Vol. 27, p. 51. See also, Mario Kessler, 'Engels' Position on Anti-Semitism in the Context of Contemporary Socialist Discussions', *Science & Society* (62), 1 (1998)

36. MECW, Vol. 42, p. 88

37. Ibid., Vol. 23, p. 363

38. Ibid., Vol. 24, p. 71

39. Ibid., Vol. 45, pp. 64, 94

40. Ibid., Vol. 45, p. 317

41. Ibid., Vol. 46, pp. 10, 152

42. Ibid., Vol. 24, pp. 267, 269

43. Ibid., Vol. 23, p. 34

44. Ibid., Vol. 24, p. 417

45. Eric Hobsbawm, *Industry and Empire* (London, 1990), pp. 192–3

46. 'Engels, Frederick' (IR 59/166), The National Archives, Kew

47. MECW, Vol. 46, pp. 434, 435, 448–9

48. *Friedrich Engels, Paul and Laura Lafargue Correspondence* (London, 1959), Vol. I, pp. 21, 51, 54, 110, Vol. II, p. 91

49. MECW, Vol. 46, p. 104

50. Ibid., Vol. 45, p. 139

51. Ibid., Vol. 45, p. 315

52. Ibid., Vol. 24, p. 567

53. Ibid., Vol. 45, p. 324

54. See Gemkow, 'Fünf Frauen an Engels' Seite', *Beiträge zur Geschichte der Arbeiterbewegung*, (37), No. 4 (1995); Yvonne Kapp, *Eleanor Marx* (London, 1976), Vol. I

55. MECW, Vol. 45, p. 321

56. Ibid., Vol. 46, pp. 89–90, 95

57. Ibid., Vol. 45, p. 379

58. See, for example, Tom Nairn, 'History's Postman', *London Review of Books*, Vol. 28, No. 2 (January 2006): 'The short-cut strategy generated by [military] defeat led to a need for larger-than-life ideas and movements, party-armies of zealots captained by supermen. Giants or angels alone could wrestle with the sorcerer, and successfully reconfigure the capitalist march of history. Marginalised in the centres of industrialisation, such trends found expression in the peripheral (or "backward") countries where traditional elites had collapsed or been discredited. The way was then open for authentic monsters like Lenin and Mao to take over: projections of a disembodied will, politics as a substitute for, rather than a realisation of, democracy. State power appeared for a time to make possible what democracy and economic growth had failed to produce. These leaders naturally claimed to have intercepted history's postman and put him right: to have seized the misdirected mail in the name of their own proletariats, as well as of the anti-nationalist aims of the now irreproachable godfathers, Marx and Engels.'

59. MECW, Vol. 24, pp. 11, 43; Vol. 47, p. 280

60. Ibid., Vol. 24, p. 48

61. Ibid., Vol. 24, p. 354

62. Ibid., Vol. 49, p. 384

63. Ibid., Vol. 27, pp. 422, 426

64. Ibid., Vol. 27, p. 426

65. Ibid., Vol. 50, p. 112

66. Ibid., Vol. 24, p. 420

67. Ibid., Vol. 46, p. 224

68. Ibid., p. 462

69. F. G. Black and R. M. Black (eds.), *The Harney Papers* (Assen, 1969), p. 296

70. MECW, Vol. 46, p. 462
71. Ibid., p. 458

Chapter 8: Marx's Bulldog

1. MECW, Vol. 24, pp. 467, 468
2. Ibid., Vol. 47, p. 25
3. *Manchester Guardian*, 4 August 1945
4. Benjamin Disraeli, *Coningsby* (London, 1963), p. 127
5. Elizabeth Gaskell, *Mary Barton* (1848) (Harmondsworth, 1996), p. 39. For a broader explication of Manchester scientific culture, see Robert H. Kargon, *Science in Victorian Manchester* (Manchester, 1977); Arnold Thackray, 'Natural Knowledge in Cultural Context: The Manchester Model', *American Historical Review*, 69 (1974)
6. MECW, Vol. 42, p. 117
7. Henry Roscoe, *The Life and Experiences of Sir Henry Enfield Roscoe Written by Himself* (London, 1906), p. 107
8. MECW, Vol. 41, p. 465; Vol. 42, p. 383
9. Ibid., Vol. 46, p. 461
10. Ibid., Vol. 49, p. 433
11. Ibid., Vol. 40, p. 551
12. Ibid., Vol. 41, p. 381
13. Quoted in David Stack, *The First Darwinian Left* (Cheltenham, 2003), p. 2
14. MECW, Vol. 45, pp. 107, 108
15. Ibid., Vol. 40, p. 326
16. Ibid., Vol. 6, p. 195
17. Friedrich Engels, *Anti-Dühring* (Peking, 1976), p. 74
18. MECW, Vol. 42, p. 138
19. Ibid., Vol. 45, p. 123
20. Ibid., Vol. 44, p. 500
21. Engels, *Anti-Dühring*, p. 11
22. See *The Philosophical Quarterly*, II (6) (1952), p. 89
23. Engels, *Anti-Dühring*, p. 12
24. MECW, Vol. 24, p. 302
25. Ibid., Vol. 25, p. 356
26. Ibid., Vol. 24, pp. 300–301
27. Engels, *Anti-Dühring*, p. 173
28. See Stephen Jay Gould, *Ever Since Darwin* (London, 1978), pp. 210–11

29. MECW, Vol. 25, pp. 452–65

30. Peter Singer has taken issue with Engels's animal–human distinction, based around control of the natural environment, by pointing to the example of fungus-growing ants which grow and eat specialized fungi that would not have existed without their activity. See Peter Singer, *A Darwinian Left* (London, 1999), pp. 21–4

31. MECW, Vol. 25, p. 460

32. Engels, *Anti-Dühring*, p. 47

33. MECW, Vol. 25, p. 127

34. Jean Van Heijenoort, 'Friedrich Engels and Mathematics', in *Selected Essays* (Napoli, 1985), pp. 123–51

35. MECW, Vol. 25, p. 354

36. Private conversation, November 2007. One obvious, British example of this phenomenon would be the pioneering X-ray crystallographer, J. D. Bernal (1901–71), who thought that 'in its endeavour, science is communism'.

37. Heinrich Gemkow et al., *Frederick Engels: A Biography* (Dresden, 1972), p. 414. For an up-to-date defence of Engels's insights into modern scientific practice and theory, see Paul McGarr, 'Engels and Natural Science', *International Socialism*, 65, 2 (1994). Also at *http://www.marxists.de/science/mcgareng/index.htm*

38. J. B. S. Haldane, 'Preface', in Frederick Engels, *Dialectics of Nature* (London, 1940), p. vii

39. See Peter Pringle, *The Murder of Nikolai Vavilov: The Story of Stalin's Persecution of One of the Great Scientists of the Twentieth Century* (New York, 2008)

40. See 'Report on Engels Society – June 1949'; 'Transactions of the Physics Group'; 'Transactions of the Engels Society, No. 4, Spring 1950'; 'To the Central Committee of the C.P.S.U (B), to Comrade Stalin. Youri Zhdanov.' Archives of the People's History Museum, Manchester, CP/CENT/CULT/5/9

41. MECW, Vol. 45, p. 122

42. See Richard Adamiak, 'Marx, Engels and Dühring', *Journal of the History of Ideas*, 35, 1 (1974)

43. MECW, Vol. 45, p. 131

44. E. Dühring, *Kritische Geschichte der Nationalökonomie und des Socialismus* (Leipzig, 1879), p. 547

45. MECW, Vol. 45, p. 175

46. Engels, *Anti-Dühring*, p. 422

47. MECW, Vol. 16, p. 474

48. Ibid., Vol. 35, p. 19

49. Friedrich Engels, 'Preface to Second Edition' (1885), *Anti-Dühring*, p. 11

50. Ibid., p. 201

51. MECW, Vol. 24, p. 297

52. Ibid., Vol. 24, p. 319

53. Ibid., Vol. 24, p. 320

54. Ibid., Vol. 24, p. 321

55. Ibid., Vol. 24, p. 323

56. Ibid., Vol. 46, pp. 300, 369

57. *Friedrich Engels, Paul and Laura Lafargue Correspondence* (London, 1959), Vol. III, p. 335

58. David Ryazonov, *Marx and Engels* (London, 1927), p. 210

59. *F. Engels' Briefwechsel mit K. Kautsky* (Vienna, 1955), p. 4

60. G. Lukács, *History and Class Consciousness* (London, 1971), p. 24

61. Norman Levine, 'Marxism and Engelsism', *Journal of the History of the Behavioural Science*, 11, 3 (1973), p. 239. See also, Terrell Carver, *Marx and Engels: The Intellectual Relationship* (Brighton, 1983) for a more refined advocacy of the same case.

62. MECW, Vol. 45, p. 334

63. Wilhelm Liebknecht, *Karl Marx: Biographical Memoirs* (1896) (New York, 1968), pp. 91–2

64. By far the most cogent and detailed explanation of this approach remains S. H. Rigby, *Engels and the Formation of Marxism* (Manchester, 1992)

65. MECW, Vol. 47, p. 53

66. Ibid., p. 16

67. Ibid., p. 17

68. *Lafargue Correspondence*, Vol. I, p. 142

69. MECW, Vol. 47, p. 41

70. Ibid., Vol. 47, p. 53

71. Ibid., Vol. 47, p. 43

72. Ibid., Vol. 47, p. 117

73. Ibid., Vol. 47, p. 265

74. Ibid., Vol. 48, p. 521

75. Ibid., Vol. 27, p. 428

76. Ibid., Vol. 47, p. 301

77. Ibid., Vol. 36, p. 20

78. Ibid., Vol. 36, p. 23

79. Ibid., Vol. 47, p. 271

80. Ibid., Vol. 48, p. 347

81. See Meghnad Desai, *Marx's Revenge: The Resurgence of Capitalism and the Death of Statist Socialism* (London, 2002), pp. 74–83

82. Carl-Erich Vollgraf and Jürgen Jungnickel, 'Marx in Marx's Words?', *International Journal of Political Economy*, 32, 1 (2002), p. 67

83. F. G. Black and R. M. Black (eds.), *The Harney Papers* (Assen, 1969), p. 351

84. MECW, Vol. 48, p. 398

85. *Lafargue Correspondence*, Vol. III, p. 344

86. Marx-Engels Archives, International Institute of Social History, Amsterdam (L5461)

87. Ibid., L5473

88. Quoted in *The Daughters of Karl Marx: Family Correspondence, 1866–1898* (London, 1982), p. 230

89. MECW, Vol. 50, p. 331

90. Ibid., Vol. 46, p. 395

91. Eduard Bernstein, *My Years of Exile: Reminiscences of a Socialist* (London, 1921), p. 168

92. MECW, Vol. 26, p. 132

93. Ibid., p. 162

94. Ibid., p. 158

95. Ibid., p. 165

96. Ibid., p. 173

97. Ibid., p. 179

98. Friedrich Engels, *The Condition of the Working Class in England* (Harmondsworth, 1987), p. 167

99. Ibid., p. 168

100. MECW, Vol. 26, p. 179

101. Ibid., Vol. 47, p. 312

102. Ibid., Vol. 26, p. 183

103. Ibid., Vol. 26, p. 183

104. Ibid., Vol. 43, p. 296

105. See Sheila Rowbotham, *Edward Carpenter: A Life of Liberty and Love* (London, 2008)

106. Kate Millett, *Sexual Politics* (London, 1970), p. 120

107. See Lise Vogel, 'Engels's *Origin*: Legacy, Burden and Vision', in Christopher J. Arthur (ed.), *Engels Today* (London, 1996)

108. Michele Barrett, 'Introduction', in F. Engels, *The Origin of the Family, Private Property and the State* (Harmondsworth, 1986), p. 28. See also, Josette Trat, 'Engels and the Emancipation of Women', in *Science and Society* 62, 1 (1998); Nanneke Redclift, 'Rights in Women: Kinship, Culture, and Materialism', in J. Sayers, M. Evans and N. Redclift (eds.), *Engels Revisited:*

New Feminist Essays (London, 1987); Terrell Carver, 'Engels's Feminism', *History of Political Thought*, 6, 3 (1985)

109. MECW, Vol. 50, p. 67
110. Ibid., Vol. 48, pp. 224, 232
111. See, for example, ibid., Vol. 47, p. 355
112. Ibid., Vol. 48, p. 253
113. Ibid., Vol. 47, p. 312
114. Ibid., Vol. 45, p. 197
115. Ibid., Vol. 26, p. 402
116. See Eric Arnesen, 'American Workers and the Labor Movement in the Late Nineteenth Century', in Charles W. Calhoun, *The Gilded Age: Essays on the Origins of Modern America* (Delaware, 1996)
117. MECW, Vol. 47, p. 452
118. Ibid.
119. *Reminiscences of Marx and Engels* (Moscow, 1958), p. 187
120. MECW, Vol. 48, p. 210
121. Ibid., Vol. 26, p. 585
122. Ibid., Vol. 48, p. 207
123. See Mike Davis, *City of Quartz* (London, 2006), pp. 46–54. Indeed, Jean Baudrillard's description of Los Angeles, quoted by Davis, is an almost exact update of Engels's encounter with New York: 'There is nothing to match flying over Los Angeles by night. Only Hieronymous Bosch's Hell can match the inferno effect.'
124. MECW, Vol. 48, p. 211
125. Ibid., p. 219

Chapter 9: First Fiddle

1. MECW, Vol. 27, p. 61
2. Ibid., Vol. 48, pp. 493–5
3. *Reminiscences of Marx and Engels* (Moscow, 1958), pp. 147, 187
4. MECW, Vol. 24, p. 387
5. Ibid., Vol. 46, p. 123
6. Ibid., Vol. 46, p. 197
7. Ibid., Vol. 47, p. 55
8. Friedrich Engels, *The Condition of the Working Class in England* (Harmondsworth, 1987), p. 45
9. Quoted in Philip Henderson, *William Morris: His Life, Work and Friends* (London, 1973), p. 308

10. Beatrice Webb, *My Apprenticeship* (London, 1926), p. 180

11. Henry Hyndman, *The Record of an Adventurous Life* (1911) (New York, 1984), p. 279

12. 'A Disruptive Personality', *Justice*, 21 February 1891

13. MECW, Vol. 47, p. 155

14. Ibid., Vol. 49, p. 494

15. Ibid., Vol. 47, p. 427

16. Ibid., p. 408

17. Quoted in J. B. Glasier, *William Morris and the Early Days of the Socialist Movement* (London, 1921), p. 32

18. MECW, Vol. 47, pp. 155, 471, 484

19. Ibid., Vol. 48, p. 108

20. Quoted in Yvonne Kapp, *Eleanor Marx* (London, 1976), Vol. II, p. 15

21. See Suzanne Paylor, 'Edward B. Aveling: The People's Darwin', *Endeavour*, 29, 2 (2005)

22. Quoted in W. O. Henderson, *The Life of Friedrich Engels* (London, 1976), pp. 685–6

23. Quoted in Kapp, *Eleanor Marx*, Vol. I, p. 270

24. MECW, Vol. 47, p. 177

25. Quoted in Kapp, *Marx*, Vol. II, pp. 171–3

26. MECW, Vol. 48, pp. 16–17

27. Ibid., Vol. 49, p. 87

28. Ibid., Vol. 48, p. 91

29. Edward Aveling, *The Student's Marx* (London, 1907), pp. viii, ix, xi

30. MECW, Vol. 48, p. 113

31. Henry Mayhew, *The* Morning Chronicle *Survey of Labour and the Poor: The Metropolitan Districts* [1849–50] (1980), Vol. 1, pp. 71–2

32. MECW, Vol. 48, p. 377

33. Ibid., Vol. 48, p. 364

34. Ibid., Vol. 26, p. 545

35. Ibid., Vol. 48, p. 389

36. *Reminiscences*, p. 313

37. MECW, Vol. 50, p. 82

38. Ibid., p. 434

39. See *The Labour Leader*, 24 December 1898

40. See Ernest Belfort Bax, *Reminiscences and Reflections of a Mid and Late Victorian* (London, 1918), p. 54

41. For the classic exposition of this question, see Ross McKibben, *The Ideologies of Class* (Oxford, 1994)

42. MECW, Vol. 50, p. 386

43. Ibid., Vol. 49, p. 243
44. Ibid., p. 67
45. Ibid., p. 70
46. Ibid., p. 68
47. Ibid., p. 346
48. Ibid., p. 416
49. *The Daughters of Karl Marx: Family Correspondence 1866–1898* (London, 1982), pp. 223–4
50. MECW, Vol. 49, p. 76
51. Ibid., Vol. 48, p. 290
52. *Friedrich Engels, Paul and Laura Lafargue: Correspondence* (London, 1959), Vol. II, p. 220
53. MECW, Vol. 48, p. 319
54. Ibid., Vol. 48, p. 352
55. Ibid., Vol. 48, p. 454
56. Ibid., Vol. 27, p. 227
57. Ibid., Vol. 49, p. 265
58. Leszek Kolakowski, *Main Currents of Marxism* (London, 2005), pp. 355–6
59. See Eric Hobsbawm, 'Marx, Engels and Politics', in Eric Hobsbawm (ed.), *The History of Marxism* (Brighton, 1982), Vol. I
60. Ibid., p. 265
61. MECW, Vol. 48, p. 36
62. Ibid., Vol. 27, p. 520
63. Ibid., Vol. 50, p. 21
64. Ibid., Vol. 27, p. 522
65. Ibid., Vol. 26, p. 112
66. Ibid., Vol. 27, p. 447. Of course, in the twentieth century, the notion of communism as a secular faith was a familiar and recurring trope. 'If despair and loneliness were the main motives for conversion to Communism, they were greatly strengthened by the Christian conscience,' Richard Crossman wrote in his introduction to *The God That Failed*. 'The emotional appeal of communism lay precisely in the sacrifices – both material and spiritual – which it demanded of the convert ... the attraction of communism was that it offered nothing and demanded everything, including the surrender of spiritual freedom.' A once true believer, the historian Raphael Samuel, sums it up thus: 'As a theory of struggle, Communism rested on a promise of redemption. Socialism was a sublime essence, a state of moral perfection, a transcendent object and end. It represented the highest form of human development, a culmination of morality, a consummation of progress, a

discovery of the greatness of man.' See Arthur Koestler et al., *The God That Failed* (London, 1965), pp. 5–6; Raphael Samuel, *The Lost World of British Communism* (London, 2007), p. 51

67. MECW, Vol. 48, p. 460
68. Ibid., Vol. 50, p. 490
69. Ibid., pp. 182–3
70. Quoted in Gustav Mayer, *Friedrich Engels: Eine Biographie* (The Hague, 1934), II, pp. 529–30
71. MECW, Vol. 27, p. 404
72. Ibid., Vol. 50, pp. 187, 190
73. Quoted in Heinrich Gemkow et al., *Frederick Engels: A Biography* (Dresden, 1972), p. 547
74. MECW, Vol. 50, p. 409
75. Ibid., Vol. 46, p. 514
76. Ibid., Vol. 47, p. 489
77. Ibid., Vol. 26, p. 451
78. Ibid., Vol. 24, p. 173
79. Ibid., Vol. 27, p. 177
80. *Reminiscences*, p. 307
81. MECW, Vol. 49, p. 76
82. William Stephen Saunders, *Early Socialist Days* (London, 1927), pp. 80–81
83. *Reminiscences*, p. 187
84. *The Daughters of Karl Marx*, pp. 247, 251
85. MECW, Vol. 50, p. 355
86. *The Daughters of Karl Marx*, pp. 253, 255
87. MECW, Vol. 50, p. 377
88. Ibid., p. 507
89. Ibid., pp. 517, 525
90. Ibid., p. 535
91. Ibid., p. 526
92. Quoted in Gemkow et al. *Frederick Engels: A Biography*, p. 579
93. See Kapp, *Eleanor Marx*, Vol. II, pp. 597–9
94. *Reminiscences*, p. 147
95. Eduard Bernstein, *My Years of Exile: Reminiscences of a Socialist* (London, 1921), p. 192

Epilogue

1. See Fred. C. Koch, *The Volga Germans* (Pennsylvania, 1977)
2. 'Address to the Conference of Marxist Students of the Agrarian Question', in J. Stalin, *Leninism* (Moscow, 1940), p. 323
3. 'Engels', *Nachrichten des Gebietskomitees der KP(B)SU und des Zentralkomitees der ASRR der Wolgadeutschen*, Vol. 14, No. 225, 21 October 1931
4. 'Engels' zum Gruss', *Rote Jugend. Organ des GK des LKJVSU der ASRRdWD*, Vol. 8, No. 97 (452), 24 October 1931
5. 'Zur Umbenennung der Stadt Prokrovsk in Engels', *Nachrichten*, Vol. 14, No. 225, 21 October 1931
6. 'Engels' zum Gruss', *Rote Jugend*
7. Quoted in Koch, *The Volga Germans*, p. 284
8. Robert Service, *Comrades: A World History of Communism* (London, 2007), pp. 52–3
9. V. I. Lenin, *Collected Works* (London, 1908), Vol. 21, p. 91
10. MECW, Vol. 50, p. 303
11. Quoted in Leszek Kolakowski, *Main Currents of Marxism* (London, 2005), p. 625
12. V. I. Lenin, *Collected Works* (London, 1960–70), Vol. 38, p. 362
13. Ibid., Vol. 14, p. 326
14. Kolakowski, *Main Currents of Marxism*, p. 629
15. Lenin, *Collected Works*, Vol. 21, p. 54
16. J. Stalin, *Anarchism or Socialism* (Moscow, 1950), p. 13
17. J. Stalin, *Dialectical and Historical Materialism* (Moscow, 1939), p. 12
18. Ibid., p. 18
19. Cornelius Castoriadis, *The Imaginary Institution of Society* (Cambridge, 1987), p. 59
20. See Orlando Figes, *The Whisperers: Private Life in Stalin's Russia* (London, 2007), pp. 155–6
21. Kolakowski, *Main Currents of Marxism*, p. 862
22. Raphael Samuel, *The Lost World of British Communism* (London, 2007), pp. 49, 94
23. Herbert Marcuse, *Soviet Marxism: A Critical Analysis* (London, 1958), p. 144
24. MECW, Vol. 25, p. 80
25. See John O'Neill, 'Engels without Dogmatism', in Christopher J. Arthur (ed.), *Engels Today* (London, 1996)
26. MECW, Vol. 49, p. 18

27. Ibid., Vol. 25, p. 80
28. Friedrich Engels, *Anti-Dühring* (Peking, 1976), p. 108
29. MECW, Vol. 50, p. 267; Vol. 49, p. 8
30. Ibid., Vol. 50, p. 461
31. Ibid., p. 356
32. Quoted in Gustav Mayer, *Friedrich Engels: Eine Biographie* (The Hague, 1934), Vol. II, p. 448
33. As David Stack has commented, 'the socialism and socialist movement that arose in the next half-century were forged and matured in an era when Darwinism was an established part of the "mental furniture".' David Stack, *The First Darwinian Left* (Cheltenham, 2003), p. 2. See also, Gareth Stedman Jones, 'Engels and the History of Marxism', in Eric Hobsbawm (ed.), *The History of Marxism* (Brighton, 1982), Vol. I
34. *http://www.marxsite.com/HobsbawnGrundrisse.html*
35. Ching Kwan Lee, *Against the Law: Labour Protests in China's Rustbelt and Sunbelt* (Berkeley, 2007), p. 235

Bibliography

Primary Sources

Karl Marx, Frederick Engels Collected Works, Vols. 2–50 (Progress Publishers, Moscow in conjunction with International Publishers, New York and Lawrence & Wishart, London, 1975–2004)
Karl Marx, Friedrich Engels Werke (Berlin, 1964–9)

Arnold, R. A., *The History of the Cotton Famine* (London, 1864)
Aveling, E., *The Student's Marx* (London, 1907)
Balzac, H. de, *Old Goriot* (Harmondsworth, 1951)
Banfield, T. C., *Industry of the Rhine* (New York, 1969)
Bax, E. B., *Reminiscences and Reflections of a Mid and Late Victorian* (London, 1918)
Beer, M., *Fifty Years of International Socialism* (London, 1935)
Bernstein, E., *My Years of Exile: Reminiscences of a Socialist* (London, 1921)
Black, F. G. and Black, R. M. (eds.), *The Harney Papers* (Assen, 1969)
Born, S., *Erinnerungen eines Achtundvierzigers* (Leipzig, 1898)
Burke, E., *Reflections on the Revolution in France* (Harmondsworth, 1986)
Carlyle, T., *Selected Writings* (Harmondsworth, 1986)
—, *Past and Present* (New York, 1965)
Cooper, T., *The Life of Thomas Cooper, Written by Himself* (London, 1873)
The Daughters of Karl Marx: Family Correspondence, 1866–1898 (London, 1982)
de Tocqueville, A., *Journeys to England and Ireland* (London, 1958)
Disraeli, B., *Coningsby* (London, 1963)
Dronke, E., *Berlin* (Frankfurt, 1846)
Dühring, E., *Kritische Geschichte der Nationalökonomie und des Socialismus* (Leipzig, 1879)

Engels, F., *The Condition of the Working Class in England* (Harmondsworth, 1987)

—, *Anti-Dühring* (Peking, 1976)

—, *Dialectics of Nature* (London, 1940)

Faucher, L., *Manchester in 1844* (Manchester, 1844)

Fourier, C., *The Theory of the Four Movements* (Cambridge, 1996)

F. Engels' Briefwechsel mit K. Kautsky (Vienna, 1955)

Friedrich Engels, Paul and Laura Lafargue: Correspondence (London, 1959)

Gaskell, E., *Mary Barton* (Harmondsworth, 1996)

Hecker, C., *Der Aufstand in Elberfeld im Mai 1849 und mein Verhaltniss zu demselben* (Elberfeld, 1849)

Hegel, G. W. F., *Philosophy of Right* (Oxford, 1942)

Heine, H., *Sämmtliche Werke* (Hamburg, 1867)

Herzen, A., *My Past and Thoughts* (London, 1968)

Hess, M., *Rom und Jerusalem* (Leipzig, 1899)

—, *Philosophische und sozialistische Schriften 1837–1850* (Liechtenstein, 1980)

—, *Briefwechsel* (Amsterdam, 1959)

Hyndman, H., *The Record of an Adventurous Life* (1911) (New York, 1984)

Jones, W. H., (Geoffrey Gimcrack), *Gimcrackiana, or Fugitive Pieces on Manchester Men and Manners* (Manchester, 1833)

Kay, J. P., *The Moral and Physical Condition of the Working Classes Employed in the Cotton Manufacture in Manchester* (Manchester, 1969)

Kliem, M., *Friedrich Engels: Dokumente seines Lebens* (Leipzig, 1977)

Knieriem, M. (ed.), *Die Herkunft des Friedrich Engels: Briefe aus der Verwandtschaft, 1791–1847* (Trier, 1991)

Körner, H. J. M., *Lebenskämpfe in der Alten und Neues Welt* (Zurich, 1866)

Leach, J., *Stubborn Facts from the Factories by a Manchester Operative* (London, 1844)

Lenin, V. I., *Collected Works* (London, 1960–70), Vols. 1–45

Liebich, A. (ed.), *Selected Writings of August Cieszkowski* (Cambridge, 1979)

Liebknecht, W., *Karl Marx: Biographical Memoirs* (New York, 1968)

Marx, K., *Early Writings* (Harmondsworth, 1992)

—, *Capital*, Vol. I (Harmondsworth, 1990)

—, *The Early Texts* (Oxford, 1971)

—, *On Colonialism* (Moscow, 1968)

Marx, K. and Engels, F., *On Ireland* (London, 1971)

Mayhew, H., *The Morning Chronicle Survey of Labour and the Poor: The Metropolitan Districts* (London, 1980)

Muller, M. F., *My Autobiography: A Fragment* (New York, 1991)

Pagenstecher, C. H. A., *Lebenserinnerungen von Dr med. C. H. Alexander Pagenstecher* (Leipzig, 1913)

Parkinson, R., *On the Present Condition of the Labouring Poor in Manchester* (Manchester, 1841)

Reminiscences of Marx and Engels (Moscow, 1958)

Roscoe, H. E., *The Life and Experiences of Sir Henry Enfield Roscoe Written by Himself* (London, 1906)

The Sack; or, Volunteers' Testimonial to the Militia (London, 1862)

Saunders, W. S., *Early Socialist Days* (London, 1927)

Southey, R., *Letters from England by Don Manuel Alvarez Espriella* (London, 1808)

Stäel, M. de, *Germany* (London, 1813)

Stalin, J., *Leninism* (Moscow, 1940)

—, *Anarchism or Socialism* (Moscow, 1950)

—, *Dialectical and Historical Materialism* (Moscow, 1939)

Stirner, M., *The Ego and Its Own* (Cambridge, 1995)

Sue, E., *The Mysteries of Paris* (Cambridge, 1989)

Taine, H., *Notes on England* (London, 1957)

Watts, J., *The Facts of the Cotton Famine* (London, 1866)

—, *The Facts and Fictions of Political Economists* (Manchester, 1842)

Webb, B., *My Apprenticeship* (London, 1926)

Weerth, G., *Sämmtliche Werke* (1956–7)

The Writings of the Young Marx, translated and edited by Lloyd D. Easton and Kurt H. Guddat (New York, 1967)

Archives

Engels-Haus, Wuppertal

International Institute of Social History, Amsterdam

Marx Memorial Library, London

The National Archives, Kew

People's History Museum, Manchester

State Archives of the Russian Federation, Moscow

State Archives, Wuppertal

Working Class Movement Library, Salford

Journals and Newspapers

Economist
Elberfelder Zeitung
Encounter
Endeavour
Hansard
Irish Democrat
Justice
Labour Leader
London Review of Books
Manchester Guardian
Manchester Times
*Nachrichten des Gebietskomitees der KP(B)SU und des Zentralkomitees der
   ASRR der Wolgadeutschen*
Neue Rheinische Zeitung
New York Review of Books
New York Times
Philosophical Quarterly
Reasoner
Rote Jugend. Organ des GK des LKJVSU der ASRRdWD
Salford Star
Sphinx
*Trudovaia pravda. Ezhednevnaia gazeta Obkoma VKP(b), TsIK i Sovprofa
   ASSRNP*

Secondary Sources

Books

Arthur, C. J. (ed.), *Engels Today* (London, 1996)
Attali, J., *Karl Marx ou l'esprit du monde* (Paris, 2005)
Avineri, S., *Moses Hess* (London, 1968)
—, *The Social and Political Thought of Karl Marx* (Cambridge, 1968)
Ball, T. and Farr, J., *After Marx* (Cambridge, 1984)
Barrett, M., 'Introduction', *The Origin of the Family, Private Property and
   the State* (Harmondsworth, 1986)

Beecher, J. and Bienvenu, R., *The Utopian Vision of Charles Fourier* (London, 1975)

Beiser, F. C., *The Cambridge Companion to Hegel* (Cambridge, 1993)

Berger, M., *Engels, Armies and Revolution* (Connecticut, 1977)

Berger, S., *Social Democracy and the Working Class in 19th and 20th Century Germany* (Harlow, 2000)

Berlin, I., *Against the Current* (London, 1997)

—, *Karl Marx: His Life and Environment* (Oxford, 1978)

—, *The Life and Opinions of Moses Hess* (1959)

Bigler, R. M., *The Politics of German Protestantism* (Berkeley, 1972)

Blackbourn, D., *The Fontana History of Germany* (London, 1997)

Blanchard, M. E., *In Search of the City* (Stanford, 1985)

Blyth, H. E., *Through the Eye of a Needle* (Manchester, 1947)

Bradshaw, L. D., *Visitors to Manchester* (Manchester, 1987)

Brazill, W. J., *The Young Hegelians* (London, 1970)

Briggs, A., *Victorian Cities* (London, 1990)

—, *Chartist Studies* (London, 1959)

Bull, S., *'Volunteer!' The Lancashire Rifle Volunteers 1859–1885* (Lancashire, 1993)

Calhoun, C. W., *The Gilded Age: Essays on the Origins of Modern America* (Delaware, 1996)

Carlton, G., *Friedrich Engels: The Shadow Prophet* (London, 1965)

Carr, E. H., *Michael Bakunin* (London, 1975)

Carver, T., *The Cambridge Companion to Marx* (Cambridge, 1991)

—, *Friedrich Engels: His Life and Thought* (London, 1991)

—, *Marx and Engels: The Intellectual Relationship* (Brighton, 1983)

—, *Engels* (Oxford, 1981)

Castoriadis, C., *The Imaginary Institution of Society* (Cambridge, 1987)

Claeys, G., *Citizens and Saints* (Cambridge, 1989)

Clark, C., *Iron Kingdom: The Rise and Downfall of Prussia, 1600–1947* (London, 2006)

Cole, G. D. H., *Chartist Portraits* (London, 1941)

Cummins, I., *Marx, Engels and National Movements* (London, 1980)

Davis, M., *City of Quartz* (London, 2006)

—, *Planet of Slums* (London, 2006)

Deak, I., *The Lawful Revolution: Louis Kossuth and the Hungarians* (New York, 1979)

Desai, M., *Marx's Revenge: The Resurgence of Capitalism and the Death of Statist Socialism* (London, 2002)

Evans, R. and von Strandmann, P. (eds.), *The Revolutions in Europe 1848–1849* (Oxford, 2000)

Farnie, D. A., *The English Cotton Industry and the World Market 1815–1896* (Oxford, 1979)

Fergusson, G., *The Green Collars: The Tarporley Hunt Club and Cheshire Hunting History* (London, 1993)

Figes, O., *The Whisperers: Private Life in Stalin's Russia* (London, 2007)

Foot, P., *Red Shelley* (London, 1984)

Fortescue, W., *France and 1848* (Oxford, 2005)

Foster, R. F., *Modern Ireland* (London, 1989)

Friends of Chalk Farm Library, *Primrose Hill Remembered* (London, 2001)

Frow, E. and Frow, R., *Frederick Engels in Manchester* (Salford, n.d.)

—, *The New Moral World: Robert Owen and Owenism in Manchester and Salford* (Salford, 1986)

Gallie, W. B., *Philosophers of Peace and War* (Cambridge, 1978)

Gemkow, H., et al., *Frederick Engels: A Biography* (Dresden, 1972)

Glasier, J. B., *William Morris and the Early Days of the Socialist Movement* (London, 1921)

Gould, S. J., *Ever Since Darwin* (London, 1978)

Greaves, R., *Foxhunting in Cheshire* (Kent, 1964)

Gunn, S., *The Public Culture of the Victorian Middle Class* (Manchester, 2000)

Hahn, H. J., *The 1848 Revolutions in German-Speaking Europe* (London, 2001)

Hammen, O. J., *The Red '48ers* (New York, 1969)

Hannay, A., *Kierkegaard: A Biography* (Cambridge, 2001)

Hayek, F. A. von, *The Counter-Revolution of Science* (Illinois, 1952)

Heijenoort, J. van, *Selected Essays* (Napoli, 1985)

Heinig, K., *Carl Schorlemmer: Chemiker und Kommunist Ersten Ranges* (Leipzig, 1974)

Hellman, R., *Berlin: The Red Room and White Beer* (Washington, DC, 1990)

Henderson, P., *William Morris: His Life, Work and Friends* (London, 1973)

Henderson, W. O., *Marx and Engels and the English Workers* (London, 1989)

—, *The Life of Friedrich Engels* (London, 1976)

—, *The Lancashire Cotton Famine* (Manchester, 1969)

—, *Engels as Military Critic* (Manchester, 1959)

Henderson, W. O. and Chaloner, W. H., *The Condition of the Working Class in England* (Oxford, 1958)

Hirsch, H., *Friedrich Engels in Selbstzeugnissen und Bilddokumenten* (Hamburg, 1968)

Hobsbawm, E. J., *Industry and Empire* (London, 1990)

—, (ed.), *The History of Marxism* (Brighton, 1982)

Holmes, R., *Shelley: The Pursuit* (London, 1987)

Howe, A., *The Cotton Masters* (Oxford, 1984)

Hunley, J. D., *The Life and Thought of Friedrich Engels* (London, 1991)

Hunt, R. N., *The Political Ideas of Marx and Engels* (Pennsylvania, 1974)

Hunt, T., *Building Jerusalem: The Rise and Fall of the Victorian City* (London, 2004)

Ionescu, G. (ed.), *The Political Thought of Saint-Simon* (Oxford, 1976)

Ivanon, N. N., *Frederick Engels: His Life and Work* (Moscow, 1987)

Jenkins, M., *Frederick Engels in Manchester* (1951)

Johnston, F. R., *Eccles* (Eccles, 1967)

Jones, C., *Paris: Biography of a City* (London, 2004)

Judt, T., *Reappraisals: Reflections on the Forgotten Twentieth Century* (London, 2008)

Kapp, Y., *Eleanor Marx* (London, 1972, 1976): Vol. I: 'Family Life' (1972); Vol. II: 'The Crowded Years' (1976)

Kargon, R. H., *Science in Victorian Manchester* (Manchester, 1977)

Katznelson, I., *Marxism and the City* (Oxford, 1992)

Kidd, A., *Manchester* (Keele, 1996)

Kiernan, V. G., *Marxism and Imperialism* (London, 1974)

Knierim, M. (ed.), *Über Friedrich Engels: Privates, Öffentliches und Amtliches Aussagen und Zeugnisse von Zeitgenossen* (Wuppertal, 1986)

Koch, F. C., *The Volga Germans* (Pennsylvania, 1977)

Koestler, A., et al., *The God That Failed* (London, 1965)

Kolakowski, L., *Main Currents of Marxism* (London, 2005)

Krieger, L. (ed.), *The German Revolutions* (Chicago, 1967)

Kuczynski, J., *Die Geschichte der Lage der Arbeiter unter dem Kapitalismus* (Berlin, 1960)

Kupisch, K., *Vom Pietismus zum Kommunismus: Historische Gestalten, Szenen und Probleme* (Berlin, 1953)

Lee, C. K., *Against the Law: Labour Protests in China's Rustbelt and Sunbelt* (Berkeley, 2007)

Levin, M., *Marx, Engels and Liberal Democracy* (London, 1989)

Mann, G., *The History of Germany since 1789* (London, 1996)

Mansel, P., *Paris between Empires* (London, 2001)

Manuel, F. E., *The Prophets of Paris* (Harvard, 1962)

Marcus, S., *Engels, Manchester and the Working Class* (London, 1974)

Marcuse, H., *Soviet Marxism: A Critical Analysis* (London, 1958)

Mayer, G., *Friedrich Engels: Eine Biographie* (The Hague, 1934)

—, *Friedrich Engels* (London, 1936)

McLellan, D., *Karl Marx – A Biography* (London, 1995)

—, *Karl Marx: His Life and Thought* (London, 1983)

—, *Engels* (Sussex, 1977)

—, *The Young Hegelians and Karl Marx* (London, 1969)

—, (ed.), *Karl Marx: Interviews and Recollections* (London, 1981),

Messinger, G. S., *Manchester in the Victorian Age* (Manchester, 1985)

Miller, S. and Potthoff, H., *A History of German Social Democracy* (New York, 1986)

Millett, K., *Sexual Politics* (London, 1970)

Moggach, D. (ed.), *The New Hegelians: Politics and Philosophy in the Hegelian School* (Cambridge, 2006)

Nova, F., *Friedrich Engels: His Contribution to Political Theory* (London, 1968)

Noyes, P. H., *Organization and Revolution: Working-Class Associations in the German Revolution of 1848–49* (Princeton, 1966)

Old, H. O., *The Reading and Preaching of the Scriptures in the Worship of the Christian Church* (Cambridge, 1998)

Olsen, D. J., *The Growth of Victorian London* (London, 1976)

Payne, R. (ed.), *The Unknown Karl Marx* (London, 1972)

Pelling, H., *Origins of the Labour Party* (Oxford, 1965)

Perkin, H., *Origins of Modern English Society* (London, 1991)

Pickering, P., *Chartism and the Chartists in Manchester and Salford* (London, 1995)

Pinkney, D. H., *Decisive Years in France 1840–1847* (Princeton, 1986)

Prawer, S. S., *Karl Marx and World Literature* (Oxford, 1978)

Read, A. and Fisher, D., *Berlin* (London, 1994)

Richie, A., *Faust's Metropolis* (London, 1999)

Rigby, S. H., *Engels and the Formation of Marxism* (Manchester, 1992)

Rosdolsky, R., *Engels and the 'Nonhistoric' Peoples: The National Question in the Revolution of 1848* (Glasgow, 1986)

Rowbotham, S., *Edward Carpenter: A Life of Liberty and Love* (London, 2008)

Ryazonov, D., *Marx and Engels* (London, 1927)

Samuel, R., *The Lost World of British Communism* (London, 2007)

Sassoon, D., *One Hundred Years of Socialism* (London, 1996)

Sayers, J., Evans, M. and Redclift, N., *Engels Revisited: New Feminist Essays* (London, 1987)

Service, R., *Comrades: A World History of Communism* (London, 2007)

Sheehan, H., *Marxism and the Philosophy of Science: A Critical History* (Atlantic Highlands, NJ, 1993)

Sheehan, J. J., *German History, 1770–1866* (Oxford, 1989)

Singer, P., *Hegel* (Oxford, 1983)

—, *A Darwinian Left* (London, 1999)

Sperber, J., *Rhineland Radicals* (Princeton, 1991)

— (ed.), *Germany 1800–1870* (Oxford, 2004)

Stack, D., *The First Darwinian Left* (Cheltenham, 2003)

Stedman Jones, G., 'Introduction', *The Communist Manifesto* (Harmondsworth, 2002)

Steger, M. B. and Carver, T. (eds.), *Engels after Marx* (Manchester, 1999)

Stepelevich, L. (ed.), *The Young Hegelians* (Cambridge, 1983)

Stokes, J. (ed.), *Eleanor Marx: Life, Work, Contacts* (Aldershot, 2000)

Taylor, R., *Berlin and Its Culture* (London, 1997)

Thompson, E. P., *The Poverty of Theory and Other Essays* (London, 1978)

—, *William Morris* (London, 1977)

Tombs, R., *The Paris Commune* (London, 1999)

Toews, J. E., *Hegelianism: The Path Toward Dialectical Humanism, 1805–1841* (Cambridge, 1980)

Trachtenberg, A., *The Incorporation of America* (New York, 1982)

Ullrich, H., *Der Junge Engels* (Berlin, 1961)

Webster, A. D., *The Regent's Park and Primrose Hill* (London, 1911)

Wheen, F., *Karl Marx* (London, 1999)

Whitfield, R., *Frederick Engels in Manchester: The Search for a Shadow* (Salford, 1988)

Wilson, E., *To the Finland Station* (London, 1991)

Zipes, J., *The Brothers Grimm* (London, 2002)

Articles

Adamiak, R., 'Marx, Engels and Dühring', *Journal of the History of Ideas*, 35, 1 (1974)

Cadogan, P., 'Harney and Engels', *International Review of Social History*, 10 (1965)

Carver, T., 'Engels's Feminism', *History of Political Thought*, 6, 3 (1985)

Claeys, G., 'The Political Ideas of the Young Engels, 1842–1845', *History of Political Thought*, 6, 3 (1985)

—, 'Engels' *Outlines of a Critique of Political Economy* (1843) and the Origins of the Marxist Critique of Capitalism', *History of Political Economy*, 16, 2 (1984)

Cohen-Almagor, R., 'Foundations of Violence, Terror and War in the

Writings of Marx, Engels and Lenin', *Terrorism and Political Violence* 3, 2 (1991)

Gemkow, H., 'Fünf Frauen an Engels' Seite', *Beiträge zur Geschichte der Arbeiterbewegung*, 37, 4 (1995)

Kapp, Y., 'Frederick Demuth: New Evidence from Old Sources', *Socialist History*, 6 (1994)

Kessler, M., 'Engels' Position on Anti-Semitism in the Context of Contemporary Socialist Discussions', *Science & Society*, 62, 1 (1998)

Kitchen, M., 'Friedrich Engels' Theory of War', *Military Affairs*, 41, 1 (1977)

Krishnamurthy, A., ' "More Than Abstract Knowledge": Friedrich Engels in Industrial Manchester', *Victorian Literature and Culture*, 28, 2 (2000)

Levine, N., 'The Engelsian Inversion', *Studies in Soviet Thought*, 25 (1983)

—, 'Marxism and Engelsism', *Journal of the History of the Behavioural Sciences*, 11, 3 (1973)

McGarr, P., 'Engels and Natural Science', *International Socialism*, 65, 2 (1994)

Neimanis, G. J., 'Militia vs. the Standing Army in the History of Economic Thought from Adam Smith to Friedrich Engels', *Military Affairs*, 44, 1 (1980)

O'Boyle, L., 'The Problem of an Excess of Educated Men in Western Europe, 1800–1850', *Journal of Modern History* 42, 4 (1970)

Paul, D., ' "In the Interests of Civilization": Marxist Views of Race and Culture in the Nineteenth Century', *Journal of the History of Ideas*, 42, 1 (1981)

Rubinstein, W. D., 'The Victorian Middle Classes: Wealth, Occupation, and Geography', *Economic History Review*, 30, 4 (1977)

Smethhurst, J. B. 'Ermen and Engels', *Marx Memorial Library Quarterly Bulletin*, 41 (1967)

Stedman Jones, G., 'The Limitation of Proletarian Theory in England before 1850', *History Workshop*, 5 (1978)

—, 'Engels and the End of Classical German Philosophy', *New Left Review*, 79 (1973)

Stepelevich, L., 'The Revival of Max Stirner,' *Journal of the History of Ideas*, 35, 2 (1974)

Thackray, A., 'Natural Knowledge in Cultural Context: The Manchester Model', *American Historical Review*, 69 (1974)

Vollgraf, C.-E. and Jungnickel, J., 'Marx in Marx's Words?', *International Journal of Political Economy*, 32, 1 (2002)

Wittmütz, V., 'Friedrich Engels in der Barmer Stadtschule 1829–1834' *Nachrichten aus dem Engels-Haus*, 3 (1980)

Index

Page references for footnotes are followed by n and those for endnotes by n and the note number, eg 380n74